SO-ECY-085

Booktalk! 3

MORE BOOKTALKS FOR ALL AGES
AND AUDIENCES

Booktalk! 3

MORE BOOKTALKS FOR ALL AGES AND AUDIENCES

Edited by Joni Bodart-Talbot

THE H. W. WILSON COMPANY
NEW YORK
1988

Copyright © 1988 by Joni Bodart-Talbot All rights reserved. No part of this work may be reproduced or copied in any form or by any means, including but not restricted to graphic, electronic, and mechanical—for example, photocopying, recording, taping, or information and retrieval systems—without the express written permission of the publisher, except that a reviewer may quote and a magazine or newspaper may print brief passages as part of a review written specifically for inclusion in that magazine or newspaper.

First Printing 1988
Second Printing 1990

Front cover: Phil Thornton's Senior English class, January 1988.

Cover photos © 1988 by William G. Tolliver, Emporia, Kansas.

Cover design by Ron Schick.

Library of Congress Cataloging-in-Publication Data

Bodart-Talbot, Joni.
    Booktalk! 3.

    Includes bibliographies and index.
    1. Book talks.   2. Public relations—Libraries.
3. Books and reading.   4. Libraries and readers.
I. Title.   II. Title: Booktalk! three.
Z716.3.B635   1988   021.7   88–17284
ISBN 0–8242–0764–5

Printed in the United States of America

CONTENTS

ACKNOWLEDGMENTS

For me, writing a book is not a solitary activity, even less so now, perhaps, than it was back when I began work on the first *Booktalk!*. There are many people to thank for *Booktalk! 3*.

First and foremost, the booktalkers from across the country who sent me talks, came to my lectures and workshops, and virtually demanded a third volume. There's nothing like positive reinforcement to keep me going, and these folks provided lots and lots of "carrots"!

My graduate assistants have been most valuable, and without them this book would probably have had a 1990 publication date! Kathleen Hwang and Kevin Hinshaw set up a database for all the index information, xeroxed piles of talks, and worried with me when a package of manuscript got lost in the mail. Sue Hecks has worked with me these last few months (undoubtedly the most frustrating period of all), helping me cope with deadlines, last-minute changes, and sudden writing blocks. She and Marcus Schlichter also managed to decipher the computer files Kevin had set up for Kathleen, after they were both long gone! I am not an easy person to work for, but Sue has put up with months of demands, revisions, and seesawing moods with unfailing good humor.

Sue isn't the only one at SLIM who has helped prevent me from tearing my hair out. My friends and colleagues on the faculty have provided regular doses of encouragement, support, laughter, companionship, and faith that I could do it once more, as well as sanity-saving jokes, occasional glasses of wine, and shoulders to lean on or cry on. Marty, Herb, Nancy, Bob, and Barb—many heartfelt thanks! Now we can all heave a sigh of relief and toast a job well done—yours as well as mine!

At the Wilson Company, Bruce and Norris are also unfailing sources of support and encouragement—and limits, of course, for pages and for time. And I'm still sure I wouldn't sound nearly so good without Norris to re-do my (our?) less-than-flawless prose.

As for my friends and family—my appreciation of your support continues to grow. I couldn't have made it without you! And a very special thank-you to Patty and Suzi, who see clearly and never pull their punches or hold back on their friendship.

For daily support, phone calls, assistance, encouragement, booktalks, and love—thank you all!

JONI BODART-TALBOT
Emporia, Kansas
May 1988

CONTRIBUTORS OF BOOKTALKS

Madeline Abath
Hockessin Public Library
Hockessin, DE

Wanda Adams

Shirley Alley
Andale High School
Andale, KS

Barbara Bahm
SLIM, Emporia State University
Emporia, KS

Mary Banach
Macomb, IL

Joy A. Basel
Williamsburg Grade and High School
Williamsburg, KS

Marie D. Bastionell
Georgetown Public Library
Georgetown, DE

Mary Beethe
SLIM, Emporia State University
Emporia, KS

Marquis N. Berrey
Galesburg, IL

Jeff Blair
SLIM, Emporia State University
Emporia, KS

Becky Blick
Prairie Hills Middle School
Buhler, KS

Joni Bodart-Talbot
SLIM, Emporia State University
Emporia, KS

Susan Bogart

Booklegger Project
Alameda County Library System,
Fremont Main Library
Fremont, CA

Michael Browne
SLIM, Emporia State University
Emporia, KS

Kay Burkett
DuPont Elementary School
Wilmington, DE

Michele Anton Cahill
Tenafly Middle School Library
Tenafly, NJ

Dorothy Carrothers
Fort Madison, IA

Roger Carswell
Wellington High School
Wellington, KS

Frances Carter
Bay County Public Library
Panama City, FL

Tracy Chesonis
Sussex Central Junior High
Millsboro, DE

JoAnne Clough
Lake Forest South Elementary School
Harrington, DE

Nell Colburn
Central Rappahannock Regional
Library
Fredericksburg, VA

Karen Cole
Prairie Hills Middle School
Hutchinson, KS

Jennifer Kaye Cooper
Student, Nallwood Junior High and
Shawnee Mission South High
Overland Park, KS

Sherry Cotter
Miami-Dade Public Library
System, North Dade
Regional Library
Miami, FL

ix

Edith Czubiak

Dorothy A. Davidson
Jackson Elementary School
Abilene, TX

Ella Deines
Abilene and West Elementary Schools
Valley Center, KS

Diane L. Deuel
Central Rappahannock
Regional Library
Fredericksburg, VA

Eitan Dickman
Student, Nallwood Junior High
and Shawnee Mission South High
Overland Park, KS

Andrea Dietze

Rose R. Donoway
Worcester County Library
Snow Hill, MD

Judy Druse
Curriculum Resources Center,
Washburn University
Topeka, KS

Larry Duckwall
Alameda County Library
System, Pleasanton Branch
Pleasanton, CA

Kathryn Dunn
Beltsville Branch Library
Beltsville, MD

Sharon Durkes
Eskridge Branch Library
Eskridge, KS

Paula Eads
Fremont Main Library
Fremont, CA

Nancy Eager
Hayward Public Library
Hayward, CA

Brad Eckols
Olpe, KS

Catherine G. Edgerton
Enoch Pratt Free Library
Baltimore, MD

Marcia P. Edwards
Alameda County Library System,
Fremont Main Library
Fremont, CA

Katherine L. Fapp
Topeka Public Library
Topeka, KS

Lesley Farmer
Corte Madera, CA

Mary Farnell
Frederick Douglass School
Seaford, DE

Patricia Farr
Central Rappahannock Regional
Library
Fredericksburg, VA

Ann Flory

Barbara K. Foster
Wilmington Library
Wilmington, DE

Brian Fowler
San Jose Public Library
San Jose, CA

Sally Fuentes
Fremont Main Library
Fremont, CA

Eileen Gieswein
Lincoln Elementary School
Concordia, KS

Charlene Graff
Robert E. Lee
Waskom, TX

Caryn Grossman
Alameda County Library System
Alameda County, CA

Nancy Guffey
SLIM, Emporia State University
Emporia, KS

Deanna Gulick
Baxter Springs, KS

Gwen Haegert

Mary Catherine Hall
Seaford High School
Seaford, DE

Gloria Hanson

Dee Hardtke
Fairfax County Public Schools
Alexandria, VA

Beverly Harvey
Royal Valley High School
Hoyt, KS

Barbara Hawkins
Lanier Intermediate School
Annandale, VA

Christine Hayes
Carrcraft Elementary
Wilmington, DE

Mary Hedge
La Porte County Public Library
La Porte, IN

Linda Henderson
Wellington Junior High School
Wellington, KS

Verla M. Herschell
Tecumseh, KS

Diana C. Hirsch
Prince Georges County Memorial Library,
Surratts-Clinton Branch
Hyattsville, MD

Donna P. Hitchens
Banneker Elementary School
Milford, DE

Betty A. Holtzen
Abilene Public Library
Abilene, KS

Martha House

Donna Houser
Iola, KS

Olivia Jacobs
SLIM, Emporia State University
Emporia, KS

Mary James

Bonnie Janssen
ACA County Library System,
Fremont Main Library
Fremont, CA

Kelly Jewett
Georgetown Library
Georgetown, DE

Zoë Kalkanis
Albany Library
Albany, CA

Carol Kappelmann
SLIM, Emporia State University
Emporia, KS

Linda Keating
Fremont Main Library
Fremont, CA

Caroline Ketman
San Jose Public Library,
Santa Teresa Branch
San Jose, Ca

Janet Knabe

Tina Marie Kopie
Central Middle School
Dover, DE

Linda F. Lapides
Enoch Pratt Free Library
Baltimore, MD

Janice Lauer
Allen Frear Elementary
Camden, DE

Linda Lee
SLIM, Emporia State University
Emporia, KS

Barbara Lesley
Smyrna, DE

Frances W. Levin
Media Specialist,
Seaman School District
Topeka, KS

Elizabeth Sue Lewis
Washington, IL

Janet Loebel
SLIM, Emporia State University
Emporia, KS

Sally Long
Worcester County Library
Snow Hill, MD

Anna Lopez
Fremont, CA

Betty H. Lynch
Frankford Public Library
Frankford, DE

Barbara Lynn
  Olathe South High School
  Olathe, KS

Carrie McDonald
  Emporia, KS

Pat McDonnell
  Stanislaus County Free Library
  Modesto, CA

Jeanne McKenzie
  Central Elementary
  Seaford, DE

Diana McRae
  Castro Valley Library
  Castro Valley, CA

Avis Matthews
  Prince Georges County Memorial
    Library System
  Hyattsville, MD

Katherine Mattson
  Knoxville, IL

Rayme Gwen Meyer
  Alameda County Library System
  Dublin, CA

Beverly Ramsey Mitchelson
  SLIM, Emporia State University
  Emporia, KS

Mary Moore
  Stanislaus County Free Library
  Modesto, CA

Peggy Murray

Alan Nichter
  Tampa-Hillsborough Country
    Public Library System
  Tampa, FL

Linda Olson
  Superior Public Library
  Superior, WI

Gail T. Orwig
  Fremont Main Library
  Fremont, CA

Elizabeth Overmyer
  Booklegger Project,
    Fremont Main Library
  Fremont, CA

Sue Padilla
  Topeka West High School
  Topeka, KS

Susan Perdaris
  SLIM, Emporia State University
  Emporia, KS

Nancy Jo F. Pepper
  Georgetown Elementary School
  Georgetown, DE

Irma Piper
  SLIM, Emporia State University
  Emporia, KS

Michelle Pollock
  Dover, DE

Faye Powell
  Prince Georges County Memorial
    Library
  Oxon Hill, MD

Marianne Tait Pridemore
  San Jose Public Library
  San Jose, CA

Ann Provost

Anne Raymer

Lynn Reeves
  Dalhousie University School Library
  Weston, Ontario

Margie Reitsma
  SLIM, Emporia State University
  Emporia, KS

Cheryl Ress
  Wellington Junior High School
  Wellington, KS

Jo Ellen Rice
  Niles Library
  Fremont, Ca

Paul H. Rockwell
  Alameda County Library
  San Lorenzo, CA

Lou Rosenberg
  Newark Library
  Newark, CA

Deborah Rowley
  Fort Madison, IA

Vicki Rubottom

Carol Sandness
  SLIM, Emporia State University
  Emporia, KS

Brenda W. Satchell
  Seaford, DE

Teresa Schlatt
  Emporia, KS

Marilyn Schlosser
  Kansas City, KS

Dee Scrogin
  Prairie Hills Middle School
  Hutchinson, KS

Sue Ann Seel
  Topeka Public Library
  Topeka, KS

JoAnn Seyfert
  Sudlersville, MD

Eileen Bluestone Sherman
  Overland Park, KS

Elizabeth M. Simmons
  Kirkwood Highway Library
  Wilmington, DE

Jan Smith
  Osawatomie, KS

Judie Smith

Lynda Smith
  Fremont, CA

Carol Spencer
  Emporia, KS

Pam Spencer
  Alexandria, VA

Shelley Standley
  Macomb, IL

Carol Starr
  Lompoc Public Library
  Lompoc, CA

Pamm Stock
  Fremont, CA

Pam Swofford
  SLIM, Emporia State University
  Emporia, KS

Sharon Thomas
  Goddard ILC/JH Library
  Goddard, KS

Sarah Thrash
  Seaford District Library
  Seaford, DE

Stella F. Tjogas
  Contra Costa County Library System
  Pleasant Hill, CA

Diane Tuccillo
  Mesa Public Library
  Mesa, AZ

Christy Tyson
  Spokane Public Library
  Spokane, WA

Michele Vessels
  Lewes Public Library
  Lewes, DE

Lola Viets
  Winfield High School
  Winfield, KS

Lana Voss
  Tulsa City County Public Library
  Tulsa, OK

Laura Walker
  Clearwater Grade School
  Clearwater, KS

Cheryl J. Warkentin
  Emporia, KS

Melinda Waugh
  Topeka Public Library
  Topeka, KS

Cheryl Welch
  SLIM, Emporia State University
  Emporia, KS

Lenna Lea Wiebe
  Clearwater Middle School
  Clearwater, KS

Pat Wilkens

Holly Willett
  University of Wisconsin
  Madison, WI

Rose William
  SLIM, Emporia State University
  Emporia, KS

Marjorie Williams
  Lake Forest N. Elementary
  Felton, DE

Ruth Wintjen
  Milford School District Libraries
  Milford, DE

Sister Patricia Wittman
  Fremont, CA

Jacqueline Brown Woody
  Prince Georges County Memorial Library
  Glenarden, MD

David Yim
  Student, Nallwood Junior High and
  Shawnee Mission South High, KS
  Overland Park, KS

INTRODUCTION

The last booktalks have been turned in, the bibliographies are almost finished, and the indexes are in the "corrections only, no additions" stage. Now it's time to write the introduction, now that I know what's really going into *Booktalk! 3*. But before I explain what it is, I'd like to share with you *why* it is.

When my editor and I were working on *Booktalk! 2*, we *knew* we had many more talks than we could use. We cut and cut and cut. Finally I said, "No more! This is it. We're cutting bone and muscle, not fat!" All the talks we had were good—good enough to publish. So I wasn't prepared for her phone call several weeks later: "You aren't going to like this, but Bruce says we have to cut down to 250 talks. The book is just too long." She was right—I *didn't* like it. And I tried every way I could to get out of it—I yelled, begged, cajoled, cried, and swore to do *anything* if only I didn't have to cut more talks. To no avail—a week later, I started cutting. But all was not lost: I had a promise from Bruce there would be a *Booktalk! 3* as soon as possible, including all the talks I had had to omit and many more. The next book would be *only* talks, and would serve as a companion volume to *Booktalk! 2*. Here at last is that book. I didn't win—but I didn't lose either!

So when I started working on this volume, I didn't have to go back to GO—I just kept on from where I'd left off, with that pile of talks I'd had to pull from *Booktalk! 2* at the last minute. Then I added the contributions people had sent in from all over the United States, the talks I'd written since 1985, and the best of the talks written by my students and members of workshops I've done recently. I tried to get as wide a variety of talks and techniques as I could, and decided not to duplicate any titles unless they were important ones and the new talks were both outstanding and quite different from those I had used before. (As you will see, this occurred very infrequently.) Again I had to stick to Bruce's page restrictions and so couldn't include all the talks I wanted, but I still think you will find a wide assortment of titles for all ages and an equally wide range of booktalking styles and techniques.

As you read through *Booktalk! 3*, you will notice many more short talks. One of my students, Margie Reitsma, coined the phrase "flash talks" for the very short ones I ask my students to do in class. These talks are the kind that you use on the floor when someone asks you to recommend a good book, or use between longer talks to vary the pace of a booktalk presentation. They are complete in themselves and can be presented as-is, but they can also serve as "starters" for longer talks of your own; some can even be used as annotations on a booklist. I included a lot of these "flash talks" because there were so many titles I wanted to cover and such tight page restrictions. It was a case of less meaning more.

In addition to the new talks, I have included several "golden oldies" from the original 1980 *Booktalk!*, which is now out of print. The instructional text of *Booktalk!* was revised and expanded in *Booktalk! 2*; the talks from that first volume that seem to have worn best are reprinted here. The index to this book covers not only the talks in this volume but also those in *Booktalk! 2*, so that you will know exactly where to look for what. Now you can have it all (I hope!) and no longer need regret *Booktalk!* being out of print.

As in the previous volumes, we have coded the talks and bibliographies by age level, and again I caution you to take these ratings with a grain or three of salt. The older I get (forty now!), the more I am aware of my lack of perfection. (I'm getting better as I get older, of course; it's just that I'm also getting more perceptive!)

With my dissertation a thing of the past and my PhD a reality, I am looking forward to working with other researchers investigating booktalking and also pursuing other research interests—communication patterns among adolescents and relationship patterns in adolescent or organizational systems. (No, they *aren't* related!) That's in addition to the lectures and workshops I still enjoy doing on booktalking, literature, and organizational relations and communications.

When I look back at the path that led to my present situation, I sometimes marvel at the chances I took. But I think the only true constant in life is the persistence of change. If we are consistently less than daring, we may end up with less to marvel at, and may limit our dreams and our lives. Even if you always said, "I never could . . . ", I challenge you to try booktalking. You may surprise yourself! You may fall on your face, but if you never dare to fall, you will never succeed at flying. So take a deep breath, get a firm grip on your smile and your booktalks—and jump!

Happy flying—and Happy Booktalking!

BOOKTALKS

ADORABLE SUNDAY   Grades 6–8
By MARLENE FANTA SHYER

If you saw her on the street, you might recognize her. It's not that thirteen-year-old Sunday Donaldson is a celebrity or anything like that. But sometimes people remember her face from TV and say, "Hey, weren't you the kid that got knocked over by the St. Bernard in the dog food commercial?" or "Weren't you the kid hanging out of the treehouse waving frozen yogurt on a stick?"

It all starts when Sunday's mother sees the snapshot of her daughter taken after Sunday's braces had come off. "Doesn't she look adorable?" Shirley Donaldson asks her husband. "She could really be in commercials now." And a week after her mother sends the letter, a reply comes from Farley's Talent Agency saying that Mr. Farley himself wants to meet Sunday as soon as possible!

The next day, Sunday and her mother take the train to the city, with Sunday in a special outfit, complete with a red belt to twist when she gets nervous. When it is finally her turn to take the videotape test, her mother pops a breath mint into Sunday's mouth and wishes her luck. The first take of the test is awful. Sunday forgets her lines, says "Sweet Thooth" cookies instead of "Sweet Tooth," and giggles like a fool. She can just picture going home and hearing her mother tell her father and brother how the talent agent tore up her yellow registration card, threw it into a waiting room ashtray, and set fire to it with a torch. . . .

But when the cameraman says he'll give her another chance, that scene vanishes from her mind. This time, Sunday says "Sweet Tooth," smiles at the camera, and her new career is launched. Being in commercials is just about the most exciting, fun thing that could ever happen to Sunday. She can't imagine it could ever stop being fun. But when kids at school start to see her as a show-off and play some nasty tricks on her, and she finds herself failing science, and her parents begin to argue about her future, Sunday gets a taste of how fun it is *not*—and she learns there's a good deal more to life than being adorable, even in commercials.

—Diane Tuccillo

1

THE ADVENTURES OF ALI BABA   Grades 3-4
BERNSTEIN
By JOHANNA HURWITZ

David Bernstein was eight years, five months, and seventeen days old when he chose his new name. There were already four Davids in David Bernstein's third-grade class. And there were seventeen David Bernsteins in the Manhattan telephone book. He knew because he'd planned to read the phone book for a book report—it was the fattest book in the house. After seeing all those David Bernsteins listed, though, David decided to do two things: change his name and find another book to read. The book he chose for his book report was *The Arabian Nights*. And in that book he found his new name—Ali Baba Bernstein. His teacher was surprised when he announced his new name. His father and mother were a little puzzled. Every once in a while they forgot and called David David.

David was very happy with his new name. Now there were three Davids in his class and one Ali Baba. He was sure that a boy with such an exciting name would have some exciting adventures. And David, I mean Ali Baba, does have adventures, with magic and princesses and a secret treasure.

—Kathryn Dunn

THE ADVENTURES OF CHUCHI   Grades 3-5
By JANE GAFFIN

Chuchi was a Siberian Husky puppy who belonged to Toby and Susie Rawlins. Many adults were scared of Chuchi because she looked so much like a wolf—the long nose, the pointed ears, the thick white ruff at the neck. Chuchi's face and legs were covered by shiny black fur, tipped with silver as the winter came on. Her sharp canine fangs could make a hambone disappear in minutes. But she had a happy disposition, and she loved Susie and Toby and all the children in the neighborhood.

Mrs. Rawlins called her kids in from playing outside and asked them to take their places around the kitchen table. The kitchen table was reserved for mealtime, homework, and family conferences, when everyone could discuss a problem. Having a conference in the middle of the day was serious, and Toby and Susie wondered what it was about.

Mrs. Rawlins explained that she had had several phone calls that morning. One of the neighbors, Mrs. Farley, was circulating a petition saying that Chuchi was a dangerous animal that ought to be destroyed before she bit somebody. Now none of the children's friends could come over and play until they got rid of Chuchi. But Chuchi had never hurt anyone. Susie and Toby felt very confused, having to choose between their friends and their pet. Their chests felt tight and tears burned in their eyes as they decided they would keep their dog no matter what Mrs. Farley said. All this time Chuchi was lying on the floor. As she looked up at Toby, her eyes revealed that she knew exactly what they had been saying about her. She raised her head, yelped her objections, then lowered her head and sighed heavily.

Since Mrs. Rawlins had not been able to convince Mrs. Farley or the other neighbors that Chuchi was not wild and dangerous, Toby and Susie decided they would go see Mrs. Farley themselves, and take Chuchi along. Their hearts beat rapidly and their hands were icy-cold and sweaty as they knocked on the Farleys' door. No one answered.

At that moment, Chuchi pulled away and darted toward the Farleys' pond. Susie saw little Pete Farley struggling and screaming in the muddy pond water. Mrs. Farley was running toward the pond crying, "Pete! No! No! Pete!" Chuchi tore by in a black-and-white streak. Mr. Farley came racing out of the barn. Susie and Toby hoped he didn't have a gun. By this time Mrs. Farley was hysterical. "Stop that dog! She's going to kill Pete! Get the gun. Shoot that dog before she kills Pete!"

Chuchi ignored the chaos. She plunged into the dirty pond, and with only her head visible above the water, she swam confidently toward Pete. Susie and Toby were frozen in fear, for they knew just what Mrs. Farley was thinking: that Chuchi was going to kill Pete!

Then Chuchi and Pete surfaced. Pete had a death-grip on Chuchi's thick, long neck fur. Relief swept through Susie and Toby as Mrs. Farley quit screaming and watched as Mr. Farley coached and encouraged the dog back to shore.

"Good dog," said Mr. Farley as Chuchi shook brown, muddy water from her coat and gave him a sloppy kiss.

Will Mrs. Farley have a change of heart and drop her petition for the dog's extinction now that Chuchi has saved her son from drowning, or will she blame Chuchi for pushing Pete into the pond in the first place? Find out when you read *The Adventures of Chuchi,* by Jane Gaffin.

—*Pat Wilkens*

ADVENTURES OF TOM SAWYER YA
By MARK TWAIN

Monday morning, and Tom Sawyer was miserable. He was always miserable on Mondays because it meant another week of suffering in school. He tried all kinds of ailments to convince his aunt that he was surely too sick to go to school. Maybe he was even dying! But she couldn't be fooled. As he slowly made his way to school, he spied Huckleberry Finn. Huck never had to go to school or to church either; he could stay up late, go fishing when he wanted, never had to wash or put on clean clothes, and he could swear wonderfully. Tom admired Huck.

This morning, Huck was carrying a dead cat. And Tom (as usual) was impressed.

"Say—what is dead cats good for, Huck?"

"Good for! To cure warts with!"

"No! Is that so?"

"Why, you take your cat and go and get in the graveyard 'long about midnight when somebody that was wicked has been buried; and when it's midnight a devil will come, or maybe two or three, but you can't see 'em, you can only hear something like the wind, or maybe hear 'em talk; and when they're taking that feller away, you heave your cat after 'em and say, 'Devil follow corpse, cat follow devil, warts follow cat, I'm done with ye!'"

Well, Huck was going to try the cat cure that very night and Tom was just itchin' to go along. Hoss Williams had just been buried and he was wicked enough.

At half past nine, Tom went to bed. He lay awake and waited. The clock chimed ten, then eleven, and shortly after that he heard Huck giving the signal. Tom climbed out his window and the two boys disappeared into the night, towards the graveyard.

They found Hoss Williams' grave and waited in silence for what seemed like a long time. The wind moaned, an owl hooted. And then— they heard it! Muffled voices! Soon they could see figures and little spangles of light. Huck and Tom just knew it was devils—until they listened carefully, and realized the voices were human.

What happened next was too much for Huck and Tom! They left the graveyard running for their lives. They swore never, ever to breathe a word about what they'd seen, and "may we drop down dead in our tracks if we ever tell!"

Tom and Huck may not have cured their warts that night but they did start an adventure full of mystery, murder, lost treasures, and narrow escapes from the men in the graveyard. And they can't tell a soul about it.

—*Kathryn Dunn*

AFTER THE RAIN   Grades 6–8/YA
By NORMA FOX MAZER

Sundays, ugh! How Rachel hates Sundays! They're always the same. She, her father, and her mother go to Grandpa Izzy's. They try to carry on lively conversations with him, when obviously he doesn't want to talk. She and her mother spend hours fixing good things for him to eat, and he complains about everything they fix. They try to interest him in television or games of Scrabble, even though he makes no effort to hide his boredom. She knows that Grandpa doesn't like them, especially her, and to top it off he is *always* rude. So—why do they keep going?

Then the telephone call comes. "Your grandfather has fallen on the sidewalk by my house. Can you come get him?"

When Rachel goes to get Izzy she doesn't realize that she is starting on an entirely new chapter in her life. The fall was caused by Izzy's inability to get enough oxygen. The doctor says it's mesothelioma—cancer of the lungs. Izzy has only a few months to live, but during that short time Rachel learns a lot about Grandpa, and about death, but most of all about herself.

—*Joy A. Basel*

AKU-AKU   YA/Adult
By THOR HEYERDAHL

Easter Island is like any other hot Pacific island except for the huge stone statues dotted all over the place, stones many times the size of a man and each weighing over fifty tons. How were these enormous stones transported from their quarry to the places where they now rest, miles away, by primitive people possessing no mechanical or engineering skills? How were they carved to resemble human heads? And what force has toppled most of them about like jackstraws?

Thor Heyerdahl went to Easter Island to find out, if he could, the answers to these questions. Instead of answers he found many more questions. In dozens of secret caves were other strange objects—carvings of skulls and strange beasts and human masks, each giving clues about the people who had made them.

As the pieces slowly fall into place, you can follow Heyerdahl's explorations into the depths of the island, into the family caves of the natives, where no stranger had ever gone before.

This is a modern detective story, an exciting adventure about mysteries hundreds of years old.

Aku-Aku, by Thor Heyerdahl.

—*Joni Bodart-Talbot*

ALDO APPLESAUCE   Grades 3–4
By JOHANNA HURWITZ

Aldo's real name is "Aldo Sossi." [Write this on the blackboard.] Aldo doesn't get his nickname just because of the way his real name sounds. He gets it on his very first day at his new school when someone accidently knocks over the applesauce in his vegetarian lunch—and it splatters everything and everybody nearby.

Aldo has not been looking forward to going to a new school. But his family moved right in the middle of the school year, and he has no choice. He expects a rough time the first day—and that's just what he has.

Not only does Aldo acquire his hated nickname, but his new teacher makes him sit next to a girl who seems rather strange. Aldo suddenly realizes that this is because she has a mustache—a big, thick, black mustache! Aldo has never seen a girl with a mustache. It startles him so much that he mixes up the name of his new teacher, Mrs. Moss, with his old teacher, Mrs. Nesse, and by mistake he calls his new teacher "Mrs. Mess!"

Aldo is relieved to get out of school that day and go home to his new house, where his cats—Peabody and Poughkeepsie—are waiting for him.

He has to go back to school on Monday, though.

Read about the rest of Aldo Applesauce's year at his new school—as he adjusts to his nickname, begins to make new friends, and finds out about that strange girl with the black mustache.

—*Nell Colburn*

ALEXANDER AND THE TERRIBLE, Grades k–3
HORRIBLE, NO GOOD,
VERY BAD DAY
By JUDITH VIORST

Have you ever had a really awful day? Then you'll understand how Alexander felt—he *knew* it was going to be a terrible, horrible, no good, very bad day the moment he woke up with his chewing gum stuck in his hair. Nothing at all went right. Everything went wrong, right down to kissing on TV and having to wear his yucky railroad-train pajamas to bed.

—Janet Loebel

ALEXANDER AND THE WIND-UP MOUSE Grades k–3
By LEO LIONNI

Every time Alexander, the mouse, comes out of his hole, people scream or chase him with a broom. Willie, the wind-up mouse, on the other hand, is Annie's favorite toy. Everyone loves him. Alexander wishes he could be a wind-up mouse like Willy. Maybe he can! The magic lizard, who lives in the garden, can change Alexander into a toy mouse if, when the moon is round, Alexander will bring him a purple pebble. Can Alexander do that? Will he be happy if he does?

—Olivia Jacobs

THE ALFRED G. GRAEBNER Grades 7–10
MEMORIAL HIGH SCHOOL HANDBOOK
OF RULES AND REGULATIONS
By ELLEN CONFORD

Alfred G. Graebner High will never be the same. During the summer the class scheduling has been taken over by a computer, and the chaos starts on the first day of school!

When Julie gets to her sophomore homeroom class, she finds out the computer has scheduled all the classes. Everyone gets a computer card with a schedule on it. Julie is horrified to discover she has *first* period phys ed. That means not only calisthenics (exercises) at 8:10 A.M. but a shower after class: her hair will look awful, every day, for her entire sophomore year! She's sitting there contemplating this depressing prospect when she suddenly notices the boy across the aisle. He is very carefully and methodically poking holes in his computer card with a pencil.

Then he puts the pencil down, folds the card in half and creases it, folds it in half again, creases it, and keeps folding it until it's just a little square wad of paper. Then he unfolds it, and begins to tear it just a little around the edge, so it looks as if the card is fringed on all four sides. Julie can't stand it anymore, and so she says, "What *are* you doing?" He looks at her, grins, and says, "Revenge!" and hands her the card. By now it's pretty bedraggled, but Julie can just barely read it. This is what his schedule is: 1 Home Ec, 2 Lunch, 3 Home Ec, 4 Study Hall, 5 Home Ec, 6 Study Hall, 7 Lunch, 8 Wood Shop. And on top of *that*, he says, he is a junior and this is a sophomore homeroom!

Julie doesn't see her two best friends until after school. They look just as unhappy as she does, and don't seem at all impressed by her first-period gym. "That's nothing," says Natalie, "I have third-period lunch! Do you know what time third period starts? 9:30! Cafeteria chow mein is awful at noon, but at 9:30, it's obscene!"

"Neither of you has any hassles at all compared to what's happened to me!" replies Isabel. You know how, in every school, in every subject, there's a teacher that no one wants to get? Maybe it's 'cause they're strict, or hard, or boring, or whatever, but everyone avoids their classes like the plague. Isabel has gotten *every one* of them! Even for study hall! She says, "I kept thinking, it has to get better—but it only got worse!" But she's thought of a way out. She gets two books—an encyclopedia of religion and a medical dictionary. (At Alfred G. Graebner, you could get excused for illness or for a religious holiday.) Isabel figures she can change religions often enough and develop enough alarming symptoms to miss at least every other day of school. (And she isn't discovered for two months!)

Julie's sophomore year turns out to be quite something, what with the computer, a new English teacher who's better looking than Robert Redford, and a Home Ec teacher who tries to teach a unit on Human Sexuality but can't describe what sex is like.

And it's all a part of *The Alfred G. Graebner Memorial High School Handbook of Rules and Regulations*, by Ellen Conford.

—*Joni Bodart-Talbot*

ALL THE CHILDREN WERE SENT AWAY Grades 7–8
By SHEILA GARRIGUE

Sara turned over in her sleep, then buried her head in her arms. The scent of appleblossoms came into her room, but with the fragrance there also came the sound of the siren.

"Get up, Sara! Get up!" her mother said. "Come, darling! It's an air raid!"

Hurriedly Sara put on some clothes and followed her mother across the moonlit yard to their air-raid shelter. Across the sky, searchlights were crossing back and forth, trying to locate the German planes that were dropping bombs on England.

That was why Uncle Duncan and Aunt Jean wanted them all to come to Canada, away from the war. Mother and Daddy could not go, but they had decided to send Sara. She spent her last night at home in that air-raid shelter.

The next day Mother took Sara to Liverpool where she boarded a ship and met Lady Drume, who was to take care of her on the voyage. Lady Drume was big. Her voice was big. Her hat and cape were big. She was such a contrast to Sara's small, gentle mother that Sara was terrified of her.

Can Sara have a happy voyage with Lady Drume? What adventures will she have in Canada? Will she ever get back to England? To find out, read *All the Children Were Sent Away,* by Sheila Garrigue.

—Ella Deines

ALL THE WAY TO WIT'S END Grades 7–8
By SHEILA GREENWALD

Drusilla Brattles has a problem. She's eleven years old, and all her life her family has lived in Coves Landing, in a twenty-six-room mansion they inherited from Grandmother Bundage. Along with the mansion, they inherited all the antique furniture and stuff inside, and Drusilla inherited her grandmother's old-fashioned clothes and, worst of all, the Bundage mouth. The Bundage mouth means that you cannot hold your lips together unless you think about it and press them shut by force. In Coves Landing, where all Drusilla's aunts, uncles, and cousins live, there are lots of people with the Bundage mouth. But now Drusilla's family is moving to Pitney Place, to a much smaller house in a town where none of their relatives live. Drusilla is very concerned about this. She thinks her family is funny-looking. They have funny old hand-me-down clothes and funny old hand-me-down furniture and funny old hand-me-down teeth. She complains to her mother, but her mother is very proud of all the antiques they have inherited and very unconcerned about the Bundage mouth (she has it herself!). When Drusilla goes to the new school, her worst fears are realized. Some of the kids do make fun of her, and she is determined to do something about it. She's going to find a way to get some braces on her teeth that will fix up her mouth. Then the neighbors do something that gives her an idea—they have a garage sale. Can you imagine what would happen if you decided to have a garage sale at your house and sold off your parents' furniture without their permission?

—*Bonnie Janssen*

THE ALMOST YEAR   Grades 6–8
By FLORENCE ENGEL RANDALL

When she arrived at the Mallorys', stones of every color and shape came raining out of the sky into the lawn, some landing with such force that they became embedded in the dirt. The stones covered the yard and blocked off the driveway, while above them the sky was clear and around them the neighbors' houses and lawns remained untouched.

For almost a year—from September till June—she was to stay with the Mallorys. Her own parents were dead, and her Aunt Cyd was too busy looking after other peoples' children to look after her. So she had been invited to spend the school year with the Mallory family in their fancy suburban home. She knew she didn't belong there, and she knew the two Mallory children, Holly and Gary, didn't want her.

But she hadn't expected the stones. Or the doorbell that rang day and night, by itself—and kept ringing, even, even after it had been disconnected. Or the books and plates that suddenly hurled themselves out of people's hands. Throughout that almost year strange forces manipulated the family, until they were forced to consider whether the violence really came from outside—or from one of them.

—*Zoë Kalkanis* and *Elizabeth Overmyer*

ALONE IN WOLF HOLLOW   Grades 5–7
By DANA BROOKINS

Bart and Arnie Cadle never dream when they move to Wolf Hollow that they will witness a murder. Bart is remembering his mother's last words—*"Take care of Arnie."* Rather than be separated and sent to live with different relatives, the brothers take the bus to Wolf Hollow to their uncle's house. Uncle Charlie is not at the bus stop to meet them, so the boys get directions to his house. Unsure of the way, they stop at a tavern to ask.

"Uncle Charlie? We haven't seen him for a week," says Madge, a waitress. "But you're on the right path. Take this flashlight and good luck!"

It's now dark and the wind is howling. As they walk, twigs snap behind them and they feel someone watching them. The boys are panic-stricken by the time they reach Uncle Charlie's, and they pound frantically on the door. No one answers for a long time, and then the door opens slowly—and a figure with horrible red eyes looms out at them.

It's Uncle Charlie. It seems that he has a drinking problem. He agrees to keep the boys on a trial basis, so Bart and Arnie try to be especially helpful.

The boys have "true grit" and are determined to stay together, especially after they stumble on a murder. What will happen to Bart and Arnie when Uncle Charlie disappears? Will they be sent to an orphanage? Will the murderer find them? Don't read this when you're alone!

—Mary Farnell

THE AMAZING AND DEATH-DEFYING DIARY   YA
OF EUGENE DINGMAN
By PAUL ZINDEL

The year Eugene Dingman is fifteen, he takes a job as a waiter at a resort in the Adirondacks. He falls in love with a waitress named Della and is humiliated by a bully named Bunker, who is dating Della. Eugene's only friend is a weird Indian named Mahatma, who keeps trying to convince Eugene he shouldn't hate himself. What Mahatma doesn't know is that he's wasting his breath—because Eugene has to figure out *for himself* how to be a waiter, a loner, a son, and (most important) how to be Eugene Dingman.

—Joni Bodart-Talbot

THE AMAZING BONE   Grades k–2
By WILLIAM STEIG

Pearl the pig decided, one beautiful spring day, that she didn't want to go straight home after school. She watched the grown-ups doing their grown-up work and some of the older locals pitching horseshoes. Then, going home the long way through the forest, Pearl decided to rest a bit among the flowers. "I love everything," she exclaimed. "So do I," said a voice nearby.

As it turned out, the voice belonged to—of all things—a talking bone. The bone could speak several languages. It could snore, sneeze, and even make the sound of a trumpet. In short, the bone could imitate any sound.

Well, Pearl and the bone, who used to belong to an old witch, were walking along together towards Pearl's house when they were besieged by robbers. But when the bone pretended it was a snake inside Pearl's purse, the robbers fled. Pearl and the bone had a good laugh. But it wasn't so easy when Pearl and the bone ran into a crafty fox. This fox liked to eat tender young pigs and wasn't fooled by the bone's imitation of a ravenous crocodile. How will Pearl and the bone get out of this mess? Find out when you read *The Amazing Bone,* by William Steig.

—Gail T. Orwig

AMERICAN HEROES   YA
By NAT HENTOFF

This book should be labeled, "Warning: Handle with Care! Do Not Open Unless You Care About Freedom and the Rights of Human Beings—Their Right to Live, and Care, and Express Their Opinions." You can't read this book and stay uninvolved and put it down and forget it. Not unless you're a lot more cold and cynical than I think most folks are. Because you'll meet people in this book that you may have only read about in newspaper headlines—people who believe in what they fight for, believe in their freedoms, and who go to the wire to fight for them, for themselves and for others.

You'll meet Joellen, who chose an antiwar quote to go under her picture in the yearbook, and you'll meet her classmates, who called her "jerk." Susan Shapiro, who chose not to stand for the Pledge of Allegiance, and whose classmates and fellow townspeople said, "Hitler didn't kill enough of you Jews; we're going to finish the job." Chuck Reineke, who decided that students *can* print anything they want in their school papers. Diane, who had to go to court to stop the police in her town from strip-searching students for drugs. And even librarians who go to court or lose their jobs to keep the censors of their communities from controlling them. All of these people and others care! And they *fight* for what they care about.

Do you care? Do you know your rights? Do you know what you can fight for? Read—and find out!

—Joni Bodart-Talbot

AMONG FRIENDS YA
By CAROLINE B. COONEY

Have you ever wanted to read someone else's diary? Well, here is your chance—you can read six of them! Six teens are assigned to keep a diary for three months. Hillary, Emily, and Jennie—The Awesome Threesome—have been friends since elementary school. Jared and Ansley are a super couple with all that they need in life. And Paul "Classified" is a mystery they would all like to solve. Outwardly they are all so successful, but their diaries tell a different story!

—*Frances W. Levin*

ANASTASIA, ASK YOUR ANALYST Grades 4-6
By LOIS LOWRY

Anastasia Krupnik, aged thirteen, feels she's on the verge of—well, she doesn't know quite what. Suddenly everything her parents do is embarrassing to her. Her father keeps his manuscripts in the refrigerator and her mother makes toy trains out of oatmeal boxes, for Pete's sake! Talk about weird! On top of that, Anastasia's three-year-old brother Sam is some kind of genius. And on top of *that*, she has to do a project for the science fair. Well, Anastasia manages to get started on the science project—she decides that mating gerbils will be an interesting experiment. But her mother *hates* gerbils!

Anastasia thinks she's in need of psychiatric help; the problem isn't her family, it's herself! And since her parents won't hire a psychiatrist for her, she goes out and finds one herself—at a garage sale.

If you want to find out who—or what—her analyst is, and how the science project turns out, read *Anastasia, Ask Your Analyst,* by Lois Lowry.

—*Gail T. Orwig*

ANASTASIA AT YOUR SERVICE Grades 4-6
By LOIS LOWRY

Twelve-year-old Anastasia Krupnik wants a summer job—and she knows exactly what she'd like to do. She wants to be a companion to a rich old lady. But her first day on the job doesn't turn out quite the way she'd planned. In her resume she'd described exactly what she wanted to do. She'd be patient and kind to her employer; she'd read aloud, advise her employer on what jewelry to wear, pull the shades when her employer wanted to take a nap and wake her up if necessary. And if her employer was in a wheel chair, she'd push her around.

Her first day on the job, however, consists of two solid hours of polishing silver spoons. She would have quit right then except that she accidentally dropped one of those expensive spoons in the garbage disposal, and now she owes Mrs. Bellingham $30.00. As if the first day wasn't bad enough, the second promises to be even worse. Anastasia is going to be the maid and serve hors d'oeuvres at a birthday party for Mrs. Bellingham's thirteen-year-old granddaughter—who probably goes to the same school Anastasia will be going to in a few weeks. Anastasia knows she is going to be humiliated. How can she possibly get out of this? Well, she can't, so she decides to try to look older and maybe the granddaughter won't notice her. She puts on loads of make-up and even wears her mother's bra stuffed with panty hose. Does the disguise work? Or does it only make things worse? In *Anastasia at Your Service,* by Lois Lowry, you will find out!

—Bonnie Janssen

AND I ALONE SURVIVED   **YA/Adult**
By LAUREN ELDER

Jim shouted at her to hurry and decide, and Lauren tried to make up her mind about going flying with his friends Jay and Jean that afternoon. Finally she decided to go—it would just be a short hop over the Sierras and back, and it was a beautiful day. Maybe she could get some good pictures. To celebrate the day, Lauren put on her favorite outfit—full skirt, short jacket, vest, and blouse with high-heeled boots. Not exactly the regulation outfit for a plane ride, but Lauren didn't care. She picked up her camera and her father's old flying helmet for luck, and was off. But Jay wasn't as good a pilot as he thought he was, and as they were going over the pass in the Sierras, they were caught in a downdraft and crashed on a mountainside, two miles up. When Lauren came to after the crash, she had a gash on her leg just above the top of her boot that went all the way to the bone, and her arm was broken. She spit out most of her teeth—but she was all right. She was alive. Jean died of massive head injuries and Jay of internal injuries during the first night. Lauren knew that search planes might not find the wreck: Jay hadn't filed a flight plan. If she stayed with the plane, she would surely freeze to death. So Lauren decided to walk down the mountain to the San Joaquin Valley. Even if she didn't make it, she'd be fighting to survive, not giving up. Her trip was to cover over twenty miles of some of the roughest terrain in the Sierras. She was alone, except for her hallucinations, and her only protection from the elements was the clothing she'd so optimistically put on the day before, for a brief flight on a beautiful afternoon. And she survived. This is her story.

—Joni Bodart-Talbot

ARE YOU IN THE HOUSE ALONE?   YA/Adult
By RICHARD PECK

You always think of being raped by a stranger, but Gail is raped by her best friend's boyfriend, and no one will believe her. Gail is surrounded by friends, family, and teachers, yet finds herself utterly alone.

How does Gail handle her problem? Does anyone ever believe her story?

—Marie D. Bastionell

ARTHUR AND THE GREAT DETECTIVE   Grades 1–2
By ALAN COREN

A storm at sea can be a terrible experience, as the passengers of the SS *Murgatroyd* could tell you. Why, after three days of wind and rain, the passengers were divided into two groups—those who groaned and turned green and those who moaned and turned white. In fact, only three people were *not* seasick and well enough to eat in the dining room. To make things easier for the waiter, the three were placed at the same table. They made an unlikely trio—one was the world-famous detective Sherlock Holmes, another was his friend and partner Watson, and the last was ten-year-old Arthur William Foskett. Arthur might have been only ten, but he was smarter than almost everyone on board the SS *Murgatroyd*. When it came to solving the mystery of the red-bearded man with the black hair, finding the stolen Gilbert and Sullivan music, and discovering why the ship's bosun kept removing his peg leg, Arthur really *was* the great detective.

And if you like this book, Arthur has been involved in several other very funny adventure stories available at the library.

—Judie Smith

ARTHUR'S TOOTH Grades k–2
By MARC BROWN

Arthur Anteater is seven years old, and he *still* has all his baby teeth. Finally, one of them gets loose. Arthur wiggles it all the time, trying to hurry it up so it will fall out. When Francine looses a tooth at school, the teacher asks how many other kids in the class have lost teeth. Everyone but Arthur raises a hand. During the next few days, Francine starts showing off and making comments about "people who still have all their little *baby* teeth." Although Arthur's family and friends try to help, he's worried. He feels different from everybody else. But in the end, it is Francine who solves Arthur's problem. If you like this Arthur story, you can read more about him in nine other books about Arthur, his friends, and his family.

—*Susan Perdaris*

ARTHUR'S VALENTINE Grades k–3
By MARC BROWN

Have you ever had a secret admirer? Arthur was receiving valentines from someone who wouldn't sign any name. Was it a joke? Was someone teasing? When the valentines fell out of Arthur's pocket, everyone laughed and teased him, calling him "Hot Lips" and "Lover Boy."

Read *Arthur's Valentine* by Marc Brown to find out how Arthur surprised his secret admirer.

—*Nancy Jo F. Pepper*

BABE, THE GALLANT PIG Grades 3–4
By DICK KING-SMITH

Have any of you read *Charlotte's Web*? Then you know it is the story of a pig who is saved from becoming pork chops by a spider. This book, *Babe, the Gallant Pig* by Dick King-Smith, is another story of a pig who is saved from the usual fate of pigs. Babe is saved by Fly, a sheep dog, who teaches Babe to be, of all things, a sheep pig. That is, Babe learns to guard the flock and round up the sheep just like a dog. Babe has something extra going for him, though: while dogs threaten and growl and push, frightening the sheep into obeying them, Babe is a very polite, gallant pig. He talks nicely to the sheep and doesn't treat them as if they were dumb, so the sheep are happy to do anything he asks.

Farmer Hoggett can hardly believe his eyes, but when Babe saves flock twice, once from rustlers and once from wild dogs, he realizes he has a very special pig indeed. And he decides to enter Babe in the Grand Challenge Sheep Dog Trials. Both Farmer Hoggett and Fly work very hard to train Babe to be a champion sheep pig. Can you imagine people's astonishment when a *pig* is entered in the sheep-dog trials? If you want to find out what happens then, read *Babe, the Gallant Pig*.

—*Diane L. Deuel*

BABY NEEDS SHOES Grades 3-5
By DALE CARLSON

When your parents are dead and you live with your 22-year-old sister who's so dumb—really dumb—that your social worker keeps trying to take you away from her, you have to watch out for yourself. Fortunately Janet had a special ability that was very useful. Every afternoon she would change out of her school uniform into her jeans and vest—her gambling clothes. Janet could predict numbers, and the day Fat Charlie saw her do this in the park, he offered her a job helping him and his gang win at floating crap games. These were, of course, illegal, but very profitable, since Fat Charlie made a lot of money from them and split it with Janet. No one found about this side of Janet's life until Big Mac from Chicago threatened to kill Fat Charlie and all his gang unless he stole some books from another gangster's safe. And of course there was only one person who could crack the safe combination—Janet.

—*Elizabeth Overmyer*

BABY-SITTING Grades 5-8
IS A DANGEROUS JOB
By WILLO DAVIS ROBERTS

Darcy thought a car followed her after she interviewed for a baby-sitting job at the home of the wealthy Fosters, and then later that day she saw the same car again.

On her first day on the job, a man pretending to be a gas company repairman came. Darcy questioned him carefully and decided he was a fake, so she didn't let him in the house.

The three children kept her so busy that she didn't have time to think about him. Melissa, who was four years old, said, "I don't want you for a sitter!*" Six-year-old Jeremy made awful faces at her. At noon, Jeremy tried to cook a whole pound of bacon in the microwave oven, burned it, ruined the platter, and got grease everywhere. Shana got into her mom's makeup later that day, and Jeremy called his uncle in Hawaii!

Darcy made it through the first day of baby-sitting, but on the second day, about the time she couldn't find Jeremy, the burglar alarm sounded. The police came, but found no burglars. Later, she heard the garage door open. When she went to see about it, suddenly from behind her a man's hand closed over Darcy's mouth! She and the three children were being kidnapped!

They were taken to an old empty house in the woods several miles from town, and guarded by two huge dobermans. Darcy had to take care of the children and at the same time try to think of a way to escape. She and Jeremy managed to leave the house one night while the little girls were sleeping, but found that they could not get past the locked gate in the stone wall outside. And getting back into the house without getting caught was very difficult!

A wasp nest and a small room at the top of a narrow winding staircase finally helped Darcy through her dangerous baby-sitting job. Just how dangerous was it? Read *Baby-Sitting Is a Dangerous Job* and find out!

—*Dorothy A. Davidson*

BACK HOME   YA
By MICHELLE MAGORIAN

Even though they had been separated for five years, it took Rusty by surprise when she got off the ship in England and her mother treated her like a stranger. She already missed her American foster family, the only one she had known since she was seven. Rusty had been looking forward to the adventure of coming back home after the war. And now her mother was acting so disapproving and cold. She didn't even like red-haired Rusty's nickname, insisting on calling her Virginia.

Every time Rusty opened her mouth, her mother cringed at her American accent. After they drove in a banged-up car to a shabby house with black curtains, her little brother Charlie, whom Rusty had never met, completely ignored her. Rusty never dreamed that coming back home would be so awful.

Soon Rusty learned that everything she did was wrong. Her voice was too loud, her accent too strong; she used too much slang; her clothes were too bright and new; she had no manners. She got punished for unladylike activities like rowing a boat or carpentry. Rusty cried herself to sleep at night remembering all the fun she had had in America, where she was loved instead of punished for her outgoing personality. How could she bear it here in England, so dull and drab with its bombed-out landscape and worn-out people in threadbare colorless clothes?

Things got even worse when they moved to London to Rusty's grandmother's house to wait for her father to return from the war. Grandmother was so strict that Rusty was relieved when her mother sent her to boarding school.

Yet boarding school truly was the most dreadful experience of all. Not only did everyone laugh at her American voice, but she got a demerit every time she said, "OK." The food was inedible. The dormitories were unheated. Rusty was behind in all her subjects, couldn't keep track of the millions of rules, and, worst of all, not one girl would be her friend because she was so different.

One day when her class went into town, Rusty heard someone yell, "Hey, Yank!" Was someone calling her? No, a boys' school group was calling one of their boys "Yank." Rusty excitedly rushed across the street to ask him where he was from. To her delight, he said he had been evacuated, just like Rusty, to the very town where Rusty's American grandparents lived.

Suddenly Rusty's chaperone yanked her away from the boy. To her horror, she had broken another rule: talking to a boy. Rusty was in disgrace. For days she was forced to sit alone in an empty classroom, even eating her meals there. Then a public announcement of her crime was made while she stood humiliated in front of the whole school. Afterwards, her hostile classmates treated Rusty as if she had the plague. They put gravel in her food and poured water in her bed.

When everyone was asleep, Rusty slipped out of bed to stare out her window high above the ground. Some scaffolding had been left along the wall by workmen. "I can't stand it any longer," Rusty moaned as she climbed out the window, looking dizzily down. "I've got to go back home."

—Catherine G. Edgerton

A BAND OF ANGELS   YA
By JULIAN F. THOMPSON

Talk 1

Jordan Paradise isn't your average teenager. He has neither a mother nor a father. He travels around the country, never settling for long in any one place. And if the US government men secretly trailing Jordan ever catch up with him, it's going to be murder. Literally. *His* murder. Jordan Paradise, a 16-year-old who wants to stop nuclear war, is the child of long-dead government scientists who discovered a secret weapon. This weapon was so awesome that Jordan's parents killed themselves rather than give it to any government. And now Jordan, his girlfriend, and three pals are being hunted down, and they don't even know it. They think they're camping, making friends, falling in love, and planning a peaceful future. They think teenagers can make a difference in the world—and they're right, if only they can live long enough to prove it.

—Stella F. Tjogas

Talk 2

Even before they started the crusade against nuclear weaponry, the government wanted them dead.

—Jeff Blair

THE BEAST IN THE BATHTUB   Grades 2-3
By KATHLEEN STEVENS

Lewis' folks tell him that he has just twenty minutes to get his bath and get in bed. They don't believe him when he says he can't because there's a beast in the bathtub. How is he going to get his bath, and what in the world can he do with the beast?

—Joy A. Basel

BEEZUS AND RAMONA   Grades 4-8
By BEVERLY CLEARY

What a terrible girl she was not to love her little sister! What would her mother think of her? Would she punish her? Would her mother stop loving her?

These were the disturbing thoughts racing around Beezus Quimby's head on what should have been one of the best days of the year, her tenth birthday.

But if you only knew this particular little sister, you'd understand. Ramona was a four-year-old hellion! Just to give you an example, I'm, going to tell you about the time Beezus tried to be nice to her bratty little sister by taking her to the public library to find a new book to read.

Everyone in the family was sick to death of reading Ramona's old favorite, *The Littlest Steam Shovel*. Even though Beezus loved books and reading, she hated having to make steam-shovel noises like "grrrrr" and "a-hooey, a-hooey" whenever she read to Ramona. So Beezus cleverly suggested that Ramona might like a *new* book. She took Ramona (who was wearing cardboard Easter Bunny ears and absolutely refused to take them off) to the Glenwood Branch Library.

After several embarrassing incidents on the walk to the library and in the library itself, ornery Ramona finally found a substitute for *The Littlest Steam Shovel*. To Beezus' dismay, the title was *Big Steve the Steam Shovel!* "You don't want *that* book!" whispered Beezus, quite annoyed. "I do too," insisted Ramona, forgetting to whisper. Since the librarian, Miss Greever, was now staring at them both, Beezus gave up. Even checking out the book was an embarrassment. Ramona thought she could buy the book and keep it. Beezus had to explain you *borrow* library books. Then dumb little Ramona insisted she could write her name by herself and have her own library card. When Miss Greever let her try, Ramona just made a big scribble. Again trying to be nice, Beezus checked out Ramona's book on *her* library card.

When they got home, Ramona demanded that Beezus read *Big Steve the Steam Shovel*. Beezus read it then and many times more over the next two weeks. Finally, to Beezus' relief (and her parents') the day came when *Big Steve* was due back at the Glenwood Branch Library. But Ramona insisted it was *her* book and even showed Beezus and Mother what she had done: she had scribbled her name in the book with a purple crayon! Not just once, but on every page!

Beezus was furious! That book was checked out on her card and was her responsibility. She was afraid Miss Greever would take her library card away from her and she'd never be allowed to check out books again.

Would she?

Well, you'll have to read *Beezus and Ramona* to find out—about this and the other obnoxious stunts Ramona pulls—that bratty little four-year-old Ramona, whom Beezus doesn't love anymore!

—*Mary Banach*

THE BELL JAR   YA/Adult
By SYLVIA PLATH

"That morning I had made a start. I had locked myself in the bathroom, and run a tub full of warm water, and taken out a Gillette blade." These are the words of Esther Greenwood in *The Bell Jar* by Sylvia Plath, who committed suicide a month after her only novel was published.

Why would Esther want to end her own life? At nineteen she had won a scholarship to college after making straight A's all through high school, and she had won a writing contest, the prize for which was a chance to work on a fashion magazine in New York for a month.

But Esther feels inadequate. She thinks that all she is good at is winning scholarships and contests, and that even that must soon end. The last time she was purely happy was when she was nine years old, before her father died.

After her month in New York, which she hates, she goes home to Boston. She learns that she has not been accepted in a summer writing course, and she starts to show signs of mental illness. She doesn't sleep at night. Her handwriting becomes like that of a young child. She quits working on a novel because she feels discouraged. Words and letters become unintelligible to her. She stops caring about her appearance.

She sees a psychiatrist, whom she immediately dislikes. He puts her in shock treatment and nearly electrocutes her. The next morning she makes a start, with the Gillette blade. To find out where this start leads Esther, read *The Bell Jar*, by Sylvia Plath.

—*Jennifer Kaye Cooper*

NOTE: The booktalker is a teenager.

THE BEST CHRISTMAS PAGEANT EVER   Grades 4–7
By BARBARA ROBINSON

The Herdmans . . . that name brought terror to the minds of all who knew. There were six of them . . . Ralph, Imogene, Leroy, Claude, Ollie, and Gladys.

They were unbelievable. Their idea of fun was to try to squash one another under the garage door. One day they even burned down Mr. Shoemaker's toolshed. They were using a "Young Einstein" chemistry set, and I guess it got out of control. You know, they weren't even scared. They were just mad that the chemistry set had burned up before they could try a *bigger* bomb! They were rotten!

The Herdmans were just as unusual as they were mean. They had a "Beware of the Cat" sign in their yard. New kids on the block laughed . . . until they met the cat. The mailman wouldn't deliver mail to the house because of that cat, and the first grade was practically destroyed by it.

The Herdmans attended my school. They didn't know math or reading or writing, but they never flunked a grade. But then, all the teachers knew that to flunk a Herdman would be asking for double trouble. You see, there was always another Herdman one grade behind. Two Herdmans in one class and we wouldn't have had a teacher! They were that bad.

You can imagine what happened when they showed up to try out for the Christmas pageant. But though it's hard to believe, that Christmas pageant turned out to be the best one ever!

Read *The Best Christmas Pageant Ever*, by Barbara Robinson, and find out how.

—Shelley Standley

BET YOU CAN'T   **Grades 4-6**
By VICKI COBB and KATHY DARLING

PROPS:
a dollar bill and two paper clips.
a penny.
a strip of paper (approximately 3˝ x 22˝), Scotch tape, and scissors.

Everybody likes to win bets or come out on top in a challenge match, but when you are a kid and surrounded by adults or bigger, older kids, sometimes it seems like you will always be the loser. Well, this book can help. There are seven chapters full of ways to fool your big brother, challenges to throw out to your father, things to make your mother scratch her head and wonder—and it's all based on scientific principles and natural laws.

Here's one I didn't believe until I tried it with my daughter and husband: a small person can force even a large strong person's fists apart. If I hold my fists like this [demonstrate from trick in book], do any of you think you can force them apart, using just two fingers? What you do is push or tap sharply with your index fingers against the backs of my fists: they will fly apart, because I am putting all of my force into up-and-down and you are pushing sideways.

Another good challenge is this: See if you can drop a penny held between your ring fingers with the knuckles of the other fingers touching.

[Demonstrate; you may need help getting the penny in; make sure they use *ring* fingers.]

There are other tricks here involving force and motion, fluids and how they work, the dynamics of airflow, and so on. Some of the most fascinating to me involve the study of form and shape, called topology. [Take dollar and paper clips.] For instance, I bet I can hook these two paper clips together using just this dollar bill. [Do trick.] Or take the Moebius strip [take the strip of paper, twist once, and tape the ends together]: An ordinary strip of paper has two surfaces, but because of the twist, the Moebius strip has only one continuous surface. When you cut it in half, it stays in one piece, and if you cut it again [cut as you talk], you get two pieces linked together.

These are just a few of the tricks and foolers you will find in this book. But there's one bet you are sure to lose. It's the one in the introduction: "Bet you can't resist trying at least one of the tricks" in *Bet You Can't*, by Vicki Cobb and Kathy Darling.

—*Jo Ellen Rice*

BETSEY BROWN   YA/Adult
By NTOZAKE SHANGE

Thirteen-year-old Betsey is growing up during the late 1950s in St. Louis, Missouri; she lives in a big roomy house with her father, who is a doctor and a musician; her mother, a social worker; her grandmother, who is hard of hearing when she wants to be; her two fresh nosy younger sisters; her older teenage cousin; and her younger brother, who likes to play with matches. Every morning Betsey has to bring her mother a cup of coffee, referee the bathroom, and prepare herself and the rest of the children, for the daily morning quiz, conducted by their father, about their Black heritage. Because Betsey is the oldest, she has some major responsibilities that she doesn't want to deal with. On the other hand, she has a romantic interest in Eugene Boyd that she *does* want to deal with, but she's not making any progress. Betsey's favorite secret place is an old tree near one of the many porches on her house where she goes to think whatever she wants, to feel whatever she feels like—until her mother hires a new housekeeper who somehow discovers Betsey's tree and commits the unpardonable sin of telling Betsey's mother. The housekeeper's days are numbered, but Betsey's life will never be the same.

—*Jacqueline Brown Woody*

BEYOND THE CHOCOLATE WAR   YA
By ROBERT CORMIER

Talk 1

Archie Costello, assigner of the Vigils, is losing his right-hand man to a girlfriend. Obie is showing more interest in Laurie Gunderson, a Monument High senior, than in the Vigils. Bunting, a sophomore, is desperately trying to replace Obie so that he can become the assigner after Archie graduates. In order to do this, he must prove to Archie that he is loyal and that there are no limits to what he would do for him and the Vigils. Bunting decides the way to do this is to do something about Obie and his girlfriend.

There was another car in Obie and Laurie's favorite spot at the Chasm, so Obie parked near a big old maple tree, with branches so low they scraped the roof of the car. Laurie had a cold and was not in a very good mood. They were seated as far apart as possible, arguing. A spotlight caught Obie and Laurie in its glare. "Lock your door," Obie called, but it was too late. The front door on Laurie's side was flung open and a lewd laugh rose out of the darkness behind the light. Obie hoped this was all a joke, a prank. A sick prank, but still a prank.

"Everybody out," a voice called, a voice he did not recognize.

"She's juicy, right?" another voice said. "Can I be first?"

Obie knew instantly it was not a prank. Rough hands pulled him out of the car. Laurie began to scream. Her screaming was cut off abruptly. The sudden silence was even worse. Was it Bunting? Had he succeeded in proving his loyalty to Archie?

Beyond the Chocolate War, by Robert Cormier.

—*Deanna Gulick*

Talk 2

An uneasy truce hangs over Trinity High. Archie, leader of the Vigils, is a senior and is picking his successor—and the enforcer for next year.

—*Mary Beethe*

Talk 3

Archie drew the black ball. Now he had to play the Fool and go under the guillotine. They should have known. Archie *never* plays the Fool.

—*Jeff Blair*

Talk 4

There was a traitor in the Vigils. Betray the Vigils and you betray Archie Costello. That's the last thing you want to do.

—*Jeff Blair*

BEYOND THE DIVIDE   YA
By KATHRYN LASKY

Meribah knows she will die here, high in the wintry California mountains, if she doesn't get some food soon. But near the doe's carcass she has found lying in the snow, two enormous vultures have landed. The huge birds try to claim the deer meat for their own, with stares like black fierce needle-points. Meribah stares back, her eyes growing large, her empty stomach rumbling. She is beyond fear. The pain of starvation is strong, and Meribah is not going to let the vultures take her meat, no matter what. With a shrill, savage scream, Meribah charges the birds, jabbing at them wildly with her rifle. The birds squawk and spread their wings, but menacingly stand their ground. Outraged, Meribah swings the rifle butt at them with all her might, slashing one of the birds' spreading wings. "Mine!" she cries, and she watches the black forms of the giant birds rise into the air and vanish over a ridge. Pulling out her knife, Meribah goes over to the doe's carcass, hoping that after the wolves and the vultures, something has been left for her: for Meribah Simon, fourteen years old, abandoned by an 1849 gold-rush wagon train; alone, starving in California's High Sierra with winter setting in. . . .

To see if Meribah can survive in this harsh land read *Beyond the Divide*, by Kathryn Lasky.

—*Diane Tuccillo*

BID TIME RETURN   YA
By RICHARD MATHESON

Richard Collier has just learned he has only about six months to live. He decides he'll spend the rest of his life doing exactly what he wants—traveling around the country. So he converts everything he owns to cash, puts some clothes in the car, and sets out. The first night out of LA, he decides to stay in an old Victorian hotel in San Diego—the Coronado Hotel (which really does exist). The atmosphere of the hotel affects Richard powerfully—the past actually seems to be alive here.

Walking through the lobby, Richard sees a photograph of a beautiful woman and immediately falls in love. Her name is Elise McKenna, and she appeared in a play at the hotel in 1896. Richard tries to find out as much information about Elise as he can—he consults books, newspaper clippings, hotel records, anything he can get his hands on. The more he discovers about Elise, the more he begins to realize that he is truly in love with her, the real woman, not just the photograph. And he begins to believe that somehow, though he doesn't know how, he once met and loved Elise. He remembers that he read some place that "what you believe is your reality," and decides to go back to 1896 and Elise by letting that time become his reality. He has nothing to lose by leaving the present; he's going to die anyway. So he changes his room in the hotel to one that had been there in 1896, gets clothes, a watch, some money, everything from 1896. He puts on the antique clothes, lies down on the bed, and begins to tell himself, "When I open my eyes, it will be 1896, and I will be able to see Elise." It's not as far-fetched as it sounds—Richard knows he'll make it. You see, during his research he found an old hotel register, and on November 19, 1896, *he* had registered at the Coronado Hotel.

—Joni Bodart-Talbot

THE BIG DIPPER MARATHON YA
By JEROME BROOKS

Horace Zweig, called Ace, his legs paralyzed and his hands weak and disfigured by polio, has tried for years to cope with his limits and frustrations. He has been "mainstreamed" at school, and both there and at home he is told he can do anything he wants, anything he aspires to do. His relatives in Chicago invite him to come visit. He is thrilled with the idea of riding a plane for the first time and making the trip alone from California to Chicago.

Ace and his cousin BC soon became good friends. Clarissa, a friend of BC's, suggests that they go to Dreamland USA, an amusement park. Ace is quite eager to go ride the Big Dipper roller coaster after seeing a poster of it in his cousin's room. Ace thinks it looks like a big silver snake as it races through the sky. His aunt, uncle, and cousin don't think much of the idea, because the amusement park requires a lot of walking. They don't say anything to Ace, though, because they are afraid of hurting his feelings.

BC chickens out when the time actually comes to ride the Big Dipper. Ace can hardly wait and agrees to ride with Clarissa. That's when the trouble begins. You see, the Big Dipper only slows down to let people on and off; it doesn't come to a complete stop. Ace has to throw his crutches into the car, unlock his leg braces, and get in—all before the roller coaster takes off again. He makes it, but just about falls in Clarissa's lap.

Like most people, Ace loves the ride. The quick dips, turns, and swerves let him feel a freedom he has never felt before. Before he knows it, the roller coaster is slowing down and people are getting off. Clarissa is no longer in the seat beside him. He can't even get a grip on his crutch or lock-in a leg brace before the silver snake is moving again. Then it hits him—he is stuck in the last car of the Big Dipper!

How many nightmarish rides does he make? How does it feel not to be able to jump over the side when the roller coaster slows down to let people off? Would you like to be in his place? Read *The Big Dipper Marathon* by Jerome Brooks and find out.

—Teresa Schlatt

THE BIGGER BOOK OF LYDIA   Grades 6–8/YA
By MARGARET WILLEY

Littlebit hates her nickname. She hates being called small, little, or tiny. It had started the day her father died five years ago. At the funeral several people commented on how small he was, how young he was. Lydia decided if he had been bigger maybe he wouldn't have died. That day she started writing her *Bigger Book*—her own survival manual, full of information on being small and how to be bigger, even information on vitamins, exercises, and ways to grow faster.

At fifteen, Lydia still hasn't grown very much, but she runs the household and everyone in her family believes she can handle anything. They don't know she still worries about her size. Then Michelle arrives. She's concerned about her size too, but for a different reason—Michelle has anorexia nervosa. She wants to shrink. They are like opposite sides of the same coin, and although neither of them can really understand the other, they have to share the same room, and they begin to talk.

—Beverly Harvey and *Joni Bodart-Talbot*

THE BIGGEST BUBBLE IN THE WORLD Grades k–3
By JANET LORIMER

How big a bubble can you blow with your bubblegum? I bet you can't blow one as big as Harvey's or Jeremy's! Read *The Biggest Bubble in the World* to find out how big that is.

—*Irma Piper*

BIRDY YA/Adult
By WILLIAM WHARTON

"Aw, come on, Birdy! This is Al here, all the way from Dix. Stop it, huh!" Al looks through the bars at Birdy squatting in the middle of the floor, ignoring him.

"Come on, Birdy. Cut it out!"

Birdy turns his back on Al. He just spins in his squat. He keeps his hands against his sides and twists around. He's staring up at the sky through a small, high window on the other side of the room.

"Hey, Birdy. This section-eight crap doesn't make sense. The stupid war's over!"

No response. The doctor-major told Al he's supposed to talk about things Birdy and he did together. They shipped Al out of the hospital at Dix to come down here. His face is still wrapped in bandages. He's between operations. It hurts to eat or talk, and he's been talking like crazy since nine o'clock in the morning. He can't think of any more things to say.

They were some pair, all right. Between the two of them, they had running away down to a fine art. Birdy wanted to fly, and Al wanted to chew nails and spit tacks. Birdy was into canaries, and Al was into tough Sicilians. World War II changed things for both of them.

The war drove Al and Birdy into separate cages. In running away, they were imprisoned. If you want to know how they found their freedom, read *Birdy*, by William Wharton.

—*Martha House*

BLACKBERRIES IN THE DARK   Grades 4–6
By MAVIS JUKES

Talk 1

Austin walked into Grandpa's barn. The room was dark; it smelled of motor oil. Austin stood by his Grandpa's workbench. It was the first time he'd been there since Grandpa died. He saw his grandfather's fishing gear: creel, rod, and rubber boots. His fishing vest and baseball cap were hanging from a nail.

"What are you thinking?" asked Austin's grandmother from the doorway.

"Do you remember, Grandma, about last summer when Grandpa took me fishing and stayed out late? We picked blackberries in the dark and brought them home and you made that pie and we ate it in the middle of the night?" He looked down at the floor. "He said this summer he'd teach me how to fly-fish at Two Rock Creek. And I was thinking about the day I wore Grandpa's baseball cap. He let met use his fishing, knife—he showed me how to clean a trout."

"I remember that day," said his grandmother. She bit her lip to keep her mouth from tembling. "Nobody knew that would be the last summer we'd all have together. Well, we can still have blackberry pie. How does that sound for dessert? Feel like picking?" Austin nodded. "You pick and I'll bake."

They walked outside the barn. "You coming?" he asked.

"These shoes hurt my bunions. And anyway, I've got chicken to fry and corn to husk. You can make it, Austin, just don't cross any fences."

Austin waved to his grandmother and walked upward through the trees. At the top of the hill he stopped and listened. Below him he heard the rush of water. "Two Rock Creek," thought Austin.

He tramped through the wood until he came to the edge of a rocky stream bank and looked down at the water below. There were blackberry bushes growing beside a boulder that rested in the creekbed.

Austin scrambled down the slope, making his way through the thick underbrush to the stream. He sat on the ground, tossing pebbles into the water. Then he stood up and began to fill the can with blackberries.

Suddenly, from the direction he had come, Austin heard the sounds of sticks cracking—as if something large was moving through the trees. His heart raced. He climbed to the top of the boulder for a better look. He listened.

It was quiet. Mosquitoes drifted in the damp air.

After a while, Austin came down from the rock. He ate a few black-berries and then dropped a few into the can. Again he heard crashing on the ridge above. He whirled around and looked up.

What was it, making all that noise? Read *Blackberries in the Dark* and find out.

—*Betty A. Holtzen*

Talk 2

Last summer Austin went fishing with his grandpa, stayed out late, and picked blackberries in the dark. This summer is different. Things have changed. Nobody knew then that would be the last summer they would have together. Even Grandma didn't know that Grandpa wouldn't be there any more. Now she and Austin remember together all the things they loved about Grandpa, and discover ways they can go on without him, and make new memories.

—*Janet Loebel*

BLIND OUTLAW   Grades 5-6
By GLEN ROUNDS

The boy could only make wordless sounds. He had some sort of impediment in his speech. So while he most probably did have a name, there was no way of knowing what it was. He'd ridden into camp with a buggy salesman, maybe a big ten-year-old or a small fifteen. Mismatched spurs, hand-me-down Stetson, boots far too large, an old saddle on his old, potbellied horse.

He pulled his weight, though, and then some. He wrangled horses, chopped and carried wood, hauled water, did a hundred small odd jobs. But his real talent was with animals. Carrying a magpie on his shoulder, he could nurse baby rabbits or a tiny coyote pup or a sick dog. Pretty soon nobody paid attention to the fact he could not speak.

But then a challenge unheard of presented itself—an outlaw horse brought in during the roundup. What's more, an outlaw horse that was blind. The ranch owner said, "I don't see how you could break him. And even if you did, what good is he? If you think you can gentle that blind outlaw, he's yours." The boy made a chirping sound. Could he do it?

—*Dee Scrogin*

A BLUE-EYED DAISY   Grades 4–8
By CYNTHIA RYLANT

The year Ellie reaches eleven is some year! She sees her uncle go off
to war, loses a classmate in a shooting accident, makes a best friend,
and gets kissed for the first time.

—*Cheryl Welch*

BONY-LEGS   Grades k–3
By JOANNE COLE

Do you think a mirror and a comb could save your life? A little hand
mirror and a wooden comb become Sasha's secret weapons when she
tries to escape the mean witch Bony-Legs in this book by Joanne Cole.

You see, one day Sasha was walking in the woods, carrying her lunch
in a basket, when she came upon a curious little house that stood on
chicken feet [show picture]. This was the home of Bony-Legs. When
Sasha opened the gate, it creaked terribly, so she scraped a little butter
off her bread and used it to grease the squeaky hinges. When Sasha saw
a very skinny dog barking at her, she gave him her bread. And when
she saw a hungry cat mewing sadly, she gave him her meat.

Then Sasha met Bony-Legs. She was a horrible, bad witch who could
run very fast on her bony legs. Her teeth were made of iron, and she
liked to eat little children. And her plan was to eat Sasha!

Luckily, because Sasha had befriended the gate, the dog, and the cat,
they returned the favor. They gave her the mirror and comb and helped
her escape—though you'll have to read this book, *Bony-Legs,* to see
how their plan worked.

—*Lynda Smith*

THE BOOK OF THREE   Grades 4–9
By LLOYD ALEXANDER

This is a book for all of you who love to travel off in your
imagination to magical lands, and make friends with brave knights and
lovely princesses who take you with them on exciting adventures and
noble quests.

When you open *The Book of Three* by Lloyd Alexander, you will find
yourself in the kindgom of Prydain, sharing the concern of Taran, the
Assistant Pig Keeper, who has just lost his most important pig, Hen
Wen. Hen Wen is special because he has magic powers and can reveal

the secrets of the future. Now Taran simply must find that pig, and soon! for there are signs that the Kingdom of Prydain may be attacked by the forces of the Horned King, and only Hen Wen knows the secret way to overcome this terrible enemy.

So off you go with Taran, and along the way you meet other companions who join him on this adventure: Gwydion, the great warrior (who is everything Taran wishes he were right now!), and Melyngar and Fflewddur Fflan, a wandering minstrel who loves to exaggerate about all the marvelous deeds he has done. But every time he gets too far from the truth, one, two, or even three strings on his magic harp suddenly pop, and Fflewddur very quickly admits how it really was.

After a long, exciting journey through enchanted forests and a strange land at the bottom of the Black Lake, Taran the Pig Keeper comes face to face with the evil Horned King. How does Taran meet this challenge? Is his own courage enough? Or do his friends come to his aid? After you find out, you can go on to read more adventures of Taran, Princess Eilonwy, and the land of Prydain in a series of books by Lloyd Alexander.

—Sister Patricia Wittman

THE BOYS FROM BRAZIL   YA/Adult
By IRA LEVIN

Yakov Liebermann is a German Jew who has dedicated his life to bringing Nazi war criminals to justice. The one man he wants to find more than any other is Dr. Josef Mengele, the "Angel of Death" who performed atrocities on the Jews at Auschwitz. One night he gets a phone call from his contact in São Paulo, Brazil, who says that he has seen Mengele with a group of former SS officers, and that Mengele told them that ninety-four men must die at certain specific times during the next two and a half years. Each of the officers received a list of people to kill and the dates they were to die. The deaths are to seem like accidents, so that there will be no suspicion of murder. The first killing is only eighteen days away. Just as the contact is getting ready to play a tape recording of the meeting for Liebermann, there is the sound of a knock on the door and the noise of a brief scuffle. Then someone else picks up the phone. Liebermann can feel hatred and evil emanating from the receiver, just as clearly as words. Then the connection is broken. Liebermann knows only one person in the world is capable of such evil: Dr. Mengele is alive, in Brazil, and it was he who had picked up the phone. What Liebermann's contact had said, then, was true—

and unless Liebermann can figure out the connection between them, ninety-four sixty-five-year-old men in government service will die, all over Europe and America, during the next two and a half years. And Liebermann has only eighteen days before the first murder.

—*Joni Bodart-Talbot*

BRAIN ON QUARTZ MOUNTAIN   Grades 3–5
By MARGARET J. ANDERSON

Dave wasn't looking forward to his summer on Quartz Mountain, away from all his friends and his baseball team, the Woodgrove Little Loggers. Things were definitely too quiet for him on the mountain—only a handful of people were working and living in the cabins at the science research center where Dave's father was the summer caretaker. But then Dave wandered into Professor Botti's lab and saw a large canning jar filled with a shapeless gray mass covered by a cloudy liquid. "Do you know what that is?" asked the Professor, and Dave was about to say he couldn't really see anything through all the murky water when suddenly the answer just came to him: "A brain," he said; "a chicken brain—and it's alive." He was right: the professor was growing a chicken brain in the jar, feeding it with a special culture to make it grow—and he wanted to hire Dave to read books to it all day to make it really smart. The job was dull until David realized just how smart the brain really was and how much bigger and smarter it was growing every day. Soon Dave found out the brain had plans of its own—it was looking for a human body to take over!

—*Zoë Kalkanis*

BROTHER IN THE LAND   YA
By ROBERT SWINDELLS

The nuclear war has come and gone. The missiles have flown, hit their marks, and completed their devastation. The long-feared nuclear holocaust is over. Now the real hell begins—for those whose fate it is to survive.

Danny is a survivor. So is his little brother Ben. *Brother in the Land* is their story. Their story of the early months after the bombs were dropped—of how they live, now that they have survived. Their old world and old way of life are no more.

As Danny describes what he sees and feels, you will feel as if you are there, struggling along with him—fighting for whatever kind of life is left in the new world that has been created by the bomb.

—Melinda Waugh

BURGLAR BILL
By JANET and ALLAN AHLBERG

Grades 2–4

Everything in Burglar Bill's house is stolen. He sleeps in a stolen bed and has stolen toast, stolen marmalade, and stolen coffee for his breakfast.

One night he goes to work, with his stolen sack slung over his shoulder, and finds a brown box with little holes punched in it. "That's a nice little brown box with holes punched in it," he says. "I'll take that!"

But the box isn't empty. Inside it is a baby.

Thinking the baby is all alone in the world, Burglar Bill decides to take care of it. He feeds it beans, diapers it with a towel, takes it for a walk in the park (at night, of course), and even teaches it to say "Runfrit," which is burglar baby-talk for "Run for it!"

That night Burglar Bill hears a noise and creeps downstairs where he hears a voice say, "That's a nice date-walnut cake with buttercream filling. I'll take that!" Burglar Bill is being burgled!

He opens the door, turns on the light . . . and to find out what he sees, read *Burglar Bill,* by Janet and Allan Ahlberg.

—Lou Rosenberg

THE CAINE MUTINY
By HERMAN WOUK

YA/Adult

The crew of the USS *Caine* were beginning to hate their new commander, Captain Queeg. The *Caine* was a DMS, a Destroyer-Mine Sweeper in the Pacific during World War II. The *Caine*'s mission was to destroy or remove all mines in front of its own oncoming fleet—obviously a dangerous job. The first commander of the *Caine* had been the respected Captain De Vreiss, but he was later replaced by a strange man by the name of Queeg.

A captain at sea has almost absolute power, but Queeg used his authority in peculiar, petty ways. Some of his actions were so bizarre that two of the ship's officers began to wonder if Queeg was insane. For example, one time the crew received a free gallon of strawberries for dessert. When the crew had had its fill, there were still some strawberries left. Later during the night, the captain asked for another serving of ice-cream and strawberries, but the container was found empty. Queeg was furious. He committed himself to finding the thief and devoted all the ship's resources to an investigation that went on for several weeks—just for a few strawberries. Another incident occurred immediately after a battle. Queeg noticed that the use of water for this particular day had increased by ten percent. This was perfectly normal on a day with battle engagements, but Queeg threw a temper tantrum and restricted all water usage for the next forty-eight hours—no joke in the tropics. No wonder the crew hated him.

Because of incidents like these, executive officer Maryk and gunnery officer Keefer decided that Queeg was sick. But not having the time to report this to higher authority, they dismissed the thought for the time being. Too bad, because on December 18th the *Caine* was in serious danger. It was caught in a typhoon, one of the most feared of storms at sea. Captain Queeg had not issued any orders when the ship entered the storm, and as the waves rose higher and the *Caine* began to wallow, he simply remained on the ship's bridge with a frozen look of terror on his face. When asked for orders, Queeg just mumbled. The *Caine* had almost capsized when Maryk finally relieved Captain Queeg, locked him in his cabin, and took over command. He brought the ship about and steered it to safety.

When the *Caine* returned to Pearl Harbor, the crew was quickly released on shore leave, but Maryk was called to a court-martial and charged with a mutinous act. If guilty, he would be finished as a naval officer, not to mention at least fifteen years in prison. His defense was based on Articles 184, 185, and 186 of Navy regulations, which say that an officer *can* take over a ship if the captain is sick or unfit for command. If Queeg could be proved unfit, Maryk had a chance.

Captain Queeg appeared before the court-martial looking neat and confident, and out for Maryk's hide. Had he really been insane? Was he *still* insane? Decide for yourself when you read *The Caine Mutiny*, by Herman Wouk.

—*David Yim*

NOTE: The booktalker is a teenager.

CALLAHAN'S CROSSTIME SALOON YA
By SPIDER ROBINSON

Have you ever known someplace where you were sure anything could happen, and it usually did? Callahan's is one of those places. If you're there at the right time you can see all kinds of people—time travelers, aliens, telepaths—sooner or later, they'll all show up. It doesn't really look like any place out of the ordinary. It's outside town and doesn't even have a neon sign, just a wooden one with a light on it. And inside, it's about as bright as any room in your home. Callahan says people who like to drink in the dark are unstable. All drinks are the same price—fifty cents—with an option. The option goes like this: put a dollar on the bar (Callahan doesn't take anything but ones) and you can either take your change from the cigar box of quarters at the end of the bar, or, when you finish your drink, walk up to a chalk line in the middle of the room, announce a toast, and hurl your glass into the big brick fireplace at the end of the room. Callahan keeps your change. And if you feel like talking after your toast, you have the undivided attention and sympathy of everyone in the room. Callahan knows there are few hurts that can't be helped by the advice, concern, and sympathy of thirty or so people who really mean it. Callahan also believes a bar should be fun, and his place always is—fun of the loudest variety, most of the time. That's how it was the night the guy with the eyes walked in. Everybody shut up and looked at him. He was nearly seven feet tall, dressed all in black, and his toast was, "To my profession, advance scout for a race whose home is many light years away." And his story was even stranger. . . . Then there was the night the time traveler explained the Law of the Conservation of Pain. And the time Callahan sponsored the Third Annual Darts Championship of the Universe, open only to his customers, and a telekinetic arrived and cleaned up—until the regulars found him out, with somewhat regrettable results. Women didn't go into Callahan's very often, but one, who was obviously somebody special, became a regular. . . . And these are only a few of the unusual visitors you'll find in *Callahan's Crosstime Saloon*.

—Joni Bodart-Talbot

THE CAMERA NEVER BLINKS YA/Adult
By DAN RATHER

I was on the wrong side of the underpass that day in Dallas in 1963. "Suddenly, I was aware that a police car had passed me, taking the wrong turnoff, going like hell. . . . All I had was this sense, an impression, of what I had observed—a police car, a limousine, then another limousine. Something had happened, but what?"

It was almost by chance that I was in the city. It was certainly by chance that I happened to be on the route of the cavalcade. But the events of that weekend would be indclibly imprinted on my memory. From noon Friday to 11:30 p.m. Tuesday I did not go near a bed or have more than a snack to eat. I have tried to tell what was going on behind the camera while the world was watching—how we got the story, and got it out.

The Memphis riots were no picnic either. We crawled on the ground and tried to be in the right place at the right time without getting killed by a mob that hated the media.

"We were the first to confirm on the air the death of the man who led the battle to win the rights promised his people one hundred years before. He had died as many, including Dr. King himself, had expected he would." And I wrote the stand-by bulletin that confirmed it.

What about Watergate? "I . . . covered the story every day to the bitter end, which came on August 8, 1974, when Richard Nixon went on national television to resign his office."

I've tried to tell you about it all, my mistakes and my triumphs and how I felt when they happened in *The Camera Never Blinks*.

—JoAnn Seyfert

CAP'N SMUDGE   Grades k–3
By STEPHEN COSGROVE

"Hey peg leg, old wooden toes!" yelled the fishermen as Cap'n Smudge limped by. "I'll get even," throught Smudge, as he leaned on the rail of his boat, eating a candy bar. He accidently dropped his wrapper in the water and watched it float away. The idea of a perfect plan was hatched. He would fill the bay with garbage; then the fishermen could not catch fish, only garbage. Soon all the fishermen were confused and angry. Only Serendipity, the pink sea serpent, could save them. If they could find her and explain the problem, she would know exactly whose problem it really was.

—JoAnne Clough

CARRIE YA/Adult
By STEPHEN KING

Carrie White was definitely different. She looked different: her mother, a religious fanatic, made her wear long, ugly dresses and fix her hair in an unbecoming style. And she had to carry a big King James Bible everywhere she went. Carrie acted different as well: her mother wouldn't let her go anywhere except to school and back—no extracurricular activities. Sports, clubs, dances, movies—everything was forbidden. The Whites didn't even go to church—Mrs. White thought that was sinful too, so they had their own church services at home, three or four times a week. And on top of it all, Carrie was the school scapegoat, the person everyone else laughed at, picked on, and mocked. She was the lowest of the low—*no one* was worse than Carrie White.

It had all started the first day of school in the first grade. Carrie had gotten her cafeteria tray of food at lunchtime, set it on a table, and knelt down on the floor to pray. Everyone had laughed, and she was marked. Even kids who were younger than she was began to copy their brothers and sisters. Carrie's days were spent in a living hell. No matter what she did, she couldn't fit in. She just took it all until she was seventeen. Then one afternoon she was walking home from school after a big scene in gym class and the little brother of one of her tormentors rode by on his bike and called her a name he'd learned from his sister. Carrie turned around and looked at him and thought, "I wish you'd fall off your bike and *kill* yourself!" And he fell off his bike! He got up and stared at her, terrified, and then ran off screaming. Carrie thought about what had happened and realized her mind had flexed in a certain way. She tried to see if she could do it again, but she wasn't as angry at the plate glass window as she had been at the boy, so instead of breaking, the glass just wavered in the afternoon sunlight. Carrie went home and began to practice until she could move anything with her mind. She could stop your heart from beating just by thinking about it! Then, almost as a joke, she was asked to the Prom, where the ultimate horrible surprise was waiting for her and her date, the surprise Carrie decided *not* to accept. Carrie freaked out and took revenge on everyone who had ever done anything to her. That's why it was called the year of the Black Prom, and why, less than two years later, the town was all but deserted—no one wanted to live there any more with the memory of Carrie White's revenge.

—*Joni Bodart-Talbot*

THE CAT ATE MY GYMSUIT   Grades 7–8/YA
By PAULA DANZIGER

Marcy is thirteen and a freshman at Dwight D. Eisenhower Junior High. She is fat and thinks she looks like a blimp. She hates her father, she hates Mr. Stone, the principal, and she hates gym. There's not much she can do about Mr. Stone or her father, but she can do something about gym—she refuses to change to her gymsuit. "The cat ate it," "My brother's using it for a security blanket," and "The Mafia stole it" are only some of her excuses.

But everything changes at Eisenhower Junior High when Ms. Finney starts to teach English. She's different—she looks different, she acts different, and she really cares. Maybe the way she teaches is unusual, but the kids in her classes begin to learn—not only English, but lots more besides. She even helps some kids start Smedley, an after-school club, where they can talk about all kinds of things that they want to discuss, but that don't fit into the English curriculum.

Unfortunately, Mr. Stone doesn't like Ms. Finney as much as her students do, and when he finds out she won't say the Pledge of Allegiance, he has her suspended. Suddenly, Marcy finds herself one of the ringleaders in the fight to get Ms. Finney back, and in even more hot water at home. She begins to realize she's got to do what's right for her, and not go along with what everyone else says is right.

—Joni Bodart-Talbot

THE CAT IN THE MIRROR   Grades 5–9
By MARY STOLZ

Erin was miserable at her new school. She was with her class on a field trip to the museum, and Fred and Faith and Rosemary were picking on her as usual. "She laughs like a hyena or something," Fred was saying as she moved into earshot. Boy, would I like to go through a mirror, Erin thought, just like Alice through the looking-glass, into another world.

Erin ran from the room, from her schoolmates, from Fred, from awareness, from the world. Somehow she would get away, away, away. . . . She ran blindly toward the big stone tablet in the Egyptian section, pitched into it headlong, and butted her forehead on a limestone corner.

"Oh, God," she sobbed, "Daddy! Somebody! Save me!"

A voice called to her from a distance. They were coming after her. To laugh or say they hadn't really meant it, or—

"Cat Queen, save me!" she screamed, and when she opened her eyes, Erin was lying in the desert with a tremendous headache.

The Cat in the Mirror, by Mary Stolz.

—*Becky Blick*

CAT WALK Grades 4–6
By MARY STOLZ

I was one of three kittens born in a hayloft of a barn in Vermont. I was different from all my family in three ways. First, I wanted to have a name of my own—and my wish was granted. I had three names. Second, I was black with the biggest white paws my mother had ever seen. I had six toes on each paw. As I grew, my paws grew with me. Third, I didn't want to be a mouser.

Our mother told us about all the other creatures besides cats that lived on farms—and also about human beings. She instructed me to learn the speech of human beings, but not to let people know I understood what they said—just listen—then I'd know what they were going to do.

Missy, the farmer's daughter, gave me my first name, Bootsy-Wootsy. She dressed me as her baby or doll. After I left her I had many experiences. One day after a big snow and ice storm I frightened a driver when I ran in front of his car in my skiing suit. Bang—he hit a tree.

Jerry, the first human I loved, named me Snowshoes. I was happy with him until I met a boy named Roddy—who completely changed my life. My last name was Max. Read Mary Stolz's *Cat Walk* to find what I found at the end of my long, long walk.

—*Laura Walker*

CATCH-22 YA/Adult
By JOSEPH HELLER

Do you like practical jokes? Well, let me tell you about the biggest practical joke of all. It was played on young Caleb Major by his own father! Or at least he thought he was Caleb Major and he'd always answered to Caleb, but when he started kindergarten he discovered a terrible secret. His father was a closet practical joker. And do you know what he had done to Caleb? He had named him Major! That's right. Major Major. Well, from this point on Caleb's, I mean Major's, life was one practical joke after another, right up to joining the Army and immediately becoming (what else?) a Major. And it's in the Army that Major Major Major meets his best and most interesting friends. There's Yossarian, who's furious because thousands of people he hasn't even met are trying to kill him; Milo Minderbinder who bombs his own airfield because the Germans make him an offer he can't refuse (cost plus six percent); the dead man in Yossarian's tent who's a great listener; and many more. Plus he learns the biggest joke of all, to which the answer is always "Catch-22."

—Caryn Grossman

THE CELERY STALKS AT MIDNIGHT   Grades 3-7
By JAMES HOWE

When the moon is up and the night creatures begin to stir, who knows what evil lurks in the hearts of lettuce? Join Chester the cat, Harold the dog, and Howie the dachshund puppy as they attempt to save the town from the vegetables that have been bitten by Bunnicula, the vampire rabbit.

—Olivia Jacobs

CENTAUR ISLE   YA
Fifth Volume in the Xanth Series

By PIERS ANTHONY

Dor, apprentice magician, age sixteen, was seated at a table, under the watchful eye of Queen Iris, who smirked at him from her place in the picture on the wall. "The Land of Xanth," he said aloud.

"Who wants to know about Xanth?" the table asked him. "I'm bored already."

"I know you are a board," said Dor. "It's the essay my tutor, Cherie Centaur, has ordered me to write as part of my training." The table sighed and settled itself.

In the mirrored surface of the table Dor could visualize his tutor. She had the forepart of a remarkably full-figured woman and the rearpart of a remarkably beautiful horse. But she was a hard tutor, nevertheless.

"I live in the land of Xanth, which is distinct from Mundania in that there is magic in Xanth. . . . "

Suddenly, he was interrupted by Irene, the palace brat, reading over his shoulder. "You are in trouble already. You can't spell. You need a

spelling bee. I will get you one. You know they can't resist letter plants."
Irene's talent was she had a green thumb and could make plants grow
instantly. She planted the seeds, watered them, and they grew and blos-
somed, each blossom a different letter. A big bee flew in the open window, going from blossom to blossom, gathering letters. "You will have
to spell for Dor before I let you out," Irene said. As she left the room
she said to Dor, "Watch the bee. It won't tell you if you have the wrong
word."

So Dor began again, saying each word and the bee spelling it, one
word at a time, no thought for continuity. "My tale is done," said Dor
finally. "Now I must take it to Cherie and I don't want to face her. She
might give me some more work to do."

"You can get a paper wasp to carry it for you, if you're asking me,"
said the floor.

"I'm not, but since you brought it up, where would I get one?"

"There is one living under my boards," said the floor, "that you could
set free." So the paper wasp set out to deliver the paper—a paper wasp
can do nothing else.

Irene, the palace brat, suddenly reappeared. "I just remembered
something. I hope you didn't use any homonyms in that essay," she
said.

"Don't worry. I wouldn't know one if I saw it."

Later, when King Trent called Dor to his chambers, Dor was embarrassed to hear that he'd made a lot of mistakes, but the king said not
to worry. "We have a job for you to do." The king and Queen Iris were
going to visit Mundania, and they wanted Dor to act as king while they
were away. How Dor and his friends handled the affairs of Xanth (land
of magic) and what they did when the king seemed to have disappeared
is the rest of the story. Dor was so busy he forgot all about that essay,
which Irene will share with you now.

The Land of Xanth
buy door

Eye live inn the Land of Xanth, which is disstinked from
Mundania inn that their is magic inn Xanth and nun inn
Mundania. Every won inn Xanth has his own magic talent;
know to are the same. Sum khan conjure things, and others
khan make a whole ore illusions ore khan sore threw the
heir. Butt inn Mundania know won does magic, sew its very
dull. They're are knot any dragons their. Instead their are
bare and hoarse and a grate many other monsters. Hour ruler is King Trent, whoo has rained four seventeen years. He

transforms people two other creatures. Know won gets chaste hear; oui fair inn piece. My tail is dun.

As you can guess from the title, *Centaur Aisle* is a very punny book.

—*Gwen Haegert*

CENTER LINE YA
By JOYCE SWEENEY

Being beaten by your father is bad enough, but to stand by and see him beat your four younger brothers is terrible. And so when Shawn is eighteen and ready to go off to college, he knows he can't leave his brothers behind. One night, all five of them agree to leave home and flee from their father's temper. Taking the family car, they just drive until they come to a town that appeals to them. Using Shawn's college money, they stay as long as they want, and then move on.

Meet Shawn, Steve, Chris, Rick and Mark; learn a little more about family togetherness, laugh at some of the crazy situations they encounter, and cry for the responsibilities Shawn was willing to shoulder just to keep his brothers safe.

Center Line, by Joyce Sweeney.

—*Pam Spencer*

A CERTAIN MAGIC Grades 3–5
By DORIS ORGEL

When Trudl was twelve, she was sent from Germany to stay with an English family and escape Hitler's persecution of the Jews. She hated the family she lived with and she hated the way people laughed when she tried to speak English, but she found a way to get back at everyone. She had an emerald ring with her, a family heirloom, and she remembered a story that all emeralds had magical powers, which could be used for good or evil. But the one time Trudl tried to use the stone, she became so frightened at what happened that she hid it away forever.

Trudl wrote down the story of the emerald and her frightening thoughts in a diary that she brought with her to America. Many years later, her niece Jenny found the diary. Jenny read it the day before she left for a vacation in England—and discovered that she couldn't forget her aunt's story. She had to return to the same village and find out more about the emerald's secrets.

—*Elizabeth Overmyer*

THE CHANGEOVER   YA
By MARGARET MAHY

Talk 1

Laura Chant and her younger brother Jacko were walking home from school one day when they passed an antique shop owned by Carmody Braque. When they talked to Mr. Braque, Laura noticed that his skin seemed to be mottled with bruises and that he smelled of peppermints and rotted, moldy mustiness; altogether a very disagreeable man. As they left, Mr. Braque stamped Jacko's hand with a rubber stamp made in his own likeness. Jacko didn't like this stamp of Mr. Braque's face, but no amount of soap and water could wash it off. And then Jacko became very ill with terrible seizures until he finally lapsed into a coma. Laura worried and wondered; she felt certain the stamp on the back of Jacko's hand was causing his illness. But what to do about it?

Join Laura as she is forced to change over—to become a witch—to save her brother in *The Changeover*, by Margaret Mahy.

—Pam Spencer

Talk 2

It was a warning to Laura. When she looked in the mirror that morning, she saw something in her reflection that scared her. The hair was the same, the eyes were the same, but the face in the mirror was older. It wasn't Laura. Then a voice said, "It's going to happen." Laura was really frightened. She asked her mother to let her stay home for the day. But her mother wouldn't write a note. Her mother was just too busy to pay attention. Of course her mother hadn't paid attention either when Laura had told her that Sorry Carlisle was a witch. Sorry was her neighbor. He was sixteen, a good student. Because Laura was a sensitive, only she knew he was a witch.

The day, though, turned out to be an ordinary one until Laura took her three-year-old brother Jacko into the curio shop. It was a strange little shop, and once she got inside, Laura realized she wanted to get out immediately. She could smell peppermint, but also something else— something very wrong. Then a man appeared behind the counter. He had a horrible smell and dark splotches on his skin, almost like bruises. It looked like his skin was rotting. The old man's name was Carmody

Braque. He seemed to like Laura's little brother Jacko, and he asked Jacko if he wanted to have his hand stamped. Before Laura could stop it, Carmody Braque pressed the stamp on the back of Jacko's hand. Jacko screamed as if his hand had been burnt. When Laura looked at Carmody Braque, she felt something very old looking back at her, something as old as the devil himself.

At home Laura tried to wash the stamp off Jacko's hand, but it was like a tattoo. That night Jacko wanted to go to bed early, and he had terrible dreams. The next morning the stamp on his hand had disappeared. Instead, his hand was red and inflamed. Overnight, the stamp had dissolved into Jacko's blood. Every day Jacko got sicker and sicker. They took him to the doctor, but no one could figure out what was wrong.

Jacko stayed in his room. He began to smell. Laura could smell the horrible sweet decay of the little shop—the shop of Carmody Braque. Jacko just continued to get sicker and sicker until he was deathly ill, and Laura knew she had to do something. Jacko was possessed. Sorry the witch told her there was only one way to save Jacko. Laura must give up her own mortality and change over to a witch herself. A changeover is a very risky thing.

Sorry tells Laura to "go while you still can." Laura has only three choices: life, death, or the supernatural.

—*Pat McDonnell*

CHARLOTTE SOMETIMES   Grades 3–5
By PENELOPE FARMER

This is a book about a girl called Charlotte who went away to boarding school for the first time. Because she was the first to arrive in the bedroom that she was to share with three other girls, Charlotte was given first choice of beds. Of course she didn't really care, but suddenly she felt strongly that she *had* to have the bed by the window, and when she looked at it closely she realized that it was different from all the others—it had funny old-fashioned wheels on it. That first day was very confusing; Charlotte met lots of new people and saw new places, but she wasn't so confused that she didn't notice the next day a tree which had not been there the day before. And the girls in her room were different: they dressed in strange old-fashioned uniforms— and they were calling her Clare instead of Charlotte. Slowly Charlotte realized that while she was still in the same school and the same room, she was back in the year 1918. She had a new name and a new sister.

As the week went on she discovered that she was actually alternating one day in the past with one day in the present, changing places each night with Clare, who lived in 1918.

Charlotte and Clare worked hard at leading two lives—they left each other notes about homework assignments, and between them they decided that it was the funny bed that was causing the time travel. But then Charlotte discovered that the girls in 1918 were to be moved to a different building with different beds, and she realized that if she were there on moving day, she could be caught in the past forever.

—*Elizabeth Overmyer*

CHARTBREAKER   YA
by GILLIAN CROSS

Finch. That's who she is now—one of the lead singers for the rock group Kelp. Tough, angry, and at the top of the charts. But that's not where it started—then she was Janis, seventeen years old, too big, too ugly, and too much in the way to suit her mother's hostile boyfriend. When her mother hit her during one of their fights, Jan walked out—in the pouring rain, with just enough money for a cup of coffee at a truck stop. That's where it happened, at that rundown truck stop. She met Kelp—Christie, the lead singer; Davc, the original blond bombshell who played guitar; Rollo, the drummer and the sensitive one; and Job, on keyboards, who wrote the song about Finch that made them all famous. [Insert partial song lyrics.]

But fame and fortune are not anything like what they expected—especially for Janis (now Finch), who finds herself turning into a completely different person, one she's not really sure she likes. Find out who she is—Janis or Finch—and whether she can really be a *Chartbreaker*.

—*Joni Bodart-Talbot*

CHASE ME, CATCH NOBODY   Grades 6–8/YA
By ERIK CHRISTIAN HANGAARD

Erik had to decide what to do with the package he was holding. The man who had shoved it into his hand and asked him to deliver it to a certain address had been arrested by the Gestapo only minutes later. The year was 1937, and Erik, a schoolboy from Denmark, was on a field trip into Germany with his classmates. World War II was still two years in the future, but Germany was already under Nazi rule. Erik didn't pay much attention to politics, but he disliked the Nazis. He decided to go ahead and deliver the package—and soon he too was being pursued by the Gestapo.

—*Roger Carswell*

CHASING THE GOBLINS AWAY   Grades 1-3
By TOBI TOBIAS

Jimmy's mommy says there are no goblins, but she is wrong. Deep in the night, when Jimmy's mommy and daddy are asleep, they come out. Jimmy knows they're coming out to get *him*. . . . Ten of them! A hundred of them! A zillion! Dad and Mom come to the rescue night after night, until the time finally comes when Jimmy must stand up to the goblins by himself. Jimmy's daddy says, "I know you can do it," but Jimmy doesn't know that at all. Alone in the dark, with the goblins, Jimmy can hear them breathing and snorting and laughing. All around him!

—*Janet Loebel*

CHICKENHAWK   YA/Adult
By ROBERT MASON

Have you ever dreamed of flying a helicopter? Did you know that to make the helicopter rise or fall, you have to use a corrective control stick? To make the helicopter pitch to the left or right, or stay level, you have a cyclic control stick to maneuver. And to cause the helicopter to turn in one direction or another, you have an anti-torque rotor to worry about. And on top of all that, you have to keep adjusting the throttle just to maintain the engine and rotor power. Now if that doesn't sound confusing enough, try to imagine remembering how all those controls operate as you come in for a landing in an area surrounded by trees with mortars and other artillery firing at you.

Read *Chickenhawk* and spend a year in Vietnam with its author, Robert Mason, a helicopter pilot. Imagine the skill you would need to land in tree-covered areas to pick up the wounded soldiers, the ingenuity and resourcefulness you would use to stay alive, and, most important of all, the sense of humor you would have to display to keep your sanity in a no-win situation.

—*Pam Spencer*

CHILD OF FIRE   Grades 6-9
By SCOTT O'DELL

The first time that Delaney saw Manuel was at the bullring. The first fights had been pretty boring, and the crowd was getting restless. Then someone shouted. A woman screamed. A young man had jumped over the wall. He staggered across the ring trying to regain his balance, dragging a red piece of cloth behind him.

Before anyone could catch him, the boy was at the bulls' entrance tunnel. There he went to his knees holding out the cloth.

The crowd fell quiet. "Huh, Toro!" the boy shouted. There is no more dangerous place in a bullring than the gate where the bull charges out of the tunnel. Cries of "No, No, No!" came from the crowd. They knew he could be killed.

Two matadors hurried across the ring to try to intercept the bull. They had reached the center of the ring when *el toro* burst through the gate. He was big and black, as black as the mouth of the tunnel. As the bull exploded into the sunlight, the boy stayed on his knees holding the cloth. He was very calm. Delaney realized that the boy would rather kneel there and be gored than run away or ask for help.

Delaney wondered how a boy not more than sixteen could kneel there calmly and face death.

The bull caught sight of the red cape—and charged.

Child of Fire, by Scott O'Dell.

—Becky Blick

THE CHILDREN OF HAM   YA
By CLAUDE BROWN

A group of kids living together in the inner city—Claude Brown writes about them in this nonfiction book, *The Children of Ham*. Claude Brown, you'll remember, is the black man who wrote about his own childhood in *Manchild in the Promised Land* and described his struggle with Harlem, growing up in the fifties and early sixties. He became a lawyer and left Harlem, but not really. Here he tells the modern-day story of what it's like to grow up in the ghetto for a group of kids who have banded together and called themselves the Hammites. They live together in an apartment in an abandoned tenement in Harlem. They run electricity in from the light in the hall (that still works) and they do without hot water. They don't have many neighbors, 'cause the building's condemned. Only junkies would stay there, but Hebro ran them all away.

Hebro's one of the oldest ones and he has no use for junkies. His idea for solving the drug problem in Harlem is to give all the addicts, say, three months to clean up and after that declare war on them—let out all the convicted murderers from jail and tell them you'll give them a week off on their sentence for every doper they kill. Hebro agrees his plan is pretty cold, but he feels it *would* solve the problem, and he thinks junkies would be better off dead anyway. Those that didn't get killed would clean up pretty quick.

Mostly the Hammites' folks knew where they are and don't care that much—it's one less mouth to feed. Forming a family of their own, they stick tight and expect everyone to speak out about what's right and wrong and stand by each other.

Salt-Noody, who likes to spray-paint the walls with his name—his territorial imperative, says Dujo—Salt-Noody also looks after the pigeons on the roof and fixes things. Jill is the big sister and mother to the Hammites. She's eighteen and she used to do everything—hustle, trick, cocaine, been busted and went into a detoxification program—swears off the stuff now.

Dujo is sixteen and though he's not the leader (the Hammites don't believe in leaders), his opinion is listened to and respected. He moved in when his mom went on a permanent nod. Dee Dee is fifteen and she has a thing going with Shaft—the only couple in the group. Dee Dee called the dime on her mother [story of dead junkie in bed with her younger brother and sister all day], so her folks were arrested. Her mother says she's gonna get Dee Dee when she gets out, but that's another two years.

They've all got dreams of escaping, mostly through college, and some are still in school trying to do well. They also dream of cars and clothes, and looking good, and some of the guys want to own a gun. Some of the younger guys think a lot about how to get their first lay. They dream about making it big in sports. They talk a lot about the life around them. And they're really street-wise: they know about heroin, unemployment, no hope, not enough food, pimping, hustling, running numbers, prostitution, having babies.

Do they realize their dreams? There must be an epilogue, Claude tells us, but time will have to write it for the *Children of Ham*.

—*Carol Starr*

CHILDREN OF THE DUST   YA
By LOUISE LAWRENCE

She saw the streets spread out beneath her, the river estuary shining silver in the distance, white piles of the nuclear power station on the opposite bank, and the Cotswold hills beyond. *She had to remember it. . . .* Gloucestershire green in the sunlight. A blackbird singing, and the wind blowing warm through her hair. *With all her senses she had to remember it.* All the sights, sounds and scents of a world she might never see again. The roadside was lacy with cow parsley, and May had covered the hedges with sweet white blossoms. Cattle grazed in the fields. A kestrel hovered, and the woods were dreamy with bluebells. She heard a cuckoo calling through the silence. *She must remember.*

It had started out a perfect day, a promise of summer with cloudless blue skies. The swallows were nesting below the eaves of the janitor's cottage, and out on the sports field the tenth graders were playing cricket and tennis. Everyone thought, when the alarm bell rang, that it was just another fire drill. But the first bombs had fallen on Hamburg and Leningrad, and a full-scale nuclear attack was imminent.

To find out what happened *after* that attack, read *Children of the Dust*, by Louise Lawrence.

—*Linda Olson*

CHIMNEY SWEEPS: YESTERDAY   Grades 4–6
AND TODAY
By JAMES GIBLIN

Suppose it is the year 1800 in London, England. You are eleven years old, and you are one of three boys who work as climbing boys for a master chimney sweep. When you were six years old, your parents sold you to the master, and you've been working for him ever since.

You must get up quickly at 4:30 every morning, or the master will hit you. You sleep in your clothes; you have no shoes. There is no time to wash your face and hands. After a small bit of breakfast you grab your blanket and a bag, a brush, and a scraper, and you go out on the streets to begin cleaning chimneys.

You must actually climb inside the chimney, scraping and brushing the soot out of it as you go up to the top and then come down again.

It is hard work and dangerous, too. Some chimneys are as small as six inches square, but most are nine by fourteen inches. Still small! Could you fit there?

Chimney Sweeps: Yesterday and Today by James Giblin tells you all about it! You'll find out
        —why chimney sweeps traditionally wear black tailcoats and top hats;
        —how it finally became illegal for young boys and girls to work as chimney sweeps;
        —and why it was supposed to be good luck to meet a chimney sweep on the street, especially on your wedding day!

—Dorothy A. Davidson

CHIP MITCHELL: **Grades 4-6**
THE CASE OF THE STOLEN COMPUTER BRAINS
By FRED D'IGNAZIO

Charlie got the nickname "Chip" after he proved to Miss Phipps, his suspicious math teacher, that using computers to solve problems is not cheating. It takes an unusual boy to outwit Miss Phipps, and Chip *is* an unusual boy. For one thing, he owns almost as many animals as the zoology lab at the University. And on top of that he's a master at solving mysteries and crimes that involve computers. Whether the problem is finding out why the electric company sent his Aunt Libby a $10,000 bill or proving that a computer really isn't a killer, Chip and his friend Leggs can usually solve the mystery. See if you can too!

—Vicki Rubottom

CHRISTINE   **YA/Adult**
By STEPHEN KING

Most teenage boys love their car. Arnie's loved him back. Loved him to death.

—Jeff Blair

THE CHURCH MICE IN ACTION   **Grades 2-5**
By GRAHAM OAKLEY

Another adventure with Sampson, the church cat, and all of his church-mouse companions. Humphrey, one of the more pessimistic of the mice, interrupts a perfect lazy summer afternoon by reminding the others that there is still a hole in the vestry roof and soon the rains will come to dampen things up a bit. Then Arthur, another of the mice, gets the brilliant (he thinks) idea of entering Sampson, who has just been washed and fussed over by the Parson's sister, in a cat show. If Sampson wins, they can use the money to fix the leak in the vestry roof.

Sampson wins the first prize—with a little help from his mouse friends, who plant themselves on the judges so that only the other cats can see them, creating total havoc during the judging. So naturally Sampson, who stands perfectly still in the middle of all the mayhem, wins by default. And by this method, he goes on to win other cat shows, collecting a total of ten pounds (that's money), a year's supply of cat litter, and three dozen boxes of flea powder. And his triumphs are published in the Wortlethorpe *Clarion.*

Little do Sampson and his friends suspect that there are others who have taken a keen interest in Sampson's winnings, others who are not very nice. If you want to find out what happens in the rest of the adventure, read *The Church Mice in Action,* by Graham Oakley.

—*Gail T. Orwig*

CIRCLE IN THE SEA   YA
By STEVE SENN

Robin Snow is a girl, a daughter of an archaeologist who lives in Florida. And Bree is a dolphin. Under normal circumstances they would never meet. But circumstances aren't normal. Bree has a strange illness the other dolphins call Nightsee—she falls under spells in which she goes into herself and sinks unconscious to the ocean floor. And Robin has a ring, a gift from her father, a strange ring carved with a dolphin, that he found on one of his underwater archaeological explorations. Robin discovers that whenever she wears the ring she becomes very, very tired. All she wants to do is sleep. And when she does, she has very, very strange dreams. But they're not really dreams. She gradually realizes that, when she wears the ring, she actually becomes a dolphin named Bree. And Bree, while unconscious with Nightsee, becomes a human girl named Robin. For Bree it's not so bad. She's fascinated with the human world she visits. But for Robin it's a nightmare, because the animals of the sea are angry, furious at the way humans have polluted their ocean. They've decided to turn on humans, to fight back. And Robin is caught in the middle—caught between her own kind and the ocean creatures she has come to love.

—*Christy Tyson*

CLONE CATCHER   Grades 4-6
By ALFRED SLOTE

The time was November 2019. The place was Australia. The mission was clone catching.

Arthur Dunn, of Dunn's Clone Catching, Inc., arrived in Australia ready for action. It was his business to catch runaway clones. And he was good at it. In fact, he was the best.

Dunn approached each job with care and cunning. He studied all of the clues carefully and always, always found his clone. This time, however, was different. Dunn sensed it right away.

Kate Montagu's clone was needed immediately. It was missing. Without the clone Kate would die. Kate's husband, Sir William Montagu, hired Dunn to find it—fast.

Dunn studied the suspects.

First was Sir William. He obviously loved his wife and did not want her to die. After all, he was the one who had hired Dunn. Dunn eliminated him as a suspect.

Next was Alice Watson, administrator of the main house. She seemed to be everywhere. Watson was responsible for running the huge house, and even though she answered all of Dunn's questions, there was always a tiny smile sparkling in her eyes. Dunn wondered what she was *not* telling.

There were other suspects, too. Billy II, Sir William's clone, was angry at everyone, especially Sir William. Kate's nurse was very cold whenever Dunn brought up the subject of the missing clone. And there was Norman, Sir William's son.

Dunn knew he would be in Australia longer than he planned. But he couldn't know what the final surprising outcome would be. The answer to the mystery was right under his nose!

—Sally Long

COLD SASSY TREE   YA/Adult
By OLIVE ANN BURNS

Hi! I'm Will Tweedy, and this here's my story about Cold Sassy, Georgia. It's really about the time back in 1906 when my grandpa, Rucker Blakslee, scandalized the whole town and shamed my mama by marrying Miss Love Simpson. My granny, Miss Mattie Lou, had only been dead three weeks; she wasn't even cold in the ground.

Oh, I'm going to tell you about Grandpa and Miss Love and her piano playing and their new Pierce Arrow automobile and about my aunt Miss Loma and her rubber bust, and about the time I got run over by the train—I got a heap of excitement to tell y'all about, in this here book.

—Pam Spencer

COME ALIVE AT 505   YA
By ROBIN BRANCATO

Danny Fetzer is the DJ for WHUP (that's 505 on your dial). Unfortunately, WHUP doesn't broadcast beyond the walls of Danny's bedroom, but that doesn't bother him. Over his high school years, he's made hundreds of tapes of imaginary radio shows. And suddenly it's his senior year, and time to make some decisions. Should he attend college, or should he go right to work at a radio station? And what should he do about Mimi Alman, this young lady who has just appeared in his life? Granted, she'a a little overweight, but she has this voice that's just fantastic for radio. For all you budding DJs, *Come Alive at 505,* by Robin Brancato.

—Pam Spencer

NOTE: Pam reads this booktalk over the PA system at her school.

COME SING, JIMMY JO   YA
By KATHERINE PATERSON

My name is James, not Jimmy Jo. I don't mind calling my mother "Olive," but why should she want us to call her "Keri Sue"? Oh well, let her call herself anything she wants, just as long as she leaves me and my name alone!

'Sides, I thought I'd never sing on the stage in front of people. I was too afraid. I could sing with Grandma or Jerry Lee, even there on the porch with no one but the dogs listening. But when people are staring, my innards turn to stone. I like singin' things like "Keep on the Sunny Side." That song just bounces the downs right up. Then if I close my eyes I'm back home—and all those faces out there disappear.

Leave it to Olive—I mean Keri Sue. She wants all of us to move to Tidewater, Virginia—leave the hills and Grandma just so we can do a show regular at some club. How 'bout me? I'll never fit in—those city kids look down on country folk.

Or would being a country music star make it different?

—*Sarah Thrash*

COMES THE BLIND FURY YA/Adult
By JOHN SAUL

The Pendleton family has just moved to Paradise Point, an old New England town. Michelle Pendleton, who is twelve, is a lively, vivacious young lady when she first arrives, but gradually her mother notices a change in her. Michelle has grown very attached to an antique doll she found in her new room and keeps referring to this doll as her only friend, Amanda. Her mother begins to wonder if Amanda is an imaginary playmate or a ghost. And when young children begin having accidental deaths, and Michelle is always close by, the whole town begins to wonder if Michelle isn't someone to be avoided.

Comes the Blind Fury, by John Saul.

—*Pam Spencer*

COMING BACK ALIVE YA
By DENNIS J. READER

My name is Bridget, and I'm a survivor. I learned it from my friend Dylan—he'd had more experience at it. I once saw his folks standing nose-to-nose, screaming at each other in the school hall, while Dylan watched, his face fading from bright red to a sick paper-white. They got their divorce a few months later, but the damage had already been done as far as Dylan was concerned. That's why, when my parents were killed in a car accident not too long after the divorce, he knew what to do. We had to get away—leave the whole mess behind us. So we made a pact that day to renounce the world, to live alone, together, by ourselves and for ourselves. Our families had rejected us, so we would be each other's family. Together, for as long into the future as we could see.

Dylan led us into an unmapped area of the Trinity National Forest, into the back of beyond. We would never go back to the suburbs again. We could survive on our own. Or could we?

—*Joni Bodart-Talbot*

THE CONTENDER Grades 6–9
By ROBERT LIPSYTE

"James, are you crazy, man? You can't shoot that dope and live. You think you're the only one with problems? Hey, man, you think I *like* working in this grocery store all my life?"

Alfred Brooks knew he would never become an addict like his best friend James, but he didn't know where his future lay. He only knew it lay beyond Harlem, beyond the black ghetto where he lived with his aunt and three cousins, beyond the grocery store that occupied all his time after he dropped out of high school.

He climbed the steps to the second floor boxing gym with uncertainty. Maybe this was a crazy idea. Maybe he'd train like a dog for nothing. Maybe he'd get his brains knocked out in his first fight. Maybe, but he had to try. He had to get out. He had to.

"I'm . . . Alfred Brooks. I come . . . to be . . . a fighter."

The Contender, by Robert Lipsyte.

—Dee Scrogin

THE COUNTERFEITER YA
By DENNIS HASELEY

James isn't your average high school junior—he's obsessed. There are only two things that are important to him: Heather, with her long legs and long, light brown hair, who doesn't know he exists, and the new piece of art he's working on. He is going to take Heather on a date, a very expensive and very stolen date. How? The new piece of art he's working on is a portrait of William McKinley, the same portrait of William McKinley that appears on the front of each and every $500 bill.

—Joni Bodart-Talbot

COWBOYS DON'T CRY YA
By MARILYN HALVORSON

My name is Casey Sutherland, and I didn't know Shane Morgan from Adam except that this was his first full day of school and he was in my Advanced Group class. Already he'd let Bart Willard pick a fight, and Bart does not fight fair. After that wicked right punch to the eye, I couldn't stand it any longer. "Knock it off, Bart!" He did, and the glare he gave me . . . but he listened, swore under his breath, turned and stalked away.

"Are you okay?"

"Yeah, sure." The typical male response.

The principal took Shane to the office. When he finally came to class, he smiled a grateful but crooked smile at me and sat down. There wasn't much to say so I didn't say anything.

That was my first encounter with Shane Morgan. The second wasn't so pleasant either. That poor palomino mare, and Shane . . . but that's what I'm not supposed to do, tell you what happened. It's Shane's story, so maybe I'd better let him tell it. He can do it better than I can. He does it in *Cowboys Don't Cry,* by Marilyn Halvorson.

—Verla M. Herschell

CRACKER JACKSON   Grades 6–8/YA
By BETSY BYARS

Talk 1

Can an eleven-year-old boy drive a car? Suppose he sits on two pillows so he can see? In this case, it was a real emergency, and Cracker Jackson was sure his best pal, Goat, would help him carry out his crazy plan—after all, Goat was the class clown.

Alma was the one who had nicknamed Jackson "Cracker"—like Cracker Jack. She had been his favorite babysitter, and even when she got married and had a baby of her own, Cracker still thought of her as a second mother. Then he saw the bruises, the black eye. Something was very wrong!

So Cracker was going to rescue Alma and her daugher in his Mom's car and make a mad dash to a safe place—if the police didn't catch up with them first, and if Goat didn't insist on taking his turn at the wheel.

—Kay Burkett

Talk 2

"Keep away, Cracker, or he'll hurt you." That was all the letter said. But Jackson Hunter knew who the letter was from. There was only one person who called him Cracker—Alma. Alma had been Jackson's babysitter when he was a little kid. She was married now and had a baby of her own, but Alma was special and the two of them had stayed friends.

"Keep away, Cracker, or he'll hurt you." The letter got heavier and heavier in his hand until he finally dropped it on the floor. Last week when Jackson saw Alma at MacDonald's she'd had a black eye. When

Jackson told his friend Goat about Alma and her husband Billy Rae, Goat's advice was, "Don't mess with him, because anybody with a python tattooed on his arm is bad news."

Jackson's best friend Goat was a lunatic, of course, and was at the moment grounded and in the doghouse. This time he was in trouble because he and Morrie had gotten bored at a movie. Spotting some girls from their class in the theater, they wet their popcorn at the drinking fountain and went back to their seats in the first row of the balcony. Then they made loud puking noises and dumped the wet popcorn over the railing. The girls had screamed and scattered like someone had yelled "Fire!" The theater manager hadn't seen the humor in the situation. Goat's mother hadn't either. And that was why Goat was in the doghouse—again.

But crazy or not, Jackson needed Goat's help. Alma was in trouble: her husband was hitting her. Only when Billy Rae *threw* their baby into the crib would Alma admit that she had a problem. What could two eleven-year-old boys do to help? Alma finally agreed to go to the battered persons center in the next small town, but the only way the boys could get her there would be to drive her themselves. Jackson was sure he could drive his mother's car—he had watched her do it so many times. And Goat even had some driving experience—he had driven his parents' car right through their laundry room!

Hilarious things happen whenever Goat is involved. Scary things happen to Alma. To find out how Cracker Jackson and Goat help Alma, read *Cracker Jackson*, by Betsy Byars.

—*Ann Provost*

THE CRAZY HORSE ELECTRIC GAME   YA/Adult
By CHRIS CRUTCHER

The Crazy Horse Electric Game was the pinnacle of Willie's athletic career. It was the last inning, and he made the impossible catch and won the impossible game. He was a hero: no one in Coho, Montana, would ever forget that game—or him. That was what he thought then. Just a few weeks later he was waterskiing, the last ride of the season, and pushed his limit a little too far. He flipped over, the tip of his ski hit his forehead, and by the time he got out of the hospital, Willie's body wasn't the finely-tuned machine it had been. He called himself a troll, and the cane his teammates gave him to commemorate the Crazy Horse Electric Game *wasn't* just for decoration—he needed it. He really couldn't walk without it. Jenny, his girlfriend, started going with another guy, and his friends acted strange around him. Then when he heard his parents fighting, arguing about him, he realized what a burden he'd become—and he left. Alone, without telling anyone, he got on a bus. He ended up in Oakland, California, at the OMLC High School— One More Last Chance—a school for all the losers, quitters, crazies, and drifters that were willing to try *once* more. There he finally realized that he too had one more chance to get his life, and maybe his body, back together. Maybe, just maybe, he didn't have to be a troll forever.

—*Joni Bodart-Talbot*

THE CRIME OF THE CENTURY YA/Adult
By HAL HIGDON

The "Crime of the Century" took place on May 21, 1924, in Chicago and was planned and carried out by two college students, seventeen and eighteen years old. Soon after Bobbie Franks, fourteen, heir to $4 million, disappeared on his way home from school, his father received a ransom note demanding $10,000 for the return of his son. He was eager to pay the ransom, but before he could do so, Bobbie's naked body was found stuffed into a culvert near Wolf Lake, on the Illinois-Indiana border. The case made headlines across the country, especially when the two students were arrested and charged with the killing. They were Nathan Leopold Jr. and Richard Loeb, both sons of millionaires and near-geniuses. They felt no guilt about the murder—only chagrin that they had been caught, since they had planned what they thought would be the perfect crime. Bobbie's death was only a minor part of their plan, and they had felt no compunction about killing him. In fact they hadn't chosen him at all—they didn't pick out a specific victim, Bobbie happened to be in the wrong place at the wrong time. Clarence Darrow agreed to defend Leopold and Loeb, and his reputation as a criminal lawyer is partly based on the fact that he won a sentence of life imprisonment for both of them, instead of the death sentence most people expected. Recently, after all the major participants in the case were dead, the author Hal Higdon went to Chicago and interviewed other people who had been involved. He did in-depth research on several aspects of the case that were too controversial to be made public in the 1920s and are revealed here for the first time. The question of who did the actual killing is raised, since Leopold and Loeb each accused the other and there were no witnesses. Their actual descriptions of what took place are horrifying [pp. 101-102, hardback edition].

If you liked *Helter-Skelter* or *Bonnie and Clyde,* you'll like *Crime of the Century: The Leopold and Loeb Case,* by Hal Higdon.

—*Joni Bodart-Talbot*

THE CROSSING   YA/Adult
By GARY PAULSEN

Thirteen-year-old Manny is alone and fighting to survive the streets of Juarez. He's begging for food and money, sleeping in doorways, and trying to stay out of sight of the others, especially the hawks. He is determined to cross the river to the Promised Land—the United States. Before he is able to make the crossing, Manny meets Sergeant Locke.

Sergeant Locke is fighting to die. Each night he drinks cheap whiskey to the point of being "brain-dead." If he isn't brain-dead, all his friends from all the battles come to haunt him. But Manny doesn't know about the ghosts. He only knows that Sergeant Locke is strange, kind, and has money; and Manny needs money to make the crossing. Do either of them foresee that, in helping Manny, Sergeant Locke too will make a crossing?

—*Sue Padilla*

A CRY IN THE NIGHT   YA/Adult
By MARY HIGGINS CLARK

Even after the children had been missing for weeks, Jenny found that her ears were still tuned for the baby's hungry cry.

The weatherman reported that the wind-chill factor was twenty-four below zero, so she dressed warmly to avoid freezing to death as she went in search of the cabin. She felt that the clue to finding her children was in the cabin in the woods. Erich had never let any of them go to the cabin because he said every artist needed an isolated place to work.

All day she skied in the woods. Just as the sun was going down she came upon the cabin. Her heart sank. The shades were drawn and dark. She kicked off her skis, pushed the door open, and was immediately surrounded by his paintings. She looked hastily through the canvases, searching for some clue.

Then she saw it. Hardly knowing what she was doing, she stumbled toward the staircase and ran to the loft. She grasped the canvas and yanked it from the wall.

Seconds later she was skiing away from the cabin. She was screaming, "Help me! Someone please help me!" The wind whipped her cry
into the woods.

—*Lola Viets*

CRYSTAL   YA
By WALTER DEAN MYERS

Crystal is black, tall, slender, gorgeous, sixteen, and a professional
model, who may be offered a part in an upcoming movie. But can she
be a professional and a normal high school student too? Will she have
to give up her friends—or her career?

—*Joni Bodart-Talbot*

THE CRYSTAL CAVE   YA
THE HOLLOW HILLS
By MARY STEWART

When someone mentions Merlin, you probably think of a very old,
very strange man with magical powers, associated with King Arthur
and his Knights of the Round Table. But who actually was Merlin? He
wasn't an old man all his life—he must have been a boy sometime. Did
he really resemble the traditional magician, white bearded, with a long
black robe and pointed hat and a staff or wand? Or is it true he was the
illegitimate son of a king or perhaps a "devil's spawn," condemned to
death as a child? Mary Stewart has taken bits and pieces of legends and
histories and woven them into a tale of Merlin's childhood and young
manhood. She explains how he found the magical secret crystal cave
that made him aware of his special powers and who Merlin's teachers
were. We first see him as a not-very-happy six-year-old boy, who
doesn't have any idea what his destiny will be.

The Hollow Hills takes up the story and tells of Merlin as a young
man, and of Arthur as a boy.

The life of Merlin the magician, a man who was and is a mystery.

—*Joni Bodart-Talbot*

THE CUCKOO SISTER YA
By VIVIEN ALCOCK

I was five years old when I found out about Emma. Before that, I'd always thought that I was an only child. I knew that the first of August was always a bad day for Mama, I just didn't know why—but that day I found out. It was Emma's birthday. She was my sister, and she'd been gone for seven years when I found out about her. And from that day, I was a different person. I had always been a good little girl—but no more! I lied, I stole, I had temper tantrums, listened at doors, and read other people's mail. And I lost things, presents people gave me, even very expensive ones. When my mother fussed at me about it, I screamed at her, "Look who's talking! Who lost her own baby? Who lost my sister? Just because you wanted a new dress!" Then my mother would go off somewhere to cry, and my father would look angry, and take me into his study for a long reproachful talk that I tried not to listen to.

Then on August 1st, the year I was eleven, Emma came back. When I opened the door, she was there—terribly thin, with short, spiky hair. Her clothes were clean, but they didn't fit her. The frilly blouse was too big, and the skirt was too skimpy. She had on ankle socks and scuffed white heels. Her arms and legs were like sticks, and her skin was sallow and dirty-looking. This wasn't the sister I'd always wanted—this was no soft and cuddly baby, this thin stranger with too much makeup and hard, suspicious eyes. But she was here, and I was stuck with her, like it or not.

—*Joni Bodart-Talbot*

DAKOTA DUGOUT Grades 4–8
By ANN TURNER

Sometimes the things we start with are best. A woman tells her granddaughter about her life in a sod house on the Dakota prairie a hundred years ago. The first year was hard and lonely, yet she could remember how the grass whispered like an old friend, and how the earth kept them warm.

—*Janet Loebel*

DANCING CARL   YA/Adult
By GARY PAULSEN

The rinks are everything in the winter. But that winter of 1958, Dancing Carl became everything.

—*Cheryl Welch*

THE DANGER QUOTIENT   YA
By ANNABEL and EDGAR JOHNSON

The year is now 2126 A.D. The ozone layer of the earth's atmosphere has been destroyed by the H-bombs of the Third World War. Because there's no longer any protection from the deadly ultraviolet rays of the sun, what's left of the population of the United States is living underground. There are two colonies, one under Colorado and one under Massachusetts.

In the Colorado colony lives KC-4, one of the genetic super-kids, bred for his brains. He's supposed to be working on the ozone layer problem, but instead he's built a time-travel machine. He's having such a wonderful time zipping back and forth between 2126 and the 1900s that he's completely forgotten about the ozone layer problem.

Then one day he finds a reference to himself in a Colorado newspaper from the 1980s, and realizes that perhaps he's lived a previous life.

Read how KC-4 solves the ozone layer problem and the mystery of his seemingly previous life in *The Danger Quotient,* by Annabel and Edgar Johnson.

—*Pam Spencer*

DAPHNE'S BOOK   Grades 6–8
By MARY HAHN

Who would want to enter the seventh-grade Write-A-Book contest with Daffy Duck as a partner? Definitely not Jessica, but she was the unlucky one picked by Mr. O'Brien to do just that. Who is Daffy Duck, and why doesn't anyone like her? You can find out in *Daphne's Book*, by Mary Downing Hahn.

—*Pam Swofford*

DARK FORCES   YA/Adult
By KIRBY McCAULEY

Do you like to be scared? Do you enjoy reading a book by Stephen King late at night? Do you jump every time the house creaks or tree branches brush against the window? If you do, then you'll love this new collection of some of the best horror stories I've ever read. You'll meet ancient, shy creatures in the sewers of New York City and zombies who become store clerks in California. A woman takes the ultimate revenge against the man who wronged her—he didn't know she was a witch. Kudzu grows on and over everything, taking over all it touches— perhaps people as well as buildings.

Mist takes over too, and since it's in a story by Stephen King, it's a deadly mist, and one that has strange, unearthly creatures in it. As it spreads, people flee before it, and some of them are trapped in a grocery store. Four creatures that look like bizarre, naked, pink bugs with long stingers crawl over the window like maggots on dead meat. But they aren't the real danger—the real danger is the huge flying things with leathery wings, albino-white bodies, and reddish eyes. They eat the pink bugs and slam into the plate glass window hard enough to make it shudder. If they can't be stopped before the glass shatters, the people inside will all die.

—Joni Bodart-Talbot

DARRYL STINGLEY: HAPPY   YA/Adult
TO BE ALIVE
By DARRYL STINGLEY

On a hot day in mid-July, 1978, Darryl Stingley checked into the New England Patriots training camp in Rhode Island. He was a five-year veteran, coming off his best season as a wide receiver. His agent was wrapping up negotiations on a half-million-dollar contract, and Stingley was in the best shape he'd ever been in.

In August, the four-game exhibition season began, with the Patriots playing the Los Angeles Rams first, followed a week later by a game against the Raiders at Oakland. Two nights before the Raiders game, Stingley told a fellow player that he'd been having strong negative vibes, stronger than any he'd had before. Although he wasn't psychic, he kept looking for something to happen. He didn't know what it would be, but he didn't think it would be related to football.

Crossing the Bay Bridge on the way to the Oakland stadium, Stingley thought about the Raiders and the tough game of intimidation they played. A New England-Oakland game, even in preseason, would not be just another NFL game. It would be a war.

Stingley was on the field for the kickoff, and was to play the whole first half. As they approached the end of the first half, Oakland led by a field goal. The Patriots had a third down and eight yards to go at the Oakland 24-yard line.

The Patriots broke out of the huddle and lined up in the Ninety-Four Slant, which was a quick pass play. The quarterback, Steve Grogan, called his signals, the ball was snapped, and the play was on. Jack Tatum was the Oakland free safety, and he had no trouble reading Grogan on the play. He knew Grogan would be throwing to only one person: Darryl Stingley.

The pass was well over Stingley's head; he never had a chance to catch it. The ball flew past his outstretched fingers as he leaped high into the air. He was coming back to earth when he saw Tatum barreling toward him at full steam. Stingley dropped his head low to duck, but it was too late. The blow hit on the head and on the back of the neck with full force.

Stingley hit the ground with a thud. When he tried to get up, he couldn't move. He felt as if an elephant had a foot on his chest. He couldn't feel any pain, but he also couldn't feel his feet or his arms or his body.

Follow Darryl Stingley on his long journey, one that began when he was a kid growing up on Chicago's tough West Side, continued through high school and college athletics to his career in pro football, and then began again—when he was carried off the field in Oakland.

—Patricia Farr

DAUGHTER OF TIME   YA
By JOSEPHINE TEY

Richard III: a villain incarnate, murderer of innocent children, one of England's most hated and wicked kings—true or false? This mystery tells of one man's search for the real Richard, not as Shakespeare described him, or as legends portray him, but as he really was. Inspector Grant of Scotland Yard was in the hospital, flat on his back from injuries received in his last case. Marta, one of his good friends, came to visit him and decided what he needed was a good mystery to take his mind off his problems—some unsolved historical mystery that he could work on while he was in the hospital, so he wouldn't have to run around looking for clues. Marta also brought a stack of portraits of famous and infamous people, past and present. Grant was a confirmed people-watcher, and she thought the portraits might keep him occupied until she could find a mystery for him. Grant wasn't really interested in any of them, but one picture caught his eye because he couldn't figure out who it showed—a man who looked as if he'd suffered a great deal, richly yet soberly dressed, a proud and gentle person. Grant turned the picture over and discovered it was the villainous Richard III. History's records of this king definitely did not fit that portrait! Who was right? Grant had his mystery, and when he began to investigate, he found some very unusual information. To learn what he found, and who Richard really was, read *Daughter of Time*, by Josephine Tey.

—Joni Bodart-Talbot

DEAD BIRDS SINGING   YA
By MARC TALBERT

Matt lay cringing in the swirl of nightmare sensations—flashing lights, siren, smell of gas and oil, the sound of metal grinding metal. His sister was sprawled on the hood. Her face was horribly mangled. His mother was a slumped figure.

Out of the jagged hole in the windshield came a man's voice, "I sho shorry. I sho shorry. I sho shorry."

Matt suddenly realized who had smashed into them.

—Janet Loebel

DEADLINE   YA
By KATHLEEN A. BEGLEY

The policeman walked into the city room and said that "a little girl" injured in a car accident had asked him to bring a photograph to the newspaper office. The "little girl" trying so anxiously to meet her first deadline was Kathleen Begley, then a naive, eighteen-year-old college student and summer copygirl on the *Daily Times* in Chester, PA. She had been gathering some information on a local young soldier killed in Vietnam. Driving her ten-year-old jalopy back to the city room and running late, she had panicked and somehow plowed up on a curb and onto a church lawn, and was brought to a dramatic halt by a large oak tree. Her name did appear in print, not for the soldier's story, but as part of the news coverage of her own accident!

Thus began the journalism career of Kathy Begley, who rose to a reporting job on the *Philadelphia Inquirer*, a nationally-known, award-winning daily. Her experiences included covering the tragic aftermath of Tropical Storm Agnes, one of the worst natural disasters in US history; the trial of the National Guardsmen who opened fire on student protesters at Kent State University; and the violence during the integration of Boston's public schools. On the lighter side, she reported on her small town's entrant in the National Spelling Bee; she almost got picked to be a TV anchorwoman; and she uncovered the seamier side of the Miss America Contest.

But this is not just a chronicle of news stories and meeting deadlines. It is also the story of one woman, and how she grew up on the job and in her own life.

—*Patricia Farr*

DEAR BILL, REMEMBER ME?   Grades 6–8/YA
By NORMA FOX MAZER

Talk 1

Dear Bill, Remember Me? is a collection of eight short stories about eight young women. You'll meet Jessie, whose English teacher makes them all keep a journal as a class assignment. At first, all she can think of to write in it is what she ate for lunch, but soon she finds she's telling the story of her first romance. Her teacher has promised she won't read anything in it; she just wants to make sure they've written regularly, but Jessie's not sure just how much she can trust that promise—how much should she tell? Kathy tries to write the perfect letter to her sister's ex-boyfriend—the letter that starts, "Dear Bill, remember me?" Louise writes about something deadly serious, something no one, not even her friends, will let her talk about. And then there's Mimi, whose mother sends her out on her first date with a packet of smelly Limburger cheese in her pocket!

—*Elizabeth Overmyer*

Talk 2

This book is called *Dear Bill, Remember Me? and Other Stories*. It contains eight short stories by Norma Fox Mazer. The one I'd like to tell you about is called "Mimi the Fish." Mimi is not a fish; she's a teenager with a very active imagination. In her fantasies Robert Rovere is in love with her. He's the handsomest boy she's ever seen. Just being in the same classroom with him makes her heart beat faster. Too bad he doesn't even know she's alive. Or at least he probably didn't until Susan, Mimi's one and only friend, passed him a note in class. Susan figured it was time they found out what, if anything, Robert thought of Mimi. So she wrote him a note: "Robert, someone with the initials MH (that's for Mimi Holzer) likes you very much. How do you feel about her? Respondez s'il vous pleeze on the other side." Well, Robert responded, all right. He wrote back. "Tell her to go pluck a duck." Not a very romantic reply. With this Mimi went back to daydreaming.

Several days later, Robert called her and invited her to a dance. She was petrified that it was a prank. Maybe it wasn't even Robert on the phone. Maybe she'd get all dressed up and ready and then he wouldn't show. How disappointed she would be. How disappointed her mother would be! (Honestly, you'd think Robert had asked her mother out, she was so excited!)

Mimi was really surprised when there was a knock on the door that Friday night. Robert had shown up. She could hardly believe it. She tried to hurry him out as quickly as possible. She was embarrassed about the way their house looked; it was really just a couple of rooms behind the family butcher shop. And she certainly had no great desire for Robert to meet her parents. She and Robert were already out in the driveway free and clear when her mother came running from the house holding a package wrapped in white paper. She forced the package into Mimi's hands, all the while chitchatting with Robert. She told Mimi to deliver the package to Milly Tea. It was limburger cheese, and she had promised it to Milly for Milly's party that night. Do you know what limburger cheese smells like? It probably has the strongest odor of any cheese in the world. Even people who love it have to admit that it stinks. Mimi protested, but her mother was insistent. The cheese went with Mimi.

Well, Robert didn't seem too put out about having to go out of their way on this errand, so they set out to Milly Tea's house. Mimi held the package in the hand away from Robert, but the smell seemed to be creeping right up her arm. At Milly's she rang the doorbell and a boy answered. She tried to offer him the cheese, explaining it was for Milly, but all the boy said was, "Phew! That stinks. There's no Milly here. You've got the wrong house."

Well, there was nothing left to do but take the cheese and go to the dance. So Mimi goes on her first date ever, with a boy she's absolutely wild about and also with a messy package of cheese that's smelling more and more like somebody's dirty feet. It's called "Mimi the Fish" and it's one of the stories in *Dear Bill, Remember Me?*

—*Rayme Gwen Meyer*

DEAR MISS MOSHKI Grades 4-6
By CRESCENT DRAGONWAGON

Jeremy and Chris are sitting out in the hall because they got into trouble in Miss Moshki's fifth-grade class. But what happens if they are still stuck outside when the famous author comes to visit? Help them think of a way to get back inside.

—Irma Piper

DEAR MR. HENSHAW Grades 4-6
By BEVERLY CLEARY

I read question number 9. "What bothers you?" I guess I'm bothered by a lot of things. I'm bothered when someone steals something out of my lunchbag. I'm bothered when my Dad telephones me and finishes by saying, "Well, keep your nose clean, kid." Why can't he say he misses me, and why can't he call me Leigh? It bothers me even more when he doesn't call at all, which is most of the time.

I wrote to my favorite author, Mr. Boyd Henshaw, as a classroom assignment, and to my surprise Mr. Henshaw sent *me* a list of ten questions to answer. Nobody else's author put in a list of questions to answer, and I didn't think it was fair to make me answer questions like number 9 when I already wrote a report. Reluctantly, I answered the questions over a period of several weeks—only because Mom made me. Mom said the least I could do was answer Mr. Henshaw's questions, since he took the time to answer mine.

I wonder if I'll ever catch the person who is stealing parts of my lunch every day. I wonder if Dad will ever find Bandit, my dog, who got lost in a snowstorm. I wonder if Mom and Dad will ever get married again. Read *Dear Mr. Henshaw*, by the popular Beverly Cleary.

—Donna P. Hitchens

THE DEATH TICKET YA
By JAY BENNETT

The ticket came like all the others: special delivery, registered—and the message: "Gil, take care of this for me. Take good care of it." And it was signed, "The Dwarf."

The ticket was one half of a New York State lottery ticket. The numbers were always the same: 25-30-32. Gil wondered who had the other half of it—what were the numbers on that half? It really didn't matter—the Dwarf never won anyway.

The Dwarf was Gil's older brother Gareth. Until he was twelve Gil had always called his brother Gareth. But Gareth finally demanded he call him the Dwarf, for that was what he was—a freak. One day the Dwarf just left home to live alone in a New York City loft. Gil loved his brother, but others who knew him said he was evil.

So Gil locked the ticket away in the small metal box, not realizing at the time that this ticket was so very different. This one carried death with it.

—*Marianne Tait Pridemore*

DEATHWATCH YA
By ROBB WHITE

Madec isn't the kind of person Ben usually takes on a hunting trip—he is cold and insensitive, and seems to enjoy hurting people. But it is nearly time for school to start, and Ben hasn't earned enough money guiding hunters in bighorn sheep country to pay for the next year of college. Madec has offered Ben more than enough money to pay his college expenses. Ben can't refuse, and since they'll only be gone for just over a week, he figures it'll be okay.

In order to hunt bighorn sheep, you have to have a license, and to get a license, you have to get on a waiting list, which can be *very* long. Once you have your license, it's good for only seven days, and for only *one* male sheep. If you don't get that sheep in seven days, it's just too bad, and you go back on the waiting list. You may never get to the top again.

Ben and Madec have been out for three days and haven't seen one sheep. By the fourth morning, Madec is getting impatient; he is sure Ben is deliberately taking him to the areas where there are no sheep. He decides to lead the way himself. He sees something moving up on a ridge and shoots it before Ben can check it out. Ben says, "Are you sure that was a male sheep? I didn't see any horns." But Madec is sure and goes up to get his sheep. Then he comes back down immediately and says he missed. When Ben gets up to the top of the ridge, he discovers that Madec has been lying—it isn't a male sheep. Madec has made a very bad mistake, because it isn't a sheep at all. It's an old prospector, and since Madec is a very good shot, the man is dead. Ben goes back down to bring the jeep to the foot of the ridge, put the body in it, take the body back to town, and report the shooting. When he gets back to Madec and explains what he's going to do, Madec is livid—"No! I'm not going to jail because of an old prospector that no one knows or cares about!" He tries to convince Ben to just bury the old man and offers him a bribe, but Ben refuses, saying only that a killing has been committed and he's going to report it. Finally, holding Ben at gunpoint with Ben's own rifle, Madec forces him to take off all his clothes and walk into the desert.

It's about forty-five miles to the highway and fifteen more back to town. Ben has no food, no water, no protection at all from the sun, and Madec is sure he will die in the desert. To make sure he does, Madec loads all the supplies into the jeep and follows Ben, keeping watch on him through the scope on his rifle, and staying far enough away to keep Ben from doubling back and ambushing him. And just in case Ben is rescued or survives all the way back to town, Madec has also altered the evidence to make it look as though *Ben* was the one who shot the old prospector, and not Madec. To see if Ben makes it back, and if Madec's plans succeed or fail, read *Deathwatch*, by Robb White.

—*Joni Bodart-Talbot*

DENNY'S TAPES   YA
By CAROLYN MEYER

When my stepfather called me a "black bastard," I left home. He was white. So was my mother. My father was black. It's funny how you can know someone for years and years, but never *really* know them. I'd known Stephanie since our parents got married when we were six and seven, but it took eleven years for me to discover how special she was— and for her to discover me. After her father found us, it only took him minutes to kick me out of the house. I went back the next morning to get my stuff and leave a goodbye note for Stephanie. I also got three addresses from my mother's address book—James Dennis Brown, my father, in Berkeley; Eugenia Brown, his mother, in Chicago; and Grace Sunderland, my mother's mother, in Nebraska. So here I am, traveling west, looking for my past to help me figure out my future, and talking into this tape recorder, since there's no one but me in this car. Where am I going? To Chicago, to Nebraska, to California—and after that, who knows? Stephanie said I needed to figure out what I was going to do with my life. I suppose I'll go looking for the answer.

—*Joni Bodart-Talbot*

THE DEVIL'S DOOR-BELL   Grades 7-8/YA
By ANTHONY HOROWITZ

I would have never believed that it might happen. My parents were struck by lightning and died, and I was placed with a foster mother. She is six feet tall with a long thin nose, a crooked mouth, and a pointed chin with a wart on it. She is named Elvira Crow. She has a cat named Asmodeus with one blue eye and one yellow eye. He was named for the demon of lascivious and lewd behavior. Her servant is named Gangree—like gangrene, rotten flesh. People in the town call me "Elvira's boy," not my name. She seems to be able to bring a car to life with a few words and gestures. And she keeps pigs, another diabolical symbol.

My dreams are hideous and strange. When I'm sick, she gives me strange medicine, black magic. I was warned to leave by a farmer who died a macabre death. I found his body, misshapen and twisted as if it had been pulled apart by supernatural forces.

Elvira's sister is named Miss Kite. They play Scrabble with words like "broom" and "bum," and are fattening a chicken called Martin to kill.

I went out one night in search of the sisters, when the hoot of an owl and whispers of the forest made the hairs on the back of my neck stand on end. I found a desecrated church filled with cobwebs, rotten pews, a twisted shattered organ, angels with broken noses, and spiders crawling out of the angels' eye sockets. There were children roasting above a fire some small animals, frogs or toads, alive. I was chased by huge hounds of hell, with flaming eyes, foaming mouths, sharp teeth, and rotting sores.

Evil forces were trying to cross into this time through *The Devil's Door-bell.*

—Michael Browne

THE DEVIL'S STORYBOOK   Grades 2-8
By NATALIE BABBITT

"Things are dull today," the Devil told himself one morning. "I think I'll go up into the world and bother someone."

Dressing like a fairy godmother, the Devil began his search. The first person he met was a woman.

"Good morning," the Devil said politely. "Beautiful day, isn't it? Because the day is so nice, I am going to give you one wish to help make it even better."

This woman was so nasty that she never spoke to people she knew, let alone to those she didn't. Besides, she didn't believe in fairy godmothers, and she wished that this one would go back to wherever she had come from. Before he could count to three, the Devil found himself back in Hell. Not being one to give up easily, the Devil returned to the world and met an old man sitting under a tree.

"What a pleasant day this is," the Devil commented, smiling at the man. "For that reason I am going to grant you a wish to use however you choose."

The old man smiled back at the fairy godmother. He really had everything he could ever want or need and didn't care to be bothered about making any wish.

When the Devil heard this, he became so angry that he took back his offer and disappeared.

Next, the Devil met a young man on horseback.

"Good day," the Devil spoke eagerly. "How would you like to have one wish on this beautiful day?"

The young man was very greedy, and he was happy to hear this news. The only problem was what to wish for—more money, finer clothing, perfect health, power, or endless youth? Suddenly he had an idea.

"Fairy godmother, I wish you would tell me what to wish for."

"Gladly," answered the Devil, "why don't you wish that every wish you make from now on will come true?"

"Perfect!" shouted the young man. "I will. Fairy godmother, I wish that every wish I make will always come true!"

"Too late," the Devil answered happily. "You used up your wish when you wished that I would tell you what to wish for."

The young man hung his head, and the Devil went back to Hell laughing, for he was very pleased with himself.

See what the Devil does next. Read *The Devil's Storybook*, by Natalie Babbitt.

—Cheryl Ress

DICEY'S SONG YA
By CYNTHIA VOIGT

You never knew where a road would end; you just knew that roads ended. The Tillermans' road had ended at Gram's house. So they were going to make a home with Gram. Home: a home with plenty of room for the four children in the shabby farmhouse, room inside, room outside, and room within Gram's heart too—the kind of room for love to grow that they really needed. That was one of the lessons that the long journey had taught Dicey—how to figure out what they needed. That long summer's journey stretched behind them now. They'd made it through; they'd made it home. Dicey still felt a responsibility to worry about and watch over the three younger children. But she now wanted to be just a little selfish too. She found an old sailboat in the barn that she began to fix up. The boat was her lucky charm, her rabbit's foot, her horseshoe, her pot of gold; it was the prize she'd given herself for leading them from nowhere to somewhere. But Dicey couldn't help but worry about the little money they had; there were so many of them to feed. Dicey felt she must get a job to help out. She knew big troubles have little beginnings. She tried to reach out, to tell Gram to let her take over the responsibility, but it wasn't until Dicey learned that you can't reach out with closed fists that she was able to let go of the past and to build a future.

—Judy Druse

DO NOT OPEN Grades k-3
By BRINTON TURKLE

Are you feeling brave? If you are, I'll tell you about this book.

Miss Moody lived in a cottage on the beach. Just about everything in Miss Moody's cottage was something that had washed up on the beach after a storm. She'd found her chairs, her clock on the wall; in fact, even her cat, Captain Kid, washed up on the beach after a storm. Miss Moody nursed Captain Kid back to health and kept him as a pet, and in return he kept the cottage free of mice.

Because of Captain Kid's experience with storms, he hated them, as you might guess. But Miss Moody loved them. One particular stormy night, Miss Moody had gone to bed with a good book, listening to the sounds of the storm, and smiling to herself as she thought of the surprises that would be waiting on the beach tomorrow. Do you know where Captain Kid was? Under the bed, of course.

The next morning Miss Moody and Captain Kid set off down the beach with a wheelbarrow. They found lots of things: driftwood (which Miss Moody could burn in her fireplace), a cookie tin (Miss Moody emptied out the soggy old cookies and kept the tin because it would be perfect for her postcard collection), and then . . . Captain Kid saw it first. It was half buried in the sand. He hated it immediately and hissed at it, as cats do when they really hate something. Miss Moody picked it up. It was a small purple bottle, and on the side were scratched the words "Do Not Open." As Miss Moody held the bottle, thinking how it might look nice on her window sill, she heard a small voice. The voice said, "Please help me! I'm a small child trapped in here by an evil magician. Please pull out the stopper and free me!"

If you want to find out if Miss Moody opened the bottle, you'll have to read *Do Not Open*—but only if you're brave. If you're not brave, do not open this book!

—*Pamm Stock*

DO YOU CALL THAT A DREAM DATE?   YA
By MARY ANDERSON

Jenny is determined to go on a dream date with handsome rock star Matt Gates. She is even willing to cheat, steal, and lie to win the writing contest. After she wins the contest, her secret is discovered. Will Jenny ever live down the disgrace, or be able to make amends? Find out in *Do You Call That a Dream Date?*

—*Barbara Bahm*

THE DOG DAYS OF ARTHUR CANE   YA
By T. ERNESTO BETHANCOURT

Arthur should never have made fun of James N'Gaweh's beliefs. It started out innocently enough with Arthur, James, and Lou sitting in Lou's living room in Manorsville, Long Island, celebrating the last day of high school and rapping about what they were going to do during the summer.

It is getting late, and the FM station starts playing a selection that James recognizes—an authentic African sacred chant used to cast out devils from a person who is possessed. James is a nineteen-year-old African exchange student, and his father is shaman (witch doctor) of his village, a job that James intends to assume eventually.

Well, Arthur tells James right out that he thinks that stuff about witch doctors and spells is just superstition. James doesn't take it well—he doesn't say anything more, but his face gets all masklike. Nobody feels like partying anymore, and just as Arthur is about to leave, James reaches into the pouch at his waist, takes out some kind of powder, sprinkles it over Arthur, and starts to chant. It's just a little prayer to give Arthur some kind of understanding of other people's ways.

When Arthur wakes up the next morning, he tries to sit up but he keeps flopping over on his side. His head aches and there is a terrible smell in the room. He finally decides that if he rolls out of bed onto the floor he may be able to crawl as far as the bathroom for a drink of water. He feels as if his tongue is hanging out about six inches, and his vision is all blurry, and everything is in black and white instead of color. Well, Arthur finally makes it to the bathroom. Turning his head he finds himself face to face with the saddest, most raggedy-looking dog he has ever seen. What an ugly mutt, with a big head, large, evil-looking teeth, and matted, shaggy, dirty gray fur with black spots. He sure looks sick. Arthur's first impulse is to yell and scare the dog away, but his head hurts too much, and besides the mutt looks as if he weighs about sixty pounds and might bite. So Arthur decides to smile, the dog wags his tail; Arthur reaches out his hand, the dog reaches out his paw. But when Arthur reaches out his hand to shake the dog's paw his fingers bump into the mirror in the bathroom door. Arthur finally gets the message—*he* is that sad-ass mutt on his bathroom floor.

He keeps closing his eyes and then opening them, hoping to see good old Arthur Cane in the mirror, but no such luck. So Arthur has to learn to make it as a dog—no easy proposition, especially in Manorsville, where everybody has a pedigreed dog and Arthur certainly isn't that. He has several run-ins with the dogcatcher, and problems with cars, subways, and even a crazy who poisons dogs, but life as a dog also has some rewards in store for Arthur. Is he destined to a be a mutt forever? Read *The Dog Days of Arthur Cane* to see.

—*Marianne Tait Pridemore*

THE DOLLHOUSE MURDERS   Grades 4-7
By BETTY REN WRIGHT

"Dolls can't move by themselves," Amy told herself when she went back to the attic and found the grandmother doll in the parlor instead of the dining room where Amy had left her. But there were scurrying sounds and small, frightening noises coming from the dollhouse when

Amy went to the attic. You see, it was Aunt Clare's dollhouse, but Aunt Clare wouldn't talk about it, and she didn't want Amy to play with it, either. Worst of all, Aunt Clare thought Amy was moving the dolls from one room to another! As creepy as it was in the attic, Amy had to find out who was moving the dolls and what was making those strange sounds!

Read *The Dollhouse Murders,* by Betty Ren Wright, to learn the secret!

—Dorothy A. Davidson

DOUBLE TROUBLE Grades 6–8
By BARTHE DeCLEMENTS and CHRISTOPHER GREIMES

Faith and Phillip may be far apart, but they can still be together. Their being twins gives them special abilities—Phillip can leave his body asleep and travel without it, and Faith can read her brother's emotions. She's sure he's in trouble now—feeling trapped, sad, in danger. His foster parents don't understand why he won't eat meat and are trying to get him involved in their weird religious cult. Faith is having problems, too. Aunt Linda won't listen to her concerns about Phillip, and she's sure her social studies teacher is doing something illegal—his cane is really a gun!

Can they help each other? Will their extrasensory powers make a difference? Read *Double Trouble* and find out.

—Joni Bodart-Talbot

DOWNTOWN YA
By NORMA FOX MAZER

For eight years, Pete has been living a lie. For eight years, he has been living with his Uncle Gene in a renovated old house downtown, going to school, hanging out with his friends, being Pete Greenwood, whose parents died when he was a little kid. He does okay in school, pretty well in sports, gets along fine with his bachelor uncle. Can't get the girls to pay enough attention to him, but maybe that's because he is shy. Generally, everyone likes Pete.

But Pete isn't really Pete . . . and he figures that someday soon, someone will look at him and sense his differentness. Somehow it will stick out all over him. Someone will look at him and know that when he tries to sleep at night, he gets engulfed in the White Terror, waking up shaky and sweaty. Someday soon, one of those cars that follow him will pull over to the curb and two guys in plain tailored suits will get out and nail him to the wall. Someday soon, someone will go through all his belongings and find his notebook full of license plate numbers of all those cars that have followed him, and his file of newspaper articles about the bomb that went off eight years ago. And that someone will know who Pete Greenwood really is.

Or maybe Pete will give it away himself. When he writes his name on a school report, maybe he'll slip and write his real name instead: Pax Martin Gandhi Connors. Pax Connors, the kid whose parents, Hal and Laura Connors, aren't dead at all. But they might as well be dead; maybe it would be better if they were. What good are they to Pete, when Laura and Hal are fugitives from the law, hiding out since that day when little eight-year-old Pax was secretly bundled off to stay with his mother's brother Gene for a while. A while that became eight years. Eight years is a long time to have lived without your parents when you're only sixteen. Eight years is a long time to wonder why your parents, political activists of the sixties who started out believing in nonviolence, bombed a lab and killed two people. Eight years is a long time to wonder why, if your parents really love you, as they write in their rare letters with no return address, they can't find a way to act like your parents.

Eight years is a terribly long time to keep such a secret. It's a long time to be afraid that if someone finds out who you really are, you could betray your own parents. Maybe someday it will just come spilling out, Pete thinks. Maybe he will just blurt it out to his new girlfriend Cary— and then would she care to keep dating the son of murderers? Maybe he will tell just anybody, some stranger on the street, anything to get rid of that dreadful weight. Maybe, Pete thinks, on the day when the car that has been following him finally pulls over and two men in suits get out and approach him—maybe they can *make* me tell.

—*Catherine G. Edgerton*

THE DRAGON AND THE GEORGE YA/Adult
By GORDON DICKSON

Jim Eckert never *meant* to become a dragon—all he was interested in was getting his fiancée back. Angie had disappeared just as he'd burst into Grottwald's lab, and Grottwald said she'd "apported." He'd been trying out his new astral projection machine and had the power up too high, so Angie's body as well as her psyche had disappeared. Jim was livid, and forced Grottwald send him to the same space, so he could find Angie and bring her back. But for one reason or another, perhaps because Grottwald had turned the power down, only Jim's mind made the transition, and when he opened his eyes, he discovered his mind was now in the body of a very large, scaly, winged, fire-breathing dragon, who seemed to be named Gorbash and was considered by his uncle Smrgol to be a somewhat stupid member of the species.

One of the first things Jim learned was that this *was* the world where Angie had gone. But since her body had come too, she wasn't a dragon, she was still a very real human female, called a "george" (all humans were called georges rather than humans). She had been captured by Bryagh, one of Smrgol's bitterest enemies. There seemed to be little chance of freeing her, so Jim went to S. Carolinus, a wizard, for help. Carolinus told him Angie had now been taken by the Black Powers and imprisoned in the Loathly Tower. So off went Gorbash/Jim and Secoh, a mere-dragon (a smaller species than true dragons like Smrgol and Gorbash); Sir Brian Neville-Smythe, a knight; Dayfydd and Danielle, archers; and Giles of the Wold, leader of an outlaw band and Danielle's father. And, of course, S. Carolinus. Together they must cross the wastelands, storm the Loathly Tower, and restore balance to this world where science and magic are equally powerful. It's a tall order; to see how well they do, read *The Dragon and the George.*

—Joni Bodart-Talbot

DRAGON FALL   YA
By LEE J. HINDLE

Lee J. Hindle wrote *Dragon Fall* when he was seventeen years old, and it won the 1982 Avon/Flare Young Adult Competition.

In *Dragon Fall* we meet Gabe, a high school senior. Gabe is rather unusual. Not only does he decorate his feet with Magic Marker drawings, but he also designs dragons for the Tally Ho Toy Company. Originally his dragons were soft and cuddly, but then a new creative director took over—Mrs. Valieri—and she didn't like Gabe's dragons. She told Gabe to redo them, to make them mean, nasty, and aggressive. It took Gabe four tries, but when he had finished, he had totally reconstructed Sid, York, and Hubub.

His dragons were now covered with green pebbly snakeskin. They walked upright and stood over five feet tall on short, powerful legs. They had huge arms and massive chests, broad mouths filled with sharp, pointed teeth, and eyes that lit up at night. Mrs. Valieri loved them, but Gabe wasn't so sure.

One day when Gabe was cleaning Sid's face, he felt a warm breeze coming from Sid's mouth. But surely that was his imagination. Sid couldn't be breathing. And at night, Gabe would zip his dragons into their body bags and hang them in his closet. But as he tried to go to sleep he kept hearing voices from his closet: voices that said, "Daddy, can we come out?" and "Daddy, it's time to play." And Gabe started to worry about these new dragons he'd created.

Dragon Fall, by Lee J. Hindle.

—Pam Spencer

THE DRAGON KITE   Grades k-3
By NANCY LUENN

Hello, I'm Ishikowa the thief, and I live in Japan. My plan is to steal those two beautiful golden dolphins from the Shogun's palace. The Shogun is the master of Japan. He is very wealthy: he could spend his days just listening to music and eating and sleeping, if he wanted.

I thought a long time before I came up with my perfect plan to steal the dolphins. The idea hit like lightning! I would fly over the gates onto the rooftop of the palace and snatch those dolphins on a dark, moonless night. But how? No one can fly! Some have tried, but all have failed. But what about a kite? . . . I mean a very large kite. In fact, the largest kite in all of Japan! I'll learn kitemaking and be the very best kitemaker ever. I'll build the largest kite in all Japan.

Why is this so important? Well, I am the Robin Hood of Japan—I steal from the rich to give to the poor. That's why my plan is important! But will I succeed? Will my kite carry me over the palace walls? You will find out in my story, *The Dragon Kite*, by Nancy Luenn.

—Sharon Thomas

DRAGON OF THE LOST SEA   Grades 5-9
By LAURENCE YEP

It was strong magic, old magic, and it carried a faint scent of the sea. It seemed to be coming from a nearby village, so the old lady stopped off the main road onto a path which led to the village.

Upon entering the village she saw a sedan chair surrounded by four creatures who looked like men. Near the inn's doorway was a guard with a cutlass. All reeked of the magic that had created them. It was Civet, the great enemy of Shimmer's clan, she who had stolen their entire sea and put it into an object the size of a pebble.

Shimmer went to the well where Thorn, the servant boy, was drawing water. He was being teased by the villagers for saying he had seen the Unicorn. When their teasing shifted to the beggar lady, he defended her by throwing water at them. He was hauled off to the inn to be beaten, but Shimmer filled his water bucket and took it after him. The boy Thorn fed her in return and asked her to stay the night at the inn.

Civet sent her guard to kill Thorn that night. As Shimmer wrestled with the creature, she suddenly found herself holding empty air while a paper cut-out of the guard drifted to the floor. The sedan chair and porters were also paper cut-outs.

Follow Shimmer and Thorn as they strive to restore the lost sea by reading *Dragon of the Lost Sea,* by Laurence Yep.

—Eileen Gieswein

DRAGONSINGER   YA/Adult
By ANNE McCAFFREY

Today we travel to the fantasy planet of Pern—that planet where people have learned to live with and depend upon their dragons to protect them from a burning, spore-like organism called Thread.

Instead of the usual dragons and their riders, we are introduced to a different side of life on Pern. Menolly is a young girl who has always loved to sing, write music, and play musical instruments. Unfortunately, her parents have forbidden her to make music and beat her if they hear her singing or playing an instrument. But she is selected by a dragon-rider and taken from her parents' home to the Harper Hall, a craft hall where people study the art of music. Here Menolly serves as an apprentice Harper and is given a chance to sing and write music. This is an overwhelming experience for her, and a considerable adjustment for the other Harpers as well, for she is the first female apprentice, and she is accompanied by nine miniature dragons, called fire lizards.

Dragonsinger, by Anne McCaffrey.

—Pam Spencer

DRAGONSONG   YA
By ANNE McCAFFREY

Drummer, beat, and piper, blow.
Harper, strike, and soldier, go.
Free the flame and sear the grasses
Till the dawning Red Star passes.

Menolly sang the deathsong solemnly, befitting the talent she had, for the old Master-Harper Petiron. He had been her only friend on Pern, the only one who encouraged her to sing and play musical instruments, for on Pern all music was controlled by Harpers, and to be a Harper one had to be male. Menolly had unusual talent, but girls had no future in music, and her folks, especially her father, the fisherman-leader, refused to allow her even to practice.

Life on Pern was largely agricultural. Farming and fishing were the main occupations. The constant danger from THREAD, a spore that fell to the ground and destroyed vegetation, made the inhabitants dependent upon the indigenous life form of dragons to destroy THREAD and save the land. Dragons were awe-inspiring: When born, they formed an instant attachment to a human and the two had a symbiotic relationship, able to talk from mind to mind (human/animal) and able to travel through time, thus finding and fighting THREAD with little damage to themselves. There were even legends of small dragon-like animals— fire lizards—but none had ever been found.

Well, after Petiron passed on, a new Harpermaster came to Menolly's sea-hold, but her folks saw to it that she was kept constantly busy gathering food, working in the kitchen, and babysitting the elderly. Life grew more and more lonely, until one day Menolly wandered further down the coastline than usual and stumbled on a clutch of— miraculous!—fire lizard eggs, and a screeching mother lizard desperately trying to move the eggs off the beach, away from the incoming tide and up to a cave in the cliff. Menolly found herself trapped on the beach by the agitated fire lizard, and somehow understood that she was to help move the eggs.

After they were safely in the cave, Menolly was allowed to leave. Back in the sea-hold, telling no one about the fire lizard, she joined the others for dinner. Afterwards there was music for entertainment from the new Harpermaster. But when Menolly started to join in the song, her mother pinched her hard, warning her to be quiet. It's not fair, Menolly thought for the hundredth time, and I won't take it anymore. The next morning she sneaked out of the sea-hold and returned to the fire lizard cave to make a new life for herself. How she did it is the tune of *The Dragonsong*.

—*Carol Starr*

DREAMSNAKE   YA
By VONDA K. McINTYRE

Snake is a healer in a future world where there are no doctors, and healers use genetically altered snakes to cure people. She has just finished her training and is now traveling through the desert on her first journey. She has with her Mist, an albino cobra; Sand, a diamondback rattler; and Grass, a dreamsnake, a small green snake that looks like a little grass snake. Grass is not able to heal anyone; he can only give dreams and ease dying. Snake had been a good student and her teachers had honored her when they named her Snake, but she is very young and trusting. The tribe of desert people she meets have never seen healers and are afraid of snakes, but they ask her to stop and heal a small boy named Stavin of a tumor. She agrees to do so. When Stavin asks to have Grass stay with him during the night while Snake gets Mist ready to cure him, she leaves Grass on his pillow. Mist has to be given a substance to alter her venom so that when she strikes the tumor, it will die and Stavin will live. Mist has convulsions all night as a result, and Arevin, one of the tribesmen, agrees to stay with Snake to help her stay awake and keep Mist from beating herself to death on the ground. In the morning, Snake goes to Stavin and finds Grass missing. Stavin's parents have killed him because they were afraid he would hurt the boy. Snake is bitter and angry, but she cures Stavin anyway, scorning his parents' fears that now she will kill their son. Arevin comes to her as she is preparing to leave and asks her to stay. She cannot, because of Grass's death. "What they did was my fault," Snake tells him; "I didn't understand their fear. Now I'm crippled without Grass and must return to my teachers and tell them I have lost my dreamsnake. They will be disappointed and they may cast me out." "Let me come with you," Arevin replies. Snakes refuses, but she promises to try and return the next spring. "Look for me next year, and the year after that, but if I haven't come in two years, forget me, because wherever I am, if I am alive, I will have forgotten you." Arevin promises to wait, but not to forget her. Snake leaves, and soon hears of a place where there are hundreds of dreamsnakes, a place where they breed. None of Snake's people have ever been able to breed the snakes—this is a chance she can't miss. She has to go further than she ever has before, and, unknown to her, Arevin has begun to follow. He has only promised to wait for her, not to forget her, and now he's decided to find her. And so this isn't just a story of Snake's search for a dreamsnake, but the story of her and Arevin's love as well.

—Joni Bodart-Talbot

DUNE   YA/Adult
By FRANK HERBERT

Arrakis is the planet known as Dune—a desert world where water is as precious as jewels. Its only export is *melange*, an addictive spice that gives Spacing Guild navigators the prescience, or future vision, necessary to guide ships through the long wastes of space. Spice is essential to the galaxy, and so Dune, its only source, is of major importance. Spice comes from the deserts of Dune and is mined by the Fremen, the free tribes of the desert.

To Dune come the Lady Jessica and her son Paul. Jessica is a Bene Gesserit, a member of a women's sect trained mentally and physically and dedicated to producing the Kwisatz Haderach—a male Bene Gesserit whose organic mental powers will bridge both time and space.

The women's sect had watched bloodlines for years and were within two generations of their goal when Lady Jessica produced, against orders, a son instead of a daughter—Paul. He becomes Muad'Dib, the leader of the Fremen of Dune and of the Bene Gesserit as well. His coming had been foretold in legends for centuries, and his power was unbeatable.

And the Guild navigators, their future vision made more acute by their addiction to spice, predict a great upheaval in the galaxy, one that will disturb the lives of everyone. Its source—Dune and Paul Muad'Dib.

—Joni Bodart-Talbot

DUNKER   YA
By RONALD KIDD

Everybody thinks that Bobby Rothman has it made. Everybody, that is, except Bobby. Bobby is a star. He's the Dunker's Donut kid. His jelly-stained face grins at the world from billboards all over town. But though he is terrific at commercials and ads and has lots of money in the bank for college, Bobby feels like a freak.

He's a sixteen-year-old sophomore who looks and sounds as though he were only twelve—that's perfect for raving to the public about Dunker's Donuts, Strawberry Delight drink, or Happy-O's cereal, but not too great for his social life at school. Bobby is tired of looking twelve when he's really sixteen. He just wants to be a normal sophomore—playing on the basketball team and getting Barbara Bell, the prettiest girl in his class, to like him. But can a guy who is only 5´4´´ ever dream of making the team? And would Barbara ever dream of giving him a second look? Believe it or not, both things happen when Bobby earns the nickname "Dunker" for an unexpected talent for basketball rather than for his ability to pose with jelly donut all over his face. And when that happens, Bobby must decide between an exciting career acting in commercials and a "normal" teenage life.

Dunker, by Ronald Kidd.

—*Diane Tuccillo*

EARTH CHILD   YA
By SHARON WEBB

How would you react if the government announced that all children under eighteen would now live forever because of a chemical put in the drinking water? To live forever! You may say, "Great!" until you read *Earth Child* and find out what happens to Kurt Kraus and the other children. Having immortality tears Kurt from his family; makes the people over eighteen attack, persecute, and even try to kill the children, "these immortal freaks of man"—all for the good of their God and their country. However, Kurt and the other Earth children do survive to watch their families and their neighbors age and die. So the first hundred years seem the hardest. Yet the second century finds Kurt one of Earth's ageless rulers, and he soon discovers the real terrible price of living forever. *Earth Child* begins the Earth Song Trilogy. Book II is entitled *Earth Song,* and Book III, *Ram Song.*

—*Faye Powell*

ELLEN GRAE   Grades 3–5
By VERA and BILL CLEAVER

Ellen Grae Derryberry has a great imagination, and she loves to talk. She is always making up wild stories to tell her friend Grover, her roommate Rosemary, and the McGruders—the people she lives with while she's going to school in Thicket, Florida. Everyone knows these tall tales are not lies, just stories that she enjoys inventing. They like to listen to them too, and Grover even makes up some of his own, almost as good as Ellen Grae's.

One of Ellen's best friends is Ira, a man who is considered simple or mentally retarded. He lives alone in a shack in the swamp and earns his living selling peanuts. The saddest thing about Ira is that he doesn't talk. Most people in town believe he can't talk, but he does speak to one person—Ellen Grae. There are a lot of people who think that Ira's talking to Ellen Grae is just another one of her stories, but it isn't. Ira really does converse with Ellen Grae. One of the things he tells her is so dreadful that she thinks it must be a wild story he has made up to amuse her. Until one day, Grover, Ellen Grae, Ira, and Ira's goat Missouri make an expedition to the swamp to look for treasure. There Ira shows her something that makes Ellen Grae believe he was telling the truth. And then she doesn't know what to do. Should she protect her friend or should she do the right thing and tell someone what Ira did?

—Holly Willett

EMERGENCE   YA
by DAVID R. PALMER

Candy Smith-Foster had an IQ of 200-plus, an advanced high school education with some college, and a Sixth Degree in Blackbelt Karate—all at eleven years old! Her only sibling was her so-called brother, Terry, a macaw (a bird) who had been hatched about the same time Candy was born. Candy's dad had built a three-story underground nuclear shelter, carving it out of the bedrock under their home. Candy called it the eighth wonder of the world. In it were more books than a public library has, films, tools, equipment, supplies, everything recording humanity's highest achievements, and everything needed to support life for years.

Candy's father reviewed the emergency procedures the day before he left on a trip to Washington, where he had to take part in some government meetings. He warned Candy how serious things had become. Together they practiced the drop down the 200-foot chute into the shelter. Candy hadn't been down there since she was three years old. They reviewed the shelter's vital components and then returned to the modest house above by way of the endless spiral staircase. Candy's father agreed she could take care of herself and Terry while he took his trip to Washington, but as he got ready to leave, she felt a little frightened. When she thought of the books in the shelter, though, she forgot her fears.

Books were a magnet for Candy. She couldn't wait to begin exploring the shelter and its treasures. After the day was over and the housekeeper had left, Candy and Terry descended the spiral staircase (in spite of Terry's squawks of protest). It all took her breath away. She didn't know where to start. Maybe she'd better wait and consult her master-teacher for a reading list. She had started toward the switchboard to power-down the shelter when a row of red lights began flashing and bells began clanging. Signs lit up that said, "Attack detected." As Candy bolted for the steps, she heard her dad's voice from a recording saying, "Red alert, radiation detected. Level above danger limit. Shelter will seal in thirty seconds . . . 29 . . . 28 . . . 27. . . . " She stood frozen as she heard the deep-toned, humming, powerful motors sliding blocks of concrete, steel, and asbestos across the top of the stairwell and the emergency-entry chute. The shelter was sealed with a final clunk. Candy and Terry were alone. She turned on the radio. The last voice told the story. The human race had been eliminated by radiation and biological warfare. It would be a long time before it was safe to venture out. How would she handle those months in the shelter alone? What would she find when she emerged? Would there be anyone else?

—*Marilyn Schlosser*

THE EXECUTIONER   YA
By JAY BENNETT

Bruce Kendall knows he is responsible for the car accident that killed his best friend Raymond. No one else knows that Bruce is responsible, and so all his friends keep telling him to forget the past and to quit feeling guilty. But Bruce can't forget what he has done, and so he keeps paying for that night—until someone decides he hasn't paid enough. *The Executioner,* by Jay Bennett.

—*Pam Spencer*

EYES IN THE FISHBOWL   Grades 3-5
By ZILPHA K. SNYDER

Alcott-Simpson's is one of those huge old department stores, high-class, with expensive merchandise. Dion wasn't the sort of teenager who went in for that kind of stuff—didn't have the money, for one thing. But he'd been shining shoes outside Alcott-Simpson's since he was about six, and he'd gotten friendly with some of the salesclerks who'd been there a long time.

So when the strange things started happening in the store, Dion was aware of them. An iguana was found in a dressing-room in Better Dress-es. New toys put on the shelf in the Toy Department at closing time looked old and scuffed the next morning. Then Dion met Sara. She drew him into the mysterious world of the department store after closing—and she led him almost to his death, before he discovered the power behind it all.

—*Nancy Eager*

THE FACE AT THE EDGE OF THE WORLD　　YA
By EVE BUNTING

Talk 1

Jed would never as long as he lived forget where he was when he heard his best friend, Charlie Curtis, had committed suicide. He was on his way to meet his girlfriend Annie on the corner of Hudson and Loma Linda when he saw the gang of kids standing on the sidewalk in front of the 7-Eleven. They'd told him. It had been on the radio and in the paper—Charlie had hanged himself from the rafters in his garage on Saturday night.

It didn't make sense. Why would Charlie kill himself? He'd won a scholarship to UC Santa Barbara; he'd had friends, a girlfriend, a loving family and talent. He and Jed had paid two months' rent on an apartment in Santa Barbara. He'd had plans, hopes, and dreams. It didn't make sense.

When Jed finally got to school that Monday morning, Lon, one of the dopers, a freshman, stopped him and said, "I saw her face. Maybe he saw it too. Maybe that's why he did it."

Jed didn't know it then, but that was the answer—the face at the edge of the world. Lon had seen it and Charlie Curtis had seen it too, and in the end it killed them both.

—*Marianne Tait Pridemore*

Talk 2

I still can't believe he did it. Charlie was my best friend. We had no secrets from each other. So why didn't he tell me he was thinking about commiting suicide?

—*Joni Bodart-Talbot*

FAHRENHEIT 451　　Adult
By RAY BRADBURY

It was a pleasure to burn. To see things eaten and blackened and changed. The great python in his hands spit kerosene, and he led a symphony of blaze and burning.

Montag had been a fireman for ten years. He loved the job. He believed in the official slogan: Monday burn Millay, Wednesday Whitman, Friday Faulkner, burn 'em to ashes, then burn the ashes. He had heard of a time when firemen put fires out instead of starting them. Now houses were fireproof, and firemen didn't have to stop fires. Their job was to start them, burn the books, and take the owners to an asylum.

He'd looked at the typed lists of the million forbidden books. At the last fire he'd even looked into a book of fairy tales, and he remembered the first line, "Once upon a time." At tonight's fire, though, the old woman's contempt had stung him. Her attic bombarded him with books. They lay like great mounds of fishes left to dry. The firemen danced and slipped and fell over them. They pumped the kerosene over each book, over each room. "Please come," Montag said to the woman.

"I want to stay here." She reached out with contempt and struck a kitchen match that engulfed her with her beloved books.

Montag gasped with horror. But was it the sight of the sacrifice, or was it fear for the book he'd hidden in his armpit? He couldn't help himself. The book had lit like a white pigeon in his hands, wings fluttering. He'd plunged the book under his arm and rushed out. But what was he to do with it now?

Fahrenheit 451, by Ray Bradbury.

—*Dee Scrogin*

FAMILY CRYPT   YA
By JOSEPH TRAINOR

When you skip school (which I know none of you would even think about doing), you try to do two things: have fun and not get caught. One of the tricks is to be home from school at the regular time—not too early, not too late.

That's what Janet Simpson tried to do when Senior Bunk Day arrived and a bunch of her friends decided to skip class. Unfortunately, Janet and her friends didn't make it home at the regular time. Or at dinnertime, either. In fact, they didn't come home at all that night. They were stranded near a small, deserted island on Lake Champlain in a boat with a dead engine.

Once rescued and safe back home, Janet is grounded indefinitely—no dates, no parties, no movies or dances, no phone calls. But being grounded is the least of the problems that begin to plague Janet after her spoiled skip day. She keeps getting ill, she's always tired and weak, and she begins to have blackouts. The worst part, though, are the dreams she starts having. They're dreams that seem to be happening in the past, hundreds of years in the past. It's like she's watching herself through a telescope. They are frightening dreams, and they are becoming more and more real.

Janet slowly begins to realize that something happened to her the night she was stranded on the island. An evil force is trying to possess her. Why? She doesn't know, and she has no idea how to stop or fight this force. Will the evil truly possess her body and her soul? The answer lies somewhere in the past. Somewhere within the *Family Crypt*.

—*Kathryn Dunn*

FAST SAM, COOL CLYDE AND STUFF YA
By WALTER DEAN MYERS

Imagine yourself as any one of the kids on 116th Street. Be Fast Sam, so named because he always wears sneakers, just in case he has to speed away from trouble. Or Cool Clyde, who thinks of forming "The Good People Club." Clyde is also the person who thinks of dressing up as a girl so that he and Fast Sam can win the $50 prize in the dance contest—now *that* is cool.

Or you could choose to be Stuff, who got his name because he's too short to stuff a basketball, but he's all heart. And then there's Binky, who got part of his ear bitten off in a fight and put everybody in jail. As Stuff said, "It was all thanks to medical science that we got sent to jail over Binky's ear."

Fast Sam, Cool Clyde and Stuff, by Walter Dean Myers.

—*Pam Spencer*

FELL YA
By M. E. KERR

It was like getting a $30,000 college scholarship. All he had to do was impersonate a nerd for two years.

—*Jeff Blair*

FERAL   YA/Adult
By BERTON ROUECHÉ

Have you ever seen a cat running across the street at night, its eyes shining in the headlights, or heard a cat howling on some black, windy night? I promise that whenever you see or hear a cat again, you won't be able to forget the horror of the wild cats in *Feral,* by Berton Roueche.

It starts innocently enough. A young couple, Jack and Amy, come to spend the summer on an island off the East Coast. They find a really nice small house out in the woods and settle down for the season. A man at the gas station gives Amy a kitten with white feet—they call it Sneakers. A couple of weeks later, they hear a horrible scream in the middle of the night. When they rush outside they see a cat—not Sneakers but a wild cat—with a baby rabbit in its mouth. They frighten the cat away, but the rabbit is dead. Next, people tell them how the indigenous wildlife seems to have disappeared. No coons or possum, no deer have been seen on the island in the last few years.

When it's time to leave, at the end of the summer, they decide they can't take Sneakers back to New York City, so they drop him off near a neighbor's house and hope he'll find a good home. That's what all the summer people do with their unwanted pets.

The next summer, Jack and Amy come back, but this time they decide to stay through the winter. Jack is a magazine writer and he is going to do his writing at home. They are only there for a short time when they find a half-grown mongrel hound in the woods. He's nearly starved, bitten and scratched, probably by cats, the vet says. They call him Sam.

Last summer the islanders noticed that there was no more wildlife in the area. This summer, even the birds have disappeared. A neighbor woman tries to feed one of the wild cats, is bitten and dies of the wound.

One day Jack and Sam go out to cut some wood, and Sam wanders off. When Jack hears a movement in the underbrush, he looks around thinking it's Sam coming back, but it isn't, it's a cat, just staring at Jack, and then another cat and another. Jack counts eight cats, just crouching there, all watching him. He yells at them to get away, but they don't move. He yells again and they finally scatter.

Sam, the dog, doesn't come home that night, so Jack and Amy go looking for him. They find him, or rather what's left of him. The cats had found him first.

The terror grows until Jack and Amy find themselves besieged in their house, surrounded by hundreds of wild, starving cats. *Feral,* by Berton Roueché.

—Edith Czubiak

FINDING DAVID DOLORES   YA
By MARGARET WILLEY

When I think of the spring I met David Dolores, I remember being thirteen, neither a child nor a woman, wandering through the town like someone lost, and finding a reason, a purpose in life, when I saw him for the first time. He was tall, older than I was, slender, with blue-black hair, with tan skin, and chiseled features. He had the same kind of aloofness and aloneness that I did that spring, but was far more elegant than I could ever be. I watched him and I dreamed, and I made up stories about him—what he might be like, and how it would be if we ever met. Of course, I didn't think we ever would. For one thing, I was sure that I would just faint before I could even say hello. And I don't think I really wanted to meet him, either; it was easier just to dream about him.

But everything changed when I got to be friends with Regina. We shared our secrets, like how she didn't think her mother really was her mother, and my secret about David Dolores. Regina wanted to see him too, but that's not all—she spotted his mother, Althea, and wanted to meet her, even talk to her! I didn't know what to do, but I knew I didn't want to go along with Regina's plan. I also knew I'd made a dreadful mistake in telling Regina about David and how I felt about him. When I wouldn't do what she wanted, she took matters into her own hands— she faked a sprained ankle to meet Althea, then lied to her mother and swore me to secrecy so she could go over to their house every day. It was almost as if she had decided to substitute Althea for her own mother, and it seemed like Althea didn't mind at all. I know it's wrong, but what can I do? I promised Regina I'd never tell.

—Joni Bodart-Talbot

FINGERS   Grades 6–8/YA
By WILLIAM SLEATOR

Dear Sam,

Mr. Jones, our English teacher, said we had to write a letter to someone we would like to know better, so I picked you. My name is Petra, and I'm in Grade 10. I read all about you in William Sleator's book, *Fingers*, and I think you're really interesting. Especially the part about how you grew up living "in the shadow" of your famous brother, Humphrey. He sounds like a real pain. I mean, he was so dumb that you had to do everything for him. All he could do was be a child piano prodigy. I don't think I'd like your mom, Bridget, either. She was always thinking up schemes to fool the public, and then you'd all have to do what she said. And her second husband, Luc—he just thought about getting rich. Nobody cared what you wanted. I understand how you must have felt: sometimes I feel like my parents just use me for babysitting and dishes and stuff.

It was really exciting when Humphrey turned 15 and you were 18, and he wasn't popular anymore because people wouldn't pay to see a fat has-been prodigy. Bridget's idea of pretending that Humphrey was possessed by a dead composer's spirit *was* original, I have to admit. Of course, it was *you* who had to write the music. After all, you're the only one who has *real* talent in the whole family. You say that you chose Laszlo Magyar because his wild music would be the easiest to copy. Are you sure that's why, now that you know the truth? I kind of felt sorry for Humphrey. You guys were all drugging him up and keeping the truth from him, saying that he went into trances to write the music.

That little old man at the concerts—the one that smelled of medicine, and looked all raggedy and dirty—he gave me the creeps. And then you read that mysterious book that just "appeared" in your train compartment—I nearly died when you told about Magyar's hands and head disappearing. If you write back (and I really would appreciate even a little note, if you have the time) please don't talk about that stuff. I get nightmares just watching Michael Jackson videos.

I think you were very brave and wonderful when you fought to save Humphrey from the evil forces around you. You may say they were just misguided people, but I prefer to think of them in more universal terms. If you answer this letter (I hope you will!) please fill me in on how you are doing now. I'm very anxious to know how the experiments are going.

Sincerely yours,
Petra Fried
—*Lynn Reeves*

THE FIRE CAT　　　　　　　　Grades k-3
By ESTHER AVERILL

Here I am. Finally I get the chance to do something *really big*. The wind is howling and the rain is pouring down. The ladder trembles and the rungs are slippery, but I have a good grip. My paws are strong! I hear a frightened cry and look up. The little kitten has climbed out to the farthest branches of the tree. The firemen tell me that I am the only one who can rescue her. Hang on, little kitty!

To learn how a bully like Pickles the cat came to rescue just the kind of cat he used to chase, and how he fulfilled his dream to do something *really big*, read *The Fire Cat*.

—*Michele Vessels*

FIRE STORM　　　　　Grades 6–8/YA
By ROBB WHITE

The fire was everywhere. Some areas close, some far away, but everywhere. The sky was dirty with smoke, no blue, no sunshine showed through. The forest had lost its color. The only colors were the awful yellowish-red flames.

The wind was insane. It was like a wild animal, blowing a gale, swirling without steadiness. The wind was so hot, so dry, so heavy with ashes that the man couldn't breathe.

He'd like to kill that kid. He'd make sure that kid went to jail. As a forest ranger he'd never understood the mentality of an arsonist. He thought about how he'd spotted that red shirt and gone to get the kid. He'd risked precious minutes of escape to save the boy. Why? Why had he risked his own life?

Because "You're an arsonist. You set these hills on fire and it's going to burn for miles, killing everything, all the trees, even the little bugs. The land's going to look like a scar. So I'm arresting you because you set this fire—on purpose."

The boy's voice was maddeningly calm. "Did you see me do it?" The man looked at him, then at the smoky air. For the first time since he had been a child, he felt like crying.

Fire Storm, by Robb White.

—*Dee Scrogin*

A FIVE-COLOR BUICK AND A BLUE-EYED CAT　　　YA
By PHYLLIS ANDERSON WOOD

Fred and Randy are sitting outside the high-school counselor's office watching kids go in looking hopeful and come out looking very depressed. Finally there are only the two of them left. The counselor comes out and says, "Why don't you two come in together?" They go in and sit down and he says, "Well, you've seen everyone leaving—I just haven't been able to find jobs for anyone." Randy says, "Oh, no! I've gotta have a job! My mother won't buy gas for my car any more!" The counselor sits up and says. "Car? Car? You've got a car? I have just one job here. It's for two boys who are friends and have a car. Are you guys friends?" Fred and Randy have never seen each other before this afternoon, but they size each other up and say, "Yeah, yeah—we're friends."

The job turns out to be working for Palmer's Pets, a chain of pet stores in the Bay Area and the Valley, picking up pets at the airports and delivering them to the stores, changing pets from one shop to another, and delivering pets to airports and to their new owners. That sounds great to Fred and Randy, and they agree to go to an interview that afternoon.

But Randy's car is out of gas and neither he nor Fred has any money, so the counselor loans them two dollars for gas. They walk out of the school and Fred looks for Randy's car. It's a block or so away, up at the top of a hill—and when Fred sees it, he suddenly feels very depressed. It's an old fifties Buick—you know the kind—huge, built like a tank, low to the ground. And this particular Buick looks as if it's been in several wrecks. Almost every piece of it is a different color from every other piece—four different colors in all! And when Fred walks around to the back, he discovers it doesn't even have a trunk lid! But Randy says not to worry, he has it all under control. So Fred pushes and then hops into the open trunk to ride down the hill to the gas station. After they get gas, Randy peels out, leaving rubber for half a block. He drives really fast, screeching around corners on two wheels, and the engine sounds as though it's going to blow up any second. Fred thinks, as he hangs on for dear life, "If we had any animals in here, we'd scare them to death!"

They get to the interview and talk to Mr. Palmer, and he seems interested. Then he wants to see the car. Fred thinks, "Well, goodbye, job!" Mr. Palmer looks a bit taken aback when he sees the car, but Randy starts telling him what a great car it is, how they don't build cars like this any more . . . but then Mr. Palmer gets around to the back and says, "No trunk lid? How can you carry animals in the trunk without a lid?" Randy says, "Oh, we wouldn't think of putting your valuable animals in the trunk! I've taken the trunk lid off so I can take out the back seat and make a platform for the animals' cages behind the front seat. Your animals will ride in absolute safety and luxury *in*side the car. And you know, this car is safe. You could hit it with a Mack truck and not

even dent it. Your animals will be well taken care of and protected."
Mr. Palmer looks at Randy, then he looks at the car again, and then he
says, "Okay, let me see how you're going to fix the car, and if it looks
good enough for my animals, you've got a job. Be back here tomorrow
morning." Then he stands outside his shop to watch them drive off.
"Goodbye, job!" Fred thinks again, when he realizes Mr. Palmer is *not*
going back inside. But Randy starts the car smoothly, quietly slips into
gear, backs up, and then drives slowly away, the engine purring, just as
if he were carrying a back seat full of raw eggs. Fred stares at him with
his mouth open. Randy turns to him, laughs, and says, "See, I *can* drive
when I have to. . . . "

And that's the start of a very exciting summer for both of them, and
a very funny one, too. Especially when they meet a parrot that does
nothing but yell cuss words and a Siamese cat that's allergic to the parrot! And wait till you see what happens when they get stuck in a traffic
jam on a hot day with a carload of animals and a horn that won't quit
honking!

—Mary Moore and *Joni Bodart-Talbot*

THE FLIGHT OF THE CASSOWARY   YA
By JOHN LeVERT

Have you ever imagined your father as an ant or your football team
as "big draft horses in the line, thoroughbreds in the backfield, and a
few tough mules as linebackers"? Or yourself as a cat (because they're
smart, not too big, quick, and tough)?

That's how it started for Paul. Then things got weirder. The first time
he became an animal was after a football game, when inner-city teenagers were hassling him and he turned into a rat. Later he turned into
a dog in French class, a lion at a football game, a rhinoceros at the zoo,
a raccoon on the freeway, a horse at the farm, a cat in biology, a squirrel
at a picnic, an orangutan in front of school, a salmon with his girlfriend,
and lastly a bird, who flew home from school.

Has Paul's infatuation with animals caused him to lose touch with
reality, or does he really have the capacity to become different animals?

—Cheryl J. Warkentin

FOOTFALLS   Grades 6–8
By ELIZABETH HARLAN

Daddy was dead! Why hadn't Mother told Stephanie and Robby that Daddy had cancer? Stephanie, Stevie for short, had run her fastest in hopes of keeping Daddy alive.

That's what fourteen had brought Stevie. In fact, it was at Stevie's fourteenth birthday party that Mother had told Stevie Daddy was bleeding and an ambulance was coming to get him. Mother told Stevie to go ahead with her party and have a good time. Now, really—"have a good time," when Stevie didn't even know for sure how sick Daddy was! That was Friday night, and on Saturday Stevie went to East Bradley to run the cross-country course she would have to race in a couple of weeks. It was an important race because Stevie had the fastest time in the 3.2-mile race, and she was the only freshman on the team. Now she knew as she followed the path through the woods that she was running for Daddy. She played a game in her mind that if she won, Daddy would live; if she lost, Daddy would die. But he died anyway, and after the race Stevie just quit! She quit running; she quit her friends; she quit her family.

And then came Jeb Gray.

Footfalls, by Elizabeth Harlan.

—Karen Cole

FOREVER   YA
By JUDY BLUME

This is one of the most controversial books written for teenagers recently. That's because it's about Katherine and Michael, two high-school seniors who fall in love and have a love affair. And nothing bad happens to them—no one gets VD, or pregnant, or has to drop out of school. No one has a nervous breakdown, or an abortion, or a fatal accident, or anything else. They survive, and they handle it, and along the way they find out that even though sometimes love lasts forever, sometimes it doesn't. Katherine and Michael, two teenagers who might be real people, in a situation that's all *too* real—*Forever,* by Judy Blume.

—Joni Bodart-Talbot

FORTRESS   YA
By GABRIELLE LORD

Teaching in an isolated one-room school house in Australia isn't really an exciting job, but Sally Jones enjoys it. Even though the Inspector will be visiting her class the next morning (never a pleasant experience), she feels she can handle it—after all, isn't she in full control of the class, which ranges in age from five to fourteen?

Sally's first feelings of dread are replaced by satisfaction. The children are cooperating beautifully in getting the classroom clean and ready. They are so busy, in fact, that no one notices the van pull up near the schoolhouse, or the four men disguised with cartoon-character masks and armed with guns creep up to the door.

When the gunmen burst into the school, Sally can't believe it's real. Even when she sees the children being herded into the van, when she hears the preposterous ransom announced—one million dollars or the death of one child an hour—she can't believe it.

After the first shock wears off and she and the now terrified children are dropped into an underground cave, Sally knows she faces the greatest challenge in her life. Somehow she has to organize these kids to fight back for their very lives. Little does she realize that these kids will do *more* than kill if their survival depends on it.

—Diana C. Hirsch

FRAUDS, HOAXES, AND SWINDLES   Grades 3-6
By DANIEL COHEN

How gullible are you? Would you fall for a fraud, hoax, or swindle? Many people have, and many people will in the future, because they either accept what they see at face value or look for easy ways to make money. And the people who invent scams know how to take advantage of this.

One of the all-time con artists was William Voight, a German shoemaker. One day back in 1906 he happened to buy a uniform of the Prussian Guards, a highly respected unit of the German army. When Voight wore his unofficial uniform, he felt like a new man—in fact, he felt like one of the Prussian guards. The ten soldiers he came across must have thought he *was* one of the Prussian guards because they obeyed his every command. He commanded the soldiers to march to the train and ride to the small town of Kopenick, where he marched them into the town hall. There he put the whole town under arrest and ordered the town treasurer to give him all of the money in the treasury—about

$10,000. Once he had the money, he sent his prisoners—the mayor and the treasurer—off to military headquarters in Berlin, where, of course, no one was expecting them.

Then there was Joseph Weil, better known as The Yellow Kid. His schemes were calculated to attract greedy people. One of his tricks took place at the racetrack—this was the two-horse swindle. He would tell certain people that he had two horses that looked just alike, only one was fast and one was slow. He told them he was planning to enter the slow horse in a race and then put in the fast horse. He would tip off the sucker when he was about to make the switch, and then offer to place a bet for him. Of course he didn't own any fast horse, and he didn't place any bet, either—he just kept the money all for himself. Would you have fallen for any of these schemes? Read *Frauds, Hoaxes, and Swindles*, and find out!

—Bonnie Janssen

FRECKLE JUICE   **Grades 1–2**
By JUDY BLUME

Andrew Marcus wants freckles more than almost anything else in the world. His friend Nicky has freckles—all over his face, his neck, and even his ears—and Andrew would do anything to have some freckles too. Then Sharon offers to sell Andrew her secret freckle juice recipe— for fifty cents. That's a lot of money to Andrew, five weeks' allowance. But after thinking about it for a while, he decides to buy the recipe. A pretty strange list of ingredients: catsup, olive oil, vinegar, grape juice, onion, salt and pepper, lemon juice, mustard, and mayonnaise—could this actually be a recipe for freckle juice?

—Zoë Kalkanis

FRIENDLY FIRE   **YA/Adult**
By C.D.B. BRYAN

On September 4, 1969, Sergeant Michael Mullen left the Waterloo, Iowa, airport on his way to Vietnam. His last words to his mother—"Don't worry yourself, now, okay? It will all be over March 1st." On March 1, 1970, Michael's body was returned to Waterloo in a silver-gray US Army-issue casket, and the Mullens learned that their son's death was attributed to "nonbattle causes."

One year later, they were under FBI surveillance because they'd tried to find out just what that meant. They kept getting the runaround, and they got more and more upset and suspicious. They felt they had a right to know how their son had died, but the Army apparently didn't. Finally they discovered that Michael had been killed by "friendly fire"—that is, he had been killed accidentally by US bullets. The Army urged them to forget about it, now that they knew. "It's just one of those things." But Michael's parents, Peg and Gene Mullen, couldn't forget. This is the story of what they did, and of what an unnecessary death and a long string of lies did to them.

—Joni Bodart-Talbot

THE FRIENDS Grades 7-9
By ROSA GUY

I did not like Edith. She always came to school with her clothes unpressed, her stockings bagging and full of holes. There were a lot of other children I didn't like in that class. Only, Edith sat across the aisle from me. She tried to be my friend. She invited me to skip school with her that first warm day. That's the day I was beaten up after school. The day I decided Edith would be my friend. She would protect me—nobody messed with Edith.

Next morning Edith stood before the class and gave fair warning: "Phyllisia is my friend. My best friend. If anybody hits on her, they hitting on me. And that goes for if I'm here or if I ain't. Or if I'm early or if I'm late." She moved to her seat.

The stunned silence held. Moments ticked by, and slowly, very slowly, the tension in the room loosened. Whispers stirred the air like a warm breeze. The girl behind me leaned over and said to Edith, "You sure did tell her off." Edith blew a big bubble that left gum on her nose. The girl touched my shoulder. "Hey, Phyllisia. You know what happened yesterday wasn't *my* fault."

It was incredible. Big, bad Beulah was so awful yesterday when she beat me unmercifully. Today Edith had made her an untouchable. I actually felt their hostility toward me fizzle.

Edith had not looked at me. I realized I needed to say something to show gratitude. I forced myself to turn. I meant to say something, but I was repulsed by her wrinkled skirt, her unpressed blouse tied in front like a halter so that every time she moved a band of brown skin showed between blouse and skirt. My gratitude turned to annoyance. Did I really have to accept her as friend? She might make a habit of walking down the street with me!

Edith caught my eye, gave me her open-faced grin and a mischievous wink. Then I knew I had to at least pretend to accept her friendship. My annoyance turned to anger. Who asked her to butt into my affairs? Rosa Guy's *The Friends*.

—Barbara Hawkins

FRIENDS FOR LIFE   YA
By ELLEN EMERSON WHITE

Seventeen-year-old Susan McAllister has moved back to her hometown of Boston after having lived in New York City for three years. She's really glad she'll be in the same school as her childhood friends, Colleen and Patrick. She's missed them a lot.

When Colleen comes over to help Susan unpack, she seems upset. She's much too thin and acts as though she were under stress. Susan questions her and discovers that Colleen thinks a kid who died at school (supposedly from a drug overdose) was really murdered, only no one will believe her. The police, her parents, even Patrick all think Colleen is overreacting to the tragedy, playing detective in an imaginary drama. Susan is not sure what to think.

The next Monday, Susan's first day at school, she gets a mysterious phone call before breakfast—the caller's voice sounds weak and muffled. It's a prank call, Susan thinks, and hangs up. When she gets to school, the police and an ambulance are there—a body has been found in the phone booth in front of the building. It's Colleen, and she's dead.

The police dismiss it as another drug overdose—maybe an accident, maybe suicide. Susan *knows* Colleen would never take drugs and she's pretty sure she wouldn't commit suicide. Then she remembers Colleen's suspicions about the previous death. Maybe she discovered something and was killed to shut her up. Only, now what happens? Can Susan find the murderer without losing her own life in *Friends for Life?*

—Diana C. Hirsch

FRIENDS TILL THE END   YA
By TOD STRASSER

You don't take a new kid like Howie too seriously. I mean, when I first met him at the bus stop, he was wearing green plaid pants, white loafers with white tassels, and a baggy yellow cardigan sweater. I had to restrain myself from asking where his golf clubs were. I'd see him at the bus stop every morning and I could tell he wanted to be my friend. But I already had my own crowd and it was my senior year, so I had a lot going on. I was goalie on our soccer team and I was so good everyone said I should go to college on an athletic scholarship. I wanted to go to med school, but no one wanted to hear that! So soccer and school took up most of my time, and any free time I had, I spent with Rena. Rena was part of the "sophisticated" newspaper-yearbook crowd; pretty, smart (some would say snobby), and always well-dressed. Anyway, I led a busy life, so when Howie was put into the hospital and Mom said he wanted me to come see him, I had no desire to go. Sure, the guy was sick. He had leukemia and that's a pretty serious disease, but I didn't really know him that well.

I had to break a date with Rena, but I did go see Howie. I'm not that big on the hospital scene, but I thought I'd run in, we'd have a nice little chat, and that'd be it. No. Howie wanted someone who would listen. He told me all about the disease and what the doctors had been doing to him. It wasn't anything like I thought it'd be. But I found myself going the next week to see him again. No one had asked me to go back; I just did. I really started getting involved in Howie and his illness. I guess I kind of changed, because my friends didn't understand me there for a while. But you'd change too if you had a friend with a cruel and ugly disease like leukemia. I tell you, it teaches you a lot about life!

—*Beverly Ramsey Mitchelson*

FROZEN FIRE YA/Adult
By JAMES HOUSTON

Kayak fell to his knees and pounded the sides of his head. Matthew ran through the snow to see what was the matter. Kayak pointed to the gas can and then to a thin yellow streak in the snow as far as they could see across the lake. The gasoline for the snowmobile was gone, and they were seventy-five miles from Frobisher, Alaska, where their homes were. And they were at least fifteen miles from the wrecked helicopter.

Using the snowmobile to rescue Matthew's dad had seemed like a good idea to the two teenagers. It had been too foggy for planes to fly, and Matthew's dad couldn't live very long in the bitter cold—no one could.

Kayak slumped in the snow again. "I brought you out here to try to save your father and Charlie, and what have I done? I may get us both killed. We have no gas and little food. And look at that storm coming straight at us across the plain!"

—*Lola Viets*

GABRIELLE AND SELENA   Grades 1-2
By PETER DESBARATS

Gabrielle and Selena were eight years old, and they had been best friends for almost that long. They were such good friends that sometimes Gabrielle seemed to know what Selena was thinking, and often Selena knew what Gabrielle was going to say even before she said it.

One day the two girls were talking together and Gabrielle said, "Sometimes I wish, Selena, that *I* were *you*." So the two friends decided to change places. That evening Gabrielle went home to Selena's house, and Selena went to Gabrielle's. But in trading places, they were in for a big surprise. How well can you know your best friend? Find out with *Gabrielle and Selena*.

—Zoë Kalkanis

GEMINI   YA/Adult
By NIKKI GIOVANNI

According to her best friend, being a Gemini only partially explains the contradictions that exist in a small, quick, harsh, gentle girl-woman named Nikki Giovanni. Her other sign is "genius," for she is one of the best and most popular Black poets. When Nikki was little, she read cheap novels, classics, books about the formation of clouds, and fairy tales. She saw every "B" movie she could squeeze from her Sunday money after bus fare. She listened to her father and mother as they sat around the table; then she would go off in secret and write stories—but only to hide them. She followed her big sister Gary's adventures out in the real world. When she was little people would come up to her and say, "Nikki, can you read?" She'd proudly say, "No, but Gary can," and they'd say, "Nikki, can you sing?" More proud, she'd answer "No, but Gary can," and maybe they'd go on to ask, "Nikki, can you play the piano?"—and she'd lean back with a smile and say, "No. But Gary can!" She was Gary's sister and that was quite enough. But now Nikki is the superstar, with quite a following. She appears on talk shows and college campuses, and travels all over reading her poetry. *Gemini,* she says, is a fictionalized autobiography—an account of growing up and growing famous.

—Jacqueline Brown Woody

GERI YA
By GERI JEWELL

Twenty-eight-year-old Geri Jewell's face is probably familiar to you if you're a fan of the TV show "The Facts of Life." On that show she plays Jo's cousin Geri.

But even if you've never seen her before, you will want to read this book about the real-life Geri.

Not only is she an actress, but Geri is also a comedian. And just like other comedians, Geri bases a lot of her jokes on her childhood experiences. Except Geri's life has always been a lot different from most other celebrities'.

Geri was born with cerebral palsy, a condition that makes people lose control of their muscles. If you ever see a person with cerebral palsy, you may think that person is drunk; if you don't think that, you'll probably be convinced that person can't do very much for herself.

But Geri was determined not to let cerebral palsy ruin her life.

And in this true story, she tells about some of the sad and funny things that have happened to her as a result of having CP and how, in spite of it, she's made it on her own to become an actress and a successful comedian.

—Avis Matthews

GHOST BEHIND ME YA
By EVE BUNTING

Strange things begin to happen when Cinnamon, a teen-aged girl, moves into a big old house near San Francisco. On her first day there she hears a car pull up to her house. It's gone by the time she looks outside, but she sees an oil stain where the car must have waited, idling. But no one else heard anything, no one else notices any oil on the pavement. Day after day Cinnamon hears the car. Gradually she begins to see it, too. At first just the outline, but then, more and more clearly, the whole car, and finally the driver. Cinnamon's father thinks that Cinnamon is just imagining things because she's still not over her mother and sister's deaths. But Cinnamon knows better. She even talks to other people who have talked to the man in the car. She discovers that his name is Felix and that he's looking for his old girlfriend Emily, whose belongings are still in trunks in Cinnamon's house. Read *Ghost Behind Me* to see what happens to Cinnamon, and whether Felix ever finds his Emily.

—Mary Hedge

THE GHOST ON SATURDAY NIGHT   Grades 1–2
By SID FLEISCHMAN

Opie can make a lot of money when a real tule fog hits town. He can guide people, just by the feel of the road and the smells of the different stores. When he guided strange Dr. Pepper through the fog all he learned of him was his ice-cold hands. But later Opie recognized him. The doctor is a famous ghost-raiser who has come to town to bring back the genuine ghost of Crookneck John—outlaw, murderer, bank robber, thief, and scoundrel. And then, during the actual ghost-raising, Opie alone realizes that the biggest scoundrel of all is not Crookneck John but Dr. Pepper himself. It's up to Opie, with the help of the tule fog, to save the town from the Crookneck ghost, and to save the townspeoples' bank accounts from the ice-cold hands of Dr. Pepper.

—Elizabeth Overmyer

NOTE: A tule (tooly) fog is a pea-souper.

GHOSTS I HAVE BEEN   YA
By RICHARD PECK

Blossom Culp, fourteen, comes from the wrong side of the tracks, lives by her wits, gets the Second Sight, and becomes the most famous girl on two continents.

It all began on Halloween night, 1913, when Blossom decided to teach Alexander Ormsworth and his friends a lesson. She knew that every year they tipped over Ol' Man Leverette's outhouse, so she hid inside it, in an old sheet with flour on her face and hair and a candle to light at the appropriate moment. But when Blossom opened the door, there was Ol' Man Leverette himself, caught, as it were, with his pants down! Blossom talked fast and explained her plan to scare the boys— Ol' Man Leverette thought it sounded like a good idea, and he had a few touches of his own to add. So Blossom hid in the outhouse, Ol' Man Leverette hid behind the compost heap, and just as the boys were about to tip the outhouse over, Blossom floated out, moaning in proper ghostly fashion. The boys scattered, but Les Dawson was last, and he was the one who got the rock salt Ol' Man Leverette had loaded in his shotgun—right in the seat of the pants! And over Les's screams of agony, the other boys heard Ol' Man Leverette shout, "Guess we showed 'em, Letty!" Blossom, you see, had thought fast, and had not told him her real name.

There was only one girl in town named Letty—she was stuck-up and proper, and would never have been in someone else's outhouse on Halloween night, pretending to be a ghost. But Les didn't think about that when he found out about it the next day. He didn't get to school till noon, having spent a very painful morning having rock salt picked out of his rear end. He waited till afternoon recess and then jumped on Letty, and started grinding her face into the ground, screaming all the while. Blossom decided to put a stop to it, and who was in a better position to know just where to kick Les so it would hurt the most, and as she put it "be the most instructive"? Les nearly turned inside out with pain, dropped Letty, and began to strangle Blossom. Just before she passed out, Blossom saw the principal coming across the school yard with a paddle in her hand, which she applied very liberally to Les—also where it would be most instructive!

As a reward, Letty's mother gave Blossom some new clothes and told her daughter to be nice to Blossom. That meant asking her to the next meeting of Letty's club, "The Sunny Thoughts and Busy Fingers Sisterhood." Blossom came, but what happened that afternoon no one had expected. Blossom announced, more to annoy Letty than because it was true, that she had the Second Sight. No one really believed her, until she saw Letty's little brother get run over by a car five blocks away! After that, word got around pretty quickly, and Blossom's adventures began—she saw the sinking of the *Titanic*, she sneaked into Madam Tussaud's Wax Museum in London in the dead of night, she met the Queen, and lots more!

—*Joni Bodart-Talbot*

A GIFT FOR MAMA   Grades 2–4
By ESTHER HAUTZIG

Sara was sick and tired of making presents. For birthdays, for Hannukah, for anniversaries, for Mother's Day, Sara always had to make a gift. Mama said the best presents were handmade presents. Papa said the gifts his Sara made were the best gifts of all. Mama and Papa loved their presents better than all the beautiful store-bought gifts they received from other people. They always told her so. But one year for Mother's Day, Sara decided that she was not going to follow family tradition. She would *buy* her mother a present; she had seen a pair of black slippers with blue leather trim that would match Mama's robe. But Sara had no savings, got no allowance, had no money to buy a Mother's Day gift. How could she get her mother those beautiful slippers?

—Judy Druse

A GIFT OF MAGIC   Grades 6-8
By LOIS DUNCAN

Nancy Garret looked pretty much like any other twelve-year-old, but she was different in one fascinating way. Nancy knew when things would happen. Not only could she tell when the phone would ring, she knew where each member of her family was at any moment and what they were doing. In short, Nancy had psychic powers, which she didn't dare admit to anyone—not even to herself. And the scariest part was that it wasn't just ESP—reading minds and seeing into the future—Nancy could *make* things happen. Like causing objects to move, or even making people do the things she wanted them to do. Nancy was particularly frightened by this aspect of her power and tried not to use her psychic gift at all. She thought she had it under control until the day she wished her sister, Kirby, wouldn't go away to study dance—and then Nancy watched in horror as Kirby fell down a flight of stairs and broke her leg.

—Zoë Kalkanis

THE GIFT OF THE MAGI   YA/Adult
By O. HENRY

O. Henry practically invented the surprise ending, the unexpected twist at the end of the story where the hero or villain gets what he or she deserves. ("Poetic justice," it's called.) His stories are short, often funny, and you can never be sure how he'll wind them up.

My favorite is a Christmas story, one that seems to express the very essence of the holiday. I've loved it from the time I first read it, which was when I was in high school—*eons* ago! It's called "The Gift of the Magi" and takes place on Christmas Eve. Della and Jim are young, very poor, and very much in love. They have only two things worth being proud of—Della's hair, which falls below her knees in gorgeous brown ripples, and Jim's gold watch, which had been his father's and grandfather's. They have no money for presents, and Della decides to sell her hair to buy a watch fob for Jim, not knowing he has sold his watch to buy the tortoiseshell combs she wanted for her hair. They each had sacrificed their most precious possession to buy a present for the other. [Read last paragraph of story "The magi, as you know. . . ."]

—*Joni Bodart-Talbot*

GIRL   Grades 3–5
By GERALD GREEN

It all began when Girl and Mr. Riddle appeared in the office of Geoff, the producer of the Don Derry show. Girl was a shaggy mongrel dog, and her ragamuffin friend was called Mr. Riddle.

"What's your act? What do you do?" asked Geoff.

Mr. Riddle explained that the dog had a vocabulary of 4,000 words. "Girl, show us the telephone," he said. "The one on this man's desk." With no hesitation Girl placed her paws on Geoff's phone.

"Show me the machine that sends the news."

"Impossible," said Geoff. "She can't know that."

The dog padded across the office, sniffed the air a few times and pressed her wet nose against the Associated Press teleprinter.

This visit was the beginning. When Girl and Mr. Riddle appeared on TV, they became overnight sensations, making believers out of the most skeptical folks. There was something magical about a performance by Girl and Mr. Riddle. Don Derry, star of the show, felt threatened by their success and was determined to discredit them or get rid of them any way he could. Would he get away with it? Or would Girl and Mr. Riddle be too smart for him?

—*Mary Catherine Hall*

THE GIRL FROM THE EMERALINE ISLAND   YA
By ROBERT S. BLUM

Ellia had never done anything as dangerous as this before, even though she had been running away from home for at least five years. This time she had enrolled at the Stone Coast Shrine—the only school on the Emeraline Island where boys could get military training. She was learning to ride and fight like a man, but if they ever found out she was a sixteen-year-old girl—what would they do to her? Would they tie her to the post in the courtyard and whip her with the electric whip that left no marks but caused horrible pain?

So far Ellia had avoided detection, but her luck couldn't last. She'd attended lots of schools over the last five years and each time she'd been found out. But she'd always managed to escape. There wasn't any future in being a girl on the Emeraline Island because women weren't taught to read or allowed to do anything outside the home. The only skills they needed were those for taking care of a house and looking after the babies they were supposed to produce year after year. Lots of boy children were needed in a land where only fifty percent of them survived to become adults. Ellia couldn't pass for a male forever, though, because all males were required to undergo a survival test in the Blasted Hills, and no Emeraline Island girl had ever come out alive. All she wanted was to be free, to choose a life for herself—but first she had to escape from the Stone Coast Shrine.

—Marianne Tait Pridemore

THE GIRL WHO OWNED A CITY   Grades 6-8
By O. T. NELSON

Lisa didn't always own a city. She grew up in a comfortable suburban family, squabbling with her little brother Todd—until the plague came, killing all the adults, but mysteriously sparing all children twelve and under. At first Lisa was just as frightened and powerless as the rest of the kids on her block, but then the gangs came and their food ran out, and she turned to looting and thieving to keep herself and Todd alive. But when the gangs got bigger and more powerful and her own house was attacked, she realized that there had to be a better way. And so she learned how to drive—and how to organize other children to form a whole army, big enough to defend the city she established in the high school.

—Elizabeth Overmyer

THE GIRL WITH   Grades 6-8/YA
THE SILVER EYES
By WILLO DAVIS ROBERTS

Katie Welker is used to people thinking she's odd. Some people are even afraid of her and think she must be a witch. The reason they feel this way is that such strange things happen when Katie is around.

For instance—Mr. Pollard lives in the apartment building where Katie has just moved. He doesn't care much for kids, Katie especially; but then, Katie doesn't like Mr. Pollard much either. Every time he sees her, some unfortunate accident occurs, and he insists it's Katie's fault. The first time they met, they collided on the stairs, sending his papers from the office flying in every direction. The next morning a rock mysteriously appeared on the sidewalk, just waiting to trip Mr. Pollard. And when the paperboy couldn't collect because Mr. Pollard claimed he didn't have any money on him, his wallet slipped up from his pocket and a wind from nowhere blew the money right out. All these incidents and many more are blamed on Katie.

But the thing that makes people immediately feel uncomfortable around Katie is that she looks so different from any other ten-year-old—or anyone at all, for that matter. Her eyes are not brown or blue or green or hazel or even gray—Katie is "the girl with the silver eyes."

With these silver eyes come very special powers. Katie can move objects just by thinking about them. This comes in very handy when she's asked to do things like set the table or straighten her room—she doesn't even need to be in the room to do it. She can also communicate with animals and read their thoughts. Katie needs to be careful when using these powers around other people, though, because most people are not very open-minded when it comes to objects floating in thin air, or children conversing with their pets.

Where did Katie get these special powers? Why are her eyes silver? Is she from another planet? Are there other people like *The Girl with the Silver Eyes?*

—*Lynda Smith*

THE GIRLS OF HUNTINGTON HOUSE   YA/Adult
By BLOSSOM ELFMAN

Huntington House is a home for unmarried, pregnant teenagers. Just like other teenagers, they have to go to school, and this is what happened to one very idealistic English teacher who came to Huntington House with lots of ambitious ideas and ended up learning as much as her students did.

This is what she has to say about her first day there. [Read from pp. 1–2, paperback edition: "Huntington House is three stories of sooty grey stone . . . And I'm tired of the joker who says 'What can you teach pregnant teenagers that they don't already know?'" and from pp. 8–9: "It was my intention on that optimistic afternoon. . . . but an unborn baby named Heather."]

For a book that'll make you laugh, and make you cry and laugh again, read Blossom Elfman's *The Girls of Huntington House.*

—Joni Bodart-Talbot

GIVE US A GREAT BIG SMILE,   Grades 4–6
ROSY COLE
By SHEILA GREENWALD

Rosy Cole is going to be famous when she turns ten. For sure. Her two sisters are already famous because when they were ten, their Uncle Ralph made books about them. *Anitra Dances* was a book like this [show one of the Jill Krementz photo-documentary books], full of photographs about Anitra and her ballet lessons. *Pippa Prances* was about her sister Pippa taking riding lessons. And now Rosy's ten years old and it's her turn.

Uncle Ralph plans a new book, *A Very Little Fiddler*, because Rosy has been taking violin lessons for two years. But Uncle Ralph doesn't know about the secret that Rosy shares with her music teacher—the woman is an old friend of Rosy's mother, and that's the only reason she keeps teaching Rosy. In fact, Rosy is supposed to have two lessons a week, but she plays so badly that she skips one and is always late for the other. She's so bad that when she practices, her neighbor, Mrs. Rosano, complains that there must be a wildcat in the apartment, and when she discovers that it's Rosy practicing, she makes Rosy's mother put carpeting on the walls so the sound won't escape. Rosy thinks a better name for a book about her would be *A Very Little Coward*, because she's too scared to tell Uncle Ralph how much she hates the violin.

Finally Uncle Ralph is all ready to start taking pictures—and he's even planned a concert where she'll have to play in front of a hundred people! Rosy knows she's in trouble, but all her parents and Uncle Ralph will say is, "Just give us a great big smile, Rosy Cole!"

—Elizabeth Overmyer

GLORY ROAD   YA/Adult
By BRUCE CATTON

Bruce Catton is one of the very few historians I actually enjoy reading. He brings out the details of history, the human details that make his books read almost like novels. The Civil War era is his specialty, and the Army of the Potomac one of his favorite topics. He's written a trilogy about the activity of that particular army during the war, and this is how I first got acquainted with him. *Glory Road* is one of that trilogy—the second book—and it tells in detail how the Army of the Potomac changed the outcome of the Civil War, at Fredericksburg, at Chancellorsville, and finally at Gettysburg. You'll meet here the enlisted men, some volunteers, some bounty men, who fought like fiends during the battles and who swapped stories and coffee with the Rebels in between them. Catton introduces you to the three generals who commanded the army: Burnside, who meant so well, and did so badly; Hooker, who was a soldier's soldier; and Meade, who took over only three days before Gettysburg. Some of the less famous people you'll find here are the man who wrote "Taps," the laundress who took coffee and hardtack to men on the firing line, and a Union private who bodily seized and captured a Confederate general.

Bruce Catton looks at history first with a wide-angle lens and then with a microscope. For a glimpse of history that's as realistic as life today, try *Glory Road*, by Bruce Catton.

—Joni Bodart-Talbot

GOING FOR THE BIG ONE   YA
By P. J. PETERSON

Jeff, Dave, and Annie Bates found themselves in a heap of trouble when their new step-mom took off and left them with only $20. Their father had taken off even earlier—he had gone to look for work in Alaska. At first the kids thought they could stay in the rental house, but the landlord insisted on payment, and to top it off, Dave got caught stealing a TV. He felt he couldn't live without a TV, and his step-mom had taken everything. The police caught Dave, and when Annie and Jeff tried to get him out, they found that that could only be done by an adult guardian. They literally carried old Mrs. Locke, a neighborhood friend so short of breath she could hardly walk, down to the station. They knew that by the next morning, when they had to appear in juvenile court, they would be split up just like before. So they packed their camping gear and headed for the mountains. There they found a way to make money—by taking care of a wounded criminal. They accepted this deal, but soon found out things weren't quite as they seemed. In fact, nothing had been as it seemed. *Going for the Big One* is always harder than it seems.

—Donna Houser

A GOOD DAY TO DIE
By DEL BARTON
YA/Adult

It is 1859. Crying Boy is fourteen years old and still carries his cradle name. In his Dakota tribe, this is considered very embarrassing. But Crying Boy has not yet proved himself through an act of bravery, and until he does he will not carry the name of a man.

Crying Boy has always been impulsive. He was born two months prematurely, but still, he was a large and lively baby. He decided he didn't want milk and grabbed for meat before he cut his first tooth. He literally kicked his way out of his cradleboard and tried to stand on his feet before they could support his weight. He climbed on a pony when his legs were too short and howled for a bow before his pudgy fingers could even hold a slingshot. And now Crying Boy is taking a wife before becoming a brave and becoming a father before becoming a bridegroom.

This also shows how impulsive Crying Boy is. His brother, Blue Feather, was married to Small Owl, who is expecting a child. When Blue Feather is killed in battle, Crying Boy turns to an old law of the tribe that says a man may marry his brother's widow to provide for her and protect her. So Small Owl becomes his wife.

It is now more important than ever to take a man's name.

The white man is moving quickly across the plains and destroying the Dakota way of life. Crying Boy's tribe is angry and fearful because of this. One day Crying Boy and his friend, Curly Fox, who also must prove himself, find a white man, the first they have ever seen, hunting in the forest. The boys capture the man, take the gun, and give the bear the hunter shot to the tribe. Now it is truly a time for feasting, because the boys have become braves. Crying Boy is given the honorable name Gray Wolf, and Curly Fox becomes Crazy Horse. Little do these two men realize that everything they do from now on will be focused on whites like the stranger they have captured—the white traders, settlers, and soldiers who are pouring into the Dakota territory.

Written by his granddaughter, this is the true story of Gray Wolf, a Dakota warrior who lived to be 104 years old. It is a story of bravery, revenge, and endurance, and also a tale of Gray Wolf's eventual love for a defiant Spanish beauty he called White Lily.

For an adventurous saga of a proud people, read *A Good Day to Die,* by Del Barton.

—Diane Tuccillo

THE GOOD SIDE OF MY HEART YA
By ANN RINALDI

When I look back on it, Josh had always been a part of my life, in the background, my best friend Gina's big brother. But the year he got kicked out of military school to come back to go to school here, he *was* my life, for a while. Gina warned me not to get involved, but there was no way I'd listen to her—Josh was too perfect, just right in every way. Except one way. Part of going with a guy is hugs and kisses, maybe even sex eventually. Josh would have none of that. I couldn't figure it out. But just the same, we were friends—we talked, we did everything together, I even got to go on the senior picnic, although that turned out to be where all the trouble started. One of the seniors was dealing drugs and left his stash on the island—*my* island—where the picnic was. He threatened to get me involved if I didn't keep my mouth shut. That's one of the reasons Josh and I were close—we shared that secret. I just wish we'd been able to share our secrets sooner. . . .

—Joni Bodart-Talbot

GOOD-BYE TOMORROW YA
By GLORIA D. MIKLOWITZ

Today is wonderful! Tomorrow promises to be even better!

Alex Weiss knows that he is the luckiest guy alive. He is in love with the nicest, most beautiful girl in school—and she loves him, too. He is the champion of the swim team. His honor-roll grades make him a shoo-in at a top architectural college next year. He has survived and recovered from a near-fatal car wreck a year ago. And he has a great relationship with his parents and his "once bratty" kid sister. What more could he ask?

Then he comes down with the flu and can't seem to shake it, and a few weeks later gets the flu again. At his mother's insistence he has a complete check-up—and the news is bad, very bad. The tests show that Alex has been exposed to the AIDS-producing virus from the blood he received in transfusions following the car wreck. Worse yet, the doctor is afraid he may already have ARC, AIDS Related Complex, which can develop into AIDS itself at any time.

Alex has to cope not only with the trauma of the disease, but also with the fear that others will find out. He knows that once the news is out, the kids at school will be terrified of him—if he is allowed to stay in school, that is.

Do his parents still love him? he wonders, when he notices that they seem afraid to touch him anymore. What about his sister Christy? She won't even carry his dirty dishes into the kitchen.

And Shannon—dear beautiful Shannon. He knows that he must tell her and he prays that he hasn't already infected her too. He also knows that he must break off the relationship before she becomes a social outcast because of her association with him.

What is to become of Alex? Alex, who only a few short weeks ago was facing such a bright future. Alex, who now can only say *Good-bye Tomorrow.*

—*Joy A. Basel*

GRANDMA, FELIX AND MUSTAPHA BISCUIT   Grades k–1
By VICTOR AMBRUS

Grandma and Felix, the cat, and Long John Silver, the parrot, all live happily together until the day Grandma brings home a little hamster in a cage. The hamster's name is Mustapha Biscuit. Do you know how he got that funny name? Well, biscuits—sweet biscuits like cookies—are his very favorite food. Whenever he sees one, he thinks, "I must have a biscuit." And Felix the cat must have a hamster. All he can think about is cooking and eating that hamster. He dreams of fried hamster, hamster on toast, and hamster à la mode.

When Grandma goes out shopping, Felix sees his chance. He works and works to pick the lock on the hamster's cage. But while Felix is working on the lock, Mustapha Biscuit is working on Felix's tail, pulling out the hair to make a nice soft hamster-nest. Grandma returns to catch Felix red-handed—and bare-tailed. Poor Felix! Grandma knits him a brightly-striped tail sweater to keep his bare tail warm—and all the other cats laugh and laugh at him. That makes Felix so mad that he is all the more determined to *get that hamster!* So the next time Grandma goes out, Felix tries a new plan. Does he ever catch Mustapha Biscuit? You can read *Grandma, Felix and Mustapha Biscuit* and find out.

—*Diane L. Deuel*

THE GREAT CHEESE CONSPIRACY   Grades 4-6
By JEAN VAN LEEUWEN

This is the story of a trio of thieves, about to pull off the greatest heist in the history of their gang. They've staked out their target and decided upon the perfect disguise . . . a popcorn box! Obviously, this is no ordinary gang of thieves. The would-be criminals are movie-theater mice, and they are about to attempt their first big job on the outside . . . what could be more tempting to a gang of mice than a store full of cheese?

But like the Swiss cheese the mice crave, their foolproof plan is full of holes. Unexpected problems occur, like a tidy shopkeeper who believes popcorn boxes belong in the trash, like shoppers with spike heels that could turn our heroes into Swiss cheese themselves, and like Giovanni the cat, who keeps careful watch over the Wisconsin cheddar. Will our heroes beat the odds? Or will the law prevail? Find out in *The Great Cheese Conspiracy*, by Jean Van Leeuwen.

—*Booklegger* class

THE GREAT CHRISTMAS KIDNAPING   Grades 3-6
CAPER
By JEAN VAN LEEUWEN

The Great Christmas Kidnaping Caper begins with Marvin the Magnificent, a New York City mouse, shivering on a street corner and trying to think of a warm safe place for a mouse to live now that winter is coming. Darting carefully through a revolving door, he finds himself in Macy's, the world's largest store. As soon as the store closes, Marvin begins to explore and is delighted to find a deli department loaded with all his favorite cheeses. He takes a wild ride on an electric train in the toy department and then settles down to sleep in a dollhouse with a bed just his size. Life in Macy's is really ideal for a mouse, so Marvin decides to share his good fortune with his friends Raymond and Fats. Raymond is very smart and likes to read the newspaper, while Fats likes to eat.

Since Christmas is only a couple of weeks away, the toy department is very busy, with loads of parents and children coming to see Santa Claus. This Santa Claus is special. His name is Mr. Dunderhoff and he has been Macy's Santa for eighteen years. Santa soon discovers the three mice living in the dollhouse, and when he leaves them a treat every day they grow very fond of this jolly fat man in the red suit. One day Santa doesn't show up for work, and the people at Macy's are extremely disappointed. (So are the mice.) A few days later Raymond reads in the newspaper that Mr. Dunderhoff is missing and the police are investigating his disappearance. Marvin, who prides himself on being a detective, suspects foul play, and the three mice decide to take action to find Macy's missing Santa. Can three mice solve the mystery, when the New York City police can't?

—*Michele Anton Cahill*

GROWING UP YA/Adult
By RUSSELL BAKER

"Something will come along."

That became my mother's battle-cry as I plowed into the final year of high school. Friends began asking her what Russell planned to do when he graduated, and her answer was, "Russ hasn't made up his mind yet, but something will come along."

I saw no possibilities and looked forward to the end of school days with increasing glumness. It was assumed I would get a job. The only thing that truly interested me was writing, and I knew that sixteen-year-olds did not come out of high school and become writers.

The notion of becoming a writer had flickered off and on in my head for some time, but it wasn't until my third year in high school that the possibility really took hold. When our class was assigned to Mr. Fleagle for third-year English I anticipated another grim year in that dreariest of subjects. Mr. Fleagle was notorious among students for dullness and inability to inspire. To me he looked to be sixty or seventy, and prim to a fault. I anticipated a listless, unfruitful year and for a long time was not disappointed.

Late in the year Mr. Fleagle distributed a homework sheet offering us a choice of essay topics. Most seemed to be dull. The topic on which my eye stopped was, "The Art of Eating Spaghetti." This title produced an extraordinary sequence of mental images. Surging up out of the depths of memory came a vivid recollection of a night when all of us were seated around the supper table and Aunt Pat served spaghetti for supper. Spaghetti was an exotic treat in those days. I recalled the laughing arguments we had that night about the socially respectable method for moving spaghetti from plate to mouth.

Suddenly I wanted to write about that, about the warmth and good feeling of it, but I wanted to put it down simply for my own joy, not for Mr. Fleagle. To write it as I wanted, however, would violate all the rules of formal composition I'd learned in school, and Mr. Fleagle would surely give it a failing grade. Never mind, I would write something else for Mr. Fleagle after I had written this thing for myself.

When I finished it the night was half gone and there was no time left to compose a proper, respectable essay for Mr. Fleagle. There was no choice next morning but to turn in my private reminiscence. Two days passed before Mr. Fleagle returned the graded papers, and he returned everyone's but mine. I was bracing myself for a command to report to Mr. Fleagle immediately after school for discipline when I saw him lift my paper from his desk and rap for the class's attention.

"Now boys," he said, "I want to read you an essay. This is titled 'The Art of Eating Spaghetti.'" And he started to read. My words! He was reading *my words* out loud to the entire class. What's more, the entire class was listening. Listening attentively. Then somebody laughed, then the entire class was laughing, and not in contempt and ridicule, but with openhearted enjoyment. Even Mr. Fleagle stopped two or three times to repress a small prim smile.

I did my best to avoid showing pleasure, but what I was feeling was pure ecstasy at this startling demonstration that my words had the power to make people laugh. In the eleventh grade, at the eleventh hour as it were, I had discovered a calling. It was the happiest moment of my entire school career. When Mr. Fleagle finished, he put the final seal on my happiness by saying, "Now *that,* boys, is an essay, don't you see. Congratulations, Mr. Baker." After that I ranked Mr. Fleagle among the finest teachers in the school.

My mother was almost as delighted as I when I showed her Mr. Fleagle's A-plus and described my triumph. Hadn't she always said I had a talent for writing? "Now if you work hard at it, Buddy, you can make something of yourself." I didn't see how.

Matters were at this stage in the spring when I discovered my great friend and classmate Charlie Sussman filling out a sheaf of forms between classes one day. I asked, "What're you doing, Suss?"

"Filling out college application forms," he said.

"What college are you going to?"

"Johns Hopkins," he said. "What college are you going to?"

"I'm not going to college."

Sussman was shocked. Dropping his pen, he glared at me in amazement. "Not going to college?" He said it in outrage. He refused to tolerate this offense to education. "You've got to go to college," he said. "Get some admission forms—they've got them downstairs at the office—and we'll go to Hopkins together."

"That would be great," I said, "but my family couldn't afford it."

"Apply for a scholarship," he commanded. "I'll get you a set of application forms," he said, and he did.

The examination was held on a Saturday in May. I hadn't been to Johns Hopkins before, so I gave myself an extra hour against the possibility of getting lost. I was directed to a huge lecture hall reeking of chemicals. I was dismayed to find the hall filled with boys, each of whom probably wanted one of the few available scholarships as desperately as I did.

Unlike my mother, I had no faith in prayer. Now, though, as I counted the boys in the room and realized the odds against me, I decided it was foolish to leave even the remotest possibility untouched. Closing my eyes I silently uttered the Lord's Prayer in my head. At the end I improvised a single line of my own and prayed, "Dear God, help me with this test." It lasted four hours.

Two weeks crept slowly past and May neared its end. I had only three weeks left of high school when I arrived home one afternoon to find my mother sitting expressionless in the glider on the front porch. "You got a letter from Hopkins today," she said. "It's in on the table."

"Did you open it?"

"I'm not in the habit of opening other people's mail," she said. "You open it and tell me what it says."

We went inside together. The envelope was there on the table. It was a small envelope. Very small. Hopkins had obviously decided I was not worth wasting much stationery on. Picking it up, I saw that it was also very thin. The message was obviously short and probably not sweet. I ripped the end off the envelope, slid out a piece of notesized paper, and unfolded it. I saw it was a form letter on which someone had typed a few words in the blank spaces.

"Well, what does it say?" my mother asked.

I read it aloud to her:

> Sir:
> I am pleased to inform you that you have been awarded a Hopkins Scholarship for two terms of the academic year 1942-43. This award will entitle you to remission of tuition fees for this period. Please let met know at once if you will accept this award.
> Yours very truly, Isaiah Bowman, President.

Something had come along.

—Linda F. Lapides

NOTE: This talk is taken from pages 183, 186-9, and 191-5 of the hardback edition, chapter 13, edited for oral delivery.

GUY DE MAUPASSANT'S SHORT STORIES   YA/Adult
By GUY DE MAUPASSANT

De Maupassant is a past master of the art of suspense and the surprise ending. His stories are brief and to the point, wasting no words, often a little cynical or sardonic in tone.

My favorite is one called "The Necklace." It is the story of a beautiful but poor woman with high-flying dreams of wealth. She was married to a clerk, and one day he brought home an invitation to a ball, and they sacrificed until they could go. They spent all their savings on her dress, and borrowed a beautiful diamond necklace from a rich friend to complete her costume.

1. the ball—compliments, etc.
2. necklace's loss discovered
3. the search, the note to the friend
4. the new necklace
5. the struggle to pay the debt
6. after ten years. . . .

[Read excerpt from story beginning "And this life lasted ten years . . . " to end.]

—Joni Bodart-Talbot

A HANDFUL OF STARS   YA
By BARBARA GIRION

Julie Ann Meyers is starting her sophomore year in high school with everything going her way. First, there's all the attention she's getting from Steve Marks, a good-looking basketball player who really seems to like her. Then Julie finds herself caught up in drama class, and she's excited about the great part she gets in the spring musical, *Guys and Dolls*. She's even enjoying her other classes, because of all the new friends she has made. No longer is it just Julie Ann and her best friend Mary Jo, but a whole circle of friends who do things together. And every Friday night, there is a party to go to. It is during one of these Friday night parties that something unusual happens to Julie. Something that will change her life more drastically than starting her sophomore year ever could.

At the end of the party, Julie, along with a few other girls, is helping her friend Elyssa clean up the mess. She is using Ajax on the corner of one wall where something had spilled, and the next thing she remembers is banging on a door and Mary Jo shaking her.

"What's the matter with you, Julie?," Mary Jo asks.

Julie feels dazed, like there are feathers floating around in her head. "What are you talking about?," she answers.

"You just walked around the room in a circle talking about algebra equations and then you started banging on the door," Mary Jo tells her. Julie looks down at her fist. It is very red where she has been banging it on the door. Her head hurts and she notices the other girls looking at her funny. It's scary because the whole thing is a blank to Julie.

This first episode does not alarm Julie too much, but the same sort of thing keeps happening, in school and at home. Now Julie is getting frightened. Why are these blank-outs happening, and why does she wake up feeling so dazed and confused? Something is going on in her body, forcing her to behave in a strange way. She just can't understand. Is it a virus? Or is she going crazy? And where are her good friends when she needs their support? Talking in whispers behind her back. Even her great part in the spring musical and her romance with Steve are on the line when the doctor finally discovers what's wrong. Julie is an epileptic, and her ordeal has just begun. To find out how Julie eventually copes and how she learns who her real friends are, read *A Handful of Stars,* by Barbara Girion.

—Diane Tuccillo

THE HAND-ME-DOWN KID　　　　**Grades 3–6**
By FRANCINE PASCAL

Don't laugh! I'm really gorgeous underneath my sister's ridiculous housecoat. You see, I'm Ari, the hand-me-down kid. Whatever my older sister outgrows, I inherit. Sometimes I think I must have been adopted just so Elizabeth would have someone for her hand-me-downs.

But then there's the bicycle. Elizabeth's bicycle, that is. It's a new Peugeot. You should hear Elizabeth roll the word Peugeot off her tongue. It would crack you up! I've heard the speech many times—"Now, Ari, you must never, ever touch my Peugeot! You know how expensive a Peugeot is!"

Well, Elizabeth never had to worry about Rhona Finkelstein! Rhona Finkelstein is the biggest girl in school, in fact the biggest girl I've ever seen in our neighborhood. And does she get her way! She ordered me to "get in the Bicycle Race at the park," and on top of that, to "borrow" my sister's bicycle. Can you believe I fell for all this? Well, maybe. She *was* big, you know. What a choice! And anyway, how would Elizabeth ever know that I had borrowed the bike for an hour while she was at the dentist's?

I shiver just thinking about all this. Because in the park, that Peugeot disappeared. It vanished. It is gone from the face of the earth.

Find out what happened to me, to Elizabeth, to Rhona—and to that Peugeot, in *The Hand-Me Down Kid,* by Francine Pascal.

—*Sharon Thomas*

HANGIN' OUT WITH CICI   Grades 6-8
By FRANCINE PASCAL

Fourteen-year-old Victoria has a reputation for being a troublemaker. It's partly deserved, but partly just rotten luck. She's *always* the one who gets caught, and sometimes the *only* one as well! Like this time—she got caught with a joint at her cousin's house-party. She was showing off, in the middle of comparing the merits of various kinds of grass (something she knew absolutely nothing about). Unfortunately, it didn't sound that way to her aunt, who called Victoria's parents and shipped her back to New York City on the next train.

On the way back, Victoria thinks about how she dreads meeting her mother at the station. They haven't been getting along lately—her mother treats her as if she were about two years old, and doesn't understand how she feels at all. It's like they're worlds apart and can't communicate anymore.

Then, as the train goes through a tunnel, there's a sharp jerk, the lights go out, and Victoria hits her head on the window sill—hard! But then the train comes out of the tunnel and pulls into Penn Station. Victoria gets off and looks for her mother, who isn't there. Instead, she meets Cici, who looks very familiar and offers to wait with her. They wait for over an hour, but Victoria's mother never comes, and the phone doesn't connect when Victoria tries to call home. She's beginning to feel strange, not only because her mother isn't there but also because everyone is dressed very strangely—the whole train station looks like a set for an old movie! Finally Cici suggests Victoria go home with her, and things get even stranger. Movies are 17¢, lunch 25¢, and shoes $2.99! Then Victoria sees a newspaper—dated May 9, 1944! That's when she suddenly realizes why it's all so strange—she has traveled, somehow, thirty years back in time. And when they get to Cici's, Victoria gets a shock that makes everything else look pale in comparison. They walk into the house and Cici's mother calls downstairs. Victoria would know that voice anywhere—it's her *grandmother*! And that means Cici isn't just Victoria's new friend who's fourteen years old and even wilder than Victoria's ever *thought* of being—Cici is her own mother!

But that's only the beginning!

—Joni Bodart-Talbot

HAROLD AND MAUDE   YA
By COLIN HIGGINS

Harold is eighteen and in love with death. Maude is seventy-nine and in love with life. This is their unique love story. Harold is making a career of suicide (he's done it fifteen times so far) because, he says, "I enjoy being dead." Maude spends her time looking for new experiences and enjoying the phenomena of life. They meet at a funeral—Maude goes because they're fun; Harold, because they're deathly. Maude doesn't own a car but she does have a set of skeleton keys, and when she needs a car, she borrows one. After the funeral she steals the Jaguar XKE hearse Harold drives, and offers him a ride home. When he tells her it's his hearse, she lets him drive her home. Harold is fascinated by the strange old lady, and they gradually become friends, the oddest of odd couples. Meanwhile, Harold's mother sets up three computer dates for Harold (she filled out the application herself), since it's high time he got married. Harold's agreeable—but he wants to marry Maude! He doesn't seem to be able to teach her much about death, but she's been teaching him a lot about life.

This is a comedy of life and love and freedom. Almost everyone can identify with what it says. We're all Harolds, in one way or another, trying to become Maudes.

It's a beautiful—and hilarious—love story that you'll never forget!

—Joni Bodart-Talbot

HARRIET THE SPY   Grades 5–7
By LOUISE FITZHUGH

As I sat in Mrs. P's dumbwaiter trying to be quiet. I heard the maid singing the Miss America theme. She was awful. What was I doing in Mrs. Plumber's dumbwaiter? I'm Harriet M. Walsh and I'm a spy. . . .

When the tray was ready and the maid left, I started pulling myself up to Mrs. Plumber's room on the second floor. My heart was beating so hard. I saw a huge four-poster bed with Mrs. P in the middle surrounded by pillows, magazines, and lots of pink fluff. She was talking on the phone, telling her friend that she found the secret of life—stay in bed and don't get out for anyone. That's the dumbest thing I ever heard—in and out is *my* motto. Mrs. P was now telling her friend she was going to get a job. *Unbelievable!!!!!*

"I think this might be too dangerous an assignment," I write in my notebook, "but I would like to know what job she takes. But how can you work lying down? How does she pay for anything just lying there? I guess she just lives off her husband's money. Does my mother mooch off my father? I'll never do that."

Then I heard Mrs. P ask the maid if she heard a creak in the dumbwaiter. Do you want to find out if I get caught? Read *Harriet the Spy.*

—*Tina Marie Kopie*

HATCHET   YA
By GARY PAULSEN

Brian's life was in turmoil. His parents had split, he was split, and he knew the secret, the reason why. However, his father didn't know what he knew. Should Brian have told his father? And before she sent him to visit his father for the summer, should Brian have told his mother that he knew her secret? No. Brian told her nothing. He didn't even tell her how silly her going-away gift was—a sheathed hatchet. When his mother saw him off on the bush plane bound for the Canadian oil fields and his father, Brian couldn't foresee that the hatchet would become even more important than the split, the divorce, the secret. That hatchet would save his life.

Brian was unprepared when the pilot of the bush plane suffered a fatal heart attack. His emotional turmoil quickly changed to survival instinct. He flew the plane as long as he could, then landed it in the flattest clearing he could find—a lake. Brian escaped a watery grave to find himself alone in the Canadian woods with only his intelligence, his instinct, and the hatchet. Brian survived fifty-four days. Each day brought another obstacle, another puzzle, another danger, as he struggled to overcome the hostile forces of nature, to reconcile himself to his parents' divorce, and to accept his knowledge of the secret.

—*Sue Padilla*

THE HAUNTING   Grades 6–8
By MARGARET MAHY

"Barnaby's dead!" it said. "Barnaby's dead. I'm going to be very lonely."

Barney stood absolutely still, feeling more dizzy than ever. Suddenly, on an ordinary Wednesday, it seemed to Barney that the world tilted and ran downhill in all directions, and he knew he was about to be haunted again. It had happened when he was younger, but he had thought that it was a babyish thing that you grew out of.

Then he saw his ghost on the pathway beside him. A figure was forming out of the air. It was quite a little one, with a curious pale face against a halo of shining hair. The hair faded into the air like bright smoke. At first the figure looked flat, like a paper doll; then it became round and real and looked alive—but it was dressed in a very strange and old-fashioned way.

"Barnaby's dead," it said again. "Barnaby's dead! And I'm going to be very lonely."

The ghost seemed to be announcing his death by using his proper name of Barnaby. And it was not just telling him he was going to die, but that he was dead already.

As he stood there, stunned by the figure before him, Barney thought, What can you do with a ghost? You can't joke with it. Can you ask it questions? Barney was afraid of the answers this ghost might give him.

The ghost dissolved in a shiver of light. Barney ran! Little stumbles in his running made him think that he mght have been struck by bullets. His hair felt prickly, and he wondered, was it turning white?

When Barney got home, he heard his sister talking. "We are in a house of mourning. No one I know has ever died before." Barney stared at her in horror!

This is just the beginning of *The Haunting,* by Margaret Mahy.

—Linda Henderson

HE NOTICED I'M ALIVE . . .   Grades 6–8/YA
AND OTHER HOPEFUL SIGNS
By MARJORIE SHARMAT

Jody Kline is fifteen. She lives with her father, who is dating a woman named Gossamer Green. Gossamer has a teen-aged son named Matt. When Jody meets Matt for the first time she almost immediately falls for him. He seems so tall and sure of himself. He says he wants to see her artwork sometime. When Jody calls her friend Alison to tell her about Matt and what he said, Alison says, "Great. He noticed you're alive. That's a hopeful sign." But Matt does more than just notice she's alive—he eventually asks Jody out. She's thrilled, but then she remembers she already has a date that evening with Alison's friend, so she has to say no. When Matt and Jody finally do go to a movie together, Jody ends the date by starting an argument. So Jody blows her second chance with Matt. Will she get a third chance? Read *He Noticed I'm Alive . . . And Other Hopeful Signs,* by Marjorie Sharmat, to find out.

—*Mary Hedge*

HEALER   YA
By PETER DICKINSON

I'll never forget the day I met her. I was at school sitting in the hallway outside the secretary's office, waiting for her to finish up some kid who'd skinned his knee. I could barely wait for her to finish. My head was throbbing, and I needed two aspirin.

"You've got a nasty head," she said.

I looked down and saw a fat little girl with glasses. She couldn't have been more than six. I tried to shrug it off, saying "I'm all right."

She replied, "Not now, but you will be soon."

Then she reached out and took my hand. Though I tried to grab it away, she held on tight and reached for my other one. Her hands were chilly, yet I felt this heat on the back of my neck and between my shoulder blades. The heat made me drowsy and I could feel myself nodding off.

She whispered, "Better now?" and I was.

That's how I, Barry Evans, met Pinkie Proudfoot.

And now, after two years of not knowing what had happened to her, I was seeing her again. She was the reason I was at the Hall of Harmony with a self-induced migraine. It was the only way I could get near her, see if she was all right, to make sure she wasn't being exploited as "The Healer."

—*Pam Spencer*

HEART'S BLOOD   YA
By JANE YOLEN

Second volume in the Pit Dragon Trilogy

Talk 1

Jakkin could hardly stand the suspense. When his beautiful red champion fighter-dragon Heart's Blood laid her hundred eggs, he had to wait patiently for at least three days until they hatched. Only then would he know how many hatchlings would live. The bondboys at the dragon nursery were betting: Would it be the usual five or six, or maybe up to ten, since Heart's Blood was such a special dragon? Jakkin couldn't understand how the others could joke and bet on such a momentous occasion. Since the day when he first held tiny Heart's Blood in his hand, until now when she was nearly thirteen feet long, his mind had been linked to hers. He had received the shimmering rainbows of her sending and sent his own thoughts and feelings back to her until their sharing made them so close, he felt at one with her. Because of their deep connection, the fight training had gone beautifully, for Jakkin could support Heart's Blood by their mind-link as she fought. Even though Jakkin was the youngest dragon-master on the planet Austar IV, his Heart's Blood was already a dexad, a ten-fight winner. Now she was ready to go to the major pit at the Rokk, capital city of the planet, where fortunes were made and lost, where off-worlders came from other galaxies to bet on the dragon fights.

As Jakkin struggled to keep calm during the hatching so as not to up-set the new mother, he received an unusual invitation to the house of Sarkkhan, head of the dragon farm. There he met Golden, a mysterious visitor who was one of Austar's senators. Jakkin couldn't understand why Sarkkhan had invited him, for political talk bored him, and all he could think of was Heart's Blood's hatchlings. He was shocked out of a daydream when he heard a special name: Akki. The senator was say-ing that Akki had sent for him!

Beautiful Akki, who had helped him raise Heart's Blood, had kissed him, and then left him suddenly with no explanation except he must wait to become a man. Now, over a year later, Akki needed him! Gol-den told him she was being held by the rebels in the Rokk. Had they discovered she was a spy for Golden? Jakkin would have to infiltrate the rebels to find Akki. Would he consent? Jakkin, who hated politics, whose whole life was dragons, who had to prepare Heart's Blood for her biggest fight yet, who had to raise her hatchlings—would he undertake this dangerous mission now for Akki, who had left him?

—Catherine G. Edgerton

Talk 2

Dragons! Fighting dragons! What could be more exciting? Especially if the action takes place on a faraway planet, Austar IV. Add to this an underground rebel group that is trying to release all the Bonders and the plot gets complicated.

A Bonder, you say? What is a Bonder? On the planet Austar IV, there are two classes of people. The Masters, who own and train the dragons and live in fine houses, and the Bonders, who wear a "bond-bag" around their necks until they can somehow earn enough gold to fill it and buy their freedom, becoming Masters in their own turn.

But can a Bonder, after becoming a Master, ever forget how it feels to be a Bonder? Can an ex-Bonder live in peace as a Master?

If you enjoyed *Dragon's Blood,* you won't want to miss the fantastic action of *Heart's Blood.*

—*Marjorie Williams*

THE HERALD   YA/Adult
By MICHAEL SHAARA

No one answered Nick's calls to the control tower, but he had to land his plane anyway, because his plane did not have enough gas to reach Jacksonville.

When he landed, Rachel roused from her sleep, yawned, looked around, said, "But where is everybody?"

Nick left his plane. The gas truck had not moved. The hangar door was open, but he saw no one moving.

He had a creepy feeling and a sudden sense that he had to go look. Rachel followed close behind him but stayed outside the building. The first man he found had been sick in the restroom; the grayness of the man's face told Nick the man was dead. Everyone they found had also been sick and had died.

Nick decided that the airport attendants had been hit by a plague. He and the girl hurried to the car that he had left at the airport and he drove toward the hospital. They passed cars sitting beside the street but saw no people. The town was empty! Nick tried to imagine what could have created the disaster.

Rachel broke into the silence when she said, "Nick, I feel awful." He went into the hospital to find help but no one was alive. As he returned to the car, he felt nauseous and slightly dizzy. He opened the car and found Rachel—dead.

—*Lola Viets*

THE HERO AND THE CROWN   YA/Adult
By ROBIN McKINLEY

Aerin stuck her hand into the fire and smiled when she felt only a pleasantly warm sensation. At last she had gotten the ingredients right: the secret ointment against dragonfire was ready. And Aerin was more than ready—ready to fight even the dangerous Black Dragon Maur to prove to the people of Damar that she was the rightful daugher of the king, and not the suspicious offspring of a witch from the North.

—*Margie Reitsma*

HIROSHIMA   YA
By JOHN HERSEY

One man was walking down a hospital corridor with a vial of blood for testing when it happened. His eyeglasses flew off his face, the bottle of blood crashed against one wall, his Japanese slippers zipped out from under his feet—but he was unharmed. Some women had the floral designs from their kimonos permanently etched into their skin. Pumpkins roasted on the vine and potatoes baked where they grew underground. Shadows of people illuminated by the flash were imprinted onto building walls at the same instant that the people themselves were vaporized. Everywhere others lay dead or dying, or were wandering in a daze. Most were badly burned and mutilated. Skin on some slipped off in huge glove-like pieces.

One group of soldiers had their faces totally burned. Their eye-sockets were hollow, and the fluid from their melted eyes ran down their cheeks. Their faces must have been upturned when it happened.

Many people without any visible injuries died mysteriously in the first few hours and days.

The place is Hiroshima, Japan, where the first atomic bomb was dropped on August 6, 1945. The bomb killed over a hundred thousand people—that's about the same number as the population of [a nearby town].

Read more about what it's like to survive, or not survive, an atomic bomb. Read *Hiroshima,* by John Hersey.

—*Caroline Ketman*

THE HOBBIT
By J.R.R. TOLKIEN

Grades 4–8

"In a hole in the ground there lived a hobbit. Not a nasty, dirty, wet hole, filled with the ends of worms and an oozy smell, nor yet a dry, bare, sandy hole with nothing in it to sit down on or to eat: it was a hobbit-hole, and that means comfort. . . . [It had a round green door with a brass doorknob in the center. The hobbit who lived in this hole] was a very well-to-do hobbit, and his name was Baggins. The Bagginses had lived in the neighborhood of the Hill for time out of mind, and people considered them very respectable, not only because most of them were rich, but also because they never had any adventures or did anything unexpected. . . . [But] what is a hobbit? . . . They are (or were) a little people, about half our height, and smaller than the bearded Dwarves. Hobbits have no beards. There is little or no magic about them, except the ordinary everyday sort which helps them to disappear quietly and quickly when large stupid folk like you and me come blundering along, making a noise like elephants which they can hear a mile off. They are inclined to be fat in the stomach; they dress in bright colours (chiefly green and yellow); wear no shoes, because their feet grow natural leathery soles and thick warm brown hair like the stuff on their heads (which is curly); have long clever brown fingers, good-natured faces, and laugh deep, fruity laughs, especially after dinner (which they have twice a day when they can get it)."

On this particularly beautiful sunny morning, Bilbo Baggins was standing in the doorway of his hobbit-hole, smoking his pipe, when a stranger came by. He invited Bilbo to share in an adventure he was going on, but Bilbo said, "We are plain quiet folk and have no use for adventures. Nasty disturbing things—make you late for dinner! I can't think what anybody sees in them!" And he began to blow smoke-rings again. However, when he realized just who the stranger was (it was Gandalf, a rather important wizard—Bilbo hadn't recognized him at first) he became quite embarrassed, invited the wizard to tea the next day to apologize, and popped back into his hole, slamming the door behind him. Gandalf just smiled and scratched a sign on Bilbo's door with his cane. The next day Gandalf came to tea, but thirteen dwarves came too and Bilbo's adventure began. The sign Gandalf had scratched on the door said, "Burglar wants a good job, plenty of excitement and reasonable reward." The dwarves were going back to the Lonely Mountains to rescue their treasure from Smaug, a dragon who had stolen it from their forefathers many years before. They needed a burglar, and

Bilbo Baggins was it!

—Joni Bodart-Talbot

NOTE: This is one of the exceptions to the "never read" rule. I know of no other way to get the actual flavor of Tolkien's writing. Another scene to use is the riddle game scene with Gollum (pp. 79-93, paperback edition), especially if you can do voices well. Tolkien himself recorded it on a Caedmon record, and you can listen to his interpretation of the dialogue to get an idea of how each character ought to sound. This scene needs to be cut and paraphrased—uncut, it's about thirty minutes.

HOUSE OF STAIRS   YA
By WILLIAM SLEATOR

In order to understand this book, you have to use your imagination. You have to imagine a place made up entirely of stairs. No ceiling, no floor, no walls, just stairs. In every direction you look, nothing but stairs. And if you try to go up, pretty soon all you find are stairs that go down. If you go down, all you find are stairs that go up. And if you try to go in any one direction, the stairs turn back on themselves, and you realize you're trapped in one section of this house of stairs. This is the situation that five teenagers, three girls and two boys, find themselves in. They get together and realize they have some things in common. They're all sixteen; they're all orphans, wards of the state; they all live in state orphanages; and none of them have any idea where they are, why they're here, or how they got here. But they do know that the two essentials are food and water, and they begin to explore. On a landing where two of the staircases come together, up nearly as high as you can go, they find a small indentation, like a bowl set down into the landing. It's full of water, fresh water. It's always fresh, and the water level never changes. So now they have water. Then on a landing further down, one of the girls finds a red light set into the landing. By now they've figured out that they've been put there by someone who's probably keeping an eye on them. The red light looks like the perfect place to hide a TV camera. So Blossom, who found it, starts to talk to it: "Let us out of here! I don't want to stay here—I want to go home!" and so on. But nothing happens. Pretty soon she gets mad and makes a face at it. And the light spits out a little pellet of food. She eats it, and it's *good!* So she tries it again—and it works again! Pretty soon she's making faces and eating as fast as she can. She isn't being very quiet about it, and when the other kids show up, Blossom explains what's going on and they try it too. But it doesn't work for anyone else, and when Blossom tries to get more food for the others, the food machine doesn't work for her either! So the group has begun to learn first two lessons from the food machine: Everyone has to do something different to get food, and the food machine only gives food at certain times, not whenever you want it to.

Gradually the machine begins to teach them other lessons, to train them as you'd train an animal, by giving them food when they do the right thing and withholding food when they don't. Eventually they learn what they call a dance. It isn't really a dance, they just stand in a circle around the light and they each do what the light has taught them to do—snap their fingers, hop around, clap their hands—all nonsense motions, but when they do them at the right time, all together, the machine will produce enough food for one day. It's never enough to keep them from being hungry or to fill them up. It's just enough to keep them from starving to death. They are *always* hungry, and so they are also grouchy and nervous.

Then one morning, they get up and perform their dance and the food machine doesn't give them anything. They try it again and again—still nothing. The two boys begin to shout at each other—"It's your fault." "No way! It's your fault!" And then one hits the other and the food machine suddenly begins to produce more food than it ever has before. They all begin to eat as fast as they can, but all of a sudden, one of the girls stops—"Wait! Can't you see what they're doing to us? Can't you see what this means? From now on we'll have to *hit* each other, *hurt* each other, maybe eventually *kill* each other in order to get food!"

This is a story of survival—who survived after that, and how.

—Joni Bodart-Talbot

HOW DEMOCRACY FAILED   Grades 6-8
By ELLEN SWITZER

What was it like to grow up in Germany on the eve of World War II? How did so many people come to accept a way of life that now seems so horrible? What would your life have been like if your father had been a German Jew, or a prosperous newspaper editor, or a dentist? Would you have joined the Resistance movement—or the Hitler Youth Brigade? Or would you have found yourself in a concentration camp? In Ellen Switzer's book, *How Democracy Failed*, she interviews people who were schoolchildren in Germany in the early 1930s—as she herself was, before her family escaped to the United States. You'll hear about Hans and Sophie Scholl, who were 15 and 12 when they joined the Hitler Youth and spent almost all their free time with the group, until Hans, whose hobby was collecting folk songs from foreign countries, was told that he could now sing only the music from the official Hitler songbook—and then one of their favorite teachers disappeared, and they began to notice other disappearances, other strange new rules. As they became concerned about what was really going on, Hans and Sophie formed their own, secret group, The White Rose, and began publishing anti-Nazi leaflets. The White Rose flourished for a year before Sophie was arrested with a suitcase full of leaflets. Hans was 25 and Sophie was 22 when they were executed.

You'll also meet Joachim, whose first job as a member of the Hitler Youth was to spy on his own mother, and Rosa, part Jewish, who survived the last six months of the war only because the supply of cattle cars and cyanide gas ran out.

It is hard to imagine that such things could happen across a whole country, and it's easy to think that of course people would never let it happen here. But did you know that *National Geographic Magazine* published a whole article in 1937—four years after the Nazis had come to power and after thousands of Germans had already been murdered—that praised the new government highly? Their photographers took wonderful pictures of the tidy streets, the clean streetcars, the pretty parks—pictures that never showed the signs on benches saying, "Jews forbidden to sit here!" or the signs in shop windows saying, "Germans, defend yourselves! Don't buy from Jews!"

She also describes the economic confusion that was so frightening in Germany during prewar years, when it seemed that street fights broke out on every corner. The rate of inflation was so bad that people had to carry knapsacks of money when they went shopping or cashed a check because prices would double or triple in a day. Workers soon demanded to be paid weekly, then daily, then hourly—and would spend all their money just as soon as they got it, because it might be worth nothing by the end of the day.

And finally, Ellen Switzer talks to these people about their lives today—what they think of their history now, and what they tell their children about the part they played in those years when democracy failed.

—Elizabeth Overmyer

HOW DO YOU LOSE   Grades 6–8/YA
THOSE NINTH GRADE BLUES?
By BARTHE DeCLEMENTS

Elsie Edwards is no longer the fat little kid she was in fifth grade. She's lost weight and is now a freshman in high school, but she's still insecure, and all those years of thinking everyone hated her because she was fat are still in her memory. So when Craddoc Shaw, the place-kicker for the football team, that gorgeous hunk that all the girls swooned over, the player who kicked the field goal that won the state football title for the school, when *that* Craddoc Shaw showed an interest in her, she reverted to her old, insecure ways.

Did Craddoc really like her, or was he just giving a freshman the big rush? Find out in *How Do You Lose Those Ninth Grade Blues?* by Barthe DeClements.

—Pam Spencer

HOWL'S MOVING CASTLE   YA
By DIANA WYNNE JONES

Poor Sophie Hatter, everyone knows that it's pretty hard to be the oldest of three sisters, but when you live in a land like Ingary, where magic is an everyday affair, the situation is even more hopeless. Anyone who reads fairy tales can tell you that the oldest of three siblings never has any glorious adventures and certainly never any success.

Well, Sophie hadn't lived all her life in Ingary for nothing. She knew the score; she was destined to spend the rest of her life as a drudge, sewing hats in the back room of the shop. And it wasn't really so bad. After all, if she were to go out having adventures, she might run into the evil and vengeful Witch of the Waste, who for some reason had recently reappeared in Ingary, and that could be dangerous. The Witch had already killed one wizard who got in her way. Sophie thought it was a shame that she didn't finish off Wizard Howl too, while she was at it. Wizard Howl, who had appeared about the same time as the Witch of the Waste, roamed about the Ingary countryside in a sort of mobile castle, a black one which spouted dark smoke over the countryside—very bad for the environment. People claimed that Wizard Howl amused himself by collecting young girls and sucking the souls from them. At least that's what some people said. Other people said he ate their hearts. Sophie couldn't imagine why he would want to do either, but then she supposed that wizards had different hobbies than ordinary people.

Anyway, wizards and witches didn't really have much to do with her life. They were more in the line of her younger sister; she was the one who was going to have the adventures. At least that's what Sophie thought until the morning when the Witch of the Waste sailed into the hat shop and turned Sophie into a . . . Never mind what she turned Sophie into. But that wasn't nearly as bad as what Sophie discovered when she got inside the Wizard *Howl's Moving Castle.*

—Margie Reitsma

HUNTERS OF THE RED MOON   YA
By MARION ZIMMER BRADLEY

All his life, Dane Marsh has liked solitary adventures—mountain climbing and other wilderness experiences—and he's on a solo sailing voyage around the world when an alien spaceship suddenly appears and kidnaps him. He finds out it's a slave ship, and he's locked up with lots of other creatures, some humanoid and some really exotic, like a giant lizard-man and a spider-man. Their captors, who are cat-men, have surgically implanted translator discs in the slaves so they can talk to each other, and pretty soon Dane has organized a conspiracy with two girls and the lizard-man to rush their guards and take over the ship.

Their attempt fails, but their captors are really pleased that they tried, because by proving their initiative and courage, they're now qualified to be sold as prey to a planet of hunters. These hunters make a religious ritual of the hunt, and they give Dane and his companions food and shelter, their choice of weapons, and time to practice. Dane has had some experience in the oriental martial arts, the lizard-man can defend himself pretty well by sheer strength and size, and one of the girls has had some judo training, but the other girl is a telepath, who is sort of frail and is deeply upset by violence around her, and the group is really worried about her chances for survival.

The hunt will last eleven days, from eclipse to eclipse of the planet's moon, and if they survive, they'll get their freedom and incredible riches. On the night before the hunt, there's a feast for the survivors of the last hunt, and they find out that of seventy-four creatures who were the prey, one survived.

No one has ever seen what the hunters look like, and Dane and his friends eventually figure out that they're shape-changers, so the hunt really turns out to be a game of wits. How do you survive for eleven days against creatures that can assume monster shapes, or can look exactly like one of your trusted companions?

—Peggy Murray

HURRY, HURRY, MARY DEAR!   Grades k-3
AND OTHER NONSENSE POEMS
edited by N. M. BODECKER

You probably know lots of nursery rhymes. But now you can learn even more, including some from Denmark, like this one that goes,

> The wood duck didn't do it,
> the woodcock didn't do it,
> a dodo never did a thing like that!
> And if whoever did it
> is too finky to admit it
> —whatever else he is, he's just a rat!
>   —*Olivia Jacobs*

I KNOW WHAT YOU DID LAST SUMMER   YA
By LOIS DUNCAN

Talk 1

Julie, Ray, Helen, and Barry were juniors in high school when it happened. Helen was Homecoming Queen, Julie was a cheerleader, Barry was a football star, and Ray managed the football team. They double-dated a lot, and this particular time were having a picnic up in the mountains. They had a little bit to eat, a little bit to smoke, and a little bit to drink. It was dark by the time they left. Barry lost the toss and was driving—too fast, as usual. Julie and Ray weren't paying much attention (Barry always drove fast) until they heard Helen scream. They looked up, heard a thump, and saw a little boy on a bike sliding across the hood. And Barry didn't even slow down! "Stop! Stop!" Julie and Ray shouted. "It'll be a hit-and-run—stop!" But Barry said, "No—I hit him really hard, and it's miles to a hospital—we've got to get an ambulance up here as soon as possible—there's not time to stop." "Then at least slow down so I can jump out and stay with him," Julie begged. "A little boy shouldn't have to die alone in the dark like that. At least let me go back." But Barry wouldn't stop, and by that time, they were almost to town anyway. Barry said he'd stop at the first telephone, but when they saw the all-night diner with the pay phone, he went by. He said that phone was always busy, and if someone was using it, they'd just be delayed that much longer. Besides, there was another phone just a mile further on, in a roadside park, and no one ever used it—they'd stop there. Sure enough, a mile later, there was the phone booth. Ray was out of the car almost before Barry put the brakes on. He ran over to the phone, called the highway patrol, and reported the accident. He was just about to give his name when Barry reached over and broke the connection. "You don't really want to do that, do you?" he said. "What are you talking about?" Ray said. "Just think about it. We've had something to drink, something to smoke. We know we're not stoned, but do you think any cops are gonna believe us? Besides, I'm the only one that's eighteen, and I was driving. They'll take my license away at the very least, and I'll probably lose my football scholarship as well. My whole life will be down the drain—and for what? Just 'cause some stupid kid was riding down the middle of the road in the dark. He didn't even have on light clothes or a light. It's as much his fault as it is mine—and I'm not going to jail to pay for it!"

Barry talked and talked, and since Ray was his best friend, he agreed not to say anything. It was easy to convince Helen—she'd do anything for Barry. But Julie wasn't so easy—she refused to go along until the others said they'd all agree that she was lying, and no one would believe her. Finally Julie gave in, and they made a pact that they'd never tell anyone what had happened that night. But Julie still felt guilty, and she sent yellow roses to the little boy's funeral. He did die, on the way to the hospital—he never even made it to the emergency room. And it was Julie who got the letter, about a year later, when she was just beginning to forget what had happened.

It came in the morning mail—a square white envelope with her name and address in square block printing. And when she opened it, there was just one line of writing, in those same square block letters: "I know what you did last summer." Julie was horrified, and called Helen. Helen found a little picture taped on her front door, a picture of a boy on a bike. And Barry got a strange phone call that told him to go to the football field after dark, where he got a bullet in his back.

Someone had found out that they had killed that little boy last summer, and now that someone was going to kill *them*.

—*Mary Moore* and *Joni Bodart-Talbot*

Talk 2

Julie's life couldn't have been more perfect. It was her senior year in high school and she had just been accepted by Smith College, her mother's alma mater. Her ex-boyfriend Ray had just come back into town, and she was looking forward to dating him again. Her friend, Helen, though only eighteen, was the Golden Girl on a local TV station, doing the weather reports and making short announcements, and earning lots of money. Helen's boyfriend Barry was just finishing his first year at the university. Life was going well for all of them.

Until Julie received the first of the threatening notes. All it said was, "I know what you did last summer," but that was enough.

—Pam Spencer

I LOVE YOU, STUPID   YA
By HARRY MAZER

Six feet tall; blue eyes; dark, curly hair; talented; popular; a seventeen-year-old senior in high school . . . that's Marcus Rosenbloom. And, oh yes, he loves girls. Standing alone on top of the cafeteria steps, he imagines that all over the room girls are looking at him. "Who's that stunning guy?" "Oh, God, it's Marcus Rosenbloom. He's a writer, you know. Isn't he gorgeous?" Although Marcus knows there are more important things in life than sex, right now he can't think what they are.

Marcus is nearly a man; he's been ready for years but has never had sex. What is wrong with him? He loves girls. He can't stop thinking about them, watching, lusting. He is on the wrong side of the wall that divides childhood from adulthood. It is no sex or first-time sex on one side, and grown-up sex on the other.

Marcus is going to be a writer, but that too is like his sex life, all talk and no action, all make-believe. He is still in kiddie-land dreaming about the great things he is going to do. And what has he done? Nothing.

Then he meets Wendy Barrett . . . again. He and Wendy had grown up together, but then she had moved away. Recently she moved back. He was in the cafeteria one day when a girl sitting alone at a nearby table looked at him and smiled. Marcus was intrigued. He knew she was a new girl in school sitting alone hiding behind a book, but she looked familiar. It was Wendy, his childhood companion. Their mothers had been best friends. But this is a new mature Wendy. The voice is unchanged, and the hair and the face too, but she is different.

The old Wendy was always a little kooky. She dressed oddly and said things that nobody else said. Now she seems beyond all that, but as a new member of the senior class, she's finding it hard to make friends.

Marcus becomes her friend, her guide through the school. She invites him over one day to say hello to her aunt, with whom she lives now. Then she asks if he wants to see her bedroom. The signs are unmistakable. Maybe he is finally going to get what he has dreamed about. But when he makes a pass, she pushes him away. He's misread the signs. She only wants to be friends, the kind of friends who can say anything to each other. "Friends who will *do* anything for each other?" Marcus wonders. Find out what kind of friends in *I Love You, Stupid.*

—Judy Druse

I NEVER PROMISED YOU A ROSE GARDEN   YA/Adult
By HANNAH GREEN

This is a look at what it's like to be insane, from inside the mind of a sixteen-year-old girl who's a schizophrenic. It's realistic because, althought it's a novel, it's based on the author's life. Deborah lives in a mental institution when she's a part of the real world. When she's not, she lives in a world in her mind, called Yr, and is outwardly catatonic, not responding to anyone or anything. Deb has a brilliant mind—Yr is marvelously complete: its inhabitants have their own language and culture, and every detail is perfect. The people there comfort Deb when she goes to stay with them, when reality has become too hard for her to handle. But then these people begin to try to pull her into their world forever, and they torture her when she tries to leave. Soon life in either world is unbearable. Deb knows she's schizophrenic and tries to help herself, but the people of Yr are too strong for her, and she begins to realize she is in danger when she goes there.

Deb's encounters with the other patients in the institution are very revealing—the patients are shown as people, trying to help each other deal with a world they are not as well-equipped to handle as people on the outside.

As Deb fights to conquer her illness she learns many things, not the least of which is that no one was ever promised a thornless rose garden, and even the most fortunate have to deal with life and its problems.

—Joni Bodart-Talbot

I, ROBOT   YA/Adult
By ISAAC ASIMOV

The Three Laws of Robotics, published in the *Handbook of Robotics*, 56th edition, 2058 A.D. One: . . . [read from title page verso].

Dr. Susan Calvin, the first robo-psychologist, saw the development of robots from voiceless nursemaids to the great machines that stood between man and destruction. Cool, rational, seemingly emotionless herself, Dr. Calvin was fascinated by the machines' cold logic.

This collection of short stories is loosely grouped around her life, the robots she treated, and the development of the science of robotics.

The first story is about Robbie, a super-specialized silent robot who was a nursemaid and risked his life to save the child he loved—or *can* a mere machine love? How about one that gets drunk? Robot SPD13 (better known as "Speedy") was in exactly that state, but without the benefit of alcohol! "Runaround" tells how it happened. "Liar!" is about Herbie, a robot who could read minds because of a mistake that was made when he was assembled—a mistake with dire consequences. Stephen Bejerly was the first World Coordinator—and in the story "Evidence," Dr. Calvin intimates that even he, too, was a robot. For these stories and others, try *I, Robot*, by Isaac Asimov, and also *The Rest of the Robots*, his second collection of short stories and short novels about these machines with psy-onic brains.

—*Joni Bodart-Talbot*

I STAY NEAR YOU   YA
By M. E. KERR

It all began with fifteen-year-old Mildred, who lived on the wrong side of the tracks. Her family worked at a laundry and lived in back of it. When Mildred wasn't helping out, she'd be studying or playing the harp. That was why she transferred to East High: to win a scholarship to Juilliard.

Mildred was not only unashamed of her family, she despised the rich. "Think their piss smells sweet!"

She confided to her girlfriend, "The *money* they leave in their pockets when they drop off their laundry! Once I found a gen-u-wine hundred dollar bill! Believe me, though, I wouldn't take it. I don't thieve to earn my money like they do." That was Mildred's way.

And then Mildred turned beautiful. And kids started noticing her for other reasons than her brains.

Like Powell Storm, Jr., only the best-looking guy in the area, and from the richest family, too.

Mildred was waitressing at the country club when she brought drinks to Powell's table.

"Hey, miss. You got the order wrong." Powell took her by the arm.

"Don't. You. Touch. Me." Mildred whirled away.

The rest of us would have died to get Powell to touch us. We'd wish the most sinful things and say some of them aloud: "Violate me in the violet time, in the vilest way that you know."

But not Mildred.

When Mildred returned, Powell tried to intercept her, to apologize and explain what he meant. He ended up holding the other end of her tray, sort of dancing with her to the newest popular song.

Suddenly they stopped, looked at each other, and smiled.

I think that was the last time that Powell's family had a peaceful moment.

Mildred and Powell's love had repercussions that lasted for three generations. Find out what they were in M. E. Kerr's book, *I Stay Near You.*

—*Lesley Farmer*

I WAS A 15-YEAR-OLD BLIMP   YA
By PATTI STREN

Gabby Finklestein is five feet tall and weighs 150 pounds. Though she longs to be accepted by the popular crowd, they only make fun of teenage blimps. Gabby finally decides to do something about it. She tries desperately to lose weight in time for the big dance the next week, so that gorgeous blond Cal Armstrong will notice her. Though she sticks religiously to her diet, her mother says she isn't eating enough to stay healthy and hauls Gabby off to the doctor for a diet that just won't take those pounds off fast enough.

At the last minute Gabby is saved by her only friend, Nicole, a slender ballet student. Nicole gives her Ex-Lax, saying that a lot of dancers she knows use it to get rid of excess weight quickly. Though Gabby spends a miserable couple of days in and out of the bathroom, the strategy works. By the night of the dance she has lost eleven pounds.

Yet instead of being the best night of her life, the dance is the absolute worst. It starts out great when Gabby finds a note in her purse, signed "Your Secret Admirer," asking her to meet by the biology lab. Imagine Gabby's disappointment when it isn't Cal who meets her but pimply-faced class nerd Mel. "If you wanted me so badly, why didn't you just say so?" Mel asks, holding out a note that is signed with her name. Before Gabby can figure out what's happening, the lights come on in the science lab and ten of the most popular kids come pouring out, laughing hysterically. Both Mel and Gabby, the two ugliest kids in the class, have been set up. And most humiliating of all, as Gabby flees down the hall in tears she runs right past Cal.

When Gabby gets home, she heads straight for the kitchen. [Read pp. 84-5 "I had never felt so bad. . . . twelve double Oreo cookies."]

When Gabby touches her bloated stomach, she does the one thing that Nicole had made her swear never to do, the terrible thing that Nicole's skinny dancer friends did sometimes. Gabby runs the water in the bathroom sink so no one will hear, sticks her fingers down her throat, and gets rid of all that fattening food.

—*Catherine G. Edgerton*

ICE STATION ZEBRA   YA/Adult
By ALISTAIR MacLEAN

When Ice Station Zebra, a meteorological outpost near the North Pole, reports a fire, a nuclear sub is sent to rescue the survivors. It's a difficult assignment, because the polar icecap shifts constantly and compasses are practically useless near the pole. Just before the ship sails, a British civilian, Dr. Carpenter, who has carte blanche clearance from the Secretary of the Navy, comes aboard and orders the captain to take him along. One of the men at the station is his brother; however, that's not the main reason he's going along. Dr. Carpenter hides his true identity behind one story after another, only revealing it at the final climax.

This is an adventure story of men against the sea, but it is also the story of men against each other, and of the tension that can build up when people are confined in a small space for weeks and months on end. Apparently the pressure of this confinement can affect people's minds, because no sooner is the sub under the icecap than a murder is committed, obviously by someone on board. For sheer excitement—*Ice Station Zebra*, by Alistair MacLean. It's not a book to read late at night. It's one of the ones you just can't put down till the last page, because only there will you find the solution!

—*Joni Bodart-Talbot*

IN THE MIDDLE OF A RAINBOW   Grades 7–8/YA
By BARBARA GIRION

Although Corrie Dickerson is pretty and a senior in high school, she has never been in love. She's been too busy working for good grades and at her part-time job in a beauty shop to have time for boys. Corrie wants to go to college and knows she'll need scholarship help to put herself through school. Her mother is a widow and is urging Corrie to have a career, not just a job, so she can support herself well. She doesn't want Corrie to suffer as she has done or to be dependent on a man to support her.

Then Corrie meets Todd Marcus. She can hardly believe he is interested in her. Todd is rich, handsome, and a soccer star. He's also understanding and generous and a lot of fun. Before she knows it, she is in love. Plans for college seem far away as Corrie spends more and more time with Todd.

They plan to go to the Christmas Snow Ball. Corrie needs a new dress but can't afford one to match what Todd is used to. Then Todd finds a beautiful dress and buys it for Corrie. She loves it, but how can she tell her mother Todd bought it? She loves Todd, but she also loves her mother. How can being in love cause so much guilt and conflict, and how can Corrie please the two people she loves most without lying or hurting them both?

—Diana C. Hirsch

IN THE YEAR OF THE BOAR AND JACKIE Grades 4-6
ROBINSON
By BETTE BAO LORD

Wham! The first punch hurt her eye terribly, but Shirley knew she was too puny to fight the tallest and strongest and scariest girl in the whole fifth grade. Instead, Shirley used a few choice words she had heard the rickshaw pullers use to insult riders who left no tips. And then, wham! Now the other eye hurt terribly too, but Shirley could not flee. A child of emperors and the ancient House of Wong could not flee. Hadn't Shirley's mother told her that she was to be China's little ambassador and that the reputation of all the Chinese rested on her shoulders? But five hundred million Chinese was a pretty heavy burden!

Shirley didn't have these problems when she still lived in Chungking with her mother, aunts and uncles, grandparents, and all the cousins. But in Chungking she was never told anything and was always treated like an ignorant child. Then the wonderful letter from Father had come, and she and her mother made the long journey across the ocean, then another long journey across the new country by train to arrive in Brooklyn, New York.

Once there, Shirley was so anxious to impress her father with her cleverness, and how she could find her way around in the new city after only one day, that she had begged and pleaded to be allowed to go to the tobacco shop by herself to buy cigarettes for him and his friends. She got there just fine (Father would be so pleased!) but the shopkeeper did not understand Shirley until she puffed on an imaginary cigarette and said the only two English words she knew, "Rukee Sike! Rukee Sike!" She had to go to still another store to purchase the cigarettes, and instead of a triumphant return home, she got terribly lost. And that was only the beginning.

Shirley had no friends among all the black, brown, spotted, and very tall kids in her class. She was not asked to play any games with them because she was always bowing to anybody who let her do anything. Shirley tried, but couldn't even learn to roller-skate. And now the best baseball player in the fifth grade—a very big, very black girl named Mabel—was furious with her for ruining the baseball game.

Would nothing ever go right for Shirley Temple Wong in the United States? Maybe she should never have come to this new country. Maybe she should have stayed in Chungking. Maybe . . . you should read this book yourself to find out if Shirley survived Brooklyn in 1947.

—Susan Bogart

THE INCIDENT AT HAWK'S HILL   **Grades 6–8**
By ALLAN W. ECKERT

Hawk's Hill is the knoll where the McDonalds build their home in Canada, on a sprawling prairie near Winnipeg in the 1870s. They have four children, the youngest being Ben, a shy, withdrawn, undersized child who rarely speaks to people, even in his own family. He is clearly not an ordinary boy, and no one knows quite what to make of him. He has developed a kind of kinship with the farm animals and wildlife in the fields, even to the point of being able to mimic their sounds and actions with amazing accuracy. Some people believe he can talk to animals, and even wild creatures accept his voice and hand. When the McDonalds' new neighbor, George Burton, arrives one day with his ferocious dog Lobo, to get permission to set badger traps on the farm, Ben is terrified by the rough, burly Burton, but he is able to subdue Lobo by imitating the dog's whines and movements!

Several miles away, a female badger has dug a burrow to raise her family in. Badgers are fierce fighters, and this one has a battle scar, a notched right ear. While out exploring the area, Ben spots the badger rustling in the grass. He gets down on all fours and imitates her chattering. Then he feeds her, and before he leaves, she actually allows him to touch her cheek and ear! Ben returns home smiling about his exciting encounter.

After the badger's babies are born, her mate is trapped and captured by Burton. The female badger, too, eventually becomes ensnared in the trap, and her babies starve while she struggles to free herself. She finally bites herself loose with her foot badly injured, but it's too late—the babies die.

Shortly after this, Ben is once again wandering the prairie, but this time he roams too far and becomes lost, just when a thunderstorm strikes. He takes refuge in a badger hole. Half asleep, he hears "a strange sound approaching, an intermingled wheezing and grumbling." A deep, solid bulk of something is entering the hole, and Ben is vulnerable and terrified. The female badger snarls viciously, and Ben screams. Then he snarls, mimicking her, and lashing at her with his hands. He tries chattering at her, as he did with the badger he met before, not realizing this is the same one.

The badger leaves, but that's not the end of the story. She returns and gradually comes to trust the boy, as he starts trusting her. The McDonald family continue to search for Ben long after their neighbors give him up for dead. What happens between Ben and the badger once they accept each other? Find out in *The Incident at Hawk's Hill*, an incident that really did happen.

—Patricia Farr

THE INDIAN IN THE CUPBOARD   Grades 3–6
By LYNNE REID BANKS

Omri received three dopey gifts for his birthday: a secondhand plastic Indian, a metal medicine cabinet that his brother had found on a trash pile, and a fancy little key that had been his grandmother's. When he went to bed that night Omri put the Indian into the cupboard and locked it with the little key. He awoke the next morning to strange little sounds coming from the cupboard. Slowly Omri opened the door to find the Indian had come alive. When Omri reached out his hand to touch the tiny man, he got a jab from a miniature knife.

Little Bear was a real Indian brave all right. Soon he was making demands. He needed food—meat! And fire! Horse! Gun! Omri turned a plastic teepee into a real one in the magic cupboard, but Little Bear was insulted. He sleeps only in the longhouse of the Iroquois! This Indian was becoming more than Omri had bargained for. This was a real person, son of a chief and scalper of thirty men, from two hundred years ago.

Keeping the Indian a secret was going to be difficult. Omri's friend Patrick finally had to be told. (After all, he was the one who had given him the Indian.) It wasn't easy to stop Patrick from turning the whole box of plastic toys into real people. While Omri was getting food for Little Bear, Patrick tried the magic on a plastic cowboy with a gun. So then the boys had Boone, a dirty crybaby cowboy with a fast draw and a hatred for Indians.

Naturally, Little Bear and Boone immediately clashed, and that was just the beginning of the adventures with *The Indian in the Cupboard*, by Lynne Reid Banks.

—Ann Provost

INSIDE MOVES   YA
By TODD WALTON

If you like basketball and San Francisco, and believe that sometimes even the craziest dreams really do come true, then Todd Walton's *Inside Moves* is the book for you. It's about Roary, who's a Vietnam vet. A land mine blew up in his back, and so now he holds his head to one side and he kind of shuffles when he walks. He's let his hair grow long and has grown a big bushy beard to hide the scars. Sometimes kids run when they see him, and even adults are nervous walking by him. They hold their kids close as if Roary might hurt them. This makes him very sad, because he really likes kids. He's listed as totally disabled, but his pension still isn't very much, so he doesn't have a lot of money for clothes, and since he knows he looks ugly anyhow, he doesn't always bother too much about the ones he has. If you saw him on the street in the city, you might think he was just a bum, drunk and stumbling down the street.

Not many people are interested in looking behind the outside to the person Roary is within. But there is one place where people do just that—it's Max's, a bar down on Irving, near the Med Center. You probably wouldn't look at it twice, or even notice whether it was open or not. The guys who are regulars there are all cripples—freaks, Roary calls them—and he fits right in. One of the first people he meets is Jerry Maxwell, who's a part-time bartender there. One of Jerry's legs is shorter than the other; he was born that way. He and Roary get to be good friends.

When Jerry isn't at the bar, he works nights in a box factory to help support his wife's drug habit (without his money, all she'd do is sleep around to raise the cash herself). Days, he plays basketball with a bunch of guys at Edison park. That's when he really comes alive—basketball is the most important thing in Jerry's life. Whenever the Golden State Warriors are in town, Jerry's right there, on the front row, the best seats in the house, and usually with Roary, since he hates to go anywhere alone. He does a lot of shouting at games, especially at the rookies, when they're not doing too well. The guys on the team notice him—they call him "The Mouth."

One night the Warriors are playing a championship game with the Bullets, and Alvin Martin, the rookie Jerry most identifies with, misses a clear shot. He freezes on the court with the Warriors behind one point and seconds to go in the game. Jerry screams at him, Martin comes to life, but by then there are guys all over him, and he misses the shot. Jerry can't stand it. He's absolutely beside himself, and fights his way into the dressing room after the game, Roary right behind him, saying, "Hey, wait, Jerry! You can't go in there! *Wait!*" Jerry ends up right in front of Alvin Martin and starts to tell him off. Martin doesn't appreciate this one bit, and before Jerry realizes what's happening, he's challenged Martin to a one-on-one game the next afternoon at two o'clock. It's so crowded in the dressing room that Martin hasn't noticed his limp.

That's when Jerry's dream starts coming true—the next day at two o'clock. As he says, "Playgrounds don't turn into Madison Square Garden, whores don't turn into virgin pompom girls, and cripples don't play for the pros," except *sometimes*, when even the craziest dreams really *do* come true.

—*Joni Bodart-Talbot*

INTERSTELLAR PIG YA
By WILLIAM SLEATOR

Poor Barney! It's summertime, and his parents have rented an old sea captain's home on the Massachusetts coast. They're spending all their time on the beach, but Barney's a redhead and burns the minute he's in the sun, their vacation home is miles from the nearest village, and there aren't any kids his age around. In short, Barney's bored.

So when three people drive up in a purple Volkswagen convertible to rent the cottage next door, Barney hopes they'll save him from his boredom. Although they seem unusually interested in Barney's summer house, at least Zena, Manny, and Joe are kind of exotic and fun-loving, not like other adults Barney knows.

They seem to spend most of their time playing this board game called Interstellar Pig. The board itself is sprinkled with glowing stars and three-dimensional planets; it looks like a huge photograph of the cosmos. The object of the game is to have possession of the piggy when the bell sounds to end the game. If you don't have possession, then you and your home planet are destroyed.

Manny, Joe, and Zena finally invite Barney to play Interstellar Pig with them. But when he does, he has this uncomfortable feeling that these people aren't really who they say they are, and that maybe they're playing for keeps.

—Pam Spencer

INTERVIEW WITH THE VAMPIRE YA/Adult
By ANNE RICE

If Louis is a vampire, he is two hundred years old. This is the story of his life, the way he told it to a boy he met in a bar in San Francisco. After two hundred years, Louis was at last ready to tell his story.

"But how much tape do you have with you?" the vampire asked. "Enough for the story of a life?"

"Sure, if it's a good life." The boy got his tape recorder ready. "I'm really anxious to hear why you believe this, why you. . . . "

"No," said the vampire abruptly. "We can't begin that way . . . I'm going to turn on the overhead light." "But I thought vampires didn't like light," said the boy. "If you think the dark adds to the atmosphere. . . . " The vampire said nothing, just reached for the light cord. [Read from Part I, p. 3, paperback edition, from "At once the room . . . " to "Just start the tape."]

It took the boy a moment to collect himself; then he turned on his tape recorder and began. "You weren't always a vampire, were you?"

"No," replied the vampire. "I was a twenty-five-year-old man when I became a vampire, and the year was 1791. . . . "

—Joni Bodart-Talbot

INTO THE FOREST Grades 3-6
By ROSAMUND SIBYL ESSEX

There were three of them—Wystan, Bridget, and Hadrian—and they were a most unusual household. They lived by themselves in a hut at the edge of a great woods, and the oldest was blind, the second was lame, and the third could not hear a single word, even if you shouted. But they were happy together.

There had been a terrible Destruction two years before. The Blast that killed all of their families and most of the other people in the world had made Wystan blind, had mangled Bridget's leg, and had made Hadrian deaf. The Blast had also made a wasteland out of all the world they knew, except for the great forest where they lived.

A few other people lived in the forest—tramps, robbers, dangerous men from whom the children hid. They had heard of another world—a new world, not destroyed by the Blast—on the other side of the dense forest. So they set out to find it, the lame girl on her crutches, the deaf boy leading the blind. The obstacles they met were staggering—a deep chasm with a frayed rope bridge, a sheer rock wall to climb, a steep mountain, tricksters who stole their food. But they were determined to find that other world, and nothing could stop them.

—Nancy Eager

INTO THE PAINTED BEAR'S LAIR   Grades 2–5
By PAMELA STEARNS

When Gregory wandered into the toy store, the first thing he saw was a display of teddy bears. They stood in front of a card table with a cloth draped over it. The top of the cloth and the sides that hung down to the floor were painted to look like a house. There were painted windows you couldn't see through and painted curtains and painted window boxes with painted flowers. A door and a mailbox and a doorbell and a nameplate that said, "Bear Lair." Under the nameplate were two more words, "Keep Out." "Keep out?" Gregory said. "You scare me to death, bears!" And so he whipped up the flap where the door was painted, bent over, and stepped in. And found himself face to face with a very large, very real brown bear. When Gregory realized that a brave and quick-witted boy like himself was just what this bear would like for dinner, he quickly escaped, and found himself in a strange land with one sign posted—"I know nothing about the toy store. Do not ask. Do not knock. I will not answer."

—Elizabeth Overmyer

INVASION OF THE BRAIN SHARPENERS Grades 3-5
By PHILIP CURTIS

Mr. Browser had a very ordinary class to teach. Oh, they were certainly not dumb, but they were not the smartest, either, and every one of them would rather have been anywhere else than in school all day long. Then one Friday, after more things than usual had gone wrong, Mr. Browser looked at the class, sighed, and said, "If only I had a brain sharpener as well as a pencil sharpener, maybe we'd learn a little more quickly."

Well, it was a silly joke and no one thought anything about it until the next Monday, when Michael was the very first person to arrive at school, in a heavy, pea-soup fog. He was there alone in the playground when suddenly all the fog on the field seemed to start blowing toward him. Then he heard a whirring sound, followed by a sudden plop and hiss. For a second or two, a gap opened up as the fog was blown away, and Michael saw a huge thing with windows sitting in the middle of the school field. It wasn't hard to find out what it was—as Michael approached, rays of light shot out of it and a voice said, "Inform Mr. Browser at once that the Brain Sharpeners have answered his call."

Michael soon learns that whatever the brain sharpeners want, the brain sharpeners get. Soon all the children have been hooked up to the brain sharpening machines, and after that they ask for at least six hours of homework a night, beg to skip recess every day, and request extra work for the weekends. The only one who's not pleased with all this is Michael—he's asked the brain sharpeners what they expect to get from the class in return, and he's the only one who knows that they're all part of a terrible experiment from another planet, with plans to take control of them forever.

—*Zoë Kalkanis*

INVINCIBLE SUMMER YA
By JEAN FERRIS

I met Rick in the hospital. I was in for tests and he was having chemotherapy. He was nothing like the guys I'd grown up with—farm boys, interested in fun and games and sex but not much more. I had more fun with Rick sitting on a cheap plastic couch in my bathrobe watching a rerun of *Casablanca* than I ever had with Ivan or any other boy. But then he was different in another way too—he had leukemia, the same kind I found out I had. Would I have made it through the next year without Rick? Maybe, maybe not. No one else understood what

I was going through the way he did, no one had his positive attitude, his joy in life, his certainty that I would make it, and no one else loved me the way he did. "In the depths of winter, I finally learned that within me there lay an invincible summer." This is the story of ours.

—Joni Bodart-Talbot

IRA SLEEPS OVER   Grades k–3
By BERNARD WABER

How many of you have slept over at a friend's house? Do you remember the first time you slept at someone else's?

Ira Sleeps Over is the story of Ira's first time sleeping away from home. When you read this book, it may remind you of how grown-up and excited you felt when you were finally old enough to sleep over. Or maybe you were a little nervous. Or maybe you were scared. Ira is all of these!

Ira has never slept without his teddy bear before. But tonight he is going to sleep over at Reggie's. He doesn't know if he should take it. His sister is no help; she says, "Reggie will laugh." That afternoon the boys play together and Reggie tells of all the plans he has made—"First I'll show you my junk collection. And after that we'll have a wrestling match. A pillow fight. Do magic tricks. Play checkers. Play dominoes. And after that we can fool around with my magnifying glass. And after that—I mean when the lights are out and the house is really dark— guess what we can do? We can tell ghost stories—scary, creepy, spooky ghost stories!"

Ira decides maybe he will take his teddy bear after all, until his sister says: "What if Reggie wants to know your teddy bear's name? He's really going to laugh, because Tah Tah is a silly, baby name."

Ira is having a hard time making up his mind. Should he take Tah Tah with him, or leave his teddy bear home . . . when *Ira Sleeps Over*?

—Lynda Smith

IS THIS A BABY DINOSAUR?   Grades k–2
By MILLICENT SELSAM

Look hard at these things you see. Are they what they seem to be? [Show pictures from the book.]

Could you string these into a necklace?

Is this a rocket streaking up into the sky?

Is this a lizard?

Are these ferns growing in a forest?
Are these baby dinosaurs? You can look that one up in . . .
Is This a Baby Dinosaur? by Millicent Selsam.

—*Lynda Smith*

THE ISLAND KEEPER Grades 6–8/YA
By HARRY MAZER

Have you ever felt like just dropping out of sight?

Cleo Murphy is rich, fat, and miserable. She lives with a father who is more interested in money than in her, a grandmother she can never please, and her sister Jam. Jam is the one person who is important to her, but then Jam is killed in a boating accident.

Cleo has thought many times of leaving, and now that Jam is dead she has no more reason not to. So on a plane flight on her way to camp, she takes out her escape plan and starts her Eight Steps to Freedom:

Step 1. The plane flight from Chicago to Kennedy Airport.

Step 2. Call the camp and, using her grandmother's voice, tell them she will not be coming.

Step 3. In the women's room, change into overalls and an old T-shirt. Then ditch everything that could identify her, carefully, a little at a time, in each trash can she walks by.

Step 4. Catch a bus to New York City.

Step 5. Disappear. Nobody in those crowds will remember a fat teenage girl in overalls and an old T-shirt.

Step 6. Go to an outdoor store and buy food and equipment.

Step 7. Buy a ticket to a town close to a Canadian lake that has an abandoned island her father owns. It's the perfect place, because nobody ever goes there.

Step 8. Steal a canoe and cross the lake without getting caught.

She makes it to the island and finds a cave to live in. Knowing the food she's bought will not last long, she learns to gather food from the island. Time goes by . . . as the days get shorter and colder, and flights of geese start passing overhead, Cleo knows eventually she will have to leave. She will never be able to survive the winter.

In mid September, a violent storm comes up and she decides it is time to leave. After it passes, she gets her things together and goes down to the canoe. But the canoe has been smashed by a tree blown down in the storm, and smashed with the canoe is her only hope of leaving the island before winter.

—*Brian Fowler*

IT ALL BEGAN WITH JANE EYRE, OR   YA
THE SECRET LIFE OF FRANNY DILLMAN
By SHEILA GREENWALD

Have you ever thought that reading could be dangerous? That it could get you in a load of trouble? Well, let me tell you what happened to Franny Dillman.

Franny *loved* to read. She would take her book into her closet and scrunch down among her clothes and shoes into the darkest corner. Then she would snap on her flashlight, delve into her bag of potato chips and her box of gingersnaps, and crunch and munch and read and read. Franny would get so completely absorbed in the world of her book, she would forget where she really was. Has that ever happened to you?

Franny's latest craze is the famous classic called *Jane Eyre,* about an English governess who lived long ago in a huge mansion, tutoring the child of her dark, mysterious master, Mr. Rochester. Despite the fact that Mr. Rochester seems to be evil and wicked, Jane falls madly in love with him. She doesn't even care that he has some awful secret locked away upstairs in a hidden room.

Soon after reading *Jane Eyre,* Franny begins to notice the uncanny resemblance between her school principal Mr. Crawford and Mr. Rochester. It is amazing how, when Franny starts following Mr. Crawford around, her heart starts to flutter just like Jane's did around Mr. Rochester. When Franny discovers that Mr. Crawford has a secret as dark and dreadful as Mr. Rochester's, her mother decides it is time to steer Fanny away from those romantic old books. So she gives her some modern novels about girls with realistic teenage problems. Franny devours all four new books in one week. All the heroines are either pregnant, have parents getting divorced, or are having nervous breakdowns. Their lives are so *interesting,* and they all keep journals. Franny decides to keep a journal too. To begin she writes [read from page 14, hardback edition, or page 18, paperback]:

Nothing. Absolutely nothing happens around here to me or anyone else. Nothing goes on. I live in a dull backwater of an exciting city. The twentieth century has not penetrated this pocket of the Bronx. My folks are still married to each other. They don't even fight. Though she is seventeen, my sister Grace has not had an affair. She hardly goes out with guys. If she did, she wouldn't tell me about it. My brother Wilson is an equal zero. At fourteen he should be a seething cauldron of erotic impulses. He should be climbing the walls. Instead he sublimates with math and science. He doesn't even have acne.

When Franny realizes how bleak and dreary her family life is, she decides to make something happen. Then she figures that maybe things *are* happening that she hasn't noticed. So she writes a new resolution in her journal: "I will make it my business to unearth the events that must be quietly erupting in my family."

And that is when the trouble *really* begins.

—*Catherine G. Edgerton*

IT'S A MILE FROM HERE TO GLORY   YA
By ROBERT C. LEE

Early MacLaren was small! He'd never thought much about it until he entered kindergarten, but in school they never let him forget it. There was always measuring—pencil marks on the walls, and big black-lettered charts for all to see, and vital statistics placed in important-looking folders.

He was the smallest child in first grade, too, and so it went, right on up through the grades. It wasn't a thing to give a fellow confidence. When he finally reached high school, it was even worse. The girls had always been bigger than he was, but now the boys were getting bigger too. Of course he grew, but he never could quite close the gap.

"I'm a freak, a midget!" he would yell at his father. "No," his dad would say calmly, "you're just small."

But that didn't help. Early was a sixteen-year-old high school junior who stood a sawed-off four feet, eleven inches tall. Life at school wasn't easy for Early, and neither were his trips to and from school. One of his chief tormentors always rode the school bus with him.

Now, life had not been particularly kind to Jimmy Plummer, either. A childhood disease had left his face paralyzed on one side, so his eyelid drooped, and one corner of his mouth. On the rare occasions when he tried to smile, his face twisted into a grotesque caricature.

On this particular morning Jimmy greeted Early with, "How's Logan County High School's chief red-headed jockey?" When the other kids muttered a few comments, Jimmy grasped Early's shoulder and sneered, "Old Early here, he's my friend, ain't ya, shrimp?" Early tried to ignore him, but the grip tightened to a painful squeeze. "I said you're my friend, ain't ya, Early?" "Oh yeah . . . sure, Jimmy, sure!" Early replied.

Jimmy leaned down close to Early and with a leer snarled, "Where'd you get a stupid name like Early anyway?" That was it! Like a shot, Early catapulted over the bus seat, smashing his geometry book onto his tormentor's head. Fists slammed, blood flowed, and Jimmy and Early found themselves standing before a very grim-looking high school principal.

As punishment Early and Jimmy were sentenced to twenty laps around the track after school. The run nearly killed Jimmy, but Early breezed through, not even breathing hard.

This punishment run caught the eye of the high school track coach, who immediately recognized Early's potential. He encouraged Early to come out for the spring track season the following week. Would this be the answer to Early's image problem? Could he run his way to glory?

—Barbara Lesley

JACOB HAVE I LOVED　　　　　　　　　　YA
By KATHERINE PATERSON

"Jacob have I loved, but Esau have I hated," was the Bible verse that her senile, spiteful grandmother had quoted to Louise. That was at the time when Louise's twin sister Caroline was given money to leave the small Chesapeake Bay island where they lived and go study on the mainland—something Louise had dreamed of for herself. Always, always, Caroline got what Louise wanted. Beauty, a promising career, even the man Louise loved.

—Frances Carter

JANE EYRE　　　　　　　　　　　　　　YA
By CHARLOTTE BRONTË

Jane Eyre had a rotten time when she was a kid. She was an orphan and had to live with an aunt who hated her. Her cousins were spoiled rotten, but she was treated like dirt.

When she finally rebelled she was sent to boarding school. She was pretty thrilled about this until she found out about the school. It was run by a man who practically starved and froze his students to death!

Well, things started to improve (after half the kids died of typhoid), the school was taken over by better people, and she ended up doing pretty well.

After she turned eighteen she got a job as a teacher to Adele, the eight-year-old ward of the mysterious Mr. Rochester. His house was a strange one, with a tower Jane wasn't supposed to enter and a servant named Grace Poole, who drank, and had a maniacal laugh.

One night a fire broke out in Mr. Rochester's room! Jane awoke to the smell of burning and the sound of laughter. She saved Mr. Rochester's life, but why didn't they fire Grace Poole?

There were other secrets Jane was to discover as she started falling in love with this dark, troubled man. Find them out as you read . . . *Jane Eyre.*

—Linda Keating

JANE-EMILY   Grades 5-6
By PATRICIA CLAPP

I want to ask you a question. How many times a day do you look into a mirror? At least once, I'll bet. Suppose that tonight, when you are brushing your teeth or combing your hair, you look into your mirror and instead of your own face looking back at you, you see—someone else's face! And suppose that it is the face of someone who is dead, someone who died a long time ago? . . . That's something to think about before you read this book.

This is the story of two girls, one alive and one dead.

The first girl is Jane. Jane is very much alive, but she has recently lost her parents. They were killed in a mysterious accident.

The second girl is Emily. Emily would have been Jane's aunt, but she died when she was only twelve years old, long before Jane was even born.

When Jane's parents were killed, she was invited to spend the summer with her grandmother, Emily's mother, in the house where Emily grew up. She is given Emily's old room and plays with Emily's old dolls and toys. She even wears some of Emily's old clothes.

Jane spends a lot of time in the lovely garden behind her grandmother's house. There she becomes especially fascinated with a large glass reflecting ball that sits in the middle of the garden. Have you ever seen those reflecting balls that some people have in their gardens? Often they are bright green or bright blue glass, very shiny, and when you look into one, it's like a mirror—you see your face reflected back.

Jane's grandmother tells her that the reflecting ball once belonged to Emily, that Emily had been fascinated by it, too. Jane isn't surprised to hear that, because often, when she looks into the reflecting ball, she sees *Emily*'s face looking back at her. . . .

Before the summer is over, Jane feels that she has gotten to know Emily, that Emily is her best friend.

Do you believe in ghosts? By the time you finish this book, you just might.

—Nell Colburn

JANET HAMM NEEDS A DATE   Grades 6-8
FOR THE DANCE
By EVE BUNTING

Janet has asked someone to the seventh-grade dance. She isn't lying when she says that he has big brown eyes, plays ball, likes to read, and is real nice. She just doesn't tell her friends that it's her five-year-old brother, and that even he has said no.

—Teresa Schlatt

JELLY BELLY   Grades 4-6
By ROBERT KIMMEL SMITH

Ned used to be the littlest one in his family until he grew. Most kids grow up, but Ned grew out—out in front and out in the rear and especially out in his belly. Ned's real name is Nathaniel Robbins. He's four feet eight inches tall and weighs one hundred and nine pounds. They call him "Ned" because when he was a little kid he used to go around either eating a piece of bread or asking for bread, and that's the way he said bread—"ned." Ned has another name: the school bully calls him "Jelly Belly." Ned really tries to diet, but how can he, when he can't resist Grandma's rich cooking? On Mondays she makes doughnuts, Wednesdays she makes a cake (usually a chocoloate one, for that's Ned's favorite), Fridays she bakes a couple of pies and cookies. Oh what cookies Grandma bakes! Round buttery ones, tan ones with sugar on top, peanut butter cookies, cookies with nuts or cherries in the middle, and of course, chocolate chip cookies.

Ned hasn't always been fat. Until he was six he was a really skinny kid. At seven he was just right, at eight he was a little chunky. He had a bit of a belly at nine. By ten his butt had started to stick out. And last year—Jelly Belly.

When Ned weighed in at twenty-five pounds overweight, his parents sent him off to Camp Lean-Too. There he found that all the other fat boys in the camp knew ways to beat the diet program. Ned loves to eat and he'd like to cheat, but how will he ever lose weight if he doesn't develop some will power?

—*Frances Carter*

JIMMY D., SIDEWINDER AND ME Grades 6–8/YA
By OTTO R. SALASSI

Dear Judge Francis, Your Honor:

So you want to know what my life, all fifteen years of it, was like before I got involved in the shoot-out at the New O.K. Corral? Mr. Harmon, my lawyer, says you even want to know about my living at the Children's Home in Vicksburg, especially since Mr. Broemel charges that I attacked him with a knife. And you want to know how I became a pool shark and a gambler? Well, to explain that I'd have to tell you about my foster family, the Rhoduses, about living in their garage, and going with "Ma" to play bingo every night. It was through them, you know, that I got started gambling, met Jimmy D., and became a pool shark. Then, because of that little incident when he was accused of shooting at the mayor's wife's brother, Jimmy D. had to leave town—and I went with him. That's when we got hooked up with Dr. Polgart, the traveling hypnotist. And of course you want me to tell you everything I know about the last of the Old West gamblers, the famous "Sidewinder" Bates. He knew Waytt Earp, you know—even had his picture taken with him! Sidewinder also knew my parents. OK, I'll tell you all about it! I'm not doing anything but sitting here in jail anyway. Maybe after you know all about me, you won't send me to prison. I hope not.

Yours truly,
Dumas Monk
—*Sue Padilla*

JOHNNY MAY Grades 3–6
By ROBBIE BRANSCUM

Johnny May lived in the Arkansas hill country with her grandparents and her two old-maid aunts, Irma and Irene—why, they were eighteen and nineteen years old and still not married! Johnny May thought she hated those two aunts as much as any one person could, but then, when Mr. Berry started courting Irene, she found out she could be worried about them too. You see, Mr. Berry's last wife only died a month ago, and that was his fourth wife—and they had all died! Would Irene be the fifth Mrs. Berry to meet with an unfortunate accident?

—*Elizabeth Overmyer*

JOSHUA, THE CZAR, AND THE   Grades 3-5
CHICKEN-BONE WISH
By BARBARA GIRION

How successful are you when it comes to making a chicken-bone wish? If you're anything like Joshua Wilson, you have no luck at all.

Joshua is the fourth-grade klutz, whom nobody wants on their soft-ball team. To make matters worse, Joshua's older brother, Benjie, is the star of his soccer team.

Then Joshua meets the Czar, or Mr. Romanoff as he now calls him-self. He is a resident of the nursing home where Joshua's mom volun-teers. He is a giant of a man who carries a riding stick. He has white hair that grows all the way down to his shoulders and a beard that starts under his nose with a mustache and continues all the way down to his chest. He wears funny shirts that button on the side by the neck rather than down the front. He wears dark pants that are tucked into high, shiny, black leather boots. It's not only his clothes that are funny, but his words, too. His w's get all mixed up with v's.

He's really the Czar of Markovo, he tells Joshua, and if his cousin hadn't broken off the winning half of a wishbone, he himself would have been Czar of Russia.

Joshua and the Czar quickly become friends and Mr. Romanoff starts collecting chicken wishbones.

To find out how the Czar's wishbone collection helps Joshua go from being a klutz who's always tripping and dropping things to being a hero, read *Joshua, the Czar, and the Chicken-Bone Wish,* by Barbara Girion.

—*Jan Smith*

JUMANJI   Grades 2-6
By CHRIS VAN ALLSBURG

It all started when Judy and her younger brother, Peter, found a long, thin box near the foot of a tree. Bored from playing in the house, they had set off to the park. The box they found there said, "Jumanji—A Jungle Adventure Game." It also said, "Free Game, Fun for Some But Not for All. ps: Read Instructions Carefully!"

Judy and Peter decided to take the game home and play it. It seemed like an ordinary board game, where the first player to reach the city of Jumanji on the board would be the winner. But once a game of Jumanji is started, it cannot be stopped until one player reaches the Golden City. Little did Judy and Peter realize the power of this rule until they started to play—and you, too, will learn what a *wild* time they had on their way to the Golden City—*Jumanji*, by Chris Van Allsburg.

—Gail T. Orwig

JUST AS LONG AS WE'RE TOGETHER   Grades 6-8
By JUDY BLUME

Stephanie and Rachel have been best friends since the second grade. This year they will be starting junior high school and many changes are happening in their lives. Alison is one of them. She is cute and popular, and soon the best friends become a threesome. But can there really be three best friends? Or will there soon be two new best friends?

—Frances W. Levin

JUST DIAL A NUMBER   YA
By EDITH MAXWELL

Imagine yourself as Cathy Shores. It's your senior year in high school and (finally!) you've got a boyfriend. No longer do the kids refer to you as the principal's daughter; now they know you as Todd's girlfriend. You've finally made it into the "in group."

Then one night you and Todd and another couple are at your house. They're all teasing you, because in the recent school play you had only one line and then you were a corpse for the rest of the play. Todd dares you to repeat your line over the phone to a stranger. Of course you can't look bad in front of your boyfriend, so you go along with the dare. Todd dials a phone number at random and then shoves the phone to your ear. Suddenly you realize that you are really saying your one line to some unknown person—your famous one-liner, "Somebody tried to kill me!" And that's when the tragedy and the terror start!

Just Dial a Number, by Edith Maxwell.

—Pam Spencer

KEEP YOUR MOUTH CLOSED, DEAR   Grades k–3
By ALIKI

Does your mom or dad ever have to say to you, "Keep your mouth closed, dear?" Oh, no! I hope you don't have the same problem Charles has! [or, Oh, good—I'm always afraid I'll find someone who has a problem just like Charles'!]

Charles' mother is continually telling him, "Keep your mouth closed, dear." Do you know why? Charles swallows things—things he's not supposed to swallow, like soap . . . a wooden spoon . . . an alarm clock . . . a can of baby powder. In fact, it has gotten to the point that every time he opens his mouth to sing or to yawn or even to ask a question, he swallows something!

If you were his mother, wouldn't you want to help Charles stop? How could you do it? Well, Charles' mother does try lots of approaches, but they're not very successful. The solution happens quite by accident, and you'll probably laugh.

Keep Your Mouth Closed, Dear, by Aliki.

—Lynda Smith

KEPT IN THE DARK   Grades 6–8
By NINA BOWDEN

All was fine at grandfather's house until David arrived. David was strange. He evoked feelings in them all that seemed unnatural, out of character. Clara had mixed emotions—she hated him and she loved him.

Boise, usually selfish, went out of his way to please David. Noel, usually kind and easygoing, didn't know why he didn't trust David. Grandfather, usually the master of the house, gave in to all of David's wishes. Liz retreated to her room, refusing to eat or come out. The entire household was under David's powerful and sinister influence. Why? Read the book and find out!

—Brenda W. Satchell

KERMIT THE HERMIT   Grades 1-4
By BILL PEET

Kermit is a crab. I mean a *real* crab. He is a scavenger crab and he can't get along with anybody. That is why Kermit lives alone on top of his pile of junk in the harbor. Kermit is used to fighting for what he wants; however, one day Kermit chose the wrong opponent. The fight was over a shiny tin can. The enemy was a large dog.

In one swipe the crab gave the dog a sharp nip on his sensitive nose, and the dog let out a yelp! "That'll teach you," Kermit snapped, "to go sniffing at me!" Then he turned himself round to head back to the sea. But the dog made a leap and seized the crab in his jaws by the back of the shell, beyond reach of the claws. He then began digging Kermit's grave and surely would have buried him alive if it hadn't been for a kind boy in raggedy clothes.

Now Kermit would like to repay the boy's kindness. But how can he do that, if he's trapped at the ocean's bottom?

—Christine Hayes

THE KID WITH THE RED SUSPENDERS   Grades 2-5
By LOUANN GAEDDERT

"Hammie, Hammie, Mommy's little lambie. Thinks he's so smart, so give him a whammie." Ham dreaded the jeering from Rob, the school bully. Ham promised himself to show all the kids at school that he didn't have to wear red suspenders, eat mother's catered lunches, get top grades, or have his mother walk him to and from school. Skipping school and going to the zoo with Jerry and Rob would definitely prove that Ham could be his own man.

The three boys decided to go to the big zoo on the other side of town. Ham knew how to get there. His mother had taught him subway survival.

After mimicking the giraffes, monkeys, and other outdoor animals at the zoo, Rob insisted the three boys visit the zoo's night house. Rob had a plan to execute in the dark house. The boys let their eyes adjust to the darkness. Ham looked at the bats, turned to talk to Jerry, his best friend. Jerry wasn't there, neither was Rob. Ham hurried around the zoo looking for the two boys. The money for the return trip home was with Rob. Only Jerry and Rob knew Ham was at the zoo. The zoo was ready to close for the day. Would Ham ever get home?

—Ruth Wintjen

THE KIDNAPPING
OF CHRISTINA LATTIMORE
By JOAN LOWERY NIXON

Christina was kidnapped from her own front porch. She was grabbed from behind and given an injection that knocked her out. She wakes up locked in a cold, empty basement. After a while, a man in a black ski mask appears with food and demands that she sign a ransom note for $25,000 addressed to her grandmother, a very wealthy executive. Seeing that the man has left the cellar door open, Christina tries to make a run for it. The man catches her and drags her down the stairs by her feet and repeats his demands. Christina throws a bowl of soup in his face . . . the man slaps her and stamps out, taking with him what's left of the food. He comes back much later with more food and the note to sign. Christina, who in the meantime has made a thorough search of the basement for escape routes without finding any, and who is very hungry, sees no alternative but to sign the note.

Days pass and no one comes to rescue her. One day, the man takes her up into the main part of the house and takes her on a tour. A woman with a gun orders her to shower and change into clean clothes. Somehow they have clothes that belong to her and some personal things like her hairbrush and makeup. Then the woman makes Christina watch TV in the living room, holding the gun on her the whole time. Suddenly there is a commotion at the front door, and the woman tosses the gun into Christina's lap. Christina grabs it, and is still holding it when the police burst into the house. They order her to drop the gun and they are all taken down to the police station. There she learns that her kidnappers claim that she was an accomplice in her own kidnapping! That she had planned it. She also discovers that all evidence of her imprisonment in the cellar has disappeared and, of course, her fingerprints are all over the house, from the tour. No one believes her, not the police, not her grandmother, who paid the ransom, not even her parents. How is Christina going to prove her innocence, or will she end up being found guilty of a kidnapping conspiracy?

—*Caroline Ketman*

KILLING MR. GRIFFIN
By LOIS DUNCAN

It was easy to hate Mr. Griffin. He was the hardest, coldest, most arrogant teacher at school. There was no such thing as an A in his class—that would mean perfection, and to Mr. Griffin, no one was perfect. He'd taught college English before he'd transferred to teaching high school, and his memory was excellent. So when Mark turned in a brilliant paper for his senior English class, Mr. Griffin recognized it as a college paper turned in to him several years previously. Mark failed the class and had to repeat his senior year. So he had a particular reason to hate Mr. Griffin, and to want to see him humbled and broken. It started as a private joke between Mark and Jeff, the idea of killing Mr. Griffin, but soon it was a fully planned kidnapping plot, involving not only them but also three other kids. They put it into action, and it worked! They blindfolded Mr. Griffin and took him up in the mountains to a secret place Mark knew about, and tried to force him to beg to be let go. But he stayed as cold and hard and arrogant as ever, even when they smashed his nitroglycerin pills to see if they would explode. They didn't—and when the kids read the label, "For Angina," Mr. Griffin didn't tell them that it meant he had heart problems. But maybe it wouldn't have made any difference if he had. They decided to leave him there, tied up on the ground, until after the game that night. It would be several hours, he'd be cold, frightened, and *then* would certainly beg to be released. But two of them got scared and went back earlier, about nine o'clock, only to find him dead. He'd had a heart attack, and without his pills he'd died. Now it was real—it wasn't a joke any longer. It certainly wasn't a joke to Kathy Griffin, Brian's wife, about to have their first child. She didn't believe the story the kids told about her husband, and began to investigate on her own. She couldn't believe anyone would hate Brian so much that they'd kill him. She knew, too, that the cold, controlled person he was in the classroom wasn't the real Brian Griffin at all, but it was a long time before any of his students (and murderers) began to realize that.

—Joni Bodart-Talbot

KILLING TIME   YA/Adult
By PATRICIA WINDSOR

Druids. Have you heard of them? They were that religious group that worshipped nature and trees, especially oaks. Well, everyone knows the Druids died out hundreds of years ago over in England . . . or did they?

After Sam's mother and father were divorced, Sam's father bought an old home out in the country. Sam wasn't too excited about moving there, but he really didn't have much say in the matter. He tried to settle in and not complain, but right away strange occurrences began. Every night this girl would appear in his room—but he couldn't tell if she was real or a ghost. And then his watch disappeared, but a few days later turned up again; their house got painted with blood; and his father fell down an outdoor shaft and broke his leg.

Sam can't figure out what is happening, but he knows every time he goes into the woods he hears strange noises and feels as though he is being watched. Is he? The *Killing Time,* by Patricia Windsor.

—Pam Spencer

THE KINGDOM AND THE CAVE   Grades 3-6
By JOAN AIKEN

I'm Mickle, the palace cat. I hate to let Prince Michael know that I can talk human language, but I have no choice. He has to know about the Under People's plot to invade and overthrow the kingdom of Astalon. And he has to learn UAL—Universal Animal Language— quickly. After all, the animals of the kingdom are the only ones who can guide him to the cave where the Under People keep the secret Magic Box they stole from the kingdom years ago. And that box, according to the old prophecy, is the only thing that can save Astalon.

—Margie Reitsma

KISS THE CLOWN   YA
By C. S. ADLER

When Viki Hill left Guatemala and started going to a new school in the US, she found it quite exciting once she finally had some friends. Marc Bruggerman was the first person to be kind to her, and he was the one who wrote the article about her that eventually broke the barrier of the new school. Marc was successful at everything, and the people around him took notice of his achievements. All seemed to be going well until Viki started looking at Marc's brother, Joel, who was older, yet had not achieved much academically because he was dyslexic, a condition that causes a person to have trouble decoding written symbols. However, Joel had compassion, and seemed to be more in touch with feelings than Marc. He understood how Viki felt when her father wrote that Viki might have to come back to Guatemala to help him with her mother, who had gotten very depressed. Everything in Viki's life seemed to be out of order. Find out what happens, and who turns out to be the clown in *Kiss the Clown,* by C. S. Adler.

—Donna Houser

KONRAD

Grades 4-6

By CHRISTINE NOSTLINGER

One morning, Mrs. Bertie Bartolotti answers her door to find a delivery man with a heavy white parcel. Inside the package there is a huge, gleaming, silvery can. Thinking it must contain corned beef, Mrs. Bartolotti pulls the metal pull-ring and finds a creature crouching inside the can. It is sort of a crumpled-looking dwarf; it has a crumpled-up head with a very wrinkled face, and crumpled-up arms, and a crumpled-up throat and chest. After mixing up the nutrient solution and pouring it over the creature. Mrs. Bartolotti learns what the parcel really contains—a factory-produced boy named Konrad. Being the product of highly developed technology, he is quite free of those faults and defects that children usually have. In fact, Konrad is trained and educated and guaranteed to please in every way.

So on the one hand we have Konrad, who knows all the rules—the "should do's" and the "shouldn't do's" of seven-year-old-boys. On the other hand we have Mrs. Bartolotti, who has no idea what's proper or what isn't, and wouldn't care if she did. For example, when she dresses herself before going downtown shopping, she grabs a pair of jeans and a T-shirt off the line, but since they are unironed she covers them up with a thick fur coat—even though it is a warm day. And of course, since she is wearing her fur coat she might as well wear her fur cap too. If she dresses herself like this, can you imagine the kind of clothes she picks out for Konrad?

But after a few weeks Konrad and Mrs. Bartolotti do adjust to each other. It is with great distress that they read the letter from the factory that explains that Konrad was sent to Mrs. Bartolotti by mistake, that it was really someone else who had ordered him, and that factory agents will be coming to collect him. Since neither of them want Konrad to leave, they must devise a plan to avoid the recall. Desperate situations call for desperate remedies—and that is exactly what Konrad and Mrs. Bartolotti come up with!

Konrad, by Christine Nostlinger.

—Lynda Smith

LACKAWANNA
By CHESTER AARON

YA

October 1929—life is great for Willy. He runs home after school to play in the carefully raked leaves in the front yard and, going into the kitchen, smells the fresh bread and apple pie his mother has just finished baking. Supper's on the stove, but he has just enough time to spend a few minutes playing football with his older brother and his friends. It seems that night that nothing can ever go wrong.

November 1929—life is very different. There are no jobs and no money after the stock market crash. Apple pies are a thing of the past. Willy's big brother doesn't play football in the street anymore, and his father sits and stares at the wall, and some days doesn't even get out of bed. His mother doesn't bake any longer, and all she has to serve for supper are potatoes.

1931—Willy is fifteen now, and no longer lives with his family—they've all deserted him, one by one. So he gathers a new family around him, a family of kids who have to survive on their own, who have to take care of themselves since no one else will do it for them. There's Carl, Deirdre and her little brother Herbie, Norman, who jokes a lot, and Slezak, the toughest of the group. They beg for food or steal it, and hop freight trains to get around. But just when it starts to looks like they've finally gotten it together—with a place to stay, food to eat, and even coal for the fire and for hot baths—Herbie disappears: he's been kidnapped! Deirdre and Carl saw him hauled into an open boxcar leaving the yard by the biggest hobo they'd ever seen. They all know about 'bos, and how some of them like to capture small boys and make them into slaves—or worse. They've got to find Herbie before it's too late!

—Joni Bodart-Talbot

THE LAND I LOST,
ADVENTURES OF A BOY IN VIETNAM
By HUYNH QUANG NHUONG

Grades 5-8

One night a terrified friend of our family's banged on our door and begged to be let in. He was fleeing the most feared sound in our village, the hiss of the horse snake. A snake as fast as a thoroughbred, a snake as long as a full-grown bamboo tree, a snake so strong its victim would never have strength enough to fight it. My father directed the buffalo horn be sounded three times to warn all the people of our village. It was done.

Shortly after midnight the frightened neighing of a horse in the rice fields broke the uneasy silence. Next morning, the search party found the old horse. Its chest was smashed, all its ribs broken. It had been the horse snake, all right, but it was gone. All day the men searched in vain.

Next afternoon Minh, a farmer, went to his fishpond to get a fish for dinner. He saw the horse snake, head hooked to the branch of one tree, tail hooked to another, and body swinging back and forth—emptying all the water from the pond. Minh fell to the ground, crawled to safety, and screamed for help.

The Land I Lost, Huynh Quang Nhuong's autobiography.

—Barbara Hawkins

THE LAST RIDE   YA
By CAROLYN HADDAD

Doug is a wimp. He knows it; most of his friends are considered wimps, but that's only because he and his friends aren't football players or cheerleaders or pompom girls. No, they just play in the band and take upper-level courses.

But then one day Cindy Ballentine says yes when Doug invites her to the Snow Ball, just the biggest dance of the year. Doug is so excited; he, Doug Valvano, going to the Snow Ball with Cindy Ballentine, one of the pompom girls. Of course, he doesn't know that she said yes to get back at Charlie Sims.

The night of the dance, Cindy and Doug double-date with two other couples, friends of Cindy's. Big, popular Red Bucknell is driving, and after the dance he takes everyone to a keg party in a field. When the cops are called, couples and cars scatter every which way. Red tries to tear out of the field, but goes in reverse most of the way. When he finally lands the car on the road, it's obvious that he's very drunk and not able to drive.

Poor little wimpy Doug does a very unwimpy thing. He hollers "Stop the car," and he gets out and drags Cindy with him, while the other two couples laugh at him. He doesn't know then what a smart move he's made—or was it really so smart? Cindy sure doesn't think so when she sees the car disappear into the night and they have to walk back to town. His one chance to stop being a wimp—has Doug blown it completely? Read *The Last Ride*, and find out.

—Pam Spencer

THE LAUNCHING OF LINDA BELL   YA
By WILLIAM F. HALLSTEAD

It all begins one day when Ms. Strickland, the tough Mass Communications teacher, gives a major assignment to her class. Each student must write a feature article on community affairs by the end of six weeks. Gordy Gordon won't be satisfied just to pass—he wants an A. And with his friends Herkimer Harnishphegger (Herk for short) and Chaunce Bramble, he sets out on a project that is a bit crazy, and harder to complete than you'd ever imagine. The project? To select one girl from the senior class—a girl who is a "nobody"—and make her into a local celebrity through a carefully orchestrated publicity campaign. All the boys need is a girl. But who?

Well, the first thing they do is go to the local photographer, who has recently taken pictures of all the senior girls. One photo catches their attention: Belinda Belinski. She was that chubby little girl all the kids teased in the lower grades and now she's a senior nonentity—perfect!

The first step in their plan to make Belinda a star is to show up at a parade in the next town with Belinda riding in the back seat of Herk's old Chevy, wearing a sash reading "Miss Gordon Hardware" (his dad's store). They figure crashing the parade will be good for a newspaper article with the headline: LOCAL GIRL MAKES GOOD IN THORNTON in the Neshannon Chronicle. But Herk spends so much time making the outside of his car look good that he forgets to check the inside. On the way to the parade, the car breaks down. There is only one way to reach the parade on time from their spot on the country road: walk. To the boys' surprise, Belinda pulls a pair of sneakers from her purse, puts them on, hikes up her long prom dress, and leads the way. It is funny—for the first thirty seconds. Then the rain smashes into them as if a dam had broken. This rain isn't the kind that just gets you wet. Oh, no. It is a real frog-strangler. And if the Crossland Fire Department truck didn't happen by at that moment, they would never have made it into Thornton. When they finally arrive, Chaunce sees an opportunity and is quick with the camera. He catches a waterlogged Belinda on the steps of the fire engine in a gigantic fireman's hat and slicker. The picture turns out great! And when they send it to the Neshannon Chronicle, it appears in not one but *three* local papers, with the caption: MISS HARDWARE MISSES PARADE. Belinda is on her way! Soon she is making special appearances, and her name gets changed to Linda Bell. And Linda Bell is a whole new person—confident, determined, ambitious. A person who *loves* fame. . . .

Herk is haunted by Belinda's father's words: "Just remember. You think you are playing a game, but you are playing with a real person."

As the three boys get closer and closer to their A, things begin to get out of hand. Have they created a monster? To find out, read *The Launching of Linda Bell,* by William F. Hallstead.

—Diane Tuccillo

THE LEFT HAND OF DARKNESS   YA/Adult
By URSULA K. LE GUIN

Genly Ai has been sent to Gethen, or Winter, to persuade the inhabitants of that planet to join with the other planets in a galaxy-wide federation. However, it isn't as easy as it might seem—the Gethians are not interested in forming alliances, and their unique sexual orientation makes them different from all the other races in the galaxy. Gethians are androgynous; that is, they are both male and female, each one of them. When the time of mating, or "kemmering," occurs, then one partner becomes male and one female, for that time. They don't always become the same sex, and one person may be mother to several children and father to several others. The rest of the time except during kemmering they are neuter, neither sex, and sex is not a motivating factor in their society. Life on Winter is strikingly different from life on other planets, since all other planets, whether hetero, homo, or bi-sexual, have sexually constant societies.

This is an excerpt from a report by one of the First Investigators, who went to the planet long before Genly Ai. [Read from pp. 93–94, paperback edition.]

Ursula Le Guin has taken psychology, mythology, and poetry and woven them together with suspense, intrigue, and politics. She has created in Winter a society totally foreign to human experience, and she has done this so skillfully that despite its strangeness, Winter is believable. It becomes almost more natural to Genly Ai and to the reader than the society that we call natural today.

—Joni Bodart-Talbot

THE LEGEND OF TARIK   YA
By WALTER DEAN MYERS

It was said El Muerte slept always alone, for any living thing that spent the night with him would be dead in the morning, such was his evil. Nor was there a living thing that he loved, or any beauty that he would not destroy.

El Muerte sold into slavery all those he did not slaughter. So it was that Tarik found himself in a sports arena awaiting death by El Muerte. He saw his father's body, heard his younger brother scream, and then the horsemen were upon him. A blow from behind lifted him into the air.

Tarik drifted into and out of knowing. When he finally reached consciousness, he was in a large room. An old man had been caring for him. This man told Tarik of his wife and child being murdered and of his own soldier's arm being sliced off by El Muerte. Tarik vowed revenge.

A second old man appeared—an old black man blinded by El Muerte. He instructed Tarik to cup his hands, draw water from a bowl, and pour the water from hand to hand while repeating the name "El Muerte." Tarik trembled with rage; the water spilled from his hands. The old scholar said, "Before you face your enemy, you must free your heart from hatred and anger. Hatred will make you as blind as I am. Each morning you are to pour water from hand to hand while repeating 'El Muerte.' When you can do this without spilling the water, come to me."

When he could pour the water one hundred times, Tarik proudly demonstrated his mastery over anger to Nongo. "It is done," said Tarik. "No, . . . it is not done, but it is well begun," replied Nongo. Thus began the training of Tarik.

The Legend of Tarik by Walter Dean Myers.

—*Barbara Hawkins*

LENNY KANDELL, SMART ALECK   Grades 5–8
By ELLEN CONFORD

"Ta-daa! Ladies and gentlemen, your favorite and mine, star of stage, screen, and radio, the incomparable, the hilarious—Lenny Dell!"

"I want to thank you for that very kind introduction. And let me tell you, it's a miracle I'm here at all. What a week I had! My teacher asked me how come geese fly south in the winter. I said. 'Why not? It's too far to walk.' Then she asked me to use the words *defeat, deduct, defense,* and *detail* in one sentence. So I said, 'Defeat of deduct go over defense before detail.'"

Lenny Kandell rehearses his act anywhere and anytime he can—on his toes in front of the bathroom mirror or while hanging the wash on the clothesline. He tries out a riddle a week on Miss Randolph, his teacher. But she never cracks a smile, not even when the answer's funny. And that time she asked him a question about the poem *Hiawatha* and he responded with the first thing that popped into his mind, his answer made the whole class laugh. But Miss Randolph kept him after school and told him that nobody likes a smart aleck. She sounded just like his mother as she told him that he was a smart boy and that if he'd use his head more and his mouth less, he could make something of himself.

Not everybody responds like Miss Randolph, though. His friend Artie is the world's best audience. He laughs at all the jokes.

Unfortunately for Lenny, he has more than jokes to think about these days. He's in a heap of trouble. He took his new pocketknife out of the house—he'd promised his mother he wouldn't. He soiled his aunt's valuable fur stole—and a policeman brought him home because he thought Lennie might have stolen the stole. He tripped a bully in the movie theater—and the guy's soda spilled all over Georgina's dress. Now Georgina won't speak to him and Lenny has to figure out how to earn enough money to have the stole cleaned and buy a new dress—*and* stay out of the bully's way.

Lenny doesn't want trouble. He just wants to make people happy. He's wanted to be a comedian for almost as long as he can remember. Before the war Lenny's father had taken the family to a show in a resort hotel. Although Lenny didn't understand all the jokes told by the comedian, he did understand the look in his mother's eyes that night—a look that said, "I love you. I'm happy. Thank you for that."

And Lenny knew then there was nothing he wanted more than to be that comedian in the white suit, making everybody so happy that they loved one another, and loved him because he could make them feel that way.

"And so now, folks, here's Lenny Dell!"

"Thank you, thank you very much, ladies and gentleman. Listen, I have this kid who's really got rotten table manners. He's always reaching for things. I keep telling him to *ask* people to please pass the plate, but *no,* he keeps reaching for whatever he wants. Finally the other night I got fed up. "Hey, sonny,' I said, 'I wish you'd stop reaching for everything. Haven't you got a tongue?' And he said, 'Yeah, but my arm's longer.'"

—*Olivia Jacobs*

LIAR, LIAR   Grades 7–8/YA
By LAURENCE YEP

I could just kill him! We've all said it. Of course, no one really means it. Or do they? Marsh was the class clown. You know—the guy who puts toothpaste in people's chairs, who tapes "Kick Me" signs on their backs. A real practical joker—only his jokes weren't very practical or even funny. When the brakes started fading on Marsh's old clunker of a car, no one noticed. When they finally failed, however, everyone noticed—because Marsh was dead. Sean had been Marsh's friend and neighbor and had been sitting next to Marsh when the car skidded on its roof down the highway and into the path of a speeding truck. Now Sean is going to find out what really happened to Marsh's brakes. Simple mechanical failure like the police said, or pay-back from a victim pushed too far? Even if Sean can find out the truth, he may have trouble convincing anyone to believe him. After all, the court psychiatrist has already labeled Sean a pathological liar.

—Tracy Chesonis

LIFE WITHOUT FRIENDS   YA
By ELLEN EMERSON WHITE

"Inside! Go to your room! I don't want to have to look at you," Beverly's father said from between clenched teeth. He'd believed Tim's lies—they had all believed Tim's lies. She'd even begun to believe them herself, and she *knew* how wrong they were! She'd been there! But she'd been too scared to tell anyone—Tim said he'd kill her if she did. He had beaten her up, just so she'd believe him, and she did.

Beverly lay down on her bed, remembering Tim's innocent face in the courtroom. He'd looked so perfect, but she knew he was crazy—*really* crazy. And now two kids were dead because he was crazy and she'd been too scared to talk. Her father wasn't the only person who blamed Beverly for their deaths. Everyone at school did too—kids and teachers. She was afraid of . . . of . . . of . . . .

So she lived alone. Senior year, life without friends. She could feel the hatred and bitterness as she walked down the hall. No one spoke to her, and conversations stopped as she walked by. She was the only one to blame—and her friends did blame her, her father too. She even blamed herself.

Then she met Derek, who just wanted to be friends—nothing more. He didn't know about her past, and Beverly didn't dare tell him. Especially not after she'd asked him if there was anything he thought unforgivable, and he'd said "Murder—you know, not an accident, *real murder.*" And Beverly knew she was alone again. If she told him about Tim, Derek would hate her too. She was truly alone, cut off, abandoned, in a *Life Without Friends,* a life she saw no way out of.

—Joni Bodart-Talbot

A LIGHT IN THE ATTIC Grades 4–8
By SHEL SILVERSTEIN

Babysitters who sit upon babies, devils who borrow kids' bikes, Backward Bill with his backward pup—these are all characters from Shel's poems. Have you ever had a hot dog for a pet? Or a tree growing out of your head? You will find Shel Silverstein's *A Light in the Attic* full of poetic curiosities.

—Pam Swofford

LISA, BRIGHT AND DARK YA
by JOHN NEUFELD

Lisa is sixteen years old, and she's going crazy. She tells her parents she needs to go to a psychiatrist, and they don't believe her. "Oh that's just a fad! This year shrinks, next year something else—we're not going to spend money on your keeping up with everyone else!" Three of Lisa's friends do believe her and they try to help, but they're only sixteen too and can't really do much. So Lisa's bright days get further and further apart, and her dark days get darker and darker, and come more and more frequently. Finally Lisa knows she has to have help or she's not going to be able to survive. She's *got* to catch someone's attention; she's *got* to make someone listen to her. And when she finds someone she thinks will listen, she does catch their attention—*she walks through a plate glass door.*

—Carol Starr and *Joni Bodart-Talbot*

LITTLE LITTLE YA
By M. E. KERR

Today you're going to meet Little Little LaBelle. She's a beautiful seventeen-year-old high school senior with long blonde hair, and she's called Little Little because she's only three feet, three inches tall.

Little Little's mother, Mrs. LaBelle, has decided that she and her husband can die happy only if they know Little Little is married and has someone to look after her. So Mrs. LaBelle has embarked on a campaign to introduce Little Little to all the diminutive people on the East Coast; "diminutive" is what Mrs. LaBelle calls midgets and dwarfs. Actually, Mrs. LaBelle has selected the person she thinks Little Little should marry—a pint-sized, Bible-thumping, hallelujah-shouting evangelist named the Little Lion. Mrs. LaBelle's plans seem to be progressing until another diminuitive person comes into Little Little's life—Sidney "The Roach" Cinnamon.

For a crazy tale of high school life through a diminutive's eyes, read about Little Little, the Little Lion, and Sydney "The Roach" Cinnamon—and then *you* decide whom Little Little should marry.

—Pam Spencer

A LITTLE LOVE   YA
By VIRGINIA HAMILTON

Some of the boys at the high school call her She-Mama but she never lets on that she hates that nickname, that it makes her feel not too good about herself. Sheema has trouble believing in herself, but she does believe in her granmom and granpop—she believes they love her and she can count on them. After all, Granmom had taken Sheema in when Sheema's mama died in childbirth. Her father left a long time ago. Sheema can't remember any of that. But very still, in the back of her mind, there are her dead mom and her missing dad. As the weather changes and spring begins, that's all Sheema can think about—finding her dad. If she could just find him, she's sure he'd make it a lot easier for her to cope with her too-large size, her slowness. Sheema finally makes a decision—she *must* find her father. She convinces Forrest, her boyfriend (who also seems to care about her in a special way), to help her search for Cruze Hadley. All she knows about her dad is that he's a sign painter and he's been sending money to her grandparents to take care of her.

So they set out, just two teenagers in love with one another, following just a few clues, hoping that they'll find him, so that Sheema can know what it feels like to have just a little love from her father.

—Jacqueline Brown Woody

LOCKED IN TIME   YA
By LOIS DUNCAN

There weren't any ghosts at Shadow Grove. What seventeen-year-old Eleanor Robbins found was harder to believe in than ghosts and far more frightening. The first warning came when Eleanor, or Nore as she was called, arrived at Shadow Grove deep in the bayous of Louisiana to meet her father's new wife Lisette and her two children—thirteen-year-old Josie and seventeen-year-old Gabe. Lisette was waiting on the steps of the mansion when Nore and her father arrived after the long drive from the airport. She was beautiful, but when Nore looked into her eyes she saw, not the promise of friendship, but something strange and sinister. But the next minute Lisette was welcoming her with open arms, and so Nore decided she had been wrong—she hadn't seen death in Lisette's eyes.

The second warning came from Nore's own dead mother in a dream. Nore had taken a nap before dinner that first evening and in her dream her mother had appeared beside her bed. She told Nore to pack her things and leave Shadow Grove immediately. When Nore replied that she was only spending the summer—she'd be going back to school in New England in September—her mother had said, "By September, it will be too late. . . . You and your father are both in terrible danger." But Nore chose to ignore this warning too.

The third warning, or hint of danger, came at dinner that evening. Thirteen-year-old Josie was chattering away about all the places she and her brother and mother had lived. She said she'd always remember Hartford because that's where the Ringling Circus tent caught fire and they almost got trampled to death trying to get out. Lisette immediately cut her off. It was only just as Nore was drifting off to sleep that night that she remembered hearing about the Hartford circus fire from her mother—a fire that occurred on her mother's eleventh birthday, forty years ago. How could thirteen-year-old Josie have been alive forty years ago?

By the time Nore began to listen to the warnings and to realize what terrible secret Lisette, Gabe, and Josie were hiding, it was too late. Her father wouldn't listen to her—it was too unbelievable, too horrible, and too late.

—Marianne Tait Pridemore

A LONG WAY FROM HOME   Grades 7–8/YA
By MAUREEN CRANE WARTSKI

Living on the streets of war-torn Saigon wasn't easy, especially for someone growing up there with no home or family. A kid had to be tough and know how to fight. It was the only way to survive. Kien is one of these kids. A fifteen-year-old Vietnamese war orphan, he learned to defend himself on the streets at an early age simply so he wouldn't starve. Kien dreams of escaping the poverty of his Communist-occupied homeland and beginning a new life in America.

Then, amazingly, a letter arrives. It is from Steve Olson, a kind American Kien once met. It says that Steve, his wife Diane, and their small son Tad want to adopt three young Vietnamese. Five weeks later, Kien, with his adoptive sister and brother, Mai and Loc, finds himself on an airplane bound for California.

Mai quickly and eagerly adjusts to American life. She's busy in school and planning her first American birthday party. Loc and Tad are about the same age, and they become friends immediately. Only Kien has a hard time adjusting, even though Steve and Diane seem to care a lot for him.

Kien can't stand the harsh English language. Most of all, he can't stand school. He would rather be out working than in classes. At first, his Vietnamese-speaking tutor and some friendly kids in school help him manage. But then Sim Evans moves to town. Sim's father lost his last factory job because Vietnamese immigrants were hired for less money than the Americans were being paid. Sim quickly learned to hold a grudge against all Vietnamese, and when he meets Kien he begins to torment him and call him cruel names. Things come to a head one day, and the confrontation that was bound to happen begins.

Kien and a friend are carrying ice cream home for Mai's birthday party when they see Sim, a gleam in his hating eyes, waiting for them. Two more boys come up from behind. One carries a metal pipe.

Suddenly Kien is back in Saigon, reacting with street-wise instinct. A scramble in the dust, a heavy stone in his hand, a swift leap . . . and Sim, his eye badly hurt, screams in pain. Kien is safe, but he knows he's in trouble. Ashamed and afraid, even though his actions were in self-defense, Kien decides to run away and start fresh in another town. Can he live on the streets again, in an unfamiliar land? Can he learn to live anywhere else?

—Diane Tuccillo

LORETTA MASON POTTS   Grades 3–6
By MARY CHASE

Loretta Mason Potts is an awful, awful, bad, bad, girl. Loretta had a cigarette dangling from her mouth by the time she was one year old. She is so bad that her brother and sisters have never heard of her: she went away when she was five. Then, when she is twelve, Loretta gets sent back to her family. Loretta swears and steals, but worst of all she introduces her brother and sisters to—*them*. This awful, bad girl may have let her whole family become captives in a mysterious, weird world. A funny, spooky book.

—Diana McRae

LOVE ALWAYS, BLUE   YA
By MARY POPE OSBORNE

Blue just doesn't fit in to her small North Carolina town. She has been more and more sure of that ever since her father left for New York City to write plays. How she longs to go stay with him in Greenwich Village, maybe go to the opening night of his off-Broadway play, meet his artistic friends in little cafes, experience the exciting sights and sounds of the big city. Left behind, Blue just can't get excited about lunch at her mother's dull country club, or trying to make conversation with the dumb boys at the drive-in. No wonder her father couldn't stand this boring little backwater. Surely Blue is her father's daughter; she likes the same things. How can her mother possibly be happy here without Dad? How could she ever have let Dad go?

When Blue sees her mother with a rich tennis-playing businessman, she feels betrayed. "You've been lying to me!" she accuses her mother, insisting that she be allowed to visit her dad in New York. Normally the mere mention of New York upsets Blue's mother, but this time, she gives Blue an odd look. "There are things you don't understand about your father, Blue," she says sadly. "I guess you'll just have to go up there and find out the truth for yourself."

Blue is overjoyed, quickly phoning her father to plan a two-week visit. Her dad sounds really happy that she is coming, though he warns her not to be put off by his drab little apartment with peeling paint on the walls.

When Blue finally arrives, everything is just as perfect as she imagined. She doesn't mind the hole-in-the-wall apartment at all, even if she has to sleep on a pillowcase stuffed with towels. There is so much life and energy all around on the streets outside. Blue and her father have dinner at a cafe to celebrate his appointment the next morning with a man who wants to produce his play. The next day, as Blue sits on the steps waiting for her father to return, another one of her dreams suddenly comes true. The most gorgeous, interesting guy walks right up to her and starts talking. His name is Nathaniel, and he is returning books that Blue's father lent him, and it turns out that Nathaniel's mother used to date Blue's father. Nathaniel is so easy to talk to! He seems to know a lot about Blue already through her father, and he enjoys her southern accent. Blue is thrilled when Nathaniel asks her to go to the movies that afternoon.

But when her father gets home, Blue knows right away that something went wrong. He is cold and withdrawn, and all he will say is that the play deal did not work out, and it doesn't matter anyway. He seems hurt that Blue made plans to go out with Nathaniel instead of staying with him.

In the next few days, her father's spirits plummet even further. When Blue can't stop him from crying uncontrollably, she knows something is terribly wrong. It hurts to love him so much and not be able to make him happy. But what in the world can Blue do?

—*Catherine G. Edgerton*

LOVE AND BETRAYAL AND HOLD THE MAYO   Grades 7-8
By FRANCINE PASCAL

Sixteen-year-old Torrie Martin thinks she has found the perfect summer job. She's going to be a camper-waitress with her best friend Steffi in a camp in the mountains in upstate New York. All they have to do is set the tables and serve three meals a day—no dishes, no cooking, no hassle. Steffi's been going to the camp for the last five years, and she says it's great—and the girls get paid $260, plus they get to participate in all the camp activities. The only problem Torrie can see is that her thirteen-year-old sister Nina (El Creepo) will be attending the same camp, but Torrie figures she can avoid her.

When Torrie sees the camp, it looks like a gorgeous hotel. There are two circles of bunkhouses, one for the boys and one for the girls, and they both look brand-new. There's a sparkling lake, green lawns, and lots of trees. The white bunkhouses even have freshly painted shutters—violets, pinks, and mauves for the girls; deep blue, brown, red, and gray for the boys. Torrie hopes for a mauve one—it's her favorite color.

They go right by the bunks though, and the only thing they see is a couple of rundown old ramshackle buildings in the middle of what looks like a garbage dump. Half the shutters are falling off and the front steps are broken. These are the bunkhouses for the camper-waitresses. Inside are eight terrible iron cots, mostly bent out of shape with sagging hundred-year-old mattresses that look like they were picked up at a prison rummage sale. The place is lit by one 40-watt bulb.

Well, it's a big disappointment, but Torrie reasons that she won't spend much time there anyway, what with all the fun things to do. Then she meets Madame Katzoff, who reads out the regulations: all the waitresses will be lined up at 6:30 a.m. in uniform. After flag-raising and the camp song, there will be instruction and the appointment of volunteers. Each waitress will have two tables of 12 kids and 3 counselors each. There will be 50-cent fines for every infraction of the rules: lateness, backtalk, spilling, dripping, unpressed uniforms, smoking, sloppy bunks, etc., etc.

For the first time Torrie asks herself, could this be a horrendous mistake?

—Diana C. Hirsch

LOVE IS THE CROOKED THING   YA
BARBARA WERSBA

Money. Rita Formica needs money, and lots of it. Rita is determined to go to Europe to find her man. And the only way to make the kind of money she needs is to write a book. Not a traditional book, but a "sizzlin' hot" paperback romance, like the ones in the grocery store. If she succeeds in this wild plan, romance will be hers. *Savage Sunset* must be written—one way or another.

—Teresa Schlatt

LOVE LETTERS   Grades 7–8/YA
OF J. TIMOTHY OWEN
By CONSTANCE C. GREENE

Owen is one of the last romantics. When, in the same day, he discovers a book—*One Hundred of the World's Best Love Letters*—and gorgeous Sophie, his imagination runs wild, and the result is disaster!

—Linda Lee

LUCIFER'S HAMMER YA
By LARRY NIVEN and JERRY POURNELLE

When they first found the comet, it was a great scientific discovery—it would pass closer to Earth than any other comet ever had. Then someone said, "What if it comes so close it hits Earth?" The chance that it would was one in a million, then one in a thousand, then a hundred, then ten—and then it did hit, and earth and its inhabitants were all but destroyed. The lucky ones went first. They didn't have to struggle desperately for survival, fighting not only the dangerous new environment but the others who had been left. For this disaster seemed to bring out the worst in people, and survivors spent a lot of time fighting each other.

Civilization was all but wiped out, modern society completely gone. Life went back to what it had been thousands of years before. An Ice Age began; the climate and the entire face of the earth were completely changed. Suddenly the human race was an endangered species! [You may wish to add a description of the changes in climate and geography in your own area. I used to say, "What was once the California coast no longer existed, and the San Joaquin Valley became the San Joaquin Sea."]

—Joni Bodart-Talbot

THE MAGIC FINGER Grades 3–6
By ROALD DAHL

I can't tell you just how I do it, because I don't even know myself.

The tip of my right hand begins to tingle most terribly, and suddenly a sort of flash comes out of me, a quick white flash, like something electric. It jumps out and touches the person who has made me cross . . . [long pause] . . . and . . .

I can't stand hunting. I just can't stand it! I used to try and stop Phillip and William from doing it, but then one day I saw them with their father coming out of the woods carrying a lovely deer!

Well, that did it!

I put the magic finger on them all. And there was no taking it off again.

If you want to find out what I did to them, put *your* fingers on the book that I'm in, *The Magic Finger*, by Roald Dahl, and watch my magic work on *you!*

—Michelle Pollock

MAKRA CHORIA Grades 7–8/YA
By ARDATH MAYHAR

Power corrupts; absolute power corrupts absolutely—and when given to someone with a twisted mind and a tainted perspective, absolute power can become absolute evil. And that is what has taken place on Sherath. Can the planet survive with a completely evil ruler? Is there any way to keep her from the throne?

—*Joni Bodart-Talbot*

A MATTER OF PRINCIPLE YA
By SUSAN BETH PFEFFER

Sometimes you can't choose the principle you're going to fight for; instead, it chooses you. This is what happens to Becca Holtz and her friends. Angered because their school newspaper sponsor won't let them publish an article they have written about students choosing the teachers for their courses, they decide to solve the problem in another way.

They start their own underground newspaper, "The Shaft." Their first issue contains the original article about student choice of teachers and some other excellent ones about student life at Southfield High. Unfortunately, it also has one rather cruel cartoon about their newspaper sponsor and the school principal.

Becca finds herself called into the principal's office and forced to make a decision—either be suspended indefinitely from school or apologize to the student body for her part in "The Shaft," and then be readmitted. Since Becca feels her First Amendment rights have been violated, she refuses to apologize and decides to fight the suspension in court.

A Matter of Principle, by Susan Beth Pfeffer.

—*Pam Spencer*

MAUS: A SURVIVOR'S TALE YA/Adult
By ART SPIEGELMAN

This is a comic book about mice, but don't expect Mickey. Whether you are a man or a mouse, a Holocaust is just the same.

—*Jeff Blair*

ME AND MR. STENNER
By EVAN HUNTER

Grades 5-6

I really don't like him. First of all, he's always kissing my mother. Every time I turn around, he's kissing her. And his breath smells of tobacco. And on weekends he doesn't shave. And he goes around with those ratty sweaters on.

Sure, I know they're getting married as soon as the divorce comes through. Sure, he helped me bury my cat. Sure, he can be really nice, but he is not my father. And I tell him so.

Last night I asked my mother if she still liked my dad. "Yes, I like him. And I loved him, too."

"But not anymore."

"No, darling, not anymore."

"Well, I love him. And I like him, too."

"Fine."

"Do you love Mr. Stenner?"

"Yes, Abby. I love him a lot."

"I hate him."

I said that to hurt her. But how can I like Mr. Stenner and still be loyal to my dad?

Me and Mr. Stenner, by Evan Hunter.

—*Dee Scrogin*

ME, MYSELF AND I
By JANE LOUISE CURRY

Grades 6-8/YA

I don't think there's anyone who hasn't seen or heard of *Back to the Future* and how Michael J. Fox went back in time and changed his parents from nerds to winners. But what if you could go back in time and change *yourself*? Make sure your project was the one to make millions of dollars, and make sure you got the foxy blonde and the Jag XKE? Sounds hard to resist, doesn't it? And JJ didn't even try to resist—he just went for it! And ended up four years in the past, face to face with himself, four years younger. And then when their plans don't work, they try again, *both* of them going back four more years to meet Mutt, who's the boy they used to be.

The only problem is, they don't realize how many problems you can create when you start changing people's lives, thir successes and their failures. And just like Michael Fox, JJ and Jacko suddenly discover that unless they can fix things up so they *do* exist in the future, they are simply going to fade away. Do they make it? Read *Me, Myself and I* and find out!

—Joni Bodart-Talbot

ME, THE BEEF AND THE BUM YA/Adult
By CHARLES HAMMER

Hi, I'm Rosie Matlock. I'm from Kansas. I am in 4-H. You city kids may not know what that is. It's a club for kids, and we do stuff like raise animals or sew, or stuff like that, and then we take it to fairs to win prizes. I myself am into cows—well, one in particular: George, my "pet" steer. Ya, you heard me. Some people have dogs; me, I've got a hunk of beef. And that's how I got myself into a real mess.

It started out OK. I mean, I won tenth place showing George at the American Royal, a big livestock show in KC. But after the show, they always auction off the animals to the highest bidder, and in George's case it was a sausage company, not even steaks! And all of a sudden, I knew that I could never see George stuffed into some sausage casing— not and ever eat again. So me and George ran away—which isn't exactly easy to do in downtown KC, Mo. I mean steers aren't exactly commonplace on city sidewalks. Anyway, that's how I met Mett. No, I didn't stutter, his name is Mett. Mett Halsey is, or was, a bum, hanging around the train yards in KC. And, being as how he didn't have much else better to do, he ran away with us.

Ya, we had problems when we ran away, like avoiding the cops, some crooks who chased us, finding food, and quicksand, all in the Flint Hills in Kansas, but I learned a lot, too. And you can read all about it in *Me, the Beef and the Bum,* by Charles Hammer.

—Sue Ann Seel

MEDICINE WALK Grades 7–8/YA
By ARDATH MAYHAR

The plane came to rest under a desert cottonwood tree. If Burr wanted to live he'd have to leave his dead father and start walking over the hot summer desert. He might not get anywhere, but he could not give up.

—Teresa Schlatt

MIDNIGHT HOUR ENCORES YA
By BRUCE BROOKS

Every year, Taxi asks her if she'd like to go see her mother, and every year Sib refuses.

Her mother had left her and her father when Sib was only one day old—they hadn't seen her since. But Taxi (her dad) knew where she was—in San Francisco. At sixteen, Sib is one of the greatest cellists in the world. She has an audition for a music school in San Francisco and tells Taxi she wants to see her mother. It's a long trip in an old '60s style VW bus from the East Coast to the West Coast, and from the '80s to the '60s, as Taxi tries to show his daughter what her mother was like when he knew her. She hears Bob Dylan and Bo Diddley and bizarre stories of hippie life. And along the way, she and Taxi compose a song—the Love and Peace Shuffle, which turns out to say more than either of them thought it might. Because when they get to the city, they discover Sib's mother isn't into macrame and Indian folklore any-more—she's into architecture, and nothing is anything like they'd ex-pected it to be.

—Joni Bodart-Talbot

MILLIE'S BOY Grades 6-8/YA
By ROBERT NEWTON PECK

All I could see was the big orange blast of the explosion. I thought I heard voices and boots scraping on the floor, but I wasn't sure because my ears were ringing. I could smell the stench of burned sulfur—gunpowder. Then I felt the wrenching pain in my gut. I'd been shot.

A hot pain in my belly overtook me, and when I moved I thought my insides were on fire. I tried to crawl, but instead I curled up. My head slid real easy along the floor and then I realized I was skidding in the slime of my own blood.

"Millie, Millie, I'm hit and bleeding. You in bed?" I asked.

I pulled myself to Millie's bed, but all I could feel was an empty bot-tle. I was hurting and bleeding real bad and knew I couldn't just stay there or I'd bleed to death.

What got me up was the wagon I heard outside the window. I stood up all doubled over, but by the time I hobbled to the window the wagon had turned the corner. Leaning on the windowsill I knew I had to get down the stairs to Doc Cushing's. I wondered where my mother was. Millie, that's what she made me call her. I decided I had walked to the window, I could walk to Doc's. Then I tripped over something.

I felt on the floor. It was Millie. I knew because I found her arm with all the bracelets and then I felt the bullet-torn flesh. She was warm, but dead.

I had to get out of there. I needed to get my bleeding stopped and I had to find out who killed Millie, and why.

Millie's Boy, by Robert Newton Peck.

—*Karen Cole*

THE MIRRORSTONE   Grades 7–8/YA
By MICHAEL PALIN and others

Paul was brushing his teeth when he became aware of a strange sensation, as if he were being watched . . . . He heard a noise, and it was coming from the direction of the mirror. Slowly Paul turned towards the mirror and saw the face of a boy. "What do you want?" cried Paul. The boy said nothing, but he stretched out his hand, beckoning Paul to follow him.

—*Janet Loebel*

MISERY   YA/Adult
By STEPHEN KING

This is the book Stephen King called a love letter to his fans—the kind only he could write. Paul has written four books about Misery Chastain, and he has hated every line! He has finally killed her off at the end of the fourth book and is drunk with both joy and liquor, celebrating her demise, when he has a wreck. He's rescued by a woman who calles herself his "greatest fan." She is a nurse named Annie and she's crazy, really crazy. His body was shattered by the wreck—legs, pelvis, ribs. Annie patches him back together, but not very well! Then she reads that fourth book and discovers he's killed her favorite person in the whole world—Misery Chastain. She goes to his room, slams the book down on his legs, and tells him he must bring Misery Chastain back to life. So he begins, and she *hates* it. He just goes back several days before Misery died and brings her out of her coma. Annie reads it and she's livid. "You *cheated*!" she screams, "you have to start with the last page and go on! Figure out a way to bring her back to life. You're a writer—write!" So he starts again, bringing back to life the woman whose death he was celebrating when he wrecked his car and ended up the prisoner of this sociopath, who has already promised to kill him if he doesn't finish the fifth book and who he knows will never let him go free even if he does!

—*Joni Bodart-Talbot*

MONDAY IN ODESSA   Grades 5–8
By EILEEN BLUESTONE SHERMAN

Imagine yourself trapped in a society that persecutes you for your religious beliefs but still refuses you the right to live elsewhere. This is the way 400,000 Soviet Jews have to live today.

On Monday mornings in Odessa, a large city in the Soviet Union, Jews who have applied for an exit visa learn if it has been granted. There are always tears. Some cry for joy; others weep bitterly. Most will not hear their names at all and will wait another fearful week in a country that has labeled them "traitors." But twelve-year-old Marina Birger doesn't want her parents to apply for an exit visa. Her mother and father are highly respected employees in Odessa's largest hospital. Besides, her parents don't seem to care about religion. Marina knows nothing about Judaism except it's a subject not to be mentioned in public.

"I won't go!" Marina cries. She is determined to change her parents' plan—a plan that could cost the Birger family their jobs, their friends, their safety, even their lives.

Marina has only one chance: if she can be chosen for the finals of Odessa's story-telling contest, Marina is sure her parents will see things her way. There's no doubt she's the best, but will the judges select a Jew to represent their school in the citywide finals?

Marina is chosen. Her parents postpone their plans and suddenly handsome Misha Pasternack is paying a lot of attention to the newest "star" in Odessa. In spite of all her problems, Marina is happy.

Only when Misha's uncle is brutally beaten and Marina's parents are persecuted because they help the bleeding old man does Marina realize that no award can ever shield her from the realities of Russian society.

But now they have no exit visa. Will they be able to escape? Or will Marina's selfishness mean they have to stay in the Soviet Union forever?

—*Eileen Bluestone Sherman*

THE MOVES MAKE THE MAN   YA
By BRUCE BROOKS

Bammata! Bammata! Bammata! Bam!

Basketball is Jerome Foxworthing's life, and he is good. Reverse spin, triple pump, reverse dribble, stutter step with a twist to the left, blind pass—"These are me!" thinks the Jayfox. (That's what Jerome calls himself.) "Yes sir, the moves make the man and moves make me."

Jerome is special and some people think he's cocky, but really he's just good at everything. He's intelligent, he knows who he is and likes himself. He's a happy survivor, and he is black, the youngest of three sons of a wonderful momma.

The very week before school is to start, life shifts for Jerome. Due to redistricting, he finds himself the only black student in a large, all-white junior high. The "crackers" were letting the "jiggaboos" in. But the Jayfox is cool, and he will survive.

Bammata! Bammata! Bam! Jerome loves to practice and practice he does, on the secret court he discovers in the woods. It's the "fake" moves he enjoys the most. Darting right then left, forward then back—he's going to outfox the best.

When Momma is in an accident and must be hospitalized for a long period of time, life again shifts for Jerome. His helpful counselor changes his schedule and puts him into a Home Economics class so he can learn to cook. One other boy is assigned to Home Ec.—Bix Rivers, a white baseball shortstop whose mother is also hospitalized.

Jerome and Bix discover they have a real bond. Both want and need to learn to cook. (By this time Jerome and his brothers are getting sick of scrambled eggs.) After days of learning the proper way of wearing and folding an apron, and some ridiculous practice making hamburger patties out of shredded paper, they finally get to cook—and an apple pie at that!

Both Bix and Jerome are dismayed at the recipe:

1/2 cup milk	2 1/2 cups of crushed Ritz crackers
1/2 cup warm water	
2 tsp cinnamon	1 pie crust
	1 cup sugar

"How much fun it is to fool people," the teacher is saying. "This pie will be so tasty no one will ever miss the apples." Bix freaks out! And from this point on, nothing is ever the same for Jerome. Read *The Moves Make the Man* to find out how Jerome learns that "If you're faking, somebody is taking. . . . There are no moves you truly make alone."

—*Elizabeth Sue Lewis*

MR. AND MRS. BOJO JONES   YA
By ANN HEAD

Respect and a sense of responsibility—not much to build a marriage on, is it? Especially when the marriage is between two crazy, mixed-up kids who have to get married. And July and BoJo not only have to contend with their own personal problems in working out a relationship satisfactory to both of them but also have to cope with alienation from their friends (since they've both dropped out of high school), two sets of overprotective and feuding parents, and the problems of making a living. BoJo has a football scholarship for college next year, but that's out of the question now. How BoJo and July meet these problems and how they handle an experience that would break up even a settled couple is the story told here. Dating and marriage are very different, as July and BoJo find out, and it takes more than sharing an apartment to make a marriage work.

To find out if the Joneses made theirs a success, read *Mr. and Mrs. BoJo Jones,* by Ann Head.

—Joni Bodart-Talbot

MRS. PIGGLE-WIGGLE   Grades k-3
By BETTY MacDONALD

Hubert Egbert Prentiss was a spoiled brat. His grandfather had given him every possible toy a little boy could want. He had an electric trains with tracks that went four times around his bedroom. He also had 1,500 toy soldiers, a real little typewriter, a real desk and radio and two cars large enough for two children to ride in. He had a hundred or more airplanes and little cars and a fire engine with real sirens and lights. And that wasn't all—any toy you could think of, Hubert had it. The problem was, Hubert would not pick up his toys. Hubert's mother picked up after him, until one day his room was such a mess all she could do was close the door and go downstairs. Then she called Mrs. Piggle-Wiggle, who gave her the Won't-Pick-Up-Toys Cure. Mrs. Piggle-Wiggle said, "Starting now, don't pick up any of Hubert's toys. Don't make his bed. In fact, do not go into his room. When his room gets so messy he can't get out of it, call me."

On the seventh day of the cure, Hubert could not get out of his room. Food was passed up to his window on the tines of the rake. His father tied the hose to the rake while Hubert put his mouth to the window opening and tried to get a few drops.

How did Hubert get out of his room?
Read *Mrs. Piggle-Wiggle*, and find out.

—Jeanne McKenzie

MURPHY'S BOY   Adult
By TOREY L. HAYDEN

Torey Hayden was happy enough, all things considered. She was working as a clinical psychologist and receiving recognition for her work. She had a good salary and more free time than she'd ever had before. Then came Zoo-boy. His name was Kevin Richter; he was fifteen years old. No one called him Kevin, though; they called him Zoo-boy. He had earned his nickname because he spent all his waking hours under tables, chairs lined up in front of him and around the perimeter of the table until he was secure behind a protective barrier of wooden legs. He sat, rocked sometimes, ate, did his schoolwork, watched TV. He lived in his little self-built cage. Kevin did not talk, nor did he make any noise when he wept. He was an elective mute. He was physically capable of speaking but for psychological reasons refused to do so. Kevin lived in fear of everything. He had been severely deprived and abused in childhood, had spent years in institutions, demonstrated violent and aggressive behavior, and was the kid nobody wanted. Torey didn't especially want the case because right from the beginning the hopelessness shone through. Kevin sounded like a lost cause. Many times Torey almost threw in the towel. But she never did. And with patience and love, she made a miracle happen.

—Judy Druse

MY BROTHER SAM IS DEAD   Grades 6-8
By JAMES LINCOLN COLLIER and CHRISTOPHER COLLIER

If you have a brother (or a sister) you know that brothers and sisters often disagree. It happens all the time. But this disagreement was *really* serious. Tim had tried to change his brother Sam's mind. It was bad enough that Sam was leaving home to join the Rebel army. But that he was planning to take Brown Bess—Father's gun—was unthinkable. Father was loyal to the British king and opposed to the war of rebellion.

But Sam wouldn't listen. And the argument that Sam had with Father was terrible. Tim overheard the whole thing. First, Father's raised voice. And then Sam's. Father yelling, "You are not having the gun!" Then more shouting. And finally, Father telling Sam to get out. The slamming of the door. And then another sound—a sound which Tim had never heard. It was Father, crying.

What was happening to this family? What was happening to this country? For the first time, the war was beginning to seem real to Tim. And he didn't know who was right. He didn't know what he believed.

What choices does Tim face, and what decisions will he make? What happens to his brother Sam?

For an inside look at how the war for independence affected one family, read *My Brother Sam Is Dead,* which was written by brothers, James Lincoln Collier and Christopher Collier.

—*Wanda Adams*

MY DARLING, MY HAMBURGER   YA
By PAUL ZINDEL

Told in the form of notes passed back and forth in class, plus diary entries, essays, and such, this is the story of what happened to Maggie and Liz and Sean and Dennis. . . . The first note tells about what happened in health class—the gym teacher was having a session on sex for the girls in her class. Afterwards she invited questions—well, one hesitant girl asked what to do, etc., etc. . . . well, what do you *do*? "Suggest going out for a hamburger," was the teacher's brilliant reply! Yes, well, the class members thought about the same thing of that answer as you do—it's not really helpful, to say the least. Face an endless stream of hamburgers or wind up in the same situation as before. The rest of *My Darling, My Hamburger* tells the story of how Liz handled "that situation" in *her* way.

—*Carol Starr*

MY FATHER'S DRAGON   Grades 2–4
By RUTH STILES GANNETT

What would you do if you met a cat who could talk? Would you be his friend? Would you tell him your secret wishes? My father did. His wish was to fly. And the cat knew a way for him to do it. But it wouldn't be easy, because he wasn't talking about flying a plane. He was talking about flying a dragon, a baby dragon with a long tail and yellow and blue stripes and golden wings. The dragon was being held against his will and overworked and treated badly by other animals in a place called Wild Island. The mere mention of the island was enough to make a fisherman shake, and all he could say was, "Many people have explored Wild Island, but no one has come back alive. I think they were eaten by the wild animals." If you were my father, would you try to make your wish come true? What adventures would await you if you did? Read *My Father's Dragon* and find out.

—*Janice Lauer*

MY FIRST LOVE AND OTHER DISASTERS   YA
By FRANCINE PASCAL

Jimmy was the kind of guy that everyone, girls and guys alike, wanted to hang out with. He had been president of his class for two years, he was captain of the tennis team, and he had a sensational body. Victoria decided that Jimmy, whom she would call Jim, was the boy for her.

The first time she talked to him was at the shoe store where he worked. She ended up buying some shoes that were way too small, so that he wouldn't think she had big feet. Then during summer vacation Victoria took a job as a mother's helper on Fire Island so she could be near Jim. On her first day, Victoria talked to Barry, Jim's best friend, and when Jim arrived he thought that Victoria was Barry's girlfriend. Things got more mixed up when Barry told her that he loved her. Of course, Victoria's main job on the island was not chasing after Jim but after the two children she was responsible for, and sometimes what she *wanted* to do didn't go along with what she *had* to do. To find out how she managed, read *My First Love and Other Disasters*, by Francine Pascal.

—*Mary Hedge*

MY LIFE AS A BODY   YA
By NORMA KLEIN

The last thing I wanted to do was spend my senior year tutoring Sam Feldman. Even Claudia said I was crazy to do it—but then she's always said I was weird, just weird enough to be her friend. She had her own problems that year—the fluffy-headed innocent blonde girls she always fell for were only interested in dating boys. Before I met Claudia, I thought being gay would be easier—now I'm not so sure.

But whether I wanted to be Sam's tutor or not, Mr. Strauch, our principal, made me an offer I couldn't refuse—for Sam's good and my own, he said. I was too supercilious, too contemptuous of other students who weren't as smart as I was. Working with Sam would give me a different perspective. He'd transferred from a high school in California, a math and computer expert, an athlete, and the son of obscenely rich parents—he had everything. Then three months before school started, he was in a car wreck and lost it all, ending up in a wheelchair, with brain damage that kept him from speaking or thinking clearly. But it might all be temporary—and that's where I and the physical therapist came in. She worked with his legs, I worked with his mind. And even though I was repulsed the first time I saw him, gradually he became more than just a cripple; he became a person—a beautiful person. And perhaps I did too. Miss O'Connell was right when she gave us that first English assignment that year—"My own experiences as a body." That's how it began. And how it ended—well, I'll let you find that out for yourselves, as you discover what happened during *My Life as a Body*.

—*Joni Bodart-Talbot*

MY MAMA SAYS THERE AREN'T ANY   Grades 2–5
ZOMBIES, GHOSTS, VAMPIRES, CREATURES,
DEMONS, MONSTERS, FIENDS, GOBLINS, OR THINGS
By JUDITH VIORST

My mama says there aren't any vampires flying over my house in red and black vampire capes. But how can I believe her, when she said my wiggly tooth would fall out last Thursday and it stayed in till Sunday lunch? So—even mamas make mistakes.

My mama says that a zombie with his eyes rolled back in his head and his arms out stiff is *not* clonking up the stairs. But this morning my mama made me wear boots and it didn't rain! So—even mamas make mistakes. Sometimes in my bunk bed I start thinking that a fiend has sneaked into the bottom bunk and he's sniffing around for a boy to eat and *I'm* the boy he's sniffing for. My mama says no fiends have sneaked in here. But even mamas make mistakes. To find out more about what my mama says, read *My Mama Says There Aren't Any Zombies, Ghosts, Vampires, Creatures, Demons, Monsters, Fiends, Goblins, or Things,* by Judith Viorst.

—*Deborah Rowley*

MY SIDE OF THE MOUNTAIN   Grades 4–8
By JEAN GEORGE

Survival? Alone in the wilderness? For a year? My father laughed at me and told me the story of the day he had run away from home to board a tramp steamer. He had hidden away on the ship, but when the whistle blew and he knew the ship was sailing, he ran down the gangplank and was home in bed before anyone knew he was gone. Then he said, "Sure, go ahead and try. Every boy should try."

In the beginning, I didn't even know how to build a fire. Before I left New York, I bought a flint and steel, a penknife, a ball of cord and an ax. My first night on the mountain was wet, cold, and miserable. Discouraged, I walked down out of the woods to the highway. When I stopped at the first house I saw, the old man who lived there taught me the one skill that I needed most to survive. He taught me how to use that flint and steel. I could now make a fire. I was ready to return and conquer the Catskill Mountains.

I am certain my father didn't expect me to last the night through. I am here now, inside my tree home that people have passed without even guessing I am here. This old hemlock tree must be six feet in diameter and as old as the mountain itself. Hollowed out, it makes a room for my bed, a fireplace, and my food. A deerskin flap covers the door.

It is now deep into December and the snow outside has piled higher than my deerskin door. I am snug and happy inside my tree home.

I dine on turtle soup, acorn-flour pancakes, nuts, dried fruit and wild vegetables, and venison. Those hunters will never guess the great favor they did for me last fall. They weren't too careful to follow up on every shot, and I didn't waste anything they left behind. Thanks to their carelessness, I have enough meat to last through the snow—I hope.

One reason I've been successful at staying here on the mountain is that I've been able so far to avoid contact with anyone who might want to take me back home. Once I spotted a Ranger waiting just outside my tree home. I had been careless with my cooking fire and my left-over food. I had to hide in the woods until he gave up.

This time, I could hear someone coming, but I couldn't see him. His boots stopped just outside my door. Had he come to take me back to the city? I was so terrified I could see my heart pounding and lifting my sweater as I lay there in the dark tree and waited.

My Side of the Mountain, by Jean George

—Linda Henderson

NATURE'S END   YA/Adult
By WHITLEY STREIBER and JANOS KUNETKA

The world ends—not with a shout, but a cough, a whimper—as mankind destroys the planet we live on.

In 1988, no one thought much about crowded freeways, LA and NYC gridlock, about plants being destroyed by pollutants, about stationary high-pressure systems and their effects on people in Denver, LA, and other cities. No one ever imagined that forests could be destroyed by pollution, that the green farmland of the Midwest might turn into a desert, or that a man in favor of killing almost half of Earth's population would have a chance to become the ruler of the planet.

But it happened—and there are only four people in the world who are trying save their planet in all its beauty, to expose this madman, show his true self to the people of Earth. In doing this, they have exposed themselves to him and his power—and his power is far greater than they and their computers have ever guessed.

They have only one out—only one hope. Somewhere there's a place called Magic. If they can find that, maybe then they will have a chance.

—*Joni Bodart-Talbot*

NECESSARY PARTIES   Grades 6–8/YA
By BARBARA DANA

I guess you could call this book a kind of self-help manual for kids whose parents are getting a divorce. Actually it's the journal I wrote when my own parents were going through the process. But don't get me wrong. It's not about how to cope with the pain and the anger; grown-ups will tell you plenty about all of that. What gets me is how they all talk a lot about how much it affects kids, but then they go on and do it anyway. Well, I decided it was time we kids did something too. So I hired a lawyer, and we discovered this interesting legal clause about "necessary parties." . . . But wait a minute, why am I telling you all this? You can read about it in my journal. After all, that's why I wrote it!

—*Margie Reitsma*

NETTIE'S TRIP SOUTH   Grades 4–8
By ANN TURNER

Dear Addie,

You asked me to tell you everything about my trip south. Let me tell you about the things I remember most. Though I'm only ten, I saw the slaves, I saw the South. I remember the sweet smell of cedar in the air, and I also remember Tabitha, the black slave in the hotel who had no last name. The slave shacks on the plantation had heaps of rags in the corners for beds. . . . Some animals live better, Addie.

Most of all I remember the slave auction and the two children, children just about our age. They clasped hands but were bought by different men, and the man in the white hat had to tear them apart. I threw up, Addie, right there with all the men and ladies about. I wanted to cry.

Addie, I can't get this out of my thoughts: If we slipped into a black skin like a tight coat, everything would change.

Write soon, dear Addie. I miss you, and I have bad dreams at night.

Love,
Nettie
—*Janet Loebel*

THE NEW KID ON THE BLOCK Grades 3-6
By JACK PRELUTSKY

Slimy-faced creatures beneath the stair,
Snillies who hop and skip here and there,
Floradora Doe who talks to her plants,
And Uncanny Colleen who got washed with the pants,
These are just a few of the sights that will shock
You when you read *The New Kid on the Block*.
(And just be glad your nose is on your face!)

—*Pam Swofford*

NIGHT KITES YA
By M. E. KERR

I used to think that India was the only country in the world that had untouchables. I was wrong; my older brother Pete is an untouchable, and he lives right here in the good old US of A. Pete is a homosexual and he's dying of AIDS. I think my dad is afraid that we'll all become untouchables if the people in our town find out about Pete. So we're not supposed to tell anyone; it's a secret. Just like my long afternoons with Nicki Marr in her room. My folks still think I'm dating my old girlfriend Dill; they don't know that I have my own secret. I've fallen in love with my best friend's girl. I'm finding out that there are all kinds of ways of becoming an untouchable.

—Margie Reitsma

NIGHT OF THE TWISTERS Grades 4–6
By IVY RUCKMAN

I remember how nice and peaceful it was at mealtime six months ago. That was before Ryan, my baby brother, was born. Now everyone, and I mean everyone, pays more attention to him than me. I rank second to whatever cutsey sound Ryan is experimenting with. Dad's head swivels like a machine gun at each "blug," and Mom gets up at the slightest "unnnh." Now even my best friend Arthur has started making eyes at Ryan and tickling and cooing at him. It's positively sickening. And our cat got banned from the table for licking Ryan's face. Ryan even took over my room! *I* got moved into the den so that they could put bunnies all over the walls!

Today, though, has been the absolute worst. On top of the weather being all hot and muggy, Ryan's been screaming at the top of his lungs because he is cutting teeth. All's pretty quiet right now; Ryan's asleep, Dad went to Grandpa and Grandma's to work on the tractor, Mom's sewing, and Arthur and I are watching TV. The weather, though, is another thing. It was while we were watching TV that the first tornado-watch announcement came on. That's really no big deal; I've spent a lot of nights in the basement during tornado season, but for some reason, Mom took this one real seriously. She decided to go tell Mrs. Smiley, a nice old lady who lives down the street, about the storm watch. Before she left, she made me and Arthur take a flashlight and a blanket down to the basement bathroom.

Not long after I had brought them downstairs the sirens started screaming, louder than Ryan. And then they died, just as if someone had cut the line. It was deathly quiet outside, and Arthur and I had just decided there was nothing to worry about when the sirens came again. The lights flickered, and I decided I had better get Ryan, but he was sleeping so nicely I chose to leave him where he was. When I got back to the living room the TV was flashing the Civil Defense Emergency signal. That's when I decided I couldn't wait for Mom any longer, I had to get Ryan. As I ran to his room, the lights started flickering again and there were these really strange sucking noises coming from the kitchen and bathroom drains. I yelled to Arthur to get into the basement. Just as I reached Ryan's door, the lights went out for good.

To find out what happens to Dan, Arthur, and their families, read this exciting book, *Night of the Twisters,* by Ivy Ruckman—based on the day the tornadoes hit Grand Island, Nebraska.

—*Janet Knabe*

NIGHT SHIFT YA/Adult
By STEPHEN KING

Let's talk about fear. We won't raise our voices and we won't scream. We'll talk very rationally about the kind of fear that takes you to the rim of madness and perhaps even over the edge.

Night Shift is about fear. It is an excursion into horror, a collection of stories about horrible things . . . about trucks—seventy, eighty, a hundred heavy Mack trucks, trailer trucks that suddenly start up without drivers, surrounding a small restaurant, holding the people inside as hostages; . . . about a laundry pressing machine called the Mangler because it caught a worker by the hand, dragged and sucked her in, and what was left they took out in a basket; . . . about rats on the third floor of a fiber mill, huge fat-bellied creatures with rabid eyes, rats that only come out of their corners during the graveyard shift between 11 p.m. and 7 a.m. to sit and watch the workers with their unblinking black eyes; . . . about the Boogeyman who comes out of the shadows by the closet in the children's room and one by one kills all the Billings children. . . .

Night Shift is about fear—fear of rats, fear of trucks, fear of the Mangler, fear of the Boogeyman, and other fears we may be afraid to talk about. . . . Stephen King, the author of *Carrie, CuJo, Christine,* and other horror stories, shows us our fears in *Night Shift.*

—*Jacqueline Brown Woody*

THE NIGHT THE MONSTER CAME Grades 3-6
By MARY CALHOUN

Andy was afraid of monsters. He was afraid of Frankenstein's monster. He was afraid of giant army ants. But what really scared him was Bigfoot. The man-beast ten feet tall.

Andy was a decent kid who sometimes pulled younger children in their wagons. He was a decent kid who sometimes lied.

"No, of course I'm not afraid," he said, when his parents left him alone in the house at night. After all he was nine years old, too old to be afraid. Not *really* afraid.

All the boys at Cub Scouts said they were scared of Bigfoot. But they laughed about Bigfoot, too. They didn't have to stay alone at night in the last house on the way to the Great North Woods. The Great North Woods where the monster lived.

Alone in the house, Andy was about to turn off the TV and go to bed early when he heard the thumping. Something was thumping against the house.

Oh, no! He was trying not to imagine things. He was *trying* to be sensible and brave, and things wouldn't cooperate.

THUMP-BUMP!

It's a tree branch. The wind is blowing a tree branch against the house. (His heart was going THUMP-BUMP too.) Or it's the neighbor dogs. The dogs are after the garbage again.

Except that Mom had brought the garbage can inside, in case it was attracting something, and the bumping and brushing sounds weren't out in back. The sounds were in front right on the other side of the livingroom wall.

Run upstairs and hide in a closet!

Like a scaredy cat.

All right, then, I'll just look!

Andy made his legs walk to the front door. He made his eyes look out the narrow window slit up and down in the door.

And he saw fur.

His head felt light. Sparks flashed in his eyes. He was going to faint.

Instead, the fur started to slide down. Next the *face* would look in the window at him. Did Andy live next door to Bigfoot?

Read *The Night the Monster Came*, by Mary Calhoun.

—*Lana Voss*

NOTE: This talk combines material from page 7 and page 44 of the book, for maximum read-aloud suspense.

NIGHT WALKERS   **Grades 7–8/YA**
By OTTO COONTZ

First the seagulls around the dump died, then a neighbor's cat was killed, and then, one by one, the children of Cloverdale came down with a strange disease. By day they slept in darkened rooms; if a light was turned on, they cried in pain—their eyes hurt. And then their skin would break out in terrible blisters. But when the sun went down, they left their darkened rooms and searched for new victims. They became

The Night Walkers, in this story by Otto Coontz.

—*Pam Spencer*

NINE PRINCES IN AMBER   YA
By ROGER ZELAZNY

He wakes up with no memory of his past. He is in a hospital bed with nothing more than a feeling he has been drugged and a strong desire to get away. Before he escapes, he extracts from a doctor the information that it was his sister who had him committed, and learning where she lives, he decides to give her a visit. When he sees her, not feeling he can trust her (or anybody else), he fishes for information without revealing his amnesia. He finds out his name is Corwin and he is in some kind of struggle with a brother named Eric who dwells in a place called Amber.

He stays at his sister's house, and the next day there is a visit by another brother named Random. He is being chased by six individuals that turn out to be not quite human. They have the general appearance of humans, but they have uniformly bloodshot eyes, sharp forward-curving spurs on the backs of their hands, and mouths full of long, sharp teeth. The brothers and sister manage to dispatch the creatures and Corwin finds out they were from "the shadows" . . . whatever that means.

Corwin's memory starts coming back very slowly, and although he still does not understand the situation, he is determined to oppose Eric. So on a drive the next day with Random, he suggests going on to Amber. As the scenery changes, as the sidewalks begin to sparkle and the sky turns green, it becomes apparent that Corwin is starting on a journey that will be a little farther than he expected.

—*Brian Fowler*

NO DRAGONS TO SLAY   YA
By JAN GREENBERG

Very little that had happened to seventeen-year-old Thomas Newman in the last six months was fair. Six months ago, he got sick. It wasn't a simple matter of taking two aspirins and drinking plenty of chicken soup. Instead, his whole life was turned around. He lost his hair, they pumped his body full of drugs, and most of the time he dragged around like some zombie escaped from Transylvania. It wasn't a nervous condition, so don't think he went bananas and ended up in a loony bin. However, there'd been times in the last six months he would have gladly traded places in a minute with some poor crazy.

When his hip started to throb during soccer practice one day, he didn't worry about it too much. But when the pain didn't go away and a hard lump formed, Thomas could no longer pretend nothing was wrong. The doctor diagnosed an inoperable, malignant tumor on his hip. Dr. Myerson point-blank told Thomas that the next eighteen months would be hell. There would be radiation followed by months of chemotherapy, with no guarantee of recovery. However, when it was all over, he might have his life back.

For Thomas, who had always prided himself on being strong and un-complaining, it was difficult to accept that he needed the help of others. However, he was eventually forced to fall back on his own inner strength because his parents' concern did not let them give him the sup-port he needed, and his friends didn't know how to react. They felt un-comfortable around him, so Thomas became more of a loner than ever. Although he wouldn't admit it, his loneliness was as painful as the dis-ease he was suffering.

Then his mother introduced him to Ana Zacharian, a young archae-ologist who treated him like a normal person and encouraged him to participate in a Midwest dig. He couldn't just lie around home concen-trating on getting well, so he went to work on the dig. Though his treat-ment had caused him to lose all his hair, suffer bouts of nausea and pain, and lose weight, the people at the dig accepted him as a person, not a freak. He began to make new friends—even got a girlfriend. Then, an accident almost killed one of his new friends. It changed Thomas' life, because it made him realize that everyone was vulnerable. He ceased to want someone or something to blame; he no longer needed to look for a dragon to slay.

—Judy Druse

NO LANGUAGE BUT A CRY YA/Adult
By RICHARD D'AMBROSIO

[Read Tennyson quote
> . . . But what am I?
> An infant crying in the night.
> An infant crying for the light:
> And with no language but a cry.]

This is a true story. It is the story of a girl the author calls Laura. Laura was an abused child, a battered child, and the experience she went through as an infant left scars not only on her body but also on her mind. She didn't talk for the first twelve years of her life. Richard D'Ambrosio is the psychologist who persuaded her that the world was not the completely hostile place she thought it must be.

Laura's parents were alcoholics. They lived in a cheap apartment over a bakery, and the neighbors complained frequently about Laura's crying. In fact, her father (who went in for killing cats when he was drunk—once he even poured gasoline on one and set it alight) said the reason they did what they did to Laura was that "she cried too much." She was brought into the hospital emergency ward by a police ambulance with second-degree burns over more than fifty percent of her body. She was barely a year old. Her parents had gotten drunk and put her in a frying pan over an open flame.

Today Laura is a nurse, and she is well. This is a story of a doctor who wouldn't give up, and who finally convinced Laura that she *did* have a life worth living.

—Joni Bodart-Talbot

NO MAN FOR MURDER   YA
By MEL ELLIS

"Jake Tabor, someday somebody is going to kill you. You hear me, Jake? Somebody is going to kill you!"

When I hurled those words in anger, I never knew how they would come to haunt me.

So here's my name in the paper. Here's my picture on the front page of the Coulee City newspaper. There's a picture of my mother with tears on her cheeks, and my father with his mouth in such a hard line you can't even see his lips.

Even my two brothers, when they rushed home from school . . . "Is it true, Danny? Is it true? You killed a guy?"

As I come out of the courthouse after the preliminary hearing, people don't look at me. . . .

They are going to try me as an adult, not as a juvenile. My lawyer was really reassuring. No death penalty in this state, he said. And so I, a seventeen-year-old boy, might be put in prison for the rest of my life. Life as I know it would end.

The court set bail at $20,000.00. My lawyer said maybe they would be lenient. Maybe only ten years. Ten years! I'll be twenty-seven by then. That's old—old enough to have a family, maybe four or five kids. Old enough to own my own farm.

It's funny now. As I await trial, school goes on without me. Scarcely anyone comes out to the farm anymore. The telephone rarely rings. At night, I lie awake, sweating. I can't eat Mom's cooking, and my black labrador, Panther, looks at me with bewilderment.

It is all around me now. The specter—the feeling of guilt. But God help me, I didn't do it. I didn't kill Jake Tabor. But someone did. Who?

No Man for Murder, by Mel Ellis.

—*Linda Henderson*

NOBODY ELSE CAN WALK IT FOR YOU YA
By P. J. PETERSON

This is Laura's first trip as a leader of a wilderness backpacking group, the chaperone for seven lively teenagers. Laura isn't worried; at eighteen she's confident that she can lead the group safely through the mountain wilderness near their hometown.

And indeed all goes smoothly until three young men on motorcycles turn up at the group's isolated campsite. The bikers seem friendly at first, but it soon becomes clear that they have mischief and worse in mind. To avoid trouble, Laura moves the group deeper into the wilderness, sure that the cyclists can't follow. But follow they do, and now they are angry. Earlier they had been content with just taunting the group. Now they attack with sadistic fury. Laura knows their only hope is to use their wits to elude their vicious pursuers. She also knows one mistake will endanger them all.

Nobody Else Can Walk It for You, by P. J. Peterson.

—*Dee Hardtke*

NOBODY'S BABY NOW YA
By CAROL LEA BENJAMIN

Livy Singer is celebrating her fifteenth birthday and thinking what a great year this is going to be. As she blows out her birthday candles, she makes two wishes—first that she'll lose weight, and then that she'll fall in love. The second wish may be the easier to attain, as she's already met Brian Kaplan and *knows* he's the love of her life.

But then Grandma Minnie comes to stay with Livy and her parents, and Livy's entire life changes. No longer can she see Brian every afternoon after school; instead, she has to hurry home to take care of Grandma Minnie. And even though Livy misses seeing Brian, she worries about her grandmother because she's quit talking. Poor Livy, all her plans for her fifteenth year are going down the drain!

Nobody's Baby Now, by Carol Lea Benjamin.

—*Pam Spencer*

NONE OF THE ABOVE YA
By ROSEMARY WELLS

When Marsha's father remarried, she suddenly discovered she was a misfit. Her stepmother was slim, intelligent, sophisticated, and ambitious—so were her two children, Chrissy and John. Marsha didn't know about things like putting tarragon in blue cheese salad dressing, or puns, or skiing, or studying French, and she did like Day-Glo pink angora sweaters, bubblegum, and David Cassidy. But she was happy being who she was until her stepmother decided to make Marsha into someone she wasn't. No matter how Marsha tried, she couldn't be another Chrissy.

She worked hard at school and got into the college prep sections, and even got accepted at an exclusive college; she lost weight. She learned a lot of ways to fake it, but she refused to compromise in one area. She insisted on dating Raymond, who wasn't the sort of person the new Marsha should have been dating at all. He liked cars, planned to be a mechanic, and sometimes rode a motorcyle. And he wanted to marry Marsha—now, just as soon as she got out of high school.

Finally Marsha realized she had to decide—who was she? The old Marsha or the new one?

—*Joni Bodart-Talbot*

NOT SEPARATE, NOT EQUAL Grades 6–8/YA
By BRENDA WILKINSON

In 1965 in rural Georgia, blacks and whites didn't go to school together. In fact, blacks and whites didn't eat or shop or play or pray together, either. But in the fall of 1965, six black students entered the white high school and started classes. Malene Freeman was one of them, although she didn't really want to be. She didn't want to deal with the hatred, the fear, the name-calling, the prejudice. But her parents said go—and she went, along with five others. This is her story.

—*Joni Bodart-Talbot*

THE OFFICIAL KIDS' SURVIVAL　　　Grades 4-6
KIT: HOW TO DO THINGS ON YOUR OWN
By ELAINE CHABACK and PAT FORTUNATO

What do you think of first when someone tells you of a new survival book? I think of books like *The Cay*, about a boy and a blind man alone on an island, or like *Deathwatch*, about a boy stripped of his clothes by a vicious hunter and left to find his way back across the desert with no food or water. *The Official Kids' Survival Kit: How to Do Things on Your Own* is about another kind of survival—the everyday kind that involves learning how things work, how the world works, and how we can cope with things on our own. It's especially written for kids who may be spending a lot of time alone—like when your parents are working—but it can help anyone who's ever been in a home or after-school situation that was puzzling or maybe even frightening.

Some of these survival tips cover minor emergencies, like cleaning up spills or dealing with a crying baby. Others concern routine problems. Do you have to do your own laundry every week? This book will tell you how to get through with it faster—and how to avoid having so much of it to do in the first place! Do you find you don't keep your money as long as you'd like? Read the tips on stretching your allowance, or the section on finding a part-time job.

But of course once in a while you may be faced with something big—like fire, fights, a broken bone, a burglar, or losing your keys. This book can show you how to help yourself in these frightening situations when you're on your own, whether you're at home, riding the bus, or walking outside at night. This book does not promise to turn you into a perfect person who can do everything right and never make a mistake. What it can do is help you face problems, tackle them, and have a fighting chance of coming out a winner—when there's no one to rely on but *you*.
　　　　　　　　　　　　　　　　　　　　　　—Elizabeth Overmyer

OLDER MEN
By NORMA KLEIN

Older men are generous, loving, and witty. They also like to spoil little girls. Elise's father is older. In fact, he is twenty years older than her mother. And Elise is definitely spoiled. Even though she's sixteen now, he still pampers her with gifts and surprises. One day, on one of their private outings, he bought her eleven silk scarves at a store on Madison Avenue. The saleslady thought he was a little crazy, especially when he wore the lime-green scarf home. Elise's mother didn't like it much either, but she was probably just jealous. She'd always acted a little different from most mothers. Maybe that's why Elise's father put her in the mental hospital.

With her mother in the hospital, Elise went to visit her grandmother for the summer. During that visit she began to have a lot of questions about her handsome, gray-haired father. What had made her mother fall in love with an older man? Did her father really care about her mother, or did he just stick her in that hospital to get rid of her? Why did he hate his twenty-four-year-old stepdaughter, Kara? She used to be his favorite companion, when she was little. Will he hate Elise, too, when she grows up?

—Rose William

THE ONE AND ONLY CYNTHIA JANE THORNTON
By CLAUDIA MILLS
Grades 4-6

A line from Cynthia's favorite book says, 'We can . . . shape ourselves into being what we want to be." But in her fifth-grade year, that poses some problems for Cynthia. How can she be herself when Lucy, her fourth-grade sister, has been moved up to Cynthia's class for math and science, and their mother still dresses them alike? How can Cynthia possibly be her unique and fascinating self with her look-alike, dress-alike sister around?

—Olivia Jacobs

THE ONE-EYED CAT
By PAULA FOX
Grades 5-9

On Ned's eleventh birthday, his Uncle Hilary presented him with a gun—a Daisy air rifle. But Ned's father disapproved and took the gun away and hid it in the attic.

That night Ned crept into the attic and found the gun, then sneaked out of the house. He wanted to fire the gun just once. He saw a small movement in the shadows and shot at it, not really knowing what it was that he had shot. It was dark out and Ned didn't think that anyone had seen him, and he crept back into the house.

A few days later, a cat turns up in a neighbor's woodshed—a cat who has recently lost an eye. Fearful and guilt-ridden, Ned finds that he cannot confide in anyone. How will a one-eyed cat survive the cold, harsh winter? What can Ned do to help the cat without making anyone suspicious?

The One-Eyed Cat, by Paula Fox.

—*Anna Lopez*

THE ONLY OTHER CRAZY CAR BOOK   Grades 4-6
By SLOAN WALKER and ANDREW VESEY

One day just before Christmas, I woke up and saw a giant hot dog parked outside on my street. If you don't believe me, I've got a picture of it right here [show picture]. It was built by the Oscar Meyer Company to advertise its hot dogs, and my neighbor is a salesman for Oscar Meyer.

That's the craziest car I've ever seen, but Sloan Walker and Andrew Vesey have seen plenty of them. Like the Bed Buggy, which has leopard-skin pillows and sheets, a telephone and a television, and ribbed wheels so it can drive on the beach.

There's also the Kopter-Rod, with helicopter blades that spin as you go.

And there's the Geoffrey-mobile, built to carry the Toys-R-Us giraffes. The sign in front of it says it runs on potato-chip power—and everywhere it goes, kids are told to feed it potato chips. Is there such a thing as potato-chip power? Find out in *The Only Other Crazy Car Book*, by Sloan Walker and Andrew Vesey.

—*Elizabeth Overmyer*

ORDINARY PEOPLE   YA/Adult
By JUDITH GUEST

Conrad Jarrett was out, back home again, back in high school, back on the swimming team, back doing things he'd been doing before he went into the hospital eight months ago. He'd spent those eight months recuperating, healing his wrists and arms, talking to a psychiatrist. It took eight months for Dr. Crawford to help Conrad face and begin to overcome his problems—the problems that had put him in the hospital in the first place. Conrad Jarrett was probably lucky to be alive. His father had had to break down the door to get to him after Conrad had tried to commit suicide by slashing his wrists.

Now Conrad Jarrett is out. And he is faced with the same problems he had before. He still has those feelings about his brother Buck's death; about his cold, unfeeling mother; about his need to stay in control; about girls and sex, about friends. Out of every hundred people to attempt suicide, fifty try again and fifteen make it. So far Conrad hasn't tried again. But there are no guarantees.

Conrad seems very close to losing it as he tries to stay in control and survive in the outside world. When he reads in the paper that a girl whom he met in the hospital, Karen Susan Aldrich of Skokie, Illinois, has succeeded in taking her own life, it could be the push that sends him over the edge, into another desperate act.

—Alan Nichter

THE OTHER SIDE OF DARK   YA
By JOAN LOWERY NIXON

As Stacy wakes up, she feels as if she has been having a long, long dream. She looks around and realizes that she isn't in her own bed. In fact, she is in a hospital room. Slowly, carefully, she moves her hands and arms. Everything seems to work all right, but there is something wrong. "I'm only thirteen years old," she thinks "and I'm in the wrong body."

Miracle of miracles, Stacy has awakened from a coma which has lasted four years. She and her mother were shot by a stranger who broke into their home. Stacy survived. Her mother didn't.

Now Stacy is faced with a new world, full of strangers with familiar names. Donna, her big sister, is married, expecting a baby. Jan, her best friend, is beautiful—she goes out with boys, and she has a new best friend of her own. Stacy doesn't even know how to put make-up on. She doesn't know about stretch jeans. She's afraid to eat pasta salad because she doesn't know what it is.

But she knows now that her mother is dead. During the last four years, the rest of the family have adjusted to her death, but Stacy finds she is haunted by that day—by the shadowy memory of the killer's face. She knows she will identify him if she ever sees him again. He knows that, too. And he wants to make sure she doesn't get the chance.

The police question her over and over. Newspapers and television reporters fight to see her. She is called "the Sleeping Beauty." She wants to cry, scream, and yell. But the tears are locked behind the hard lump of hatred that grows and chokes and burns inside. Why? Because Stacy doesn't have a mother anymore. She has come back to life, but her mother is dead.

—*Carol Kappelmann*

OUT OF BOUNDS   YA
By LORI BOATRIGHT

Judie clearly remembers Coach Arthur's words: "Don't forget, Meier High is a lot bigger than your old school. Competition is really stiff. Maybe you ought to think more seriously about the girls' team. . . . " But Judie has her mind made up. She knows she's good. At her old school, Bookner High, she had been a star on the boys' varsity basketball team. Except for the fact that she changed in a different locker room, the guys on the team respected her abilities and treated her as an equal. Now that her family has moved, she has to start all over from the beginning again, proving that her talent is of boys' varsity caliber and that she can play as well as the best of them.

Tryouts are tiring and hard, but when the list of those who made the team is posted on the bulletin board in the hallway, Judie finds her name there. She can hardly believe her eyes! She made the boys' varsity team at Meier High! Judie feels that the toughest part is over, but she doesn't realize that the worst is yet to come.

First, Franky Warnik, a guy who also made the team, is very resentful of a girl's playing on it. When he's not shooting baskets, he's giving Judie a very hard time. Then, during Homecoming Week, Judie walks into school and sees a massive sign above the Junior Class bench. It reads: "Good Luck to All You Meier Boys! (And We Do Mean *Boys*!)." Judie is furious, but when she tells off the Pep Club member who made the sign, she ends up in the principal's office. Mr. Vance, the principal, *hates* the fact that there's a girl on the boys' varsity team in his school, and he'd love to have an excuse to kick Judie off the team. On top of all that, how can Judie get Russ, a fellow team member whom she has a crush on, to see her as a girl instead of just "one of the guys"? When life seems too confusing and complicated, Judie is really glad that her best friend Tack, who is also on the team, is there to share all her problems and worries. It's so nice to have a guy to talk to seriously, without getting involved in a romance—she thinks.

As the season moves on and the championship comes within reach, Judie has to come to terms with a lot of things. *Out of Bounds* is her story.

—*Diane Tuccillo*

OUT OF TIME   YA
Compiled by AIDEN CHAMBERS

"The Zone of Silence," by Monica Hughes

The sun beat down upon the triangle of desert and the ancient rocks bore its heat silently. Nothing seemed to move. Beneath the surface the Stranger stirred restlessly. It reached upward, searching for . . . what was it searching for? Not food—it could have eaten the nearby turtle; companionship perhaps? But there was nothing out there. Only overwhelming heat and silence. The Stranger retreated into the cold loneliness at the center of its being and waited. Sometime, sometime. . . .

Dad banked and the white houses of El Paso came up to meet them. Then he straightened out and climbed. Roger leaned back and pulled out a guidebook that was tucked into the map pocket behind Susan's seat. He flipped the pages idly. A chapter title caught his eye—"The Zone of Silence":

> The desert area of northern Mexico, at the junction of Chihuahua, Coahuila, and Durango, harbors an electronic vortex that will not permit the propagation of hertzian waves. There appears to be a magnetic field below the ground, the force of which, rising in a funnel shape past Earth's atmosphere, also attracts meteorites and other objects flying over it.

Weird, thought Roger. He glanced past the seats at the instrument panel. Dad had changed course—130 degrees—a bit off.

Beneath the rocks the Stranger stirred. What had wakened it? A dream of the last visitor? Or perhaps . . . a *new* visitor?

—Linda Olson

THE OUTSIDERS   YA
By S. E. HINTON

Ponyboy's a greaser, from the wrong side of the tracks; he has long hair and sometimes carries a switchblade, but he's a dreamer too. he lives with his older brothers, Darry and Sodapop. Their parents are dead.

Ponyboy's best and only friends are the boys in his gang—Dallas, wild, restless, hard; Steve, whose specialty is cars, both stealing and fixing; Two-Bit, a wisecracker, famous for shoplifting and his long, black-handled switchblade; and Johnny, the youngest, who looks a little like a small, dark puppy lost in a crowd.

Johnny's the gentlest and the most vulnerable of the gang, but he is the one their enemies, the Socs, the rich kids with Mustangs, choose to beat up, one night when they find him alone. From then on, Johnny carries a huge switchblade and swears that he'll kill the next guy who tries to mess with him. Not long after that, the same gang of Socs in a nasty mood find Johnny and Ponyboy alone, and Johnny gets a chance to use his blade. Then they have to split just ahead of the police.

To find out what happens next, read *The Outsiders*, by S. E. Hinton.
— *Joni Bodart-Talbot*

THE PALADIN   YA/Adult
By BRIAN GARFIELD

It was a fateful day when fifteen-year-old Christopher Creighton was summoned by his Uncle John to a mysterious appointment in London. After being sworn to silence, Christopher left school, took a long train ride, and was met at the station by a rumpled man who introduced himself as Winnie-the-Pooh and hurried him into a long, official-looking, black car.

Arriving at the British Admiralty, Christopher was ushered into an office and found himself suddenly face to face with a very familiar person: Winston Churchill, the Prime Minister of England, but also Christopher's neighbor in the country—that fat, grumpy man who lived next door.

"You told no one you were coming here?" asked Mr. Churchill. "No, I hardly knew myself," answered Christopher.

"You will call me by the code name of Tigger," said Churchill. "And you will be Christopher Robin. Your Uncle John will be called Owl, and I am about to send you on a secret mission to Belgium which may help us win the war."

While Christopher had been growing up next door, Churchill had observed special qualities in the boy, qualities that would make him a perfect spy: intelligence, courage, quick wits, an uncanny ability to wriggle out of any tight spot, and an unbelievably innocent face.

So Christopher found himself going off to Belgium as a personal favor for his fat neighbor, on the surface just to visit a school friend who happened to live in a castle where important policy meetings were held. Christopher was to secretly gather any information he might overhear at these meetings and report it back to England. For someone as smart as Christopher, this was not at all difficult . . . until the Germans invaded Belgium and moved into the castle as well.

—*Catherine G. Edgerton*

THE PAST THROUGH TOMORROW   YA/Adult
By ROBERT HEINLEIN

Some science fiction authors write many unconnected stories. Heinlein, on the other hand, has written many stories that fit together, forming a "Future History" series. They are collected in this book. In fact, Heinlein has drawn up a huge chart of "Future History" which includes main events and important technological advances, starting in the late 1980s and going into the twenty-second century.

These stories are among the most famous of his works, and are where some of his best known and most durable characters originated. For instance, there's Lazarus Long, the oldest person in the world, who also has a leading role in several of Heinlein's later books. And D. D. Harriman, "the man who sold the Moon," in the story by the same name. In "Requiem," Harriman finally does get to go to the Moon. Johnny Dahlquist, in "The Long Watch," can make a Geiger counter go crazy just by blowing cigarette smoke at it. Holly Jones, at fifteen, realizes that she has to deal with "The Menace From Earth" or she'll lose her best friend and business partner, Jeff, to a sexy blonde bombshell. Andrew Jackson Libby, a mathematical genius, has the title role in "Misfit," but discovers he has his own niche too.

My favorite character is Rhysling, the Blind Singer of the Spaceways, in "The Green Hills of Earth." Rhysling is blinded by a leaking jet and spends the rest of his life cadging rides on the jets that shuttle around the solar system, writing hauntingly beautiful poetry about the sights he will never see again. Finally he decides to go back to Earth one more time and loses his life because of yet another faulty jet. This is how some of his poetry goes. . . . [Read "Green Hills of Earth" and other poems. Leonard Nimoy reads the story "Green Hills of Earth" on a Caedmon record of the same title, and you might get some good hints about effective recitation from it.]

—*Joni Bodart-Talbot*

PATH OF THE PALE HORSE   YA
By PAUL FLEISCHMAN

The last time you had a high fever, what did your mother or your doctor do for you? Give you an aspirin or a cool sponge-bath or maybe a shot of penicillin?

What if the doctor had come in with a vinegar-soaked cloth over his mouth and nose, given you an opium pill, and put a mustard plaster on your throat? Then, to top it off, made three slashes on your arm with a knife and removed a quart of your blood?

Doesn't sound too healthy, does it? But that was the way doctors practiced medicine during the 1700s when our country was beginning to really grow. Doctors didn't attend medical schools as we know them. A young boy was apprenticed to a practicing doctor so he could learn by watching his master heal people.

Lep is fourteen years old and lives near Philadelphia in 1793—the year yellow fever killed thousands of people in that city during the summer. At a time when most people were leaving the city to try to escape from the terrible plague, Lep was entering Philadelphia with Dr. Peale to stock up on pharmaceuticals. He had been allowed to go along on the trip to look for his older sister Clara, who had gone into the city earlier and hadn't come back.

When Lep arrived in Philadelphia, he found people firing muskets into the air in hopes of clearing the fever from the atmosphere. The streets were almost empty, for people were either too sick or too scared to go outside.

The first minute Lep was left on his own he got separated from Dr. Peale in that strange city. He'd been sitting in the buggy minding the horse when the muskets fired. The horse had bolted and raced through the city and down side-streets and alleys. There he was, lost, not remembering where Dr. Peale was and having no idea how to locate his sister.

—Lenna Lea Wiebe

THE PENCIL FAMILIES   Grades 3-5
By SUSAN TERRIS

For years, no pencil in the Mendel household had been safe from Emily. Left alone, she would scoop up every pencil in sight and carry them off to her room, where she would name them, introduce them into one of her pencil families, and invent elaborate stories about them all. The stories sounded a lot like soap operas—like the one about Mrs.

Susannah Choice who was "about to divorce her husband because of that brain surgery and because they argued when he didn't laugh at her joke about the elephant's wrinkle. But before she could divorce him, he committed suicide. He jumped off the Golden Gate Bridge, and then Mrs. Choice had her name changed in court to appeal to her new (and much younger) husband."

Most people who knew about them thought Emily's pencil-family games were pretty stupid, but harmless. And then came the summer when Emily and her older brother were left alone for two weeks while their parents were on vacation. And one day Emily and her friend Carla biked to Bolinas Bay and found a dead body. And after the police came, Emily, just from habit, took a silver pencil from the body. And from then on, nothing in the Mendel household was safe, during the most frightening week of Emily's life!

—Elizabeth Overmyer

THE PEOPLE COULD FLY: Grades 4–8/YA
AMERICAN BLACK FOLKTALES
Retold by VIRGINIA HAMILTON

They say that long ago in Africa, some of the people knew magic and could fly. When they were captured for slavery however, they shed their wings and they stopped flying. But they kept their power, their secret magic, even in the land of slavery, and there were times when the people who could fly, did fly away, when the suffering became too great. And this is only one of the black folktales you'll find in this book, born of sorrow and passed on in hope.

—Janet Loebel

THE PET-SITTING PERIL   Grades 5–7
By WILLO DAVIS ROBERTS

It was the summer Nick worked as a pet-sitter. He worked for several people, as a matter of fact. There was Mr. Haggard, whose dog Rudy he walked each day. And he gave Mrs. Sylvan's cat Eloise her medicine each day while her owner was at work. Just catching Eloise was a job! And when Mrs. Monihan went to visit her sister, Nick fed her cat and dog, Fred and Maynard.

Strange things began happening in the apartment house to make Nick's pet-sitting job a peril—a dangerous experience!

The hall lights inside the building were out several times in one week, even the day after the light bulbs had been changed. Then the boxes next door were apparently moved to the back wall of the apartment building, and a fire was set! Nick had a hard time convincing the fire inspector that *he* had not set the fire.

Two strange repairmen came to work late one Saturday afternoon and left the entire building without electricity—and that was the night Nick had to stay in Mr. Haggard's apartment *alone.*

To make matters worse, both the dogs in the building were sick—sleepy-sick, as thought they'd been doped!

Read *The Pet-Sitting Peril* by Willo Davis Roberts to learn how Nick and the pets spent the night in the dark, creepy, spooky apartment building.

—*Dorothy A. Davidson*

THE PIG-OUT BLUES   YA
By JAN GREENBERG

It's bad enough to be fifteen and plump and to have someone tell you your arms are thick as tree trunks, but it's even worse when your Mom has a figure that's a perfect 10. Poor Jodie! She loves to eat, and her mother loves to complain about her eating, which of course makes Jodie eat all the more.

Then Jodie hears that the school drama club is putting on the play *Romeo and Juliet.* Now, Jodie may love to eat, but she also loves Shakespeare and she knows that she would be the perfect Juliet, if only she weren't so plump. And then she hears that her heart-throb David is going to try out for the role of Romeo. Drastic measures are called for, and Jodie goes on a crash diet.

Oh, she's so good, eating carrots and celery instead of cream pies, Doritos, bagels and cream cheese, and those marvelous Milky Ways. By the afternoon of tryouts, Jodie looks wonderful. Even though she hasn't eaten for twenty-four hours and is feeling weak, she knows that she looks superb and that the part will soon be hers. And she certainly knows she will be a better Juliet than that Maude St. James, even though Maude does have a British accent.

Finally it is Jodie's turn to audition. She walks on stage and gets set to say her lines, when suddenly she feels a dizzying pain between her eyes, followed by waves of nausea—and she faints before she has a chance to say the first word. Is this the beginning of Jodie's *Pig-Out Blues?*

—*Pam Spencer*

THE PINBALLS   Grades 7–9
By BETSY BYARS

"Stabilizes! Whooooo, that means I'll stay until I'm ready for the old folks' home!" said Pig. But Carlie was tough! She never said anything polite. Her favorite responses were, "What's it to you?" or "Bug off!" Her favorite pastime was TV. She threw things at people who blocked her view. Carlie was in a foster home because she couldn't get along with her stepfather.

Two boys were sent to the foster home that same summer. Thomas J. had spent the last six years with the elderly Benson twins. Their names were Thomas and Jefferson, but they were women! He had been dropped off in front of their farmhouse at the age of two, and the twins had just kept him. Thomas J. was in the foster home because the twins were in the hospital.

Harvey (aka Pig) had two broken legs. His father had run over them with his new car—by accident. Pig was supposed to stay in the home until his father stopped drinking and could provide a safer environment.

Carlie likened their lives to "pinballs in a machine," bouncing from experience to experience by chance.

Read this book to discover why she changed her mind and the role she found herself playing. If you have ever been disappointed by your parents, you'll relate to this one!

—Kelly Jewett

PLAYING MURDER   YA
By SANDRA SCOPPETTONE

Talk 1

It begins as a game. A game called Murder. Then suddenly one player is dead, another a killer, and the game turns into a nightmare.

—Barbara Bahm

Talk 2

It was only a game until someone they *all* knew turned it into murder. The eight teenagers had been playing the game all summer.

They each drew a slip of paper—six were blank, one was marked D for detective, and the other was marked M for murderer. The detective ran the game—when he or she said "go," everyone had three minutes to run and hide; then he blew a whistle and the murderer had three more miutes to find his victim, tap him, and say "You're dead!" Then everyone but the victim ran back to where the game started, and it was up to the detective to solve the murder.

Only tonight the murderer had done more than tap his victim—he had killed Kirk with Kirk's own penknife.

Anna couldn't believe that Kirk, with his blond hair, blue eyes, and winning personality, was dead. She and her family had only been on the island for five weeks, but she and Kirk had been attracted to each other immediately, even though Kirk already had a girlfriend. He had told Anna that he couldn't break up with Charlotte because she'd already had one nervous breakdown—but his smile, his kisses, his touch had told Anna that she was the one he loved.

When Anna's twin brother Bill is arrested for the murder, Anna decides she must find the real killer. As she begins to question the list of suspects—the other teenagers who had played the game that night—she learns some disturbing facts about Kirk. His own brother and sister hated him, maybe enough to kill him, and Charlotte . . . well, she'd never had a nervous breakdown. Maybe everyone in the game that night had had a reason to want Kirk dead. As Anna asks more and more questions and gets closer to discovering the real murderer, she may be the next victim.

—Marianne Tait Pridemore

POPCORN DAYS
AND BUTTERMILK NIGHTS
By GARY PAULSEN

Grades 7–8/YA

Carley was a tough city kid, sent to his country uncles to be straightened out after getting in trouble for vandalism. When he got off the bus and wasn't met at the store as planned, Carley took a look around the tiny town and came to the blacksmith shop. It was impossible not to stop—the smell of horse sweat and coal and burnt hair would have stopped a truck. The man shoeing the horse smiled at him and said "Hello-den." It was his uncle David.

"You are going to stay with either Harvey or me," he said. "We wasn't sure which, because we heard you was coltish and a little wild. Are you?"

"No, I don't think so," Carley said. "I got in some trouble, is all. But it's done now, I think."

"So why don't you stay with me, and we'll see what happens?" asked Uncle David. It was decided, and that's how Carley came to know David—all in fire and heat and the ringing of steel and the smell of thick smoke.

But that was just the beginning of Carley's stay in the Minnesota farm country, an experience he never forgot that included not only the joys of spring and summer, but the harshness of a fall that brought a grim problem seemingly beyond solution—until David found a way to work his amazing magic and change the lives of everyone.

—Patricia Farr

PORTRAIT OF JENNIE YA/Adult
By ROBERT NATHAN

This is a love story, but not a typical one at all. Eben first meets Jennie when he is a struggling, discouraged young artist (complete with an unheated garret room) in New York City. She comes up to talk to him while he's sitting in the park one day, and he notices she has on a rather old-fashioned-looking black dress. She says her parents work as jugglers in the Hammerstein Music Hall, and suddenly Eben realizes that the building was torn down years ago, when he was a boy. As she leaves, Jennie tells him to wait for her to grow up, and she sings him a little tuneless song—"Where I come from nobody knows,/And where I'm going everything goes./The wind blows,/The sea flows,/And nobody knows."

Each time Eben sees her after that, she's a little older than she should be, and she always asks him to wait for her, and says she's hurrying as fast as she can.

There is something elusive and haunting about Jennie, and Eben manages to capture this quality in a portrait of her. Almost overnight he's a huge success—he sells all his pictures, even the ones he painted years earlier.

And then he realizes that Jennie comes less often, but now Eben's in love with her, and so he still waits for her.

—Joni Bodart-Talbot

PRAIRIE SONGS   Grades 7–9
By PAM CONRAD

Emmeline Berryman in her frilled lavender dress was the most beautiful woman Louisa had ever seen! Next to Emmeline, Louisa's mother Clara looked like a wrinkled brown nut, tanned by the sun.

Louisa was ten years old and lived a long time ago in Nebraska, a wide open place with no trees and hardly any neighbors—the closest were two miles away!

Louisa loved this open space, but Emmeline hated it. She was used to nice houses, a lot of people, and servants to do her housework. She was afraid—of snakes, of Indians, and of being alone. Some said she'd never make it, she was too used to the city. Clara said Emmeline would feel better when her baby came.

To help Emmeline out, Clara did her washing for her in exchange for Emmeline teaching Louisa and her brother to read. They loved it; they only had three books at home, and Emmeline had hundreds! Paul, their other neighbor, hated it. When his mother dragged him over to be taught too, he ran into the house, grabbed a shotgun, and started blasting away at her! Emmeline began to scream and wouldn't stop. . . . then her baby started coming—too soon. Rough times lay ahead as winter approached—would she really be tough enough?

Read *Prairie Songs*, by Pamela Conrad.

—*Linda Keating*

PREMONITIONS   YA
By FRANK BONHAM

Klutzy Kevin, high school newspaper editor, seems to have a terminal case of fear of females. He sits in front of the phone for over an hour, sweating and doodling and trying to gather up the courage to call Anni, the pretty, mysterious girl in his French class. He knows that as soon as he hears Anni's sexy French voice on the other end of the line (Anni really is French and she calls him Kayvan) he will start to hyperventilate. His breath will come in quick ragged gasps and he won't be able to talk at all. Maybe he will stop breathing altogether.

Fear of females and fear of hyperventilation—Kevin never makes the call. But a few nights later, miraculously, the phone rings, and it is Anni calling Kevin! She asks about a rumor that his school paper wanted to run a column on her predictions of the future. Now, Anni had become a school legend after she had casually mentioned the coach was sick—the day *before* the stroke. She had also known, beforehand, about the fire in the school office. No one is surprised at her ESP abilities—her older brother Dante had been famous for them too, before he died in a drowning accident. As newspaper editor, Kevin had squelched the idea of using Anni as a crystal ball, because even though he doesn't know her as well as he wishes he did, he senses that Anni is embarrassed by her abilities. Her uncanny future knowledge makes her seem strange, but even more fascinating to Kevin.

And now Anni is actually phoning *him*, and somehow Kevin is able to breathe long enough to invite her to go to the beach late that night for the grunion run.

For those of us who don't live on the California shoreline, grunion are fish which choose a very few beaches for laying their eggs every spring. No one knows which beaches will teeming with millions of the silver fish, washing in with the waves, glowing in the dark. The kids at Kevin's school make a party out of the grunion run every year, trying to guess which beach to have the party on. Though Anni's brother Dante had been famous for predicting the grunion run, Anni now tells Kevin a secret: that it was she who knew where the fish would come, and she will know tonight, too.

How could Kevin resist a great news story like that? Yet when he and Anni find the grunion on a dark, deserted beach, Kevin also finds something else: that there are disturbing secrets about Anni and her dead brother, secrets that make Anni shiver and turn away from Kevin just as he thinks he is getting closer to her. And suddenly, with a cold sense of certainty, Kevin has his own premonitions.

—*Catherine G. Edgerton*

PRESIDENT'S DAUGHTER　　　　　　　　YA
By ELLEN EMERSON WHITE

Meg Powers was sixteen years old. For as long as she could remember her mother had been involved in politics. Meg's mother had gone from being a member of the town council all the way to being a United States Senator.

Meg was used to her mother's routine. For instance, she knew her father, her brother, and herself would only see Senator Powers on weekends because the Senator worked in Washington, DC, and the family lived in Boston. Meg knew when her mother *was* home with the family, she still spent half her time being interviewed by reporters, meeting people, and going to formal dinners and balls. Meg knew she could pick up the newspaper just about any day and see her mother's picture or name. Senator Powers was just that important!

So when Senator Powers told Meg she was going to run for President of the United States, Meg knew knew her mother had all the right stuff: Mrs. Powers was very smart, very elegant, very poised, and very popular.

But Meg was nothing like her mother. And what she was not so sure of was whether *she* had the right stuff—the right manners, the right attitude, even the right clothes—to be the *President's Daughter.*

—Avis Matthews

PRINCESS ASHLEY   YA
By RICHARD PECK

Talk 1

It was like having Princess Diana want to be your friend. That's the way the new freshman girl, Chelsea Olinger, felt when Ashley Packard, the most beautiful, glamorous, and powerful girl at Crestwood High, started singling her out for friendship. It was like being admitted into the royal court of Crestwood. Why couldn't her mother understand that? Instead of going on and on about how selfish and manipulative Ashley was. No matter what her mother said, Chelsea would have given everything she had to keep Ashley's friendship. And she almost did.

—Margie Reitsma

Talk 2

There are some books that say what you don't want to hear. There are some people who tell you to be independent—to pay attention to what *you* care about, not to what everyone else says you *should* do. Maybe Chelsea should have read those books, listened to those people. It was her sophomore year when Ashley picked her out to be part of her special crowd—the in crowd. Chelsea was willing to do anything to belong. And she did—even when things turned wrong, even when she knew it could not be the way it had been, could never be the way she wanted it to be. But belonging was everything—wasn't it?

—Joni Bodart-Talbot

PRISONER OF VAMPIRES   Grades 4–8
By NANCY GARDEN

Alexander Darlington, twelve years old, has just gotten into trouble with the law. He and his pal Mike were stealing hubcaps to make birdbaths, and Alexander got caught. Now he'll be put on probation, which will include cutting short his beloved movie-viewing hours.

As if that weren't bad enough, Alexander has been given a very tough homework assignment. He must do a paper on a subject he can research from primary sources. The problem is, Alexander's favorite subject is vampires. He *loves* vampires—he reads books about them, watches films about them. But where will he ever find a *real* vampire?

Alexander's research leads him to a private library where he meets an eccentric librarian named Dleifner and a sinister fellow named Radu, who has a penchant for rare roast beef sandwiches and promises Alexander that he will lead him to "the greatest primary source of all." And this is just the beginning of Alexander's adventure in *Prisoner of Vampires*, by Nancy Garden.

—Gail T. Orwig

PURSUIT   YA
By MICHAEL FRENCH

High school senior Gordy Dobbs and his thirteen-year-old brother Martin are on a six-day hiking trip in a remote section of the Sierra mountains with Gordy's friends, Roger and Luke. Roger, the oldest and strongest, has planned the trip, and Roger thinks Gordy should have left young Martin at home. Martin thinks Roger's a bully, with his arrogant demands to "hurry it up" and his relentless pursuit of the most difficult areas to climb.

The group comes to a sheer rock formation; Roger is intent on climbing up and Luke and Gordy don't want to be thought chicken so they keep quiet. Roger makes his way up easily, and, miraculously, Luke struggles to the top. It's Martin's turn. Gordy insists he wear the safety rope. Halfway up Martin freezes—he's obviously terrified. Roger keeps up the jeers at Martin—telling him he's got a safety rope on and he's *still* a baby. Martin, in hysterics now, says he's not a baby and he doesn't need a rope. At that Roger bends own and cuts through the rope with a knife. Martin tries to hang on but he slips and falls to his death.

Gordy, in shock, knows he has to get help and he knows Roger is responsible for Martin's death. But Roger doesn't want Gordy to get help. He doesn't want the *real* story to get out. Gordy decides to go on his own for help. Then he discovers Roger is not continuing the hike. He's following him, and Gordy fears he will become another "accident" in *Pursuit*.

—Diana C. Hirsch

PUTTING IT TOGETHER: YA/Adult
TEENAGERS TALK ABOUT FAMILY BREAKUP
By PAULA McGUIRE

Who's going to take care of me? Do they love me? Was it my fault? Fear, insecurity, and guilt are often the feelings that accompany divorce, separation, or death. The breakup of the family is something that happens, but what really matters and makes the difference is what the family does about it. Eighteen teenagers tell the stories of their families and how they coped with divorce—or how they didn't. Quentin and Peter learn that divorce isn't like what is shown on TV. "It doesn't shatter us all at once." It may mean the end of one family but the beginning of a new family. And Michael discovers that many times help doesn't come from outside but from inside. You have to learn to help yourself, and that may take time. But sometimes you may want someone else to talk to—someone else who's been there too. Maybe you could find that person here, in *Putting It Together: Teenagers Talk About Family Breakup,* by Paula McGuire.

—Beverly Harvey and *Joni Bodart-Talbot*

RAMONA THE BRAVE Grades 3–5
By BEVERLY CLEARY

Ramona had a good teacher last year in kindergarten, but she's going to have to be brave to put up with Mrs. Griggs, her teacher this year. Terrible things keep happening all term. One time, when Ramona tries to make herself feel better by walking to school a new way, she runs into a huge, fierce dog. Ramona takes off her shoe and throws it at the dog. Then a horrible thing happens! The dog grabs her shoe and starts to chew on it. When Ramona gets to school, Mrs. Griggs picks her to lead the flag salute. In one shoe! She's in trouble!

—Zoë Kalkanis

RAMONA THE PEST Grades 2–5
By BEVERLY CLEARY

Ramona had waited and waited—now finally she could go to school! It was the very greatest day of her whole life! Today she could go to kindergarten and learn to read and write and do all the things that would help her catch up with her big sister Beezus.

When she got to school, Ramona met her teacher, who was named Miss Binney. She was so young and pretty Ramona knew she couldn't have been a grown-up very long. "Hello, Ramona," she said. "I'm so glad to have you in kindergarten. Sit right here for the present." A present! thought Ramona—and on the first day of school too! She decided to be *very* good. Miss Binney didn't tell anyone else they were going to get a present if they sat in a certain chair. Just Ramona. So Ramona didn't budge—she stayed in her chair no matter what happened, even when Miss Binney took them to the cloakroom to see where they were supposed to hang their coats. Not even when they were all supposed to stand up and sing. Not even when the class all got up to go outside and play Grey Duck. By this time everyone in the class (except Miss Binney) knew that Ramona was sitting in her chair because *she* was going to get a present—and no one else was. But Miss Binney didn't know. She asked Ramona why she wouldn't go out and play Grey Duck. Ramona said, "I can't leave my seat. Because of the present. You said if I sat here I would get a present, but you didn't say how long I had to sit here."

"Ramona, I don't understand—"

"Yes, you did—you said sit here for the present, and I've been sitting and sitting and you haven't given me a present."

Miss Binney's face got all red and she looked very embarrassed. Ramona was confused—teachers weren't supposed to look that way. Then Miss Binney said, "Ramona, I'm afraid you misunderstood—you see, 'for the present' means 'for right now.' I just meant sit in that chair for now."

"Oh." Ramona was so disappointed she didn't know what to say. Words were so confusing.

But that was only Ramona's *first* day at school. Tomorrow there would be Show and Tell—Ramona could hardly wait!

—*Joni Bodart-Talbot*

THE REAL THIEF   **Grades 1–2**
By WILLIAM STEIG

Gawain was chief guard of the Royal Treasury; he was in charge of the king's pile of gold, silver, and rubies. For a long time the job was actually boring—until one day the King discovered that twenty nine rubies had disappeared! Who had keys? Only Gawain and the King! Soon gold pieces disappeared, precious silver ornaments, and then the prize of the treasury, the world-famous Kalikak diamond! Gawain hadn't done it, but no one knew that except the real thief, and so when

Gawian was arrested and sent into exile, there was only one person who could set things straight.

The Real Thief, by William Steig.

—*Elizabeth Overmyer*

REBELS OF THE HEAVENLY KINGDOM   YA
By KATHERINE PATERSON

The sun was high in the summer heaven as Wang Lee dug his hoe into the warm, fragrant, red earth. It was 1850, in a China ruled by the Manchus but overrun by marauding soldiers, deserters, and bandits roaming about like packs of wild dogs. Wang Lee was digging the last spindly turnips left to him and his parents when suddenly the short shadow of his body lengthened at his feet. Lunging for his hoe, he was swung around by his pigtail to find himself facing a bandit and his companions.

Invading Wang Lee's home, the bandits filled baskets with all the family's portable possessions and food, loaded the baskets onto Wang Lee's shoulders and left his parents to their empty house, taking with them the only son the farmer and his wife had.

Within three hundred steps, Wang Lee had left the land worked by his ancestors for generations. Three hundred more and he had passed the rocky hillside that held their whitened bones. Soon he had gone farther from his people than he had ever traveled in his life.

The bandits were headed for the river, and from there into the mountains. Wang Lee and the bandits finally arrived in a city. Resting in the courtyard of a filthy inn, Wang Lee found himself sitting next to a man who drove a hard bargain with Red Eye, the bandit leader, and bought the boy.

Little did Wang Lee realize that this "man" who saved him was a woman, Mei Lin, a member of the Taiping Tienkuo, a secret religious society of rebels dedicated to overthrowing the incompetent Manchu emperor. Wang Lee was allowed to join the society, and he and Mei Lin, through battles and sieges, struggled to establish in China what the rebels hoped would be a Heavenly Kingdom of Great Peace.

—*Patricia Farr*

RED SKY AT MORNING   YA
By RICHARD BRADFORD

After Pearl Harbor, Josh Arnold's father decides to send his family someplace safe. Safe is Sagrado, New Mexico, a little town up in the mountains, about as far from Atlanta's shipbuilding yards as you can get. It's the kind of place that has a population of six cows, four dogs, seventeen chickens, and almost no people. Josh has to get used to a whole new way of life, and he gets into trouble his very first day at school.

He's watching this beautiful girl walk down the hall and notices that no one else is looking at her. It's as if she doesn't even exist. Just at that moment, Josh feels a knife stick in the back of his neck, and a voice growls, "You look at my sister like that, I cut your ear off!" It is Chango, the town bully, and that's why no one is looking at his sister. Then Josh hears, "Oh, lay off, Chango, he's new—let him go," and Chango skulks off down the hall, muttering under his breath. Josh turns to his rescuer. It's Steenie, the local doctor's son. Steenie decides that Josh needs some lessons on how to survive in Sagrado. He enlists to help of Marcia, the daughter of the local minister. They are without doubt the two best poeple in town to teach Josh how to survive in Sagrado. Steenie read all his father's medical books and knows all the Latin and Greek medical terms for all the parts of the body. He can cuss you out for ten minutes, and you'll never have any idea what he really said—and what's better, neither will his teachers! Marcia, on the other hand, is a typical "preacher's kid"; she specializes in dirty jokes. Every year she goes to church camp and comes back with a whole year's supply—the *worst* ones in town! Marcia and Steenie decide that the first thing Josh needs to learn is how to play Chicken, Sagrado-style.

On Saturday, they take him out to lunch: the greasiest, hottest tacos and burritos they can find—as many as Josh can eat, and really more than he wants. (Remember, Josh is from Atlanta, and his stomach isn't used to Mexican food.) Then they go for a walk. Josh isn't used to the high altitude, and he's lagging behind, panting for breath, his stomach feeling worse by the minute, when he notices that Steenie and Marcia have stopped and are talking. They're at the top of this little rise and are pointing to something below them, and saying things like, "Boy, this is gonna be a great game of Chicken—the best we've had in a long time!" "Yeah, Josh is really gonna learn to play the right way!" "He's one lucky fellow—it wasn't this good when I learned to play," and so on. Josh is really wondering what's going on, till he gets to the place where they're standing and looks down. There in front of him is the town dump, and in the middle of the dump is a dead horse, a *very* dead horse—bloated, covered with maggots, and smelling *horrible.* The object of the game is to walk, or run, up to the horse, touch it, and walk, or run, back to the starting point, which is back just far enough that you can take a deep breath without throwing up. If you walk up, you have to walk back, which takes longer, but you aren't so likely to get out of breath. If you run up, you run back, which won't take as long, but you may lose your breath, and have to take another. Marcia says, "Ladies first!" Marcia is a walker. She walks up to the horse, touches it—"nice horsie"—and walks back. Steenie is a runner. He dashes up to the horse, gives it a kick—"Hey horse"—and runs back. Josh just can't *believe* this stupid game! And he's so busy thinking about these small-town kids and their dumb games that he doesn't see the empty beer bottle lying right in front of the horse—the bottle Steenie and Marcia have very carefully avoided. He trips and falls and slides right into home plate, which is, of course, the horse.

Now, what do you do when you fall down suddenly? You lose your breath. And what do you have to do when you lose your breath? Take another one. Well, that's what Josh does, he can't stop himself, and that's when Josh loses both his lunch and the game of Chicken. When he gets back to where Steenie and Marcia are, they're still howling with laughter, hardly able to talk. But when she gets her breath back, Marcia says, "You know, Josh, we've been playing the game wrong all these years. You're not supposed to just *touch* the horse—you've got to get in there and hug him like a *brother!*"

And that's only the first of many lessons that Josh learns about how to survive in Sagrado, New Mexico!

—Joni Bodart-Talbot

REMEMBERING THE GOOD TIMES   YA
By RICHARD PECK

Three friends—Buck, Kate, and Trav. Their friendship started in eighth grade and carried on into high school.

Three friends—as close as anyone could possibly be. They spent all their spare time together and really didn't care for anyone's company but their own. They were a kind of family. Buck's parents were divorced and he lived with his dad. Kate had never known her father. And though Trav lived with both of his parents, he couldn't talk to them. They were too far away. But Trav, Kate, and Buck had each other, and it was good.

Sure, they had their problems off and on, but mostly everything was easy. They all knew everything about each other and understood each other. After all, they were best friends.

Three friends—for a long time. Then there were only two. Two left wondering "why?" and feeling that they should have seen the signs and done something to help. But they didn't know. Their best friend, and they didn't know.

Remembering the Good Times will ask that of you: How well do you know your best friend?

Remembering the Good Times, by Richard Peck.

—*Melinda Waugh*

REPRESENTING SUPERDOLL YA
By RICHARD PECK

They seemed an unlikely pair—Verna, fresh off the farm, and Darlene, the beauty-contest winner. In fact, they didn't want to be together really but Darlene's mother had decided what would be best and she'd swept them all along, just the way she always did. It had started the year before, when Darlene had won her first beauty contest. And, with Darlene's looks, it wasn't hard—blonde hair, baby-blue eyes, and gorgeous! The kind of person who comes out in beauty marks instead of pimples. And she was just as dumb as she was beautiful— maybe that's why she let her mother keep her under her thumb the way she did. She just didn't know any better. But she did know how to look beautiful, and won one contest after another. Finally she'd won the Central United States Teen Superdoll contest, and would go to Las Vegas for the national contest. But first there was a trip to New York and a chance to appear on *Spot the Frauds*, a TV contest show like *To Tell the Truth*. Since Darlene's mother couldn't go, she had decided that Verna, the most presentable of Darlene's friends, would be superdoll's companion, and before they knew what was going on, the two girls were on their way to New York. The morning they were supposed to film the show, one of the two frauds that were to appear with Darlene got sick, and Verna got drafted to fill in! They rehearsed her lines, fixed her hair and face, and pinned her into the long white gown with a ribbon over her shoulder. Then Verna got a chance to look into the mirror and saw a stranger staring back at her—a stranger who looked almost pretty.

And then they were on stage, and as Verna said, "My name is Darlene Hoffmeister," suddenly she knew that nothing would ever be the same again!

—*Joni Bodart-Talbot*

RIDE THE RIVER   YA
By LOUIS L'AMOUR

This is a "shoot-em-up" adventure of the early 1800s told from a girl's point of view. Echo Sackett is a sixteen-year-old girl from the mountains of Tennessee who has been sent to Philadelphia to bring home an inheritance. Echo can ride, shoot, use her "Arkansas toothpick" (that's a knife), hunt, follow a trail, and paddle a canoe better than most men. She needs all these skills to see her safely home with the three thousand dollars of gold.

How does she manage to outmaneuver a group of ruthless killers who want to steal her gold? You'll just have to read *Ride the River* by Louis L'Amour to find out.

—*Pam Spencer*

RITE OF PASSAGE   YA
By ALEXEI PANSHIN

Mia Havero lives on one of the seven giant spaceships that are all that's left of earth's civilization. There are a few primitive colony-planets that the spaceships visit to get raw materials, but the ships are the real centers of science and culture. With so little room on the ships, the population has to be strictly limited, so one of the things the people do is make all teenagers go through a thirty-day period of trial, where they are put down on a primitive planet with some simple weapons and equipment and have to survive on their own. After thirty days the spaceship comes back to pick them up, and if they've survived, they're considered adults with all rights and privileges. If they haven't, the ship doesn't have to worry about them anymore.

At the beginning of this story, Mia has two years to go before her trial. She's a pretty shy, meek person, and her father is afraid she won't make it, so he moves to a different section of the ship, where she gets a new tutor and meets Jimmy, a guy who has the same tutor. Now, Jimmy is far from meek, and pretty soon they get to be friends and start doing things together, like exploring the outside of the ship where they aren't supposed to go and getting into trouble, but all their activities really increase Mia's confidence in herself.

A year and a half before trial, they start survival class together, where they learn things like how to build shelters in the wilderness and how to stalk and kill wild animals with their bare hands. By this time, they have become romantically interested in each other and they plan to go down for trial as a team, which increases Mia's confidence still more. Then, three days before trial, Mia has a big fight with Jimmy, and they decide to go down separately. So if you want to find out if they make it and ever get back together, read *Rite of Passage*, by Alexei Panshin.

—Peggy Murray

RUN FOR YOUR LIFE Adult
By BARBARA ABERCROMBIE

Sarah's house is like a three-ring circus. Sarah has three teenage children, a new husband, a cat, and men working on an addition to her house, coming in and out all day long.

Really, this is a fairly normal California household. But then things start happening. First Adam, Sarah's new husband, gets mugged at the beach by a teenage boy when he goes to Baskin-Robbins. Then the cat appears in the house even though no one let it in. Sarah and Adam's wedding picture turns up missing. The dog they get to guard the house howls during the night, and then Adam discovers footprints in the new addition. On another day the family's calendar is missing from the bulletin board. The cat dies. The carbon copy of the book that Sarah is writing disappears. The flower garden is destroyed.

Of course everyone tries to figure out who is doing this. The children think it is Adam. Adam thinks it's the guy who mugged him.

All Sarah knows is that it's someone who has read her manuscript, because everything that happens is just like she has written it. The thing is, Sarah is the character who finally gets killed in the book. The killing takes place at the end of a marathon, so Sarah decides that the only way to solve the mystery is to run the real marathon herself. To find out who the culprit is, read *Run for Your Life*, by Barbara Abercrombie.

—Mary Hedge

RUNNING LOOSE YA
By CHRIS CRUTCHER

Louie Banks doesn't have everything, but he's satisfied. He has Becky. With Becky he can face anything. But then he finds out that life doesn't always play fair, and some people aren't playing fair either.

—Nancy Guffey

'SALEM'S LOT   YA/Adult
By STEPHEN KING

Ben Mears, a writer, returns to his home town of 'Salem's Lot after twenty-five years and before long strange things begin to happen. The old Marsten house, which has stood vacant since its owner killed his wife and committed suicide thirty-six years ago, is rented to a very mysterious stranger. A dead dog is found hanged, head down, from the stakes on the cemetery gate. A little boy disappears and shortly afterward his brother, who had been with him when he disappeared, dies of severe anemia, as if all the blood had been drained from his body.

Being a writer and naturally curious, Ben does a little research and finds that the last time the Marsten house was occupied four children had disappeared from the area without a trace. When he discusses what he has learned with other people, he becomes increasingly alarmed by the strange things they tell him about. Small scratches on the neck of the boy who died of anemia. Townspeople who have disappeared. Corpses that get up off the slabs in the morgue at night.

Twelve year-old Mark Petrie doesn't need any research or discussion to figure out what is going on. One night his friend, the boy who died of anemia, appeared outside Mark's second-story bedroom window begging to be let in. Mark knew there was nothing to stand on outside that window. There could be only one explanation for his friend's presence.

'Salem's Lot, by Stephen King.

—Gloria Hanson

SARAH, PLAIN AND TALL   Grades 3-6
By PATRICIA MacLACHLAN

Talk 1

Sarah brought something from the sea for us. For Caleb she had a shell, a moon snail which curled and smelled of salt. She gave me the smoothest and whitest stone I had ever seen. Sarah had a faraway look on her face. Papa didn't see it, I know, but Caleb did, and so did I. I wished that Papa and Caleb and I could all be perfect for her. But what if Sarah didn't like us, or what if she was too lonely for the sea, or what if she thought we were too pesty—would she go back to the sea before the preacher came to marry them at the end of the week?

Papa began to sing again. Sarah learned how to plow the fields. We made dunes of haystacks and rode them to the ground. One morning Sarah got up early, put on her blue dress and yellow bonnet, climbed up into the wagon, and drove off to town. Papa and Caleb and I watched Sarah leave for town. It was sunny and warm—a day just like the one when our Mama went away and didn't come back.

"What has Sarah gone to do?" "I don't know." said Papa. "Ask if she's coming back," whispered Caleb. But I would not ask the question. I was afraid to hear the answer.

To find out if Sarah came back, you'll have to read this story.

—*Barbara K. Foster*

Talk 2

"What did I look like when I was born?" Caleb asked. "Well, you didn't have any clothes on. Mama handed you to me in a yellow blanket and said, 'Isn't he beautiful, Anna?'"

I remember what I thought. You were homely and plain, you had a terrible holler and a horrid smell. But that was not the worst of you. Mama died the next morning.

It was hard to think of you as beautiful. It took three whole days for me to love you, sitting by the fire, Papa washing up the supper dishes, your tiny hand brushing my cheek.

"Did Mama sing every day?" Caleb asked. "Every single day," I said, "and Papa sang too."

Papa leaned back in his chair and said, "I've placed an advertisement in the newspaper. For help."

"A housekeeper?" asked Caleb.

"No, not a housekeeper," said Papa slowly. "A wife."

Caleb stared at Papa. "A wife? You mean a mother!"

Papa reached in his pocket and unfolded a letter written on white paper. It was an answer to his ad.

> Dear Mr. Jacob Whitting,
>
> I am Sarah Wheaton. I am answering your advertisement. I have never been married, though I have been asked. I am strong and I work hard. I would be interested in your children and where you live. And about you.
>
> Very truly yours,
> Sarah Elizabeth

When Papa finished reading, no one said a word. Then I said, "Ask her if she sings."

Caleb, Papa, and I wrote letters to Sarah. We all received answers.

> Dear Anna,
>> Yes, I can braid hair.
>
> Dear Caleb,
>> I have a cat named Seal.
>
> Dear Jacob,
>> I will come by train. I will wear a yellow bonnet. I am plain and tall. Tell them I sing.
>
>> Sarah

Sarah came in the spring. Papa drove off along the dirt road to fetch her. Papa's new wife? Maybe. Our new mother? Maybe. Find out when you read *Sarah, Plain and Tall.*

—Katherine Mattson

SAY HELLO TO THE HIT MAN YA
By JAY BENNETT

Fred Morgan isn't really Fred Morgan. He's the son of a famous gangster. And when he found this out, he began to run. But he didn't run far enough, because one day the phone rang and a voice told him: "You're going to die. You won't know where, you won't know when, but you are going to die."

Who wants to kill Fred? Is it his father's enemies? Or his friends? Who can he trust?

There's only one way to find out. And that's to go back. Back to his father's world, where he finally comes face to face with the killer. Who is it? Read *Say Hello to the Hit Man,* by Jay Bennett, and find out.

—Lou Rosenberg

SCARLET MONSTER LIVES HERE Grades k-3
By MARJORIE SHARMAT

Have you ever moved into a new neighborhood and wondered why no one came to visit you? Scarlet wonders, and she's even hung out a welcome sign and sung a song at the top of her lungs inviting the neighbors over. She's built a cheerful fire in her fireplace and baked special treats for her visitors. And still no one comes! Maybe it's because she's ugly: she does have evil-looking eyebrows, her fangs need braces, and she weighs three hundred pounds (she's a monster!). But she does like to kiss and was hoping this would be a kissing neighborhood. Why aren't her neighbors welcoming her?

To find out the reason, read *Scarlet Monster Lives Here*, by Marjorie Sharmat.

—Ann Flory

NOTE: Show pictures of what she's done and what she looks like.

SCARY STORIES TO TELL IN THE DARK Grades 4-6
By ALVIN SCHWARTZ

Here is a collection of "scary stories to tell in the dark." If you like to stay up late and scare friends with gruesome stories, this book is a sure thriller. It's the only book I know with a ghost that has bloody fingers and moans all night, "Bloody fingers, b l o o o o d y fingers!"

If one of your friends claims "You can't scare me," tell the story about a boy who finds a big toe in the garden, puts it in his soup, and has it for supper. In the middle of the night he hears a voice. "Where is my tooe?" In another tale, two boys meet "The Thing," and one of them decides to *touch* it.

Some of these stories are "jump stories"—sure to make listeners jump in fright. Others are "shine-ons" with funny endings. There's a gory poem and a prank called "The Dead Man's Brains." Schwartz also gives hints on how to tell each story.

One word of caution: Never tell more than two or three of these tales in a single night. Otherwise, your friends may never come back—alive.

Scary Stories to Tell in the Dark, by Alvin Schwartz. And after that, try *Witches, Wit and a Werewolf,* retold by Jeanne Hardendorff, or *The Thing at the Foot of the Bed,* by Maria Leach.

—Paul H. Rockwell

THE SEA WOLF   YA/Adult
By JACK LONDON

Humphrey Van Weyden, a respectable young gentleman, is going on a short trip from San Francisco to Sausalito on a ferry steamer, the *Martinez,* when all of a sudden, boom! the *Martinez* is struck by a steamboat coming out of the fog. This is how Humphrey Van Weyden begins the adventure of his life.

He is rescued by a schooner, the *Ghost*. The captain of the *Ghost* is Wolf Larsen, a strong, cruel man who can kill with his bare hands, unlike Humphrey, who is skinny and weak and has never had to work in his life. Humphrey offers any sum of money for his safe return to San Francisco, but Wolf Larsen decides to take him with him to the offshore waters of Japan, where they will be hunting seals.

At first Hump, as he is known on the ship, has a terrible time adjusting to shipboard life. Wolf Larsen makes him work as a cabin boy, helping the cook and cleaning up the ship. As the voyage continues, Hump and Wolf Larsen develop a sort of friendship, like the friendship between a tyrant and a hostage. Sometimes they carry on long and interesting conversations, but at other times Wolf seems on the verge of killing the younger man. Wolf believes in survival of the fittest, and he takes pleasure in triumphing over others.

As Hump becomes more familiar with the ways of the sea, he is promoted and begins to enjoy the trip a little. But he sees such brutality on board the *Ghost* that he sometimes gets sick at his stomach. One day the ship's cook is thrown overboard for fun and has his foot bitten off by a shark. And there are vicious fights among the men, egged on by the sadistic Wolf, who personally beats up anyone who challenges his rule. Some of the men try to desert by taking the ship's rowboats and heading for the Japanese coast. But Wolf Larsen is determined to keep all of his sailors: he goes after every single person who tries to escape.

One day a small boat is spotted on the horizon, and Wolf Larsen thinks it must be one of the deserters. When the *Ghost* catches up with the boat, however, it turns out to contain four men and a woman. They are survivors of a ship that has gone down, and they too are taken aboard Wolf Larsen's ship. Humphrey is attracted to the woman, Maud Brewster, and eventually falls in love with her. However, Wolf Larsen has also taken a liking to Maud. During one of their late-night conversations, Wolf dares Hump to kill him. Will Hump take up the challenge? Is he a match for *The Sea Wolf?*

—*Eitan Dickman*

SECOND STAR TO THE RIGHT   YA
By DEBORAH HAUTZIG

Leslie Hiller had the perfect relationship with her mother. Unlike so many daughters and mothers, she and her mom were friends. No problems of communication at all: Leslie told her mom everything—except why she was starving herself to death.

—*Margie Reitsma*

SECRET SELVES   Grades 5–8
By JUDIE ANGEL

Are people always what they appear to be? In *Secret Selves,* Julie returns to school after summer vacation to find the "boy of her dreams" right there at school. But how is she going to get him to notice her?

When Julie discovers that Rusty plays on the soccer team, she becomes very interested all of a sudden in watching soccer practice after school. That doesn't work. He doesn't even know she's there.

On a dare from her best friend, Julie telephones Rusty. She is too embarassed to use her own name, so she makes up some names—she calls herself "Barbara" and she calls him "Wendell." He goes along with the game and pretends he knows "Barbara." They become secret phone pals—"Barbara and Wendell." Talking with him as "Barbara," Julie gets to know Rusty and finds that he is kind and sensitive. But at school he seems to be the ultimate male chauvinist, and they argue every time they meet.

Julie wonders how a person can be so different. Why does Rusty act so tough at school and yet so sweet and caring on the telephone? To find the real Rusty and to see what happens next, read *Secret Selves,* by Judie Angel.

—*Anna Lopez*

SECRETS OF   Grades 7–8/YA
THE SHOPPING MALL
By RICHARD PECK

Barney and Theresa were in *big* trouble. They had stood up to the worst gang in school, the King Kobras, so the Kobras were out to get them. Since Barney and Theresa didn't have such terrific home lives, they figured the best thing for them was to leave town. So they pooled all their money—four whole dollars—and hopped a bus headed for Paradise Park.

Paradise Park turned out to be a big surburan shopping mall, not a nice quiet retirement community where some sweet little old lady could take them in. But they had no more money and no place else to go, so

Barney and Theresa decided to live there in the mall. They chose a big department store, like Hecht's or Woodies [use the names of local stores] and that night, just before the store closed, they snuck under a bed in the furniture department until the lights went out and the night watchman had made rounds. They got food from the bakery and deli department.

On the third night, while they were trying to find some clothes to exchange for their own, Theresa noticed a female dummy or mannequin that had not been there before. She really liked the dummy's sweater, so she went to touch it—and the thing grabbed back at her! Just when Barney and Theresa thought they could live alone together in the shopping mall forever, they found out the real and scary secrets of Paradise Park.

—Jacqueline Brown Woody

SEE DAVE RUN   YA
By JEANNETTE EYERLY

Dave Hendry is a runaway! He's wearing jeans, Adidas, and a green windbreaker. Notify the police!

As Dave Hendry starts out on a search for his long-absent father, you will hear his story through the people he meets on his journey. His father moved away when he was a child, but Dave has high hopes of finding him and a better way of life.

"I'm Dave's best friend. He said the next time his step-dad laid a hand on him, he'd split for good."

"I gave this kid a ride. He seemed like a nice kid, but awfully lost. I offered him some money, but he wouldn't take it. Said his step-father had given him a little going-away present just before he left home."

The police dispatcher remembered Dave's mother calling to report him missing. He'd been gone two days then. From the yelling in the background, the dispatcher figured they were drunk.

"I'm a hooker, and even for me, it was a rotten thing to do. When I met Dave in the laundromat, I'd had to stop and think how old I was. I stopped having birthdays when I was twelve, four years ago. I think, maybe, if I hadn't cleaned him out—if I'd left him a dollar or two . . . but I took it all, even the change. I'd met a lot of guys on the street, but Dave was the only nice boy I'd ever met."

"I figure it's not my fault if he gets what's coming to him. Take his mother, Lillian—I think she enjoys getting slapped around a little. But the other night, I roughed her up a little. Dave turned on me like a little wildcat. He damned near killed me. I noticed this morning that my wallet was missing. The truth of it is, it would be worth a hundred eighty bucks if I never had to lay eyes on that spoiled brat of hers again."

This isn't just Dave's story. It's also the story of twenty-five people, each one who had a chance to care. Dave is on the road, heading for Colorado, when he meets the sheriff. Dave Hendry is a runaway.

—Linda Henderson

SEE YOU THURSDAY   YA
By JEAN URE

The last, absolutely the *last* thing Marianne wanted was for them to get another boarder. Especially since the extra money went to pay her fees at a private school that she secretly hated. But not only was it a new boarder, it was a man—a music teacher. "And you might as well know now," her mother said, "you'll have to keep your things picked up and not lying around on the stairs and in the hall—he's blind." "Oh, Mother! The last one was bad enough—and she was only senile! . . . How does he cook?" "I don't suppose he does much—he'll have to have breakfast with us—" "A stranger at breakfast!" That was too much for Marianne. The day was spoiled. She even refused to stay at home when he arrived later that week.

But the next morning she ran right into him at the top of the stairs, and was appalled discover he wasn't old at all—maybe not even twenty-five! And he was also quite good-looking, dressed in an ordinary pair of cords and a yellow sweater. Not what she'd been expecting!

Just the same, it was still embarrassing to have to escort him to the bus stop. How do you treat a blind man, anyway? Drag him along by the arm? Offer him your elbow? At least he couldn't see her turn first pink and then red—but it was almost as if he *could* see how uncomfortable she was. As the week passed, even Marianne had to admit that having a boarder wasn't the pain she'd expected. In fact, she'd quit thinking of him as the blind boarder—now he was just Mr. Schonfeld, who couldn't see. And then gradually, he was Abe, and the fact that he couldn't see and was eight years older than she was didn't make any difference. They were in love, and they belonged together.

—Joni Bodart-Talbot

A SEMESTER IN THE LIFE OF A GARBAGE BAG   YA
By GORDON KORMAN

Raymond Jardine describes himself as having no luck, a garbage bag. "Have you ever seen the commercial for garbage bags where they test the strength of the bag by seeing how many pounds of pressure they can put on it before it breaks? So that's Jardine—a garbage bag hooked up to a hydraulic press, doing his best not to fall apart in spite of the guy who keeps turning the knob up."

Raymond decides that winning a trip to an exotic Greek island will be the perfect way to change his luck. To win the contest, Raymond plots, along with his reluctant English partner, Sean, to bring to life an obscure and long-deceased Canadian poet, with the help of Sean's eccentric grandfather. Their antics lead to national notoriety for Gramps and the destruction of a multi-million-dollar government project. Does the Garbage Bag survive?

—Jan Smith

SENTRIES   YA
By GARY PAULSEN

Talk 1

Sue, a bank teller; Peter, a rock star and a composer; David, a Mexican wetback; Laura, the daughter of a sheep rancher; and the veterans of three wars have nothing in common—except that each of them is at a turning point in life. Afterwards, nothing will ever be the same.

—Mary Beethe

Talk 2

Change never comes when you expect it, or when you're prepared for it. But sometimes it does come when you most want it.

Sue is seventeen, working in a bank, and out on a date with Bob when Alan walks up to her and says, "Are you whole?" He is drunk, and he is an Indian. And Sue is a little afraid of him, and of Bob's reaction to him, because she is an Indian too, although she doesn't like to admit it. And then two days later, Alan shows up at the bank to take her to lunch, and won't take no for an answer, so she breaks a date with Bob and goes with him.

David is fourteen when he comes across the Rio Grande somewhere in New Mexico. He has made it! He is in the United States, and now he can get a good job working in the beet fields and send money back to his family. He will get three dollars a day, food, and a dry place to sleep. What more could he want?

Laura is on her way to school when she stops in the barn to talk to her father about lambing. She's always helped with lambing, ever since she was in the first grade, and she is in high school now. But her father is away, and Louie, the hired man, passes on a message from him—she is not to stay home this year, she has to go to school. Laura can't believe it—it is as if she'd been slapped in the face. She'll have to talk to her father when she gets home this afternoon—surely then she can make him understand that to her, being a sheep rancher is the most important thing in life.

Peter is a rock star and leader of his own group, and he realizes that he needs a new sound—something different that can say what's going on inside him. The group has a gig at Red Rocks in Colorado, and he needs something fine. So he closets himself in the beach house, doesn't answer the phone, drinks Cokes and eats macaroni and cheese from boxes he got at the store, and after a while, it comes—the first chord. And it is fine.

For Peter, for Laura, for David, for Sue, change is something that they want, though maybe they haven't gone looking for it. But woven in with their stories are the stories of three soldiers from three different wars who didn't want the changes that happened to them, who fought against those changes, and lost. Change happens when we least expect it, when we're not looking, and suddenly we are different from the people we were yesterday. And it will happen to you just as surely as it did to these teenagers, and you will never be the same again.

—Joni Bodart-Talbot

SEVENTEEN AND IN-BETWEEN   YA
By BARTHE DeCLEMENTS

Craddoc was pushing Elsie to get some birth-control pills. How else would he know if Elsie truly loved him? Yet something was holding Elsie back. Was it her own family life, which always seemed to be in some kind of turmoil? Her mother had a new boyfriend now, and her father's wife seemed to take her anger out on her baby. Elsie's sister, Robyn, was responsible for Elsie's mother not liking Elsie any more. Or was she? How was Elsie going to get all of this turmoil in her life straightened out? She couldn't ask her best friend, Jennifer, for help, because Jennifer had problems of her own. Jack! Her long-time friend who was away at a lumber camp, she'd write him. Nothing seemed to go together, though . . . problems just kept surfacing. That's how it feels to be *Seventeen and In-Between.*

—*Donna Houser*

SHEILA'S DYING   Grades 6–8/YA
By ALDEN R. CARTER

Before becoming a hero, Jerry Kincaid was a pretty average guy—a B+ student, a benchwarmer on the varsity basketball team, a popular kid at school. His friends were a little surprised when he began dating the crazy-acting, unpredictable Sheila, but Jerry found her funny and sexy and exciting—in the beginning, anyway. But just when he has decided to let their relationship drop, Sheila is rushed to the hospital. Cancer. Can Jerry walk away now—while Sheila's dying?

—*Carrie McDonald*

THE SHELL LADY'S DAUGHTER   YA
By C. S. ADLER

Kelly's mother's best friend is her daughter Kelly, age fourteen. Kelly tells her mom about everything that happens to her, and they do a lot of things together like biking and shopping. At least, this is the way things always used to be. Lately, Kelly has been spending so much time with friends that she has been neglecting her mother.

Her mother always allows Kelly to go out and do the things she wants to with her friends. But she always smiles in a wistful, sad way when Kelly leaves. And then she looks sort of like she does when she tells Kelly sad stories about the ladies who live in seashells.

One day when Kelly comes home she discovers that her mother is being taken to the hospital. Kelly can't believe it, because her mother looked all right when she last saw her a few hours ago. But Kelly is not allowed to see or talk to her mother for a long time. Kelly doesn't understand why, and she wonders if she is the cause of her mother's illness. Is she? Read *The Shell Lady's Daughter,* by C. S. Adler, to find out.

—*Mary Hedge*

THE SHERWOOD RING   Grades 6–10
By ELIZABETH POPE

Peggy had never been happy in her life, and she didn't think things would get better when her father died and she went to live with her only living relative, her uncle Enos, at the ancestral home, called Rest-and-Be-Thankful. Once, before he died, Peggy's father had told her that the house might be haunted, and that made the trip seem a bit more interesting.

When Peggy got off the train, there was no one to meet her, and she had a long walk before she got to the house. But before she'd gone too far, the path split into two, and she didn't know which one to take. She was nearly in tears when suddenly, silently, a girl in a long scarlet cape on a black horse came up behind her and said if she took the lefthand fork, she'd find a man who could tell her the way to Rest-and-Be-Thankful. She found him, and he told her the way to the house and gave her a ride as well. But Peggy met her uncle, who reacted very strangely to her new friend. She had meant to ask him about the girl she met on the road, but she didn't have a chance to—her uncle nearly had a heart attack when he saw Pat, the man who had given Peggy a ride to the house. Peggy found out when she started upstairs. On the landing there was a full-length portrait of the girl she's seen—red cape, black horse, just as she'd been that afternoon. And the plaque beneath the picture read, "Barbara Grahame, painted at the age of 16, by John Singleton Copley, 1773," and Peggy knew that she'd seen her first ghost.

—Joni Bodart-Talbot

THE SHINING   YA/Adult
By STEPHEN KING

This is the story of the Overlook Hotel, high up in the mountains of Colorado. It's also the story of Wendy and Jack and their six-year-old son Danny. Jack was all but an alcoholic, and their marriage was about to break up because of it. So when they learned that the Overlook needed a caretaker over the winter, they decided to take a job. The hotel would be snowed in for four months; their only connections with the outside world would be a CB radio and a snowmobile. By the time they left, their marriage would either be a success or a failure. The decision about divorce would be clear. What Wendy and Jack didn't know was that Danny had been having dreams about the hotel and what they would find there. Danny sometimes knew things and saw things that no one else could. And when he thought about the hotel he could hear voices shouting at him, and a word, written on walls or on mirrors—REDRUM. He didn't know what a redrum was, but he knew it was dangerous. When they got to the hotel, the cook, Halloran, could see right away that Danny had the same ability that he himself had—Halloran called it "shining." It meant he and Danny could see things that had left an impression on the place where they'd happened, rather like a psychic photograph. They could also see and feel things no one else could, and Halloran was sure they could also communicate telepathically over long distances. He explained to Danny that the things he'd see at the hotel couldn't hurt him—just like seeing something on TV. But if Danny ever needed him, he could call Halloran mentally and Halloran would come immediately. And he told Danny never to go into one of the rooms in the hotel—*never*. Of course, since Danny was a normal boy, as soon as Halloran had left and he could get hold of the key, he opened that door and walked in. When he did, Danny realized why Halloran had told him not to. The hotel had been owned by the Mafia at one time and because of its isolation was the scene of many Mafia executions. This room was where some of them had taken place, and to Danny's eyes, it was as if they had happened only minutes before. The floor and walls were covered with blood and gore. Danny fled, followed by the voice chanting, "Redrum . . . redrum . . . redrum. . . . " Danny began to notice strange things after that. His parents were changing, especially his father, who didn't do anything any more except sit in the basement and look at the old hotel scrapbooks. His mother was different too. Then Danny saw the most frightening thing of all—the topiary animals on the lawn were changing! They were just carved out of shrubbery, but they were moving closer and closer to the house, and looking more and more dangerous.

Danny began to understand that Halloran had been wrong when he told Danny that the things he saw and heard couldn't hurt him—it wasn't like TV after all. The forces that possessed the hotel were real, and so were the things Danny saw. They *could* hurt him and his parents. But by now they were snowed in. The snowmobile had crashed, and the radio was broken beyond repair, and his father was getting worse and worse. They were trapped—there was no way to escape.

—Joni Bodart-Talbot

THE SHOOTIST   YA/Adult
By GLENDON SWARTHOUT

J.B. Books is the last survivor of the famous gunfighters, and he rides into El Paso in 1901 with a terrible pain in his groin. He's looking for the doctor who operated on him the only time he was ever shot in a gunfight, because Books knows he can trust him. If the doctor tells him what he wants to hear, he's going to turn the town upside down! Wine, women, and song, and lots of all of them! But this doctor tells him just what other doctors have told him—he has an advanced cancer of the prostate and only has about two months to live. He will die a slow and incredibly painful death, and nothing the doctor can give him will help the pain at the end. And the more morphia he uses now to kill the pain, the less effective it will be at the end. Most men in this situation have only two choices: suicide or a slow death from natural causes. As Books thinks about this, he realizes that because he is who he is—the last of the really good gunfighters—he has a third choice other men don't have. There are many people who would like to say, "I'm the man who shot J.B. Books." He can arrange a fight and let himself be killed, and die without the stigma of suicide. He picks out three men: a flashy card-sharp, a cattle rustler, and a pimply-faced kid. One of them will be his killer. And then Books begins to plan his own death, using these three— how, where, and when he will die, and finally, who will kill him.

—Mary James and *Joni Bodart-Talbot*

THE SHORT LIFE OF SOPHIE SCHOLL   YA
By HERMANN VINKE

Sophie Scholl didn't start out as a radical. She did all the childish things everybody else does. She kept a journal; she enjoyed school and the friends she made there; she played with her brothers and sister. But Sophie's times weren't ordinary times. Sophie's home wasn't an ordinary house.

When Hitler came to power, she was twelve. And like most young German girls, she joined Hitler Youth. For a while the children disagreed with their father, who was opposed to Hitler. Gradually, Hans, her older brother, began to question the endless marches and the lists of forbidden books. He and his friends formed a club. They read banned books, sang banned songs, and exchanged prints and postcards by banned painters. Hans and Sophie were among the many young people arrested in November 1937 for subversive activities, and put in jail for a while to teach them a lesson.

Several years later, Sophie joined Hans at college in Munich. She discovered his association with the White Rose, an organization that published and then distributed flyers calling on young Germans to rise against Hitler. Sophie joined the organization. Through her letters and journals and in interviews with her surviving sister, Inge, Sophie's story unfolds. On February 23, 1943, Sophie, Hans, and Christoph Probst were executed. Hitler called it high treason. Sophie said, "With all those people dying for the regime, it is high time that someone died against it."

The Short Life of Sophie Scholl, by Hermann Vinke.

—Barbara Hawkins

SIGN OF THE BEAVER   Grades 4–7
By ELIZABETH SPEARE

Have you ever tried to imagine what it was like around your home when only the Indians lived here? When there were more wild animals than people, no cars to need freeways, and there were no supermarkets where you could buy food for dinner? In *The Sign of The Beaver,* by Elizabeth Speare, thirteen-year-old Matt lives in that kind of world. He and his father have traveled to the wilderness of northern Maine to set up a homestead: a small garden and a log cabin.

When his father goes back to Massachusetts to fetch Matt's mother and sister, Matt is not really worried about staying alone—he has his father's good gun, and he feels confident that he can look after things for the six or seven weeks his father expects to be gone. The first few days everything goes well. Then Matt has a visitor. His name is Ben, he says, and he's a trapper just passing through. He accepts Matt's offer of supper and a bed on the floor and repays him by stealing the precious gun. Now Matt can no longer hunt for meat, but he can still fish, and you *can* live on a diet of fish, if you have to. But when an ornery bear breaks into the cabin and makes short work of Matt's supply of cornmeal and molasses, Matt begins to think about stealing himself. He knows where there is a bee tree, and he can't resist going after some of that honey. Unfortunately, the bees go after him, and he is soon so badly stung he might have died except for the help of two unexpected friends. They are Indians—an old man and his grandson—and they soon strike a bargain with Matt: they will help him to survive if he will teach the younger one, named Attean, to read and write English. From then on, Matt finds new ways to live in this wild country, and learns many things about the people who already live there. But will the Indians learn to accept Matt, whose people are taking their lands and the game they need to live on? And, after the six weeks go by and there is no sign of his family, will Matt be able to survive on his own through the cold winter ahead? Read *The Sign of The Beaver,* by Elizabeth Speare, and live the adventure!

—Jo Ellen Rice

SIMON PURE   YA
By JULIAN F. THOMPSON

Simon Storm is not your average freshman in college. He's fifteen, skipped grades like most kids skip school, and is on an island by himself as far as girls are concerned. He wants to fall in love with an intellectual like himself and graduate from college before he's legally old enough to drink. Both these plans are threatened when a plot to overthrow the university is unveiled—with a key role for Simon in the evil process. It's now up to Simon to see that the plans fail.

—Teresa Schlatt

SIMPLE GIFTS   YA/Adult
By JOANNE GREENBERG

Talk 1

Hi ya'll, my name's Kate, and I'm here to tell you about how our family got "perfect authenticity." To get here you have to ford two creeks and go halfway up a mountain. We're in one of the rising valleys on the east leg of Croom Mountain, and the road is so rutted that it about shakes your car apart. You can see our place as you come up over the last rise, the barn, corral, and house, at the end of one of our fields. Mr. Kelvin nearly had a fit the first time he saw it—he said it was an example of "perfect authenticity." He wanted to sign us up for the SCELP program. That was a government program that helped people live like they were in another century so other people could come and visit them and see what the past was really like. He wanted us to go back to the 1880s. So we did—but we found out that it wasn't as easy to live like pioneers as we'd thought it would be. Having strangers around all the time was no picnic either, especially when they found out about some of our secrets, things that we just hadn't told Mr. Kelvin or any of the other government people who came up to inspect us and show us how to live like we were supposed to. There was that doctor who found out about Daddy's sleeps—he just goes to sleep every seven hours, no matter where he is or what he's doing, sometimes even in the middle of a sentence. It only lasts about fifteen minutes, so we just let him stay wherever he falls. But that doctor called it by some special name and wanted to take Daddy off somewhere so he could study him! And that man who thought his little girls were so pure and holy—ha! They found our still and got drunk every single day they were here, until old One Eye caught them at it one day and put the fear of God into them. And then there was the day the longhorns got out of their pasture and the doctor's wife had to go for help to round them back up again. We were all glad to see that family go! But there were good visitors too—seemed like the worse the weather got, the better they liked it, even the snowstorms and having to string rope to get to the barn and the privy. . . . But I've got to go—there are new folks about to get here and I have to make sure Louise and Jane have on their button-top shoes, and that Robert Luther and I have an excuse to get Daddy away from the visitors when he's about to go to sleep. Living in 1880 sure isn't always what they told us it would be!

—Joni Bodart-Talbot

Talk 2

"Authentic" does not necessarily mean real. That's what the Fleuris discovered when they let the government transform their old dilapidated ranch into an authentic version of an 1880s homestead, for a tourist attraction. The farm could look authentic, as though it were back in the frontier times, but the people on the farm couldn't *really* have a moonshine still, or a herd of illegal Texas longhorns hidden out in the hills. At least, according to the books they couldn't. But they did. You see, the Fleuris weren't just authentic—they were *for real.*

—Margie Reitsma

SIXTEEN: SHORT STORIES   YA
BY OUTSTANDING WRITERS FOR YOUNG ADULTS
Comp. by DONALD R. GALLO

There's nothing like a good short story. A quick hit. Now you can read your favorite authors in that form: Cormier, Kerr, the Mazers, Peck, Sebestyen, Sharmat. Sixteen of them, cram-packed into one concentrated volume. Take M. E. Kerr's story, "Do You Want My Opinion?", for instance. . . .

"I've heard you're getting serious about Eleanor Rossi," John's father accused. "Spending all night talking with her."

John kept silent, waiting for the inevitable lecture.

"You've got lots of time to get intimate with a girl," his father started. "Don't let one get a-hold of you."

"Don't worry, Dad. I think about a lot of them."

"That's your problem. You think too much. Just stick to lovemaking and keep your ideas to yourself. OK, son?"

John knew he was going through a phase. But it was hard to escape the temptation. On the bathroom walls were scribblings: "Josephine Merril is a brain! I'd like to know her opinion." Leering things like that. If only he could stick to hugs and kissing, not this confiding business. . . .

Then there was Lauren, who nearly caused a scandal imagining a world where people openly shared their thoughts but kept lovemaking private. Where would that end?

Sound thought-provoking? Wait till you read the other stories in this great collection!

—Lesley Farmer

SKINNYBONES   Grades 3–6
By BARBARA PARK

T.J. Stoner is the kind of kid that kids like me hate. He's a superstar; I'm a supergoof. My name is Alex Frankovitch, but T.J. Stoner calls me Skinnybones. Why? Because I'm a munchkin, and when I put on my size-small Little League uniform the neck hangs down to my stomach.

I play ball about as good as I look. For six years in a row I've won the Most Improved Player trophy. Big deal! I know that the only player to get the trophy is the one who stinks to begin with. So now on the door of my room I have this sign: "This room belongs to Alex Frankovitch, the only boy in the whole world who has gone from stink-o to smelly six years in row!"

I may not have athletic ability like T.J. Stoner, but I've got a sense of humor. Making people laugh is a lot of fun. I've been able to make people laugh since I was in kindergarten. The teacher had us do Show and Tell. She always called my talks Show and Fib.

This year's sixth grade teacher had us stand up and tell about ourselves. Braggart T.J. Stoner stood up and said that his team won the state baseball championship in California and he was voted the most valuable player. Yuck! When I was called, I said my mother was a land turtle and my father was a raisin. The whole class roared. T.J. Stoner and the teacher didn't. Teachers aren't funny people. I ought to know. My goal in life is to try and find a teacher who appreciates my sense of humor.

When T.J. Stoner grew to be the biggest kid in class, I thought it might be wise to make friends with him. T.J. didn't seem to be interested. His exact words were, "Get lost, creep-head." "Does that mean no?" I asked. He grabbed me by the shoulders and looked me straight in the eye and said, "It means I hate your guts." "Aw, come on T.J., can't our guts be friends?" He didn't think that was quite as funny as I did—I could tell by the way he sat on my head.

One day T.J. Stoner was bragging to a bunch of kids that his Little League team hadn't lost a game all year. (Every team that I've played for came in in last place.) It was when I heard his bragging that I did a very dumb thing. How dumb? Read my story *Skinnybones* and find out just how dumb.

—*Marquis Berrey*

SLAM BOOK   Grades 6–8/YA
By ANN M. MARTIN

Anna wants to be Miss Popularity—not Miss Invisibility—on her first day at Calvin High. Her slam book will prove to everyone that she is not just a little nobody freshman. The book is passed around at slumber parties and in the cafeteria. A page is devoted to whomever Anna chooses—the kids she likes, the ones she hates, the cute boys, the dorks. Then people write what they really think about those kids. The book is a success, and so is Anna. She and her friends are having a million laughs—until somebody starts to cry. The slam book is not for laughs anymore.

—*Carrie McDonald*

SLAVE DANCER   GRADES 6–10
By PAULA FOX

Most of us don't associate the slave trade with music, and Jessie Bollier certainly didn't until the night he was kidnapped and taken to play his pipe aboard a slave ship. Jessie had been sent on an errand by his mother that night and found himself trapped in a canvas bag, destined for the slave ship *The Moonlight*.

Jessie usually made spare change playing his pipe on the New Orleans docks where the ships from every part of the world loaded and unloaded their cargo, and he had seen the slave ships with their human freight.

One of these ships needed someone to dance the blacks that were bought in Africa for rum or tobacco, or a price of $10 a head. The ship's captain, Captain Cawthorne, wanted to be able to deliver a shipload of muscular young blacks to the Portuguese in Saõ Paulo, and he needed some way to encourage them to exercise. Jessie's pipe-playing seemed just what he needed, so he kidnapped the boy.

On the ship, Jessie got used to the stench, the bugs, and the constant thirst, and he learned how the slavers avoided the law with such tricks as changing flags, presenting Spanish papers, or forcing the slaves off the boat and into the water as the inspection party boarded on the other side.

He came into contact with cruel men such as Ben Stout, who claimed to be Jessie's friend and then stole his fife and threw it down into the hold. Jessie had to retrieve it from among the packed bodies, his stomach retching from the stench.

This story is built around an incident that really occurred in 1840—a slave ship was wrecked in the Gulf of Mexico on June 3. There were two survivors, a white boy and a young black.

—*Mary James*

SMALL WORLDS CLOSE UP   Grades 4-6
By LISA GRILLONE and JOSEPH GENNARO

[Introduce this book by having children close their eyes and pretend they are taking a mysterious fantastic journey.]

Small Worlds Close Up takes you on a fantastic journey into the world of magnification. By using a powerful instrument known as the Scanning Electron Microscope, it is now possible to take pictures of the minutest details of ordinary objects. For example, have you ever wondered what a pinhead looks like? No, I don't mean your friend—I mean a *real* pinhead. Here, let me show you, this is what a real pinhead looks like, magnified two hundred times. Some other things that can be found around your house are also included in this book: table salt, newspapers, aluminum foil, and even a razor blade with tiny bits of skin attached to it. Now that I have shown you a few examples and told you what they are, let's see how good you are at guessing what this might be [choose a picture to show] and what about this [show another picture; in both cases any identifying text should be covered]. To find out the answer, all you need to do is enter the hidden world found between the pages of *Small Worlds Close Up.*

—Sally Fuentes

THE SNAKE THAT COULDN'T SLITHER   Grades 1-3
By PEGGY BRADBURY

Simon was a handsome young snake who couldn't slither. All the other young snakes slithered as they hastened over the jungle floor. Simon couldn't even climb trees. Whenever he tried he would fall to the ground. All the other snakes said he was a slob and a poor excuse for a snake. One day when all the snakes were asleep some poachers came into the jungle to capture them. How did Simon save all the other snakes when he couldn't even slither?

—Betty H. Lynch

THE SNARKOUT BOYS   Grades 7-8/YA
AND THE BACONBURG HORROR
By DANIEL PINKWATER

Winston Bong and his pal Walter Galt like to snark out together. "Snarking is the art of sneaking out of the house when your parents are sleeping, and having an adventure late at night," is how Walter explains it. These adventures usually take the form of forays to the Snark Theatre. The Snark is a great theatre because it is open 365 days a year and has a different double bill every 24 hours. What more could a movie buff want?

It was while snarking out one evening that Winston and Walter met Rat. Actually, Rat's name was Bentley Saunders Harrison Matthews, but everyone called her Rat—even her family.

Rat's uncle, Flipping Hades Terwilliger, told her about this neat coffeeshop, known as the Dharma Buns coffeehouse. All kinds of interesting folks hang out there, including a poet named Jonathan Quicksilver, who has written a poem about Rat's favorite actor, James Dean. But poets, artists, and snarkers aren't the only ones who like to hang out at the Dharma Buns. Rumor has it that a werewolf likes to frequent the coffeehouse as well. Could this be possible? And will the Snarkout Boys find out the truth? Read *The Snarkout Boys and the Baconburg Horror,* and you, too, will find out.

—Gail T. Orwig

SOMEONE IS HIDING ON ALCATRAZ ISLAND YA
By EVE BUNTING

It was only three days ago that Danny had made his fatal mistake. When he'd seen the kid throw the old lady down on the sidewalk, he'd chased him, caught him, knocked him down, and sat on his fat belly till the cops came. If the kid had been big and mean-looking, Danny probably wouldn't have done anything, but he was small like Danny. How was Danny to know that fat, soft, wimpy kid was Priest's younger brother?

Priest was a member of the Outlaws—the toughest, meanest gang at San Francisco's Jefferson High. To stay alive at Jefferson, it was best to stay out of the gang's way. Things happened to kids who didn't. One kid had imitated one of the Outlaw's voices—the next day he found all his pet pigeons with their throats cut. Another kid had kicked Priest by accident in gym class—he was jumped by four guys and had an ice pick jabbed through his foot. Priest always carried an ice pick.

Danny had knocked down Priest's brother three days ago, right at the start of spring vacation, and instead of hiding out at home he'd gone to Fisherman's Wharf, where the Outlaws had spotted him. Danny had never run so fast in all his life, just fast enough to jump aboard the boat for Alcatraz Island, leaving the Outlaws standing on the dock. Danny figured he'd hide out on Alcatraz—go on the tour and then sneak back into San Francisco in the middle of all the tourists—but when he started back toward the boat he saw the Outlaws again. They'd followed him. Danny was trapped on Alcatraz Island with no way to get off—just him and the Outlaws.

—Marianne Tait Pridemore

SPACE STATION SEVENTH GRADE Grades 5-9
By JERRY SPINELLI

Life's not easy for Jason, once a sixth-grade big shot, now a seventh-grade big nothing. Jason is finding out the hard way just how different things are in junior high, where seventh-graders are lowly and ninth-graders are kings. To make the going easier, which actually makes things harder sometimes, Jason and his friends resort to pranks.

In seventh grade, everyone has to take Home Economics, both girls and boys. The Home Ec teacher is Miss Perch, who is about ninety-nine years old. No matter what the class cooks, Miss Perch takes a bite, rolls her eyes, and exclaims "Glorious!"

Well, one day Miss Perch announces that the class will be making food for Herman the janitor's retirement party. Jason and his friend Richie are class cooking partners, and they decide to make fudge. They only know two kinds, vanilla and chocolate, and they vote on chocolate.

"What are we gonna put in it? Nuts? Coconut? Peanut butter?" Jason asks Richie.

Richie answers, "Bugs." Now, at first Jason thinks Richie is crazy, but then he sees Richie is serious. Pretty soon, Jason agrees. After all, people ate locusts in the Bible, and no one could get poisoned, because once you cook a bug the germs all die.

First they have to decide on what kind of bug. Since it's winter, most bugs are gone. And nobody they know has roaches in their house. But Richie gets a brilliant idea. There's an ant farm in the science classroom. After school, he and Jason sneak in, use some taffy as bait to collect some ants, and put them into an empty cole-slaw container. Then they go to Richie's house to make the fudge.

The boys decide the ants should be crispy, but should they fry them with or without butter? Then Richie gets another brilliant idea. "Popcorn popper!" he yells. They put in some oil, plug in the popper, and pretty soon there they are: unsalted, unbuttered, popped ants!

The boys proceed to use this secret ingredient, and they bring a whole batch of the fudge to their classroom. To find out what happens, read *Space Station Seventh Grade,* a funny, crazy, happy, and sad book by Jerry Spinelli.

—*Diane Tuccillo*

SPACE 3: YA/Adult
A COLLECTION OF SCIENCE FICTION STORIES
Selected by RICHARD DAVIS

This is a collection of stories written by some of the biggest names in science fiction. My favorite is "Scoop," by Peter L. Cave.

From cities all over the world, the news buzzed along the wires and was fed into computers to be analyzed, edited, checked, rechecked, and cross-checked. There was a great rush to get the paper out on time. Robots handled every phase of the reporting, and every job from copy-boy to managing editor. Automatic typesetting, automatic proofreading; and electronic gadgets set up page after page of newsprint. Finally the finished pages were bundled together by robots and loaded onto trucks. They were delivered to automatic news vendors.

The *Daily Globe* carried the biggest scoop of all time. HUMANITY DESTROYED, in letters three inches high—it was the greatest headline of recorded history. It was the scoop to end all scoops. . . . They didn't sell a single copy.

—Janet Loebel

SPECTACLES   **Grades 4–6**
By ANN BEATTIE

Alison's great-grandmother is too ill to come to Alison's birthday party, so after the party Alison goes to her grandmother's room and lies down across the foot of the bed.

Alison wants to tell her great-grandmother of the wonderful gifts her friends have given her. But Great-grandmother has a faraway look in her eyes and begins to wish for things the way they used to be. Alison asks, "Don't you like anything the way it is?"

It really upsets Alison. Her great-grandmother is in a world of her own, and she just does not see things the way Alison does.

That night, as Alison lies in bed, she thinks of all the day's events. She decides to go look for the leftover brownies. As she finishes eating them, she sees a pair of glasses lying on the kitchen table. They belong to her great-grandmother.

Alison picks them up and looks through them. Everything is fuzzy and strange. The stairs look like pools of water, the rug seems like a long sandy beach.

In her bedroom, the white shades become valentine cards, and the painted walls now have flowered wallpaper. And a large pillowy sofa is where her bed had been only minutes earlier. On the sofa a man and a woman are sitting closely, intent on one another.

As Alison looks around she recognizes the birthday gifts she received. The hair ribbons are alive, Alison's new hat is listening, the colored pencils are ready to spring into action.

Discover what you might see when you look through Ann Beattie's *Spectacles*.

—Rose R. Donoway

SPIRITS AND SPELLS
By BRUCE COVILLE
Grades 7-8/YA

The old haunted Gulbrandsen mansion was the perfect place to play the new fantasy game, Spirits and Spells, that Jerry had purchased at the gaming convention. The mansion was said to be haunted by the ghost of a servant girl, Charity Jones, whose head had been severed from her body. The head was perfectly preserved in a box in the attic, but 150 years later Charity was still looking for her body. So Charity was waiting for Jerry and his five friends in the attic, and in the cellar deep below the house was the guardian of the sword, a huge ugly monster with long slimy tentacles.

Jerry and his five friends would be the first to play this new game, which its inventor said had come to him in dreams from beyond. If only Jerry had known the horrors from which this game had sprung! It wasn't a game at all; it was real—quite real and quite deadly. And Jerry and his friends might be the first—and the last—ever to play *Spirits and Spells*.

—Marianne Tait Pridemore

SQUEAK
By JOHN BOWEN
YA/Adult

When Squeak's parents disappeared, the people they had lived with took the orphaned baby into their home to raise. In the beginning there was a little confusion: the people thought Squeak was a "he," and Squeak just *knew* she was exactly like them.

Squeak soon convinced them that she was a girl, when she fell madly in love with the both of them and decided to have a baby. But it didn't take her long to realize that these two guys were slightly backwards when it came to a serious relationship, for they never seemed to get the hint. She would have to be the aggressive one—that is, if she wanted to have her baby. But what could she do?

Then she entered the kitchen and saw the oven mitt, and she knew everything would be all right. She would start to love nest. But even though she tried her hardest to make them understand what she was doing, they kept shooing her away from the oven mitt! And eventually they exiled her from the kitchen altogether!

How was she ever going to have a love nest if they wouldn't build one for her, or let her make one out of the mitt, or even out of a dish towel? For, you see, little Squeak, who thinks she's human, is really a lovelorn homing pigeon.

—Faye Powell

THE STALKER   YA/Adult
By JOAN LOWERY NIXON

Talk 1

I killed Stella Trax. I don't want to think about it anymore. It happened. What's done is done.

Just one thing worries me. Where did she keep the stuff? I should have made her tell me.

The news said the police have arrested Stella's daughter Bobbie. Now they have their suspect. Maybe they'll stick the kid with it. Let's see what I can do to make sure.

Jennifer, Bobbie's best friend, is like a gnat. A small nuisance. Why is she getting in the way? It's not her business. For her own sake, she better not become more than a nuisance.

There's no way the girl can connect us. I'm careful. And I know what to do with people who become dangerous to me.

Careful, careful, little girl. I'm keeping track of you.

Better scare off, or you'll be next.

—*Cheryl Welch*

Talk 2

When 17-year-old Jennifer Lee Wilcox first heard the news that Stella Trax had been murdered and her daughter Bobbi, who was Jennifer's best friend, had been charged with the killing, she couldn't believe it. Then the police showed up to question Jennifer. Bobbi had disappeared—did Jennifer know where she was? Of course Jennifer knew where to find Bobbi, but she wasn't telling the police. Instead she borrowed her boyfriend's car and went to find Bobbi at the old lean-to tucked away in the sand dunes. Bobbi was there; she'd run off after having a huge fight with her mom, and Jennifer had to tell her that her mom was dead—murdered. One look at Bobbi's face told Jennifer the truth: she hadn't done it. Just as the two girls were getting ready to return to town the police appeared. They had followed Jennifer. Both girls were taken to the police station where Bobbi was charged with her mother's murder and Jennifer was questioned and released. It was an open-and-shut case; the police were through investigating—they had the killer. Only Bobbi, Jennifer, and the real murderer knew the truth.

The police wouldn't listen to Jennifer. She tried to hire a private detective, but they all wanted $500 to start. Even Bobbi wanted her to give up—afraid of what she might find out. Finally Jennifer convinced a retired detective, Lucas Maldonaldo, to help her. Together they'd find Stella's killer—or he'd find them. Stella's killing is only the first in *The Stalker*, by Joan Lowery Nixon.

—*Marianne Tait Pridemore*

THE STOLEN LAW   YA
By ANNE MASON

"There is no doubt," Kira thought, after four days at her new assignment, "this is going to be the worst experience of my life." As an EXO-communicator assigned to the famous Vallusian commander Ertex, it was her duty to translate messages between the Vallusians and the Arraveseans, and in addition to observe the Vallusians and explain them to the Arraveseans so the other alien culture could work with them more easily. That was no problem—the problem was Ertex himself. He hated Earth-people, and hated Earth E-comms most of all. He had refused to give her Valued Aide status and made her part of a security squad instead, expecting her to fail so he could refuse to work with her and send her back to her own station. But he didn't know Kira very well. She was small, but she was also stubborn. Not only did she manage to keep up with her group, she even saved the life of one of her squad leaders when he fell into a river during training maneuvers. But not even that could change Ertex's mind about her. Then she discovered the reason for his hostility—he believed that an Earth E-comm had betrayed him and his bond-partner, and his partner had died. He and the E-comm had lived, but she had refused to tell anyone what had happened to them, to explain why his partner's body had never been found.

Ertex didn't know about the law of sector status—an E-comm who revealed what had been heard under sector status was immediately executed, and any person that he or she had talked to also died. There were no exceptions, and no appeals. The E-comm who had been working with Ertex and his partner had been under sector status, and could not have said anything without condemning to death both of them and anyone else who heard. But no one ever told Ertex about the law, and he had nursed his hatred for years, and now was determined to take it out on Kira. What he didn't know, and what Kira was horrified to discover, was that she was the daughter of the woman Ertex believed had betrayed him.

—Joni Bodart-Talbot

STOTAN!   Grades 6–8/YA
By CHRIS CRUTCHER

Stotan: a week of endurance for Jeff, Nortie, Lionel, and Walker. They endure, but then one of them comes up with a challenge that may be too difficult even for Stotan.

—Carol Sandness

STRAWBERRY GIRL   Grades 4–8
By LOIS LENSKI

We all know what a Cracker is, right? Wrong! Birdie Boyer's a Cracker and that's because she grew up in the Florida backwoods long before any of us was born. She loved animals, piano-playing, hard work, and most of all strawberries! She hated rattlesnakes, lazy people, and braggarts. What would life without cars or electricity be like? Find out in Lois Lenski's *Strawberry Girl.*

—Pam Swofford

STRICTLY FOR LAUGHS   Grades 7–8/YA
By ELLEN CONFORD

When the going gets tough, Joey Merino goes for the laughs. Since she was twelve, she has gone for the laughs. But when Joey starts high school, she realizes she is deeply, passionately, hopelessly in love with her longtime friend Peter Stillman.

Unfortunately, Peter is deeply, passionately, obsessively in love with his uncle's radio station. Somehow Joey's got to get Peter's attention. But can she stop joking long enough to let him know she's serious?

—Olivia Jacobs

SUMMER IN THE SOUTH   Grades 3–5
By JAMES MARSHALL

Who were the guests assembled in a small hotel on a quiet beach—and was their vacation really going to be as quiet as they thought?

Some of the guests were exactly who they seemed to be—there were the rowdy squirrel twins, who liked to go furry-dipping (without their bathing suits); there was Mr. Foster Pig, who was shocked by the twins and was so fussy and cantankerous that he carried a feather duster everywhere he went, just in case some dust got in his way. And there were the Cootie Family—so small they could travel through the mail in an envelope.

Other guests were a bit more complicated. Miss Marietta Chicken was a most beautiful lady with a mysterious past. She had been a famous circus chicken, and had performed all over the world. Miss Eleanor Owl and her assistant Mr. Paws were a celebrated detective team, who had already solved twenty-nine important cases, including the Puzzle of the Talking Bubblegum. Eleanor Owl thought she was here for a rest until she met the strangest guests of all—The Travelling String Quartet, a group of lady baboons who carried musical instruments wherever they went. But were they really musicians? Eleanor began to wonder. They refused to play or even to listen to music at the hotel, and they said their favorite living composer was Beethoven!

But at least the hotel was quiet—or was it? The night the string quartet arrived was the night the first ghost was seen. Soon Miss Chicken's room had been broken into, and before long, everyone knew that she had been cursed by the Mummy of the Great King Kluk! Even the Cootie Family were called upon to perform a dangerous mission as the curse came true in *The Summer in the South,* by James Marshall.

—*Elizabeth Overmyer*

SUMMER OF FEAR   YA
By LOIS DUNCAN

It's been four years now. I'm still not rid of it. Perhaps I never will be. I still remember the very day it began, June 2. School was just out, but summer had not really begun. I lay in bed, watching the sunlight filter through the blinds and listening to my family below, enjoying the smell of bacon cooking and coffee perking and feeling a little lazy and a little guilty. The phone rang. I waited to be paged. When no one called my name I swung out of bed, dressed, and went downstairs.

No one was in the kitchen. The bacon was draining on a paper towel, the coffee was still perking on the back of the stove. Eggs and milk sat waiting to be turned into French toast. Gradually I became aware of muffled sounds coming from the living room.

My mother was crying. My father had his arms around her. Mom's only sister, Aunt Marge, and her husband, Uncle Ryan, had been killed in an auto accident. My cousin Julia, who had stayed at home, would come to live with us.

Julia. She was a plain, thin girl with long black hair that hung halfway to her waist. Her face was narrow and sallow, her eyes were riveting. Haunting eyes, dark and full of secrets.

No one else thought her plain or saw what I saw in her eyes. They loved her. My older brother Peter, who didn't even like girls, my parents, my best friend, they all loved her. Even after she killed my dog they loved her. They said my dog was sick and that I was dreadfully wrong. Even my boyfriend, Mike, fell in love with Julia. I saw into her eyes, I saw her power.

They wouldn't believe me. Father grounded me, Mother exiled me from her studio. They loved her. I was terrified. How could I make them believe me? Even if I could convince them, would it be in time?

Summer of Fear, by Lois Duncan.

—*Barbara Hawkins*

THE SUMMER   Grades 7–8/YA
OF MY GERMAN SOLDIER
By BETTE GREEN

"Every German oughta be taken out and tortured to death," said Patty Bergen's father. It was wartime, and the Nazis were slaughtering Jews in Europe.

Still, even though they were Jewish, Patty couldn't understand how her father could talk that way. She really discovered how wrong he was about all Germans being the same the day the German prisoner-of-war came into her father's store—and she met Anton.

Patty was twelve, and she found a friend in the German who wanted to be a doctor. When Anton escaped, she tried to help him. She had the most exciting, the happiest, and the saddest summer of her life.

To find out how Patty was hurt, humiliated, and grew up, you'll have to read *The Summer of My German Soldier.*

—*Madeline Abath*

SUMMER OF THE MONKEYS   Grades 4–8
By WILSON RAWLS

Up until I was fourteen years old, no boy in the world could have been happier than I was. Like most boys my age, I didn't have a worry or a care. In fact, I was beginning to think it wasn't going to be difficult at all for me to grow up. But wouldn't you know that just when things were really looking good for me, something up and happened? I got myself mixed up with a bunch of monkeys, and right then all my happiness just flew out the window. Those monkeys all but drove me out of my mind.

Grandpa is my pal, so I got him mixed up in it (which was my first big mistake), and I even coaxed Rowdy, my old blue-tick hound, into helping me with the monkey business. I didn't realize that monkeys could make me so miserable, until I was laughed at, bitten, robbed, made a fool of, and even had my britches stolen.

Those twenty-eight little monkeys wouldn't have been so successful at making me miserable if Jimbo, the chimpanzee, hadn't master-minded the whole plot by giving them instructions in his monkey talk and gestures.

You will never believe all the problems, trials, and tribulations those monkeys caused me, until you read *Summer of the Monkeys*.

—Dorothy Carrothers

SUMMER RULES   YA
By ROBERT LIPSYTE

"I hear there's an opening at Happy Valley" Bobby's father said at dinner one night.

"Better close it quick before all the happiness spills out," Bobby cracked. His father smiled—which Bobby later realized should have set off his alarm that something was wrong.

"An opening for a counselor. I think you'll get it," continued his father.

"What makes you think I'm going to apply for it?"

"You already have," his father said. "You are going to work at Happy Valley this summer."

When his father threw in the threat of not letting him use the car that summer, Bobby knew the case was closed. He would be working at Happy Valley, like it or not. And he didn't. Happy Valley. What a laugh! They should have called it Pathetic Molehill or Death Valley

Day Camp. How was he supposed to become a great writer like Ernest Hemingway if he had to spend the summer wiping the noses of a bunch of soft city kids? What was worse, his sister Michelle would be working there too. Neither one was happy with the arrangement. But neither one had a choice.

A few days later they headed to the first counselor's meeting of the season. They were late, so Michelle made them sit in the first row, and Bobby felt like a fool when he was introduced to the rest of the group. Then Moe Bell, director of the camp, started talking about camp spirit:

"'More in Fifty-Four means that the summer of 1954 is going to be a Super-Duper, Extra-Special, Yankee Doodle Ipsy-Dipsy A-Number-One True-Blue Hot-Diggety Bell-Ringing Wing-Ding for all the folks at Happy Valley!'"

Bobby didn't know it at that meeting, but Moe Bell was right. It was the kind of summer Bobby had waited for all his life.

—Kathryn Dunn

THE SUMMERBOY   YA
By ROBERT LIPSYTE

The summerboy, Bobby Marks, is once again looking for a summer job. After spending recent summers mowing lawns and being a camp counselor, he's looking for a real job. And he finds it at the Lenape Laundry, becoming the first Rumson Lake summer resident to ever work there.

Although Bobby is concerned about the horrible work conditions at the laundry—things like leaking steam pipes and delivery trucks with faulty brakes or bald tires—he still manages to have some summer fun.

While attending a party one night at the home of a very rich friend, he meets two young French girls, Marie and Mignon, and immediately sets out to impress them. He suggests they meet down at the dock for a midnight skinny-dip. They giggle a reply which he assumes means they'll meet him. At midnight he heads to the dock. Thinking he's seen the girls, he sheds his clothes under the boathouse stairs and prepares to dive. [Read from pages 58–59, hardback edition.]

Bobby seems to have a natural ability to dive into uncomfortable situations, and his exploits at the Lenape Laundry prove no different. He is a true *Summerboy*.

—Pam Spencer

SURROGATE SISTER   YA
By EVE BUNTING

Cassie is sixteen and her widowed mother is pregnant. One day she walks into English class and there's a message on the blackboard: "Cassie Dedrick's Mother Does It for Money!"

—*Cheryl Welch*

SWEET WHISPERS, BROTHER RUSH   YA
By VIRGINIA HAMILTON

"Tree was on her way home from school, walking down the street with the dudes catcalling to her, when she first spied Brother Rush. She saw him at once, the way you see something that has been there all the time, but you never had eyes open wide enough to see. It was like Brother Rush jumped right out of space at her, in one never-to-be-forgotten impression. She hadn't realized that it was the message out of Brother's eyes that had captivated her. It had all happened too fast."

The next time Tree saw Brother Rush, she fell more in love with him. He was standing on the avenue and again she did not speak.

But Tree wouldn't *ever* have known Brother Rush was a ghost if it hadn't been for the little room at home. Tree would go to the little room to draw on the big round table, to relax herself, and be alone.

One evening, Tree came to the little room. To peel away her worries, to draw.

She saw the strangest light. And Brother Rush. The way he had been on the avenue, although Tree hadn't seen him today on her way home. It shocked her, seeing him. But she wasn't scared. She was about to say to him, "What you *doin'* in here—how you *get* in here?" but then she saw. Saw and couldn't help seeing, couldn't keep herself from believing.

Brother Rush was in the middle of the table. Not standing on the top of it in the middle, but *through* the middle. He was standing *in* the table. Brother Rush was smack through the hard wood of the round table of the little room. And Tree knew. Brother Rush be a damned ghost.

To find out why Brother Rush appeared to Tree and where he took her, read *Sweet Whispers, Brother Rush,* by Virginia Hamilton.

—*Sherry Cotter*

THE SWORD OF SHANNARA   YA
By TERRY BROOKS

Two thousands years into the future, and one thousand years after the last of the Great Wars, the world is slowly rebuilding. But this is a much different world from the one we know today.

For one thing, humans are no longer the dominant race on earth but must now share the planet with others, such as dwarves, elves, gnomes, and trolls. For another thing, the huge, centralized nations of our world have now given way to small, separate communities, made up of people who travel little and know even less of life beyond the boundaries of their territory.

In one of these communities, the Shady Vale, two brothers, Shea and Flick Ohmsford, live with their father, the innkeeper. Shea, the older of the two brothers, is an adopted son and is half human and half elf. Unknown to him, he is also a descendant of Jerle Shannara, the greatest of the Elven kings who a thousand years before, vanquished Brona, the Warlock Lord who ruled the evil Northern Kingdom. But Shea knows nothing of this and feels that his beloved Shady Vale is a haven of un-disturbed peace.

Then a stranger comes into the Vale. He is the huge and forbidding wizard/historian Allanon, and he reveals to Shea that the Warlock Lord, long thought to be dead, is alive and once again plotting to de-stroy the world. Against his power the only effective weapon is the Sword of Shannara, which can only be used by a true descendant of Jerle Shannara. Shea is the last heir, and upon him all the hopes of the people rest.

At first Shea and his brother Flick try to convince each other that Allanon is only a faker and that the Warlock Lord and the Sword are merely myths, but before long a Skull Bearer, the dreaded messenger of the Warlock, comes into the village seeking to destroy the heir. Shea and Flick are forced to run for their lives.

Realizing that Shea will never be safe as long as the Warlock Lord is in power, the two brothers decide to search for the only thing that can defeat him, the Sword of Shannara. And so begins an almost hope-less journey, on which the brothers cross many strange lands, face many dangers, and make many friends and enemies. Through it all, they know that eventually they will have to make a stand alone against the greatest evil the world has ever seen.

—Larry Duckwall

TAKERS AND RETURNERS
By CAROL YORK

Boredom can strike anyone at any time, and in *Takers and Returners* it leads to the invention of a game.

Every summer for seven years, the Carter family and their three kids and their two cousins and their folks rent a house at Green Hills Lake. By mid-July the cousins are bored. Julian, who's fifteen and the oldest of the cousins, makes up a game. He calls it Takers and Returners. It's really quite easy. If your team takes something, there are two rules. You must take something that adults will miss and it must be something that adults will look for. If your team takes it without getting caught, you get points. If the other team returns the item without getting caught, they get points. At the end of the summer the team with the most points wins.

Julian's team starts right away and takes a bust of Charles Dickens from the library. Not caught. Points. Ellen's team returns it. Not caught. Points. Ellen's team then takes the weather vane from the roof of the house Julian's folks have rented for the summer. Not caught. Points. Julian's team has to wait a while before they can return it because there's always an adult around. About a week later their patience pays off. The folks go out to dinner and the weather vane is returned. Not caught. Points.

By this time, Julian has had it with this kiddy stuff. His team takes Dr. Drover's car. This poses a real problem for Ellen's team. Not only is no one old enough to drive, no one is tall enough to operate the pedals, steer the car, and look out the windshield at the same time. Ellen's team takes Miss Mindy's dog. Now that doesn't sound like much, but this dog will bite anyone at any time for absolutely no reason. But this time, when each of the teams tries to return the items taken, tragedy strikes.

If you'd like to know how far kids will go to win a game, read *Takers and Returners,* by Carol York.

—Paula Eads

TAKING CARE OF TERRIFIC
By LOIS LOWRY

I have always hated my name. Enid Irene Crowley. Now really—it would be a terrible name even for an old lady. I was named after my father's aunt. My father is a lawyer, but I just couldn't ask him to change my name legally.

My mother is a radiologist. She's one of those people who can see even the most microscopic objects, but she can't do everything herself. She hires people both at work and at home.

Mrs. Kolodny was hired fourteen years ago. She's a real space cadet. She can't remember anything. She's the type of person who cleans between soap operas and chapters of books. She also forgets—she has a memory that doesn't work. That's how I got the job baby-sitting Joshua Warwick Cameron IV. We changed his name too! Tom Terrific. It was a pretty good summer . . . until the kidnapping.

—Katherine L. Fapp

THE TALKING EARTH   Grades 6-9
By JEAN CRAIGHEAD GEORGE

"Billie Wind, what do you think will be a suitable punishment?" the medicine man asked.

Billie was a modern-day Seminole Indian girl, just a little older than you are. She had been to the Kennedy Space Center school, where her father worked, but her tribe still believed the old legends about animals that talk and little people who live underground and play tricks on you.

All except Billie, that is. . . . So she had to be punished for not believing. The punishment which she suggested was that she go to the Everglades swamp and stay there until she heard the animals talk and saw the little people who live underground.

Alone in the Everglades, Billie made friends with a baby otter, a baby panther, and a gopher turtle. She survived a flash fire and a hurricane, and discovered an ancient Indian cave. And she found answers to her questions about animals talking and little people who live underground!

—Dorothy A. Davidson

TANCY   Grades 6-8/YA
By BELINDA HURMENCE

Tancy loved to read. She practiced every chance she had. Before the war she had devoured *The Carolina Watchman* and *The Knoxford Express*, but they weren't available now. In 1864 there was no paper to spare.

While her mistress napped she continued to read the letters, papers, and plantation records lying on the library table. One February day she discovered her own birth record: "6/17/48—Lulu delivered of Tancy. Both well." Where was Lulu? She must have been sold. When? To whom? None of the old slaves would tell her.

After Emancipation, when almost all the slaves left the plantations, Tancy stayed. She felt an obligation to Miz Gaither. Besides, it was home. Still, she wondered about her mother. When Julia came, looking for her husband, she and Miz Gaither agreed on a salary for Julia's housekeeping services. Miz Gaither wouldn't be alone, now.

In the milky blue dawn, Tancy plaited her hair securely over her silver dollar and tied a turban over her head. She bid a silent farewell to Miz Gaither and crept from the room. One last stop to read again the words she knew so well: "9/9/49—Lulu sold to Thad Shurford . . . $600.00." "My mother, and I wasn't even two years old."

She left home, taking the high road to Charlotte. Hours later she met a man on horseback. He took her to an old ambulance transporting freed blacks to Knoxville. She was going to find her mother.

Tancy, by Belinda Hurmence.

—Barbara Hawkins

A TEACUP FULL OF ROSES   YA
By SHARON BELL MATHIS

This is a story about three brothers: Paul, who painted like a god and who took drugs to forget he hadn't made it with his art; Davey, the youngest, smartest, and tallest, who was a natural athlete with a brain that wouldn't stop working; and Joey, who wasn't anyone special, except to his girl Ellie. But Joey could tell beautiful stories. He promised Ellie they'd be happy and live in a teacup full of roses, and he promised Davey he'd help him go to college. This is also a story about being black and living in a ghetto, when your father can't work and your mother's working too hard and nobody's ever *really* happy.

When this story begins, Paul has just gotten back, clean, from a drug rehab center. Joey is about to graduate from night school, after going for two years with a full-time job during the day, and he and Ellie want to be married soon. And Davey has been chosen as one of nine high-school juniors to participate in a special academic program the next year. Everything looks good.

Then, in one week, it all falls apart. Joey realizes that Paul's hooked again, that Davey's caught, and that he and Ellie may never have their happiness, their teacup full of roses, after all.

—Joni Bodart-Talbot

TELL ME SOME MORE   Grades 1-4
By CROSBY NEWELL BONSALL

"I know a place where I can hold an elephant in my hands," said Andrew to Tim. "I don't believe you," said Tim. "It's true!" said Andrew; "if I tell you about it would you believe me?" "Sure!" said Tim, "tell me and see!" "Well, I know a place where I can hold a camel, a river, a boat, and a rocket ship in my hands. I can take the lions home with me, too." "Tell me some more!" said Tim. "No!" said Andrew, "I won't tell you, but I will take you there."

—JoAnne Clough

THE TEMPERED WIND   YA
By JEANNE DIXON

The questions were to the point: What could Gabriella do? Could she milk cows? Tend chickens? Cook? Clean? Shoe horses? Plow? Naturally she said yes, yes, yes. Gabriella needed this new chance at life. She had spent most of her childhood alone in her small bedroom, locked in by an uncaring mother. After her mother died, she had been passed from one aunt to another. Tante Eloise had fulfilled her Christian duty by providing shelter (in a damp basement) and an education (at a strict girls' academy). Although Gabriella had been the brightest student, she had not been liked by the others. But to travel out to frontier Montana and work as a chore girl—that could be the opportunity she craved. Someone would love her for herself, for her abilities. It would not matter that Gabriella was a misshapen dwarf, seventeen years old and barely over three feet tall.

—Carol Spencer

THAT MEAN MAN   Grades k-3
By LIESEL MOAK SKORPEN

I knew a man, and he was mean.

I mean he was *mean.*

He kicked cats and growled at dogs. He frightened little children and made them cry. He popped other people's balloons. And when children flew kites, he clipped their strings. I mean he was *mean!*

But one day he met a woman, a mean woman. With one glance they knew they were meant for each other. They had a lovely wedding, but of course they didn't invite anyone.

And then, it happened! They got just what they deserved.

That Mean Man—find out just what he deserved!

—*Lynda Smith*

THERE'S A BAT IN BUNK FIVE   Grades 7–8/YA
By PAULA DANZIGER

Marcy Lewis, the main character in *The Cat Ate My Gymsuit*, is back, two years older and several pounds thinner. She's been asked by her former teacher, Ms. Finney, to be a junior counselor for the summer at a new creative-arts camp. Marcy is thrilled—not only will she have the chance to work with her favorite teacher again, but she will also have a chance to get away from home for an entire summer. Things are better at home since the entire family went through family counseling, but her father had a serious heart attack the previous fall and Marcy and he still have a very strained relationship. Marcy does hate leaving her younger brother Stuart, who has put aside his famous teddy bear, Wolfe. Now he has this thing about becoming a football player and he wears his football helmet all the time. Marcy is a bundle of nerves as her parents drive her up to the camp. Little does she imagine that it will be the most exciting summer of her life—especially after she meets a hunk named Ted and a brat named Ginger.

—*Barbara Lynn*

THERE'S AN ALLIGATOR UNDER   Grades 1–4
MY BED
By MERCER MAYER

I had the perfect alligator bait: soda and candy by the bed, cookies in the hall, vetegables on the stairs. Now all I had to do was wait and watch.

—*Teresa Schlatt*

THE THING AT THE FOOT OF THE BED   Grades 4-6
By MARIA LEACH

Here's a whole book of scary stories. Many of the stories are about ghosts or other haunts. Some are about strange, unearthly creatures, or people possessed by demons. The story "Milk Bottles" tells of an occurence many years ago in a small country village in Alabama. One day a strange pale ghostlike woman, dressed all in gray, came into the town store. She didn't speak, just pointed to a bottle of milk. The storekeeper handed the bottle to her and she took it and left, without speaking or paying. After this happened several days in a row, some of the villagers decided to follow the woman. Out of the town she led them, past the church and up the hill to a graveyard, where she disappeared. The villagers noticed that she had vanished right beside a fresh grave—the double grave of a woman and her infant daughter who had died just three days previously of a fever. The villagers fetched shovels and soon unearthed the mother's coffin. Then, just as they were moving the coffin, they heard a tiny muffled wail. Quickly, they opened the coffin, and inside they found the corpse of the woman in gray . . . and in her arms the baby girl, ill and weak, but still alive. Scattered in the coffin were the empty milk bottles.

—Zoë Kalkanis

THINNER   YA/Adult
By RICHARD BACHMAN

Thinner. . . .

Billy Halleck weighed around 250 pounds when he ran down the old Gypsy lady in the street with his car. The judge let him off easy.

Thinner. . . .

Halleck and his wife had been fooling around, and he hadn't been paying attention to the road. Killing the old lady was an accident, but it was an accident that shouldn't have happened.

Thinner. . . .

That's what the old Gypsy man whispered to Halleck as he was leaving the courthouse. He was going scot-free after killing someone. The old man with the rotting nose touched his cheek and whispered, "Thinner."

And Halleck began to get thinner, thinner by several pounds a day, thinner no matter how much he ate.

Thinner. . . .

what would happen between us before the summer was over.

Joni Bodart-Talbot

WHEN NO ONE WAS LOOKING   Grades 7–8/YA
By ROSEMARY WELLS

Kathy Bardy is ranked twelfth in New England girls-fourteen-and-under tennis. She trains faithfully and says she'd run to the North Pole barefooted if it would help her take the New England championship.

But Kathy has a problem. Her best friend Julie explains, "You let everyone who wants it have your number. You let people rip you to pieces. You don't get even, you get mad and take it out on your insides instead of the other person."

Kathy's invitation to the National hinges on her beating a fairly good but not spectacular player whose quiet, stubborn arguments about nothing are calculated to test Kathy's well-known temper.

The night before the match, a freak accident eliminates this obstacle and fingers begin to point.

Was it really an accident?

Who has an alibi?

What actually happened *When No One Was Looking*?

—Marcia Edwards

WHEN THE BOYS   Grades 4–6
RAN THE HOUSE
By JOAN CARRIS

Can you imagine the four hundred kinds of trouble four brothers can get into when their dad is in Europe on a business trip and their mother is sick in bed? Of course, everyone has to *eat*. Fixing cold cereal and peanut butter sandwiches was pretty easy for the boys, but they did get tired of eating that day after day. So they decided to try something a little fancier. For their first big meal they fixed spaghetti, ravioli, black olives, waffles with syrup, celery stuffed with peanut butter, and banana splits. You can imagine what they felt like (and what the kitchen looked like) after all that.

Then they realized they would have to go grocery shopping. Jut, the oldest boy, sent Nick into the supermarket. When Jut came to get him Nick had really filled up their cart—three boxes of Twinkies, a row of Ding Dongs, a row of chocolate cupcakes, root beer, cola, ice cream,

The judge was cursed too. He began developing scales. The chief of police was cursed. He developed the world's worst case of acne. And Halleck *just keeps on getting thinner.*

No one believes it's happening because of a curse. They think it's a physical problem—or a mental one. His only hope is to hunt down the old Gypsy and get him to remove the curse.

But Halleck's time is running out. He's down to 130 pounds and still getting thinner.

Thinner, by Richard Bachman—a pseudonym for (who else?) Stephen King!

—*Melinda Waugh*

THIRD GIRL FROM THE LEFT   YA
By ANN TURNER

"First," Sarah's aunt said severely, "There was the day you put molasses on the minister's saddle. Then there was the time you put a pinch of gunpowder in the school stove. And I won't even mention the time you stole the clothes from the men's swimming hole and Charlie Blackmun had to crawl home naked through the blueberry bushes! That ruined several good proposals, Sarah. Don't you *want* to get married?"

But Sarah had other ideas—she wanted to *run* a farm, not drudge for some man, have a houseful of babies, and die before she was forty! And in 1855, what else could she be, except perhaps an old-maid schoolmarm? It seemed there was no way out—until she saw the ad in the Portland paper: "Wanted, a wife of docile temper to care for husband and hands. Ranch in high country with one thousand head of cattle. Wife must be able to cook, sew, read, and (God willing) talk. Direct all replies to Alex T. Proud, High Ridge Ranch, Dillman, Montana."

That sure didn't *sound* like the same old boring stuff, day after day—and on a ranch, it'd be hard to feel closed in. Just thinking about answering that ad made her tingle—it shouted excitement, maybe even danger! What a way to leave town—what drama and style!

"Dear Sir, I read your advertisement and am interested. I've a mind to come west and marry—especially to someone who wants to talk. . . . "

Just a few weeks later she was on the way to Montana and Alex. But things didn't turn out the way she'd expected. For one thing, the picture he sent showed a man in his forties. However, after they'd been married, when Alex took off his hat for the wedding picture, she discovered he was closer to sixty or seventy. She'd just married an old man! Alone in her hotel room that night she realized she'd done it again. She'd jumped into this before she'd thought about it—and now she was in over her head, with no way out. She couldn't go home again—all she could do was make the best of it.

—*Joni Bodart-Talbot*

THE THIRTEENTH MEMBER   Grades 3-5
By MOLLIE HUNTER

Imagine that you live in 1590, nearly four hundred years ago, in a little village in Scotland. You are a sixteen-year-old boy, a servant who sleeps in a shed on a pile of straw. Late one night hunger wakes you. Through a crack in the wall you see a strange bluish glow traveling along the track between your village and the next. Despite your better judgment, you are curious and get up to investigate. Someone else from the household is ahead of you, though. It's Gilly Duncan, the timid housemaid. Your curiosity grows. Trying to follow Gilly, you find that you're getting closer to the blue light. Then you lose sight of the girl, but see the light coming nearer. You crouch behind some bushes by the side of the road, waiting, watching. Muffled hoofbeats approach. To your horror, as the blue light comes around a curve in the path, you see that it is the Devil himself riding horseback. You know it is the Devil, because he looks and smells just as the minister says he does.

You think that he will surely carry you off, but somehow he misses you and disappears down the track. Then you remember Gilly Duncan. You are sure the Devil will kill her, and you will be blamed for her death. But the next day Gilly is at her work, cleaning the kitchen fireplace. When you tell her what you saw, she begins to cry and say strange things you don't understand, begging you to tell no one else, warning you that death will follow. In confusion, you seek out your only friend, Mr. Grahame, the alchemist. Somehow he knows just what you're talking about, and asks, "Adam, how much do you know about witchcraft?"

If you were Adam Lawrie, this would have been the way the terrifying adventure began. Before the end of it, you would meet witches, the Devil, and the King of Scotland himself, and learn the terrible secret of Mr. Grahame's past.

—*Holly Willett*

THIS CHILD IS MINE   YA
By CELIA STRANG

Living in poverty with a widowed mother and selfish older sister has never been easy for Tally. But the summer she's fourteen, things get both harder and better than ever before. That summer her unmarried sister, Leta, finally has the baby she's been expecting. The day she comes home from the hospital is when Tally's world changes.

When Leta enters their house that day, she hurries as if she can't wait to put down the bundle she holds in her arm. As soon as she gets inside, she dumps the baby on Tally's bed, like a worthless pile of laundry. Then she begins to get dressed up fancy to go out! Leta completely ignores her baby, as if he doesn't exist at all. She doesn't even give him a name.

Tally can't believe her sister can be so cold. The baby is only five days old, tiny, wrinkled, and beautiful. He's lying on her bed, hungry and wet, crying for someone to feed him and change him. Tally decides to do it, and it's after all the baby chores are done that it happens. Tally picks the baby up and looks at his face. He gives a little hiccup and looks back. And Tally is sure that he tries, at that moment, to smile at her. Tally's heart gives a funny jump, her throat gets hot, and her eyes fill up. From that time on, she knows they belong to each other. From that time on, it doesn't matter that his natural mother ignores him, because the baby has a special aunt to be his mother. Tally can feed him and clothe him, and, hopefully, get a neighbor to babysit when school starts in September. Tally names her baby Sean.

At the end of the summer, Tally learns that finding a babysitter is not her biggest problem. One day, a young couple come to the door when she's home alone and Sean's sleeping. They tell Tally they are anxious to see the baby—the baby they are paying Leta to let them adopt!

In a panic, Tally tells them the baby is at the sitter's. She'll go get him. While they wait in the living room, Tally grabs Sean, some clothes and money, and the baby carriage and rushes out the back door. She succeeds in escaping down the road. Now, a teenager running away on his or her own usually has a tough enough time, but with a baby to care for, getting by is nearly impossible, in *This Child Is Mine*, by Celia Strang.

—Diane Tuccillo

THIS LIFE   YA/Adult
By SIDNEY POITIER

He was fifteen years old when he came to Miami from Cat Island in the Bahamas. He came believing that, for poor people like himself, America was the land of opportunity where the streets were paved with gold. All you had to do was get there. When he came, he had his passport, the new clothes he was wearing, and three dollars left over. He moved in with his brother, sister-in-law, and their six children, in a three-bedroom house. He soon realized that his sister-in-law was not too thrilled about having him around. She made it known he would have to get a job right away and not go to school as he'd planned.

He found a job at a department store delivering packages—that lasted about one day, because he went to one of the homes in the wealthier neighborhood and refused to go around to the back door. Next he decided to try parking cars at a lot because it seemed so glamorous to be an attendant, zipping around in all those different cars. The trouble was, he didn't have the faintest idea how to drive. So he went to one lot and stood around for a while watching what the attendants did with their hands and feet. Driving a car was obviously just a matter of coordinating your hands and feet. He figured he was ready to give it a shot. He went to another lot and asked about a job. They asked if he could drive. "Of course," Sidney replied—so the guy gave him a car to park and of course it was a disaster. The guy threw him off the lot, but Sidney didn't give up; he went to six or seven other places that day, banging up cars, trying to learn to drive. After a year of doing other things— trying to join the Navy, washing cars, cleaning out garages, running away from his uncle's—Sidney finally decided that Miami wasn't ready for him. He went to the bus station to buy the ticket that cost the most because he figured it would take him the farthest. When the attendant told him $11.35 for a ticket to New York City, he figured that was far enough. Knowing no one in New York, but with $27.00 in his pocket, Sidney Poitier was on his way to fame and fortune.

—*Jacqueline Brown Woody*

THIS PLACE   Grades 7–8/YA
HAS NO ATMOSPHERE
By PAULA DANZIGER

The year is 2057, and life for fifteen-year-old Aurora couldn't be better. She's popular with her school friends and Matthew has just asked her to the homecoming dance. But there she finds out her parents' plans and her world falls apart.

Her parents, who work for the space agency, have agreed to live and work in a moon settlement for five years. Moving to another state would be bad enough, but living on the moon seems impossible even to imagine. The last thing she wants is to become a "man in the moon"!

—*Jan Smith*

THIS TIME, TEMPE WICK?   Grades 1–4
By PATRICIA GAUCH

Hiding a horse in the bedroom is a bit surprising, but then Tempe Wick was a most surprising girl. She grew so big people said she looked more like the family bull, Joshua, than she looked like her parents. She was strong enough to toss her friend David out the kitchen door. And ever since the age of nine, Tempe had been able to beat her father in a race, on her horse Bonny.

Tempe lived during the Revolutionary war, when men fought against England to make our country free. Although the farmers helped out, it was difficult for the soldiers to last through the cold winter. Some of the soldiers decided to quit fighting and go home. Tempe was angry when the soldiers wanted to give up, and she was downright furious when one of them wanted to quit *and* take her horse Bonny. That soldier did not know how many surprising ways Tempe could hide Bonny, because no time was right for Tempe Wick to give up her horse.

—*Judie Smith*

THROUGH A BRIEF DARKNESS   YA
By RICHARD PECK

When Karen was twelve years old, she walked into the girls' restroom at school and saw this rhyme written on the mirror:

Andrea's daddy's a fireman
Carmen's father's a cook
Rachel's dad is a doctor
But Karen's old man is a CROOK.

Her father was away on a business trip, but when he got home, she told him about it. He was livid! He took her out of public school immediately—"I don't want my little girl going to school with trash like that!"—and put her in a very expensive private school. She expected to go back there the next fall, but one afternoon, when she got home from a shopping trip with her father's secretary (her mother was dead), she found a letter on the floor of her father's office. It was full of long sentences that didn't say anything clearly—"illegal connections of any parent of a student . . . responsibility to other students and their parents . . . Karen is no longer a suitable classmate . . . I am returning your check for the fall semester's tuition." On the floor by the desk was a little pile of paper scraps—the check. So Karen went to a boarding school that fall, a school a long way from New York, where no one knew about her father. And to another school the next fall, and the next. She spent her summers at camps and hardly saw her father, even on holidays—he was always off on a business trip somewhere.

But when she was in the eighth grade, Karen met Bea, who finally explained to Karen why she kept changing schools—it was dirty money that was sending her there. As Bea put it, "Your dad practically *is* the New York operation—he can work both sides of the street and still come out looking like Mr. Clean!" Karen didn't believe her—almost. It seemed to answer so many questions, but the *Mafia*? Her *father*?

Karen was sixteen, daydreaming through English class at yet another boarding school when she was called to the principal's office and told that her father wanted her to meet him in London for the Easter holidays. But when she got to the meeting place in New York, neither her father nor his secretary was there. Instead, she was met by a girl from his office whom she'd never seen before and put on a non-stop jet to London. About midway in thir flight, there was an announcement that they would have to land at Shannon, Ireland, because of a bomb threat. They landed and the plane was searched, but there was no bomb. But when Karen started to get back on the plane, a man in an overcoat who said he was from the airlines tried to pull her away. When someone else saw what he was doing, he let go of her and ran. In London Karen's cousins were there to meet her, just as they were supposed to be, and Karen thought it would be all right after all. But it wasn't—the big dark house seemed more like a hotel than a home, and the maid and chauffeur were sinister-looking. And then Karen overheard a conversation that let her know that the uneasy feelings she'd had all along were right—these people weren't her cousins, this wasn't their old family home, and the chauffeur wasn't a chauffeur, and the maid was only hired by the week, just like the house. And her father hadn't been delayed on business; he wouldn't be arriving in just a day or so. "They might have killed him and then where would we be? . . . Hired to give him a scare . . . but he's been in a coma for a week—some scare!" And suddenly Karen knew who her cousins were—they were her father's enemies, and she'd been kidnapped. Her father was hurt, maybe dying. But what can you do when you're all alone in London? Who's going to believe you when you tell them you've been kidnapped? Karen didn't dare go to the police, but there was one other person. It wasn't really much of a chance, but it might work, and it was her *only* chance.

—*Joni Bodart-Talbot*

TO RACE THE WIND YA/Adult
By HAROLD KRENTS

Hal grew up in Scarsdale, New York, went to school, learned how to read and write, and became a hero in the first grade because of the demonstration he led against his teacher. He went to high school, was elected student-body president when he was a senior, learned to drive a car, graduated with honors, went to Harvard, played touch football in the Harvard quad, and was nicknamed "Cannonball Krents" because when he got the ball, he'd duck his head and charge for the goal line as fast as he could go, and if you got in his way, it was like being hit by a cannonball. He graduated with honors, went to Harvard Law School, was classified 1A for the draft, and almost had to drop out of school to join the Army! He graduated, was admitted to the New York Bar, and went to England for a year on a scholarship. When he returned he married a beautiful woman named Kit, joined a law firm in Washington, D.C., and began to practice law.

He and Kit now have a son Jamie, who's about three and who loves to have his daddy read picture books to him. Hal and Kit have divided the labor in their marriage—Hal takes out the garbage and Kit drives the car and rides in the front seat of their tandem bike. The one detail I've left out that makes this very ordinary life something special, and also explains why Kit is always in the driver's seat, is the fact that since Hal was about eight years old, *he has been totally blind.*

He's done all of these things without being able to see. He decided to not let the fact that his eyes don't work keep him from enjoying life to its fullest—and he has succeeded. He has lots of funny stories about the scrapes he's gotten into because he can't see, but the funniest, I think, is the story about how he learned to drive a car.

Hal and some friends were spending a fall evening partying, and it was about midnight when they ran out of booze and decided to go get some more. They were all so drunk they could hardly walk, and most of them forgot all about the mud puddle at the end of the sidewalk. Five people fell in—Hal wasn't one of them, but by the time he'd pulled them all out and loaded them into the car, he was as muddy as they were. It was a little cramped in the car—it was a VW *Beetle*! Hal was in the back seat, with a 103-pound cheerleader on his lap. Any other time, Hal would have been delighted, but she was covered with mud, and when she threw her arms around him, squealed, "Oh Hal, I liiike youuu!" and gave him a great big kiss, it was like being kissed by a 103-pound mud-pie! Yick!

But suddenly Hal realized they had another problem—"We're not on the road!" he said. The driver stopped the car, opened the door, looked out, and said, "Whaddaya know? The blind guy's right!" "Huh! I bet even Hal could drive better than you." "Yeah, why don't we let Hal drive?" Hal said, "Oh no, that's okay." "Come on and drive, Hal—" "No, no, I'm fine right here." "Whatsa matter Hal—you chicken?" "*I'll drive.*" So, everyone got out so Hal could get in the driver's seat; they showed him the wheel, the pedals on the floor, the gearshift; then everyone piled back in and they started off. Have you ever been in a car with someone who's just learning to drive a standard transmission? First gear is awful—rather like a motorized earthquake! Everyone started shouting, "Shift! Shift! Put the clutch in!" After a few false tries, Hal managed to find the clutch and even got into second. Like magic, it all smoothed out, and they were going down the road just fine. Hal was thinking, "Huh, there's not so much to driving a car—" Just then one of the girls screamed, "There's a curve up ahead! We're all going to *die!*" Then everyone started screaming hysterically, and no one remembered they had to tell Hal two things—when to turn and which way! So he had to depend on his good old Krents intuition—which was also drunk that night. He made a *beautiful* turn. Unfortunately, it had nothing to do with the turn in the road. They went through some underbrush, cutting a new road as they went, through someone's front lawn and into a large bush next to their front porch. There was a short silence, then someone in the back seat said, "Thank God—we're alive!" "Right—but what're we going to do about that cop?" "What cop?" "The one that's been following us—and here he comes!" "I know! I know! We'll tell him we picked up a blind hitchhiker, and he kidnapped us and held us at gunpoint and forced us to let him drive our car!" "No, I don't think that'll work."

Just then the cop walked up and knocked on Hal's window. He rolled it down and the beer fumes drifted out. "Okay, lemme see your license!" "I haven't got a license." "Aha! I *knew* you weren't eighteen!" "Oh I'm eighteen all right—I just don't have a license." "Okay, let's hear your excuse!" "I'm blind." "Huh? *Sure* you are—*you* can't be blind!" It took Hal and his friends five or ten minutes to convince that policeman that it was true. Then he decided not to give Hal a ticket—if anyone at the station ever found out he'd given a drunk-driving ticket to a *real* blind drunk, he'd never hear the last of it! So if Hal would promise he'd never drive again, he'd let him go. Hal promised, and that's why Kit is the one in their marriage who does the driving today!

—Joni Bodart-Talbot

TO THE TUNE OF A HICKORY STICK   Grades 6-8
By ROBBIE BRANSCUM

After Nell's father died, she and her brother JD were sent to live with their Uncle Jock and his family while their mother worked in the city. Every month their mother sent them $40.00—enough money in those days to buy food and clothes for them and for Uncle Jock's family too. But they never saw any of it. The only clothes they got were ones Nell stitched herself out of old flour sacks. Even her underwear had "Baker's Best" printed across the seat. Most nights they were sent to bed without supper—and their school lunches were just one biscuit and a bit of fatty sidemeat. Uncle Jock's own children did a lot better—they had eggs for lunch, and they got to wear shoes all year long. Nell and JD had to wait until the first frost of each year, no matter how rainy or cold it might be before.

Going to school in the one-room schoolhouse was the only thing Nell really enjoyed. She had her enemies there, like Bessie Belle Cisk, who was fat and stuck-up, but most people kind of ignored her—she liked that, and she liked the quiet, and the books she got to read. But then one day she discovered that school would be closed all winter, and that same day Uncle Jock told them that their mother had been killed in a car wreck. Without the monthly checks from Nell's mother, Uncle Jock became meaner than ever. One day Nell discovered him in the barn, standing over JD, who had passed out from the brutal beating he had given him. Nell could take it no longer. She picked up the first thing that came to hand—a pitchfork—and left it hanging out of Uncle Jock's rear end. And then she knew she really had to get away. She couldn't go far with JD so badly beaten—she didn't even know if he would live. And then she thought of the empty schoolhouse. To find out what happened after she and JD ran away to the schoolhouse, how they survived the worst blizzard in a hundred years, and how they finally got revenge on Uncle Jock, read *To the Tune of a Hickory Stick*, by Robbie Branscum.

—Elizabeth Overmyer

TOBY, GRANNY AND GEORGE   YA
By ROBBIE BRANSCUM

Some said that Preacher Davis done it—drowned Ole Minnie in the baptizin' hole. But everyone knows that she was jest plain too fat for the Preacher to hold up in thet shallow water. Some blamed Deacon Treat—if'n he'd let the hole be dug deeper . . . but then, ol' Deacon Treat ended up daid too . . . in the baptizin' hole. When them bullets came whizzin' by my haid . . . well, it was a mystery all right!

Toby, Granny and George, by Robbie Branscum

—*Verla M. Herschell*

TOO MUCH MAGIC   Grades 3-6
By BETSY and SAMUEL STERMAN

Wouldn't it be great to get anything you wished for? That's what Jeff Hastings was able to do after he found that metal cube in the playground, but he discovered that it could also cause a lot of problems he hadn't planned on.

—*Joy A. Basel*

TOO MUCH T.J.   YA
By JACQUELINE SHANNON

What do you do when you suddenly discover that the boy you're madly in love with is not only the school Don Juan but also the son of your mother's new husband? And you not only have to live in the same house, you even have to share the same bathroom! Everyone told Rozz how great it would be to have T.J. as a brother, but she didn't feel like his sister at all—she felt like just exactly what she *wanted* to be: his girlfriend! Find out how she copes with *Too Much T.J.*

—*Joni Bodart-Talbot*

TOUGH-LUCK KAREN   Grades 4-6
By JOHANNA HURWITZ

Some people have good luck and some have bad luck. Karen Sossi usually had no luck at all, except for one recent week. Then her luck was all bad.

It started on Monday morning. She dropped half of an English muffin on her good gray wool slacks. Of course it fell with the butter side down. Karen rushed upstairs to change her clothes and then raced to catch the school bus. A rotten start for a rotten week.

When Karen got to school she thought her luck might change. No way. Her science class was going on a field trip, and Karen's five-dollar fee was still in the pocket of her gray wool slacks. She had to borrow money from her teacher.

As soon as Karen got home, she rushed to find the gray pants with the five dollars in the pocket. But her mother had already taken the pants to the cleaners. When she phoned them, they said the pockets were empty.

On Tuesday Karen's mother asked her to mail a letter and then go to the store. She gave Karen a five-dollar bill. Karen stopped first at the mailbox, then went on to the grocery store. When she arrived at the store, the letter was still in her hand. . . . the money was in the mailbox!

On Wednesday Karen had the second-lowest grade on her math test. On Thursday she picked up the wrong brown paper bag. Instead of finding her lunch inside, she discovered a pound of raw ground beef. Even Friday was a disaster. She forgot her locker key.

Tough luck, Karen! Will it ever change?

—*Sally Long*

THE TREASURE   Grades 4–8/YA
OF ALPHEUS WINTERBORN
By JOHN BELLAIRS

After stumbling upon a clue one day while dusting in the Hoosac public library, Anthony Monday, a library page, begins a wild and dangerous hunt for a treasure long rumored to have been hidden in the library by a wealthy, eccentric citizen. The late Alpheus Winterborn was an inventor, archaeologist, and most of all, a practical joker. So no one has ever been sure whether or not he hid a treasure in the town library which he built in 1929. But Anthony Monday feels sure the day he accidentally discovers the first clue—a note and a gold coin behind a wood carving hanging in the library. Mr. Winterborn's nephew, Hugo Philpotts, is also searching for the hidden treasure, and nothing will stand in his way. With the help of Miss Eels, the town librarian, Anthony discovers another clue. Together they survive assault and robbery, broken bones, and a threatening flood as they race against time and Hugo Philpotts to piece together the mysterious and difficult clues. A very strange reward awaits the first person to discover *The Treasure of Alpheus Winterborn.*

—*Michele Anton Cahill*

THE TROUBLE WITH FRANCIS   Grades 3–6
By BEMAN LORD

Why can't parents wait until you are old enough and then let *you* decide what you want to be called?

According to Francis Harrison Ward III, his only problem is his first name, Francis. It sounds like a girl's name, even though it is spelled with an i, not an e. He doesn't have a nickname. His father is called Frank, so that's out. Francis decides to go visit his friends Pokey and Squarehead and ask them how they got their names, but unfortunately their stories don't apply to him.

Francis finally gets his own nickname and in a very funny way. You'll find out how in *The Trouble With Francis.*

—*Charlene Graff*

THE TROUBLE WITH TUCK   Grades 5–8
By THEODORE TAYLOR

Some neighborhood cats got into a noisy brawl along our back fence, spitting and screeching. To Friar Tuck, our golden Labrador, this was a unpardonable sin. The cats were invading his private kingdom. Even worse, they were creating an ear-splitting disturbance. His answer was immediate attack—as usual.

Mom was in the kitchen and heard him scramble on the slick linoleum, trying to get traction with his paws, and as she turned, she saw him plunge straight through the closed door, ripping a gaping hole in the screen.

I was sure that Tuck was far too intelligent to do a thing like that. I said, "Maybe he was dreaming?"

Mother scoffed, "Helen!"

I looked out at him, thinking of excuses. My mother shook her head and went outside, quickly crossing over to him, maybe to scold him properly. He deserved it. Instead, she bit her lip and frowned as she looked into his eyes. "Have you noticed anything different about Tuck lately?" she asked.

We made an appointment with Dr. Tobin, our vet. He confirmed our fears by saying simply, "He's going blind. I'm sorry, but it isn't fair to Tuck unless you know exactly what this is all about. Helen, he may have to be put to sleep."

I shouted, "No!" I'd find a solution. Secretly, Tuck and I began to make our plans.

The Trouble With Tuck, by Theodore Taylor.

—*Becky Blick*

TROUBLE WITH WEDNESDAYS   Grades 6-9
By LAURA NATHANSON

Dr. Rolfman does other things besides checking Becky's braces each Wednesday—frightening things. Must she keep them secret? Can she?

—*Carol Kappelmann*

THE TWISTED WINDOW   Grades 7-8/YA
By LOIS DUNCAN

Talk 1

Brad and Tracy meet in the high school cafeteria in Winfield, Texas. Brad says he's moved there from Albuquerque. Tracy says she's moved there from New York City. Who's lying?

—*Mary Beethe*

Talk 2

"I've got to find her! Help me find my little sister—she's been kidnapped!" It's hard to resist Brad's plea, and Tracy doesn't even try. Mindy, his little sister, has been kidnapped by her father—and Brad must get her back.

But then when it all seems so sure, things begin to crumble—and Tracy begins to wonder, is she doing the right thing after all? Is Brad for real, or is this all a game? A game whose rules she doesn't know? A game where only Brad wins—where Mindy, Tracy, and everyone else loses?

—*Joni Bodart-Talbot*

UNCLE LEMON'S SPRING   Grades 4–6
By JANE YOLEN

It was so dry that year the stream beds puckered up and fish practiced breathin' air.

"'Bout time to do somethin'," said Uncle Lemon, so away he went carryin' his walkin' stick for protection to see Old Merlie, the witchin' man, who lived in a cave, top of the next hill. (I followed.)

"Old Merlie! Old Merlie!" called Uncle Lemon, standin' before the cave. He dropped his walkin' stick, stood on one leg, and spat through his second and third fingers so no bad magic would fall on his head.

Suddenly there was this yawnin' and growlin' inside the cave and out came Old Merlie himself. He stood there scratchin' and lookin' like a big black bear. He had a great big black beard and long black hair that covered his head and the backs of his hands. (Witchin' men always have too much of somethin', and with Merlie it was hair.) He looked at Uncle Lemon through slitted eyes, not at all surprised at his funny pose.

Uncle Lemon, seein' he wasn't gonna be witched, yelled, "Peace, Merlie."

Merlie nodded, "Peace."

Uncle Lemon told him 'bout us needin' water, and next thing they were off down the mountain with Merlie graspin' his divinin' stick. (I followed.) Into our farmyard we went, Old Merlie's stick pullin' him and shakin' him like a big wind. Uncle Lemon cheered, "Go to, Merlie." The stick dove to the ground and Merlie stopped too. He stood like he'd died standin' up, then opened his mouth and said one word—"Dig!"

"Get me that shovel, girl." I ran to the shed, grabbed the shovel, and started to dig. 'Bout five minutes later Uncle Lemon took over. After maybe eighteen shovelfuls he hauled himself out of the hole and not a minute too soon, 'cause Old Merlie let out a grunt and the pit commenced a-spoutin' pure ice-cold, crystal-clear blue-white mountain water, fifteen feet straight up into the air, takin' our shovel with it. Old Merlie pounded once on the ground with his stick and the spring stopped singing and settled down.

Now witchin' men always get something from you in return, so we gave him our last old hen and that started a whole pack of troubles for Uncle Lemon and me. And you'll find out about some of them in *Uncle Lemon's Spring,* by Jane Yolen.

—Sharon Durkes

US AGAINST THEM YA
By MICHAEL FRENCH

"Staying up here together with our friends. Showing every adult we're independent." Marcy was confused; she wanted to stay, but there was something about Reed's plan that bothered her. The gang had gone to the mountains to prove they didn't need adults. Hadn't they proved it already? Why should they continue their stay? They didn't need to stay any longer. But then the nightmare began and they didn't seem to have a choice. Sometimes "life's a little easier when you don't always buck the system."

—Teresa Schlatt

VIEW FROM THE CHERRY TREE Grades 7-8
By WILLO DAVIS ROBERTS

Have any of you ever had an older sister get married? If so, you have some idea of what Rob had to go through. All those last-minute preparations and all the things that went wrong. The bakery had the wrong date for the cake, one of the bridesmaids came down with the measles, and more relatives arrived than planned for. Well, as you can imagine, Rob's family were too busy to pay much attention to him— they wouldn't even listen to his best stories. This all made him feel pretty left out of things, so he spent most of his time in his favorite place—up in the cherry tree.

He liked it up that tree because no one else in the family could get up there and because he was so close to the neighbor's house that he could easily spy on Old Lady Calloway. And she was very interesting to spy on. She was about the most crotchety old lady anyone could have for an neighbor. Why, she called the police when someone ran over her garden hose even though she had left it in the gutter herself! Now she had it in for Rob—Rob and his cat SOB. I mean, that cat was hard to control. He was always getting on Mrs. Calloway's property and sometimes he even went inside her house. Rob was hoping he'd see Mrs. Calloway have one of those fits his mother was always talking about. Well, he never did see her have a fit. Instead, he saw her get murdered. Only no one would believe him. No one would even listen to him, no one, that is, except the murderer. To find out if Rob convinced anyone else of the murder before the murderer could take care of him, read *View from the Cherry Tree*, by Willo Roberts.

—Bonnie Janssen

VISIONS
By DONALD R. GALLO

Seth feels like a kid trying to imitate someone truly cool. He's never smoked before, and his denim jacket will never look as authentic as Adam's leather jacket. Adam is really tough; he tells Seth about beating up a guy who had tried to push him around. And Adam is daring; up on the overpass, he pretends to toss rocks down onto passing cars. Seth will never forget what happens after Adam flicks his cigarette butt onto the windshield of a black Camaro. Suddenly, facing three guys bigger than he is, Adam isn't nearly so cool or so tough.

Jason knows he's not the kind of guy most women are looking for. In fact, Jason's just the opposite—a wimp. But when the Wendy's where he works is held up, Jason begins to look at himself and his co-workers differently. Maybe he isn't a cool stud, but maybe he isn't a complete wimp either!

Ghosts aren't always who they seem to be—I once knew a ghost named Seth who spoke to me from the shadows in the corner of my bedroom and who learned the ABCs and the multiplication tables with me. It was only later that I learned that ghosts don't grow up.

These are some of the people you'll meet in these nineteen stories, each with fantasies, with problems, with dreams and realities to discover. To see how each of these characters handles life with its many unknowns, help yourself to some *Visions*.

—*Susan Perdaris* and *Joni Bodart-Talbot*

WAIT FOR ME, WATCH FOR ME, Grades 5-9
EULA BEE
By PATRICIA BEATTY

An agonizing howl from Rascal, my blue-tick hound, first warned me that something was wrong. Then came a terrible screeching. I knew it wasn't a panther in the woods: it was a human voice. Then I saw them—five men on ponies. "Their black painted faces were horrible to look at, and their half-naked bodies gleamed a copper color—Indians!"

Pa and Johnny had gone off to join the Confederate army and left us—my Ma, Old Uncle Joshua, young Daniel, four-year-old Eula Bee, and myself, Lewallen—on our own. Nearby were the no-good Cabrals; Pa said to keep away from them. Ma said Old Cabral was truly someone to watch out for.

I was to care for Eula Bee and keep her out of trouble. I tried to, but when the Comanches came I shot a couple of them and they hit me in the head with a club. I didn't see them put three arrows into old Uncle Joshua. I didn't see them club Ma to death. I didn't see young Daniel killed by a lance as he fired at them and missed. And I didn't see Eula Bee dragged out of the house sobbing and wailing.

What I did see was a brown hand holding a blood-smeared knife a few inches from my face. Then I was instantly jerked to a sitting position as he grabbed my hair and pulled the knife tight against my scalp. But I wasn't scalped and stabbed. I was saved by an older warrior. It was then that I saw Eula Bee—we were to be kept alive and taken captive. Would I be able to escape and ransom my little sister from the Indians? She was all the family I had left.

Wait for Me, Watch for Me, Eula Bee.

—*Elizabeth M. Simmons*

WAITING FOR AN ARMY TO DIE: Adult
THE TRAGEDY OF AGENT ORANGE
By FRED A. WILCOX

As one veteran put it, "I died in Vietnam, but I didn't even know it."

Paul Reutershan, who made that statement on the Today Show in the spring of 1978, died of cancer of the liver, colon, and abdomen on December 14, 1978. Like many other veterans of the Vietnam War, Reutershan came to believe that his terminal illness was the direct result of his exposure to the herbicide Agent Orange in Vietnam, where the deadly chemical was routinely used by the US Army to defoliate the jungle.

In this book Fred Wilcox tracks down the testimony of veterans and their families, of the physicians, scientists, and lawyers who have been involved in cases of long-term dioxin poisoning. And he chronicles the bureaucratic stonewalling, as the government refuses to acknowledge the veterans' claims or compensate them in any way. This is a human story—about brave men who were in top physical condition fifteen or twenty years ago, and who now, after serving their country, are sick and dying. This is the story of their children—born with severe birth defects. It is the story of the dangers we all face from the continued use of herbicides in this country—herbicides sprayed on our national forests, which are annually visited by millions of Americans. Herbicides sprayed on highway and railroad right-of-ways all across the country. Herbicides like those that created the tragedy of Times Beach, Missouri. From the jungles of Vietnam to the American national parks of the 1980s, herbicides are a part of our lives, a deadly part.

Waiting for an Army to Die, by Fred Wilcox.

—Barbara Lynn

WAITING FOR JOHNNY MIRACLE   YA
By ALICE BACH

Life's a bitch. It used to be great for Becky and her twin sister Theo. Good students, great athletes, popular and pretty. Then Becky falls down on the basketball court and can't get up. X-rays show nothing. Becky hides the pain and makes up excuses to avoid games and practice. Finally, she tells Theo, "My leg. First it was numb, then it throbbed. I figured it was the fall, but it's been three weeks, and now it *burns.*"

There's a tumor the size of an orange in Becky's leg. The treatment is chemotherapy and surgery to replace the diseased bone with a metallic prosthesis. No more basketball, no more Jay—her boyfriend, who fled in a panic as soon as he heard the word "cancer." No more being mistaken for Theo.

—Andrea Dietze

WALKING UP A RAINBOW   YA
By THEODORE TAYLOR

Y'all want a bok 'bout cowboys? Y'all want a story 'bout good guys 'gainst bad guys? Well then, Hoss, this here's the book for you.

It's mostly 'bout this teenage girl, Susan Carlisle. Her folks got theirselves killed in a buggy accident. But one mean feller, G. B. Minzter, don't feel too sorry for her. He's fixin' to collect on the $15,000 that Susan's daddy owed him. An' if it means takin' the big ole Carlisle house 'way from the girl instead, well G. B. Minzter'd do it without battin' an eye.

Well the li'l lady's a feisty one, an' somehow she gits the judge to give her thirteen months to produce the money. All hope o' savin' that house is wrapped up in the 2,000 sheep she's bin left with. So to save the place she up an' hires a team o' herders to drive them critters from Iowa to California an' sell 'em to gold miners.

Now, Drover Bert Pettit an' his six herders don't take too kindly at first to the idea o' that Carlisle girl goin' 'long, but when they take out 'cross the frontier, there she is, right with 'em. There's plenty o' adventures waitin' for 'em out on the trail. Susan's out to round up a husband, an' she's got her eye on Clay Carmer, one o' the cowboys from Texas. An' nobody's ever quite sure who's workin' for G. B. Minzter an' who's on the Carlisle girl's side Y'see, G. B. Minzter wants that big ole house awful bad, an' he's the type to try an' ruin even a teenage girl's plans. An' 'bove all, the whole trip's a race 'gainst time 'cause Susan has to git that money back to Iowa, an' the days keep goin' by so fast y'all can't hardly count 'em.

—Brad Eckols

THE WAR BETWEEN THE CLASSES   YA
By GLORIA MIKLOWITZ

Each of us, whether we realize it or not, is prejudiced in some way, shape, or form. That is what *The War Between the Classes* is about— bias and prejudice.

Amy Sumoto is Japanese. Adam Tarcher is a typical Wasp. They have been dating for quite some time and care deeply about each other. But Adam's family is not happy about his dating someone who is so far beneath him socially—and a Japanese, at that. Amy's parents are unhappy because Adam is white, not one of them. But Amy and Adam feel that that type of prejudice is part of their parents' generation, not theirs—until the Color Game begins.

The Color Game is a class experiment that runs for a month. The class is divided into four different social classes. Blue is the elite—the best, and Orange is the lowest of the low. And in each level, women have a higher status than men.

Amy and all the others from minority groups in the school become Blues, while Adam and those like him are Oranges. They have to wear armbands denoting their new social class at all times. They have to bow before people of a higher color class. They are fined and penalized for breaking any of the rules of the game, and the Blues always seem to get off a lot easier than the Oranges. The rules are enforced by a police force and a network of spies.

Soon the Color Game is no longer a game for many of the students. They begin to learn things about themselves that are not too pleasant. It's a lot different being on the other side of things, even for a short time.

But Amy is worried for a different reason. Can her relationship with Adam survive the Color Game? He doesn't much like being of a lower social status than Amy—and Amy is wondering why. Why does it bother *him* so much to be in the position that *she* is normally in?

The War Between the Classes, by Gloria Miklowitz.

—Melinda Waugh

THE WAR ON VILLA STREET   YA
By HARRY MAZER

Willis Pierce has spent his entire life as a loner. He figures it's easier to have no friends than to have to explain about his alcoholic father. So Willis stays a loner—and runs to forget about his troubles.

He also runs to get away from Rabbit Slavin and his gang, who are threatening to beat him up. He runs to get away from those two cute girls in his class, Sue and Marion, because he doesn't know what to say to them. And he runs so no one can see he's coaching Richard, a young boy who's mentally handicapped.

Willis Pierce knows he's spent his whole life running away from everything—but then the day comes when he has to stop running.

The War on Villa Street, by Harry Mazer.

—Pam Spencer

WART, SON OF TOAD   Grades 7–8/YA
By ALDEN R. CARTER

Have you felt that no one likes you? Are you not able to communicate with your dad? Well, you and Steven should get along, then. Ever since Steven's mother and sister were killed in a car wreck, Steven's dad has been bugging him. Steven's grades aren't high enough, Steven's goals in life aren't good enough, Steven's attitudes aren't right. That isn't the half of it. The "in crowd," the football heroes, are threatening him and his so-called "dirt friends." Steven's father, a biology teacher, makes the students mind. The students hate him and take it out on Steven. They call his dad Toad, and they rename him Wart, Son of Toad.

To find out how Steven copes with the jocks and his father, read *Wart, Son of Toad.*

—Donna Houser

WATCHER IN THE DARK YA
By BEVERLY HASTINGS

Taking care of four-year-old Abby Peters while Mr. Peters is away is not how I had hoped to spend spring break. But I had just broken up with Greg and thought it would give me time to sort out my feelings.

Babysitting is usually uneventful, but my experience turned into a nightmare. The terror began with phone calls. Shrill, insistent ringing and deadly silence on the other end of the line. After the first call, I thought, "wrong number." But when the second, third, and fourth came, I got scared. Even Abby seemed afraid. Besides the calls, I had a sense that someone was watching us.

Coming up the path after taking Abby to the park, I thought I saw a shadow move across the living-room window. I just knew someone was in the house. The neighbor came and checked out the house and could find no sign of anyone. But later that night, I stood transfixed in horror. I had been right after all! Somebody had been in the house—somebody had been in that very room, carefully removing the picture of Abby and Mr. Peters and then systematically destroying it.

My mind raced. Who could it have been? Why would anyone do such a thing? I couldn't think of any rational motive. And the weirdest part was that nothing else in the house had been disturbed. I sank into the desk chair, trembling as a wave of fear washed over me. What was going on? As I sat there in silence, I heard a click and then a scraping noise coming from the kitchen. It was the unmistakable sound of a key being turned. I froze with terror—someone was coming into the house!

—*Barbara Bahm*

WHAT DO YOU DO Grades 5–9
WHEN YOUR MOUTH WON'T OPEN?
By SUSAN BETH PFEFFER

Reesa, who was twelve years old and in the seventh grade, had a problem. She had a phobia. Now people have all kinds of phobias. For instance, there's a rather common one called claustrophobia, which means you're afraid of being in a tight space. But Reesa had a more unusual kind of phobia. She was afraid to read out loud. In fact, she had never read out loud in school in her whole life.

But when Reesa found out that an essay she had written had won a contest, things began to change. She realized she would have to read it out loud in order to compete in the next phase of the contest. Her parents wanted her to read it, and so she thought about it. But she kept dreaming of people laughing at her, up on the stage, because her mouth wouldn't open.

She asked her friend Heather if she would read it for her, but Heather said that would be cheating. Then a psychologist recommended a book with some good ideas on speaking in it. As a result, Reesa began to practice reading out loud. The first thing that she read out loud was the Gettysburg Address—one day she practiced it seventy-nine times. Another thing she practiced was jiggling. This is a way of moving parts of your body before a speech to relax yourself.

To find out whether Reesa ever read her essay in front of five hundred people, read *What Do You Do When Your Mouth Won't Open?*, by Susan Beth Pfeffer.

—Mary Hedge

WHAT I DID FOR ROMAN   YA
By PAM CONRAD

What did I do for Roman? Well, it was wild—and crazy—and somehow it was really the right thing to do at the time, although I don't think anyone else saw it that way.

It all began that horrible summer I was sixteen, when my mother got married for the first time and went off to Europe with her new husband. I had to spend the summer with Aunt May and Uncle George, working in their restaurant at the city zoo. It was weird having a man in the house—it had always been just Mom and me. I never even saw a picture of my father, or knew his name. It was the first evening I was there I found the old photo album, with a picture of Mom on her sixteenth birthday. And standing behind her was a boy, a boy with hair and hands like mine—my father. Now I knew why I didn't look like my mother—I looked like him. I had a million questions to ask Aunt May, questions I'd never dared ask my mother because of the hurt in her eyes whenever I tried, but just then Uncle George walked in and started yelling—I was never to mention his name again! Never! I ran upstairs, still clutching the picture—at least now I had that much.

It was the next day at the zoo when I saw Roman. He was standing in the sunlight, in the center of the seal pool, feeding them. The sun shone on his dark curly hair, and somehow he seemed to shimmer in the light. And when he was through feeding the seals, he bent down and kissed the oldest one right on the nose—just as if it were the most natural thing in the world. I knew even then that he was special and that maybe he could make me special—but I never, even once, imagined

Fudgsicles, chocolate yogurt bars, potato chips, pretzels, and (squashed in the middle) a loaf of bread. Then there was the time that Marty took Gus, the youngest, who was two, to the bathroom at a World Series game. Marty let Gus go in by himself, and Gus never came out. He had disappeared. Announcements were made, and finally someone found Gus eating an ice cream cone at the other end of the stadium.

To find out about other incidents—involving things like bees in the kitchen, a fat pet cat, and crow pie—read *When the Boys Ran the House*, by Joan Carris.

—Mary Hedge

WHEN THE LEGENDS DIE YA/Adult
By HAL BORLAND

"When the legends die, the dreams end. When the dreams end, there is no more greatness." This novel is about what happens when an American Indian rejects his heritage and the beliefs of his fathers. Although it's about an Indian, it could be true for anyone else—Black, Chicano, Oriental—whatever the heritage.

Tom Black Bull grew up with his parents in the old Indian way. When his father died, he and his mother continued in the way, and when she died Tom continued alone, until Blue Elk, an old Indian, found him and took him to the Indian school. Tom hated living inside, acting as the white man forced him to act, but he was a boy and had no choice. He was kicked out of the school and was helping an old man herd sheep when he discovered he could ride broncos. He was a natural. A cowboy tricked him into riding a horse that was unrideable, and Red Dillon saw it, brought Tom from the reservation, and set him on his way to becoming a star. Tom won prizes, but he didn't make many friends, and he rode as if there were a demon on his shoulders. It was a long time before Tom realized it and could start to deal with it, so he could find out just who this person named Tom Black Bull really was—a bronco rider famed for his rough treatment of horses? or an Indian named Tom Black Bull, who lived in harmony with nature, in the old way?

—Joni Bodart-Talbot

WHEN THE PHONE RANG   Grades 6–8/YA
By HARRY MAZER

Talk 1

Had he known what the voice would say, Billy probably wouldn't have answered the call. But that wouldn't have changed the facts: the airplane had crashed, and both of Billy's parents were dead.

—*Beverly Ramsey Mitchelson*

Talk 2

Sometimes it seems as if the bad times don't know when to stop.

Take our moving. Delmar was a pleasant place to live, but Mom and Dad decided to move to the Big City for more opportunity. Get a brownstone and renovate it. And my sister Lori and I are supposed to like the New School and New Friends. Well, it doesn't work that way. I don't like the chained doors, the chained playground, even chained garbage cans.

And then we're left to grub for ourselves while Mom and Dad bask in the Bermudas. That means last-minute cleaning before they get home and think they've inherited an instant ghetto.

So you can guess that I wasn't prepared when the phone rang.

"May I speak to the head of the house?" a strange woman's voice asked.

"That's me," I grabbed the phone from Lori.

"Isn't there someone older?"

"My folks are on their way home; probably switching planes in Miami about now," I answered defensively. Is sixteen that young?

"This is Pan-Con Air," the woman spoke tentatively. "Your parents' plane crashed into the Caribbean at four-twenty this afternoon."

I hung up.

I didn't want to talk to anyone. Not Lori. Not my brother in college, Kevin. I just wanted to be little again. To hear a lullaby. To promise to never do anything bad again so that my parents would come back.

And then it got worse.

Our Aunt Joan and Uncle Paul visited, pretended to console us. But Uncle Paul kept criticizing the half-done carpentry work, and Aunt Joan bugged Lori about her weight. They wanted to sell our house—and separate us! They wanted to destroy all the family that was left after that terrible phone call!

The outcome of the Kellers story is told in Harry Mazer's book *When the Phone Rang.*

—*Lesley Farmer*

WHEN WE FIRST MET   YA
By NORMA FOX MAZER

When Jenny saw Rob for the first time, he was sitting behind her in the school auditorium. Every time she turned around to sneak a look at him, he was leaning forward in his seat staring at her, too. And the only thing she could think was that this boy had the face of an angel.

During that week at school, Jenny saw Rob several more times. Once as she walked past the band room she stopped and looked in, and he looked up and saw her standing there. But they didn't speak. One day when school was letting out he was walking ahead of Jenny, and he turned and looked at her, as if he knew she was behind him. But they still didn't speak. And one afternoon when Jenny was in the school library he came and sat at the very same table, right across from her; when she looked up from her book, he was staring at her again. But neither of them said a word.

When Jenny Pennoyer and Rob Montana finally met, they fell in love like something that would happen in the movies.

But of all the things Jenny and Rob did together and of all the places they went, there was one place Jenny could not take him. She couldn't take Rob home to meet her family because she knew they would hate him.

Three years ago Jenny's older sister Gail had been hit by a car and killed when she was riding her bike home from the store. Rob Montana's mother had been the drunken driver behind the wheel of that car.

Jenny wants to be loyal to her family and her dead sister, but now she's in love with Rob and he's in love with her.

—Avis Matthews

WHEN YOU FIGHT THE TIGER   Grades 5-9
Text by JOAN HEWETT
Photographs by RICHARD HEWETT

Do you know how animals are trained for TV commercials and movies? Tana is sixteen years old and has grown up with wild animals on her parents' ranch, but this summer is the real thing—she will actually work as a trainer instead of being a helper as in past summers. Here are a few facts which she shares with you:

Did you know that animal trainers must see and work with their animals every single day?

Did you know that "Affection Training" is the modern method of training animals, without whips, guns, or clubs?

Did you know that you should never stand between a trainer and his animal? And did you know that a large cat like a lion, no matter how well trained, may pounce on a small child? Trainers watch their animals even more carefully when young children are near.

Did you know that animal trainers actually "speak animal"? They learn to understand and make the same sounds the animal makes, whether it is chuffing, yelping, whining, barking, or whatever. This helps the trainer communicate and understand the animal better.

What do you know about a hyena? Well, scientists don't know very much about their signs and behavior either, so they are very dangerous to handle.

And bears . . . they are *so* powerful and unpredictable, and they have short tempers and long memories: they can carry a grudge for a very long time! They too have few distinct signals, so only a few people—mostly men—are willing to work with them or fight them in movies or on TV!

Did you know that the ultimate test of an animal trainer's skill is to "fight" the tiger—to simulate a tiger fight in which the trainer, acting as victim, spars with an attacking tiger? The test is to make the fight look real without letting it become real, and that's really difficult—and dangerous!

This is Tana's story in *When You Fight the Tiger,* by Joan and Richard Hewett.

—*Dorothy A. Davidson*

WHERE ARE THE CHILDREN?   YA/Adult
By MARY H. CLARK

Almost seven years ago, Nancy ran away from California, changed her identity, cut and dyed her hair, and began a new life in an old house on Cape Cod. Now she is happily married to Ray Eldredge, a real estate man, and has two lovely children, Missy and Michael, but she's still haunted by the tragedy that occurred seven years ago on her twenty-fifth birthday.

Then she had been Nancy Harmon, the wife of a university professor and the mother of three-year-old Lisa and five-year-old Peter. She had taken Lisa and Peter with her to get candles and chocolate for her birthday cake but had left them in the car while she went into the store. When she came back, Lisa and Peter were gone, and she was charged with murder when their multilated bodies, their heads covered by plastic bags, were washed up on the shore of the ocean.

Nancy Harmon was sentenced to die in the gas chamber, but her conviction was overturned because two women jurors were overheard discussing the case in a bar midway through her trial and saying she was guilty as sin. By the time a new trial was ordered, the leading prosecution witness had disappeared. Nancy was released with the prosecuting attorney's promise that her nightmare wasn't over, that someday he would find a way to convict her.

Now, seven years later, the nightmare is beginning again. Today is Nancy's thirty-second birthday and Missy and Michael—her and Ray's two children—are outside playing on the swing at the edge of the woods behind the house. Fifteen minutes to do some housework, look at the paper, and then time to call the children in. Nancy picks up the paper and there is the story—"Somewhere today Nancy Harmon is celebrating her thirty-second birthday and the seventh anniversary of the deaths of the children she was found guilty of murdering."

In a panic Nancy runs outside to the children, but they are gone—only Missy's red mitten is left behind, caught on the swing. She runs to the lake and plunges into the icy water, but there is nothing. Where *are* the children, and will they ever be seen again alive?

—Marianne Tait Pridemore

WHERE THE KISSING NEVER STOPS   YA
By RON KOERTGE

I couldn't believe it! Why couldn't she get a job selling clothes at Sears or Penneys or even waitressing at Dennys or someplace? But no—she's got to go get a job at Ye Olde Burlesque as a stripper! And it was in Love Park, Kansas City's sleaziest suburb! I'd sneaked over there to the movies a couple of times—it wasn't the place where anyone's mother should be working—least of all, *mine!* What if my friends find out? What if *Rachel* finds out? There's no way she'd date a stripper's son! And there's no way my mom's gonna quit—she *likes* it! What am I gonna do?

—Joni Bodart-Talbot

WHISPER GOODBYE   Grades 4–8
By DOROTHY MORRISON

Katie had finally found a way to stay in Rollin and keep her horse, Whisper. But it meant not moving to a new town with Grandad and Gram, the only family she had known since her parents' death. Was she really going to be able to say good-bye?

—Cheryl Welch

WHO KNEW THERE'D BE GHOSTS?   Grades 4–6
By BILL BRITTAIN

Many townspeople think the old Parnell House is haunted by ghosts. But Tommy and his friends Book and Harry the Blimp use the place as their playground, until one day they overhear two strangers planning to rip the whole place apart to find something. What is it they're looking for? What secrets does the house hold?

—Olivia Jacobs

WHO PUT THAT HAIR IN MY   Grades 6–9
TOOTHBRUSH?
By JERRY SPINELLI

The other day I heard my parents talking. . . .
"Next time it won't be donuts. Next time they'll kill each other." "That's a trifle overreactive." "Tell that to my headache. . . ." "Sibling rivalry, honey." "Sibling homicide."

Megin (Megamouth), age twelve, and Greg (Grosso), fourteen, were at war. They used any weapon that they could lay their hands on, and enlisted the aid of anyone who would help. They take turns telling their own sides of the story and explaining how each of the battles began.

First there was the Great Shower Caper, which involved flushing the toilet and running water in the bathroom sink while Megamouth was in the shower the last night before school started. She got frozen and scalded by turns. Then there was the hair-in-the-toothbrush trick. Megin found it—a long brown hair, woven in and out, around and around the bristles of her toothbrush. Grosso had brown hair.

There was only one way for her to respond to all this underhanded sabotage: torture—donut torture! Grosso would *kill* for a creme-filled donut. Megin got out a dozen leftover donuts she'd gotten the night before. She set them out in the kitchen and went up to Grosso's room to put her plot into action. It worked perfectly! She walked back into the kitchen just as Greg was about to bite into the only creme-filled donut. She screamed and pounced. Filling splattered all over Grosso's face. Megamouth howled with laughter, but in the middle of it all, she got a punch in the mouth, everything went black for a minute, and she suddenly tasted blackberries. The Donut Battle had begun! Donuts flew thick and fast, landing everywhere, on Greg, on Megin, and all over the kitchen. Suddenly their mother stood in the doorway. She listened to Megin's explanations without saying a word, and then she just turned around and left the house. A horrible thought occurred to Megin—"What if this time we went too far? What if she never comes back? What if I never see her again?"

To find out what happens—if their mother ever does come back, if Greg and Megin really do start using weapons more dangerous than donuts, and to see who wins the war, read *Who Put That Hair in My Toothbrush?*

—*Joni Bodart-Talbot*

WILD CHILD YA/Adult
By MARI HANES

This is a true account of a child who was abandoned at the age of five or six in the streets of Los Angeles. The two things Sandy had going for him were that California has a warm climate and that he was intelligent. On the other side, Sandy had so many strikes against him, it was amazing that he lived. He had an arrest record from the age of six, never bathed or changed clothes, couldn't speak properly, needed surgery to clarify his sex, was the victim of beatings so severe his hearing was damaged, and became addicted to drugs and alcohol—you can understand why one social worker referred to him as "human garbage."

Sandy would eventually have died on the streets, except for meeting a very loving, caring woman named Naomi.

The Wild Child, by Mari Hanes.

—*Pam Spencer*

THE WILD CHILDREN
Grades 5–9
By FELICE HOLMAN

Talk 1

Alex clutched his ticket and tried to push himself aboard the train. He wanted to get away from the swarms of dirty, shabby boys who roamed through the crowds on the station platform. Those boys had already stolen the schoolbag which held all his money and possessions. If he didn't get away, they'd steal his ticket too. Just then the crowd lurched forward, and Alex found himself jammed into a second-class carriage of the train. When the train began to move, he felt a surge of hope. Just a few more hours and he'd be in Moscow with his uncle. His uncle would take him in, and he'd have a home again. In the middle of his daydreams, Alex felt the train jerk to a stop. Russian soldiers crowded into the corridors, ordering people off the train. In just a matter of seconds, Alex found himself in a crowd of people standing on the ground beside the railroad tracks. As the train disappeared out of sight, a man beside Alex spoke to his wife.

"We'll have to walk to Moscow. The next train may not come for days."

The woman's answer echoed Alex's own thoughts. "How can I walk to Moscow? It must be a hundred miles, and I have no heavy boots for the snow."

The man looked at her and smiled gently. "What are the choices?" he answered and began walking.

Alex stood still, thinking about what the man had said. "It's true," he told himself. "If I wait here, I'll either starve or freeze to death." So he too began walking. In the days that followed, Alex tried to stay close to groups of adults, because many children like the ones at the train station were also walking on the roads. All of them were dressed in rags, and most traveled in groups. "How long have you been walking?" Alex asked one ragged boy beside him on the road.

"Three or four months," the boy muttered with a sideways look at Alex's warm coat.

"Months!" Alex cried, horrified.

The boy looked at him and gave a mocking laugh. "Just wait," he said. "You'll see."

"No, I won't," Alex thought. "I have an uncle in Moscow. He will give me a home; there I can have food and shelter again!"

But when Alex finally got to Moscow, a strange woman answered the door of his uncle's house, and she told Alex that his uncle had been arrested a month ago. Alex was still homeless. He hadn't eaten in three days, and he had no money for food and nowhere to go for shelter. As he stood there, Alex saw a few dirty, ragged children, like the bands he had passed on the road, and he remembered the boy's warning. Alex looked down at his once clean coat, now foul with mud and grime. Already he was beginning to look like them. What was going to happen to him?

They called them the wild children, and in the 1920s in Russia, people were terrified of them. Groups of homeless children whose parents had been killed in the war or taken away by the secret police—these bands of wild children roamed through the city and the countryside, stealing to survive. Although Alex had heard his parents talking about what a problem these bands had become, he had never really paid that much attention. It didn't really matter to him. Until one morning he woke up to a strangely empty house and slowly realized that the impossible had happened to him. His family had disappeared.

We still have wild children with us today. Have you ever wondered what happens to all the homeless children in cities like Beirut or Belfast? Does someone take them in, or do they roam the streets like the wild children, stealing to survive? A well-known song about the results of war asks, "Where have all the children gone?" Read *The Wild Children* and find out for yourself.

—Margie Reitsma

Talk 2

It had happened to them! When he came down to breakfast there wasn't a sign of anyone. The first thing that had alerted twelve-year-old Alex was an overturned chair in the front hall. His mother, tidy as she was, would never have allowed a chair to remain that way for more than a moment. A very cold feeling started in his chest. Like birds in winter, people had been disappearing for months, years now. Everyone knew that. And yet when Alex found his whole family had been taken away—his mother, his father, his young sister Nadya, and his old grandmother—he couldn't quite believe it. He hadn't heard a thing because of his crazy room, just a little cell on the second floor that had been used for storage. It was probably that crazy room that had saved him. When the GPU, the secret police, came to take everyone away, they had overlooked the storeroom.

Now Alex's family had been taken away, and he knew he would be in danger himself. At first he didn't know what to do or where to go. He felt uncertain and insecure. But he couldn't go anywhere without speaking to Katriana Sergyeva, his teacher and friend, and telling her what had happened. Katriana decided to send Alex to his uncle in Moscow, but she also told him of a friend in Leningrad who might help him to leave the country one day.

On the way to Moscow, Alex saw many other families dragging themselves to something or someplace better, going from the known to the unknown. Alex arrived to find his uncle had also been arrested. He was alone.

And then Alex fell in with a gang of Moscow's homeless children, the *bezprizorni*, the wild children. Homeless, desperate, criminal, living in cellars and caves, they ran in packs through city and country, pillaging and terrorizing. At first Alex found it hard to adjust to the *bezprizorni* way of life. But he soon realized it was the only way he could survive. And as part of this band, Alex found his way to a new life.

—Judy Druse

WILL THE REAL   Grades 4–6
GERTRUDE HOLLINGS PLEASE STAND UP?
By SHEILA GREENWALD

Gertrude was very good at pretending and play-acting—whether she did it to entertain her stuffed owls or to get the best of her know-it-all cousin Albert.

Her play-acting or pretending was OK until she had to spend three weeks with Albert and his parents while her own parents went to Greece.

That's when she got in *big* trouble! You see, Albert was super-smart, and he never let Gertrude forget it. How she wanted to win his respect—maybe even be friends with him! And she found the way when she began telling him Greek myths.

She pretended to be Athena carrying the thunderbolt, and Albert believed her! Then at the lake cabin that weekend, she pretended again . . . this time she was an oracle, a priestess, and she warned Albert, "Beware of the Babe . . . the Babe who will take your place!" This, of course, reminded Albert that he was soon to have a baby brother or sister!

To find out what Albert did next, when he heard "Beware of the Babe . . . ," and to see where the play-acting ends, read *Will the Real Gertrude Hollings Please Stand Up?* by Sheila Greenwald.

—Dorothy A. Davidson

WINNING   YA
By ROBIN BRANCATO

He woke up and couldn't figure it out. Where was he? He looked down and saw a white sheet covering his six-foot frame, his mother nodding sleepily in a chair, and a nurse walking by his door. What had happened? He tried so hard to remember who he was.

He was Gary Madden. Gary Madden belonged in the winner's circle. Tall, handsome, senior, good student, middle linebacker on the football team. On top of that he was in love with Diane, and she loved him. The world he inhabited was a charmed place, full of charming people and future possibilities.

So why was he here? Try to remember. The last thing he remembered was the football game and the other team rushing him and his being tackled and his blanking out and . . . and . . . and. . . .

Winning, by Robin Brancato.

—Dee Scrogin

THE WISH GIVER   Grades 4-6
By BILL BRITTAIN

At the annual Coven Tree Church Social, a strange man named Thaddeus Blinn sat in a tent with a sign that read, "I Can Give You Whatever You Ask For, Only 50¢." When people approached, he warned them they had to be careful because they would get exactly what they asked for. Find out if the four people who wished got what they really wanted, or what they asked for!

—Cheryl Welch

THE WITCH IN ROOM 6   Grades 4-6
By EDITH BATTLES

A lawnmower cutting grass with no one pushing it, a milk-carton windmill flying around like a helicopter, and an unexpected bus trip to Disneyland are just a few of the amazing, unbelievable events that start happening when Cheryl Suzanne Endor joins the fifth grade. Is Cheryl the cause of all this commotion? Sean, seemingly her only friend, can tell us a thing or two about *The Witch in Room 6.*

—Pam Swofford

WITCH WEEK   Grades 5–7
By DIANA WYNNE JONES

"Someone in 6B is a witch," reads the note Mr. Crossley finds among the tests he's correcting. A joke, he thinks, but not a very funny one. For Mr. Crossley teaches in Larwood House, a boarding school where many of the pupils are witch orphans—children of men and women who were burned as witches. It is quite possible that some of the children have inherited magic powers, and of course if they have—and if they're discovered—they too will be burned. That's just the way things are nowadays in England, where the Emergency Witchcraft Act permits anyone to be arrested on the merest suspicion of witchcraft.

Mr. Crossley decides to ignore the note at first, but it's not so easy to ignore the flock of birds that comes swooping into Room 6B—just after the music teacher has made the class sing three bird songs in a row. And nobody can ignore the night when every shoe in the entire school vanishes—and then reappears in the hall. What with six hundred pupils and all the school staff, there are hundreds and hundreds of shoes—far too many to have been moved around by human hands.

Then there's Simon, the kid who has all the best friends and the best grades and never gets into trouble. Suddenly everything he says comes true, just like the game Simon Says, only it isn't so funny in real life. "I've got the golden touch," he jokes, and from then on, everything he touches turns to gold—including Theresa's hand. When he tries to make it better by saying, "You haven't got a golden hand," her hand disappears altogether!

Is Simon a witch? What about Nan, who was named after the most famous witch of all time? What about Charles, who finds himself becoming invisible one night, or Nirvipam, whose brother, a student at the school last year, was actually burned as a witch?

Before the week is over, the witches in 6B are out in full force, a portal between two worlds has been opened, and only a desperate trick can save the witches—and the world.

—Elizabeth Overmyer

THE WITCHES' BRIDGE   Grades 3–5
By BURTON OLIVER CARLETON

"Out of the night and the fog and the marsh, these three, Doom shall come for thee." That was the curse that old Samuel Pride hurled at the world just before he was killed, accused of being a witch. He refused to plead either guilty or not guilty, so instead of hanging him or drowning him, they forced him to the ground, put a long board over him, and piled stones on it until he was crushed to death.

Through all the years since then, whenever a particularly dense fog rolls in, the sound of a violin is heard near the bridge that leads to the house Old Samuel built. They call it a Fiddler's Fog, and some terrible thing always happens after the fiddler's music is heard. Sometimes there is also the howling of a dog, and folks say that Old Samuel the violin player has summoned the devil out of the marsh in the shape of a great black dog.

Now young Dan Pride has come back, many generations later, to the family home. He doesn't believe in the old superstitions—he has enough trouble in the present, in the real world. Dan's parents were killed in a plane crash, and now he has to live with his Uncle Julian, his only relative. But the townspeople don't like the Pride family, and when they see young Dan Pride arriving with a violin case in hand, they act as if *he* were a witch; they'll have nothing to do with him.

Dan was hoping for a good home, but his uncle turns out to be a bitter, sour old man who will scarcely speak to him. And the house is dark and cold and unfriendly too—oaken beams, age-blackened walls, cold stone floors. After Dan has been there just a few days, a dense fog rolls in and Dan himself hears it—the sound of a violin, out over the marsh near the Witches' Bridge. He hears it clearly—and feels certain that the disaster is coming for him. But he doesn't sit in his room and wait; he goes to the bridge to meet it. And it's there, the disaster—not a ghost, but a very real danger. Dan must fight for his life, at *The Witches' Bridge.*

—*Nancy Eager*

WITCHWOOD   YA
By TIM LUKEMAN

In the ancient land of Therrilyn, magic was alive. Crystal cores of stars glimmering with molten gold sometimes fell to the earth, bringing their finders instant wealth. Everything was the gift of the Lady of the Witchwood, who created the green land. But men were forgetting her magic and turning away.

Fiona, trapped in the dreary orphanage of Balestone House, held the Fire of the Lady in her strange green eyes with their flecks of gold, but she didn't yet realize it. One night, after sulking along the edge of the nearby cliffs, she turned to follow the path leading back to town. Then it happened. Fiona caught her breath. The air tasted of ginger, and ashes began to fall softly upon the clover, touching the standing pools of sweetwater with a hiss like quenched candles. Fiona wished upon the falling star, and then a fiery thread of pain seared along her cheek. She looked up in amazement. The drifting ashes were shot through with silver and gold, as the glistening star plowed into the field at the edge of the Witchwood.

Fiona hesitated, remembering the old wives' tales about the dark, haunted wood. But the unexpected hope of ruling her own life was stronger than her fears, so she made her way to the edge of the Witchwood, and the beginning of an exciting, dangerous quest.

—Patricia Farr

WOLF RIDER   **Grades 6-9**
By Avi

Talk 1

The caller said, "I just killed someone." His father and the police said it was a joke. To Andy, talk of death was never a joke.

—Jeff Blair

Talk 2

The kitchen phone rang three times before Andy picked it up. "I just killed someone." "What?" "I killed Nina. . . . Now I don't know what to do." "Who is this?" "Zeke . . . I loved her, now I don't know what to do." The man named Zeke went on to explain how it happened and who Nina was. Andy scribbled a note to his friend Paul—"Guy killed someone. Go call police—trace call—I'll keep him talking." Finally Andy heard several clicks on the line—and then it went dead. But when Andy tried to go to the police, no one believed him—they said it was only a gag. Paul didn't believe him; his father didn't believe him.

Then one day he's in his father's office (his father teaches math at the local college) and sees the college phone book. On impulse he looks up Nina Klemmer—and she's listed. But when he calls, he can't figure out what to say—and later, when he *does* figure it out, she thinks he's crazy, simply harrassing her. Andy *knows* she's the right person, though. She looks like the person Zeke described, she drives the same kind of car—there are too many coincidences to ignore. So Andy continues to try to find Zeke, to try to save Nina from a murder that, so far, has only occurred in Zeke's imagination. But no one believes him—everyone accuses him of crying wolf. Somehow he must get to Zeke before Zeke figures out who he is—and kills both him and Nina.

—Joni Bodart-Talbot

THE WOMAN WHO LOVED REINDEER   YA
By MEREDITH ANN PIERCE

Caribou, not yet thirteen summers old, has lived alone in her frozen world since her father died. Her house is set far out from the village, and no one visits her now that they have heard she sees visions. She has been managing on her own until Branja, the sister-in-law who refused to take her in, suddenly arrives on her doorstep after an exhausting two-day journey on foot, carrying a sleeping baby whom she insists that Caribou keep.

Caribou realizes that her brother's wife is giving up her baby because her brother, long away hunting, is not the father. But it is not so easy to understand why Branja seems afraid of the child himself. Before Caribou can stop her, Branja thrusts the fur-wrapped child into Caribou's arms and runs off across the cold tundra. Caribou has never even held a baby before. How can she care for him?

Reluctantly Caribou carries him inside her cabin to the warmth of the fire. Pushing back his fur wrap, she is surprised to see that the baby's hair is yellow like the sun, so different from the dark hair of her people. When the babe opens his eyes to stare into hers, Caribou gasps, for his eyes are golden, their gaze infinite.

And so Caribou warms to the child. How good it is to have company in the cold winter! He never cries, only looks at her with those melting eyes.

One day when Caribou has carried the baby far from her cottage to forage for food, a great golden stag reindeer appears. Caribou has never seen such a color, for reindeer have silver coats. The stag calls, and her child answers him, until the huge animal lunges upon her and scoops the baby out of her arms into the nest of his antlers, bolting off into the woods like lightning.

Sobbing with fear and dismay, Caribou tracks them, searching for hours until darkness falls and the cold descends. When Caribou has nearly given up hope for her own life as well as the child's, she suddenly comes upon the fallen stag, pierced by a hunter's arrow, with the child still cradled—alive!—within his antlers.

After this brush with disaster, Caribou names the child Reindeer, for she cannot forget how he answered the stag's call and screamed with delight as he was carried away. A nameless fear lives within Caribou, for as the child grows up, she knows he is different from other children. He does not laugh or cry, he seems without human feeling. Yet he is always obedient and loyal to her in his strange way. Caribou loves Reindeer completely, for she has no one else on earth, but she does not understand him. Why is he so restless when the reindeer run in their silver stream, thundering through the valley on their way to the unknown country on the other side of the Pole, across the Land of Broken Snow where no man has ever been? And why, when she catches Reindeer's reflection in the smooth surface of the water, does she see a golden-furred young buck, and not a boy at all?

—*Catherine G. Edgerton*

WORDS BY HEART
By OUIDA SEBESTYEN   Grades 7-9

"Lena," Claudie said quietly, "Lena, this kind of game—can't everybody win. So you mustn't take it hard if you don't. Second place, or third place—"

Lena pulled away as though the hand had scorched her. I'm going to win, she said inside. It's not a game, and I'm going to win. But she couldn't say that to Claudie—she couldn't say, I'm going to show you and Papa and Winslow Starnes and everybody! She wasn't sure she could.

Mr. Jaybird Kelsey announced the rules. Quote a verse of Scripture when it's your turn, or drop out. There would be a prize for the winner. Lena looked around her. She had but one real opponent, Winslow Starnes, although there were other entrants. She gave her verse, Winslow gave his, time and time again. After Winslow Starnes recited his fiftieth verse, Mr. Kelsey stood up and said: "Brothers and sisters, that was fifty verses for Winslow Starnes. Let's give him a big hand."

Everybody clapped. Lena flashed with anger, waiting to say her fiftieth verse, began "Eye for eye, tooth for tooth . . . " Somebody began laughing, and then other people started to applaud. Mr. Kelsey ducked his head embarrassed, but he laughed, too.

After five more rounds, Winslow stopped in the middle of one verse, and then began another. The audience questioned with their eyes, "Is that fair?" Mr. Kelsey's eyes referred the question to the preacher, Winslow's dad. Reverend Starnes complimented Lena and his son and suggested the contest was a tie. Lena said "I want to go on." They did. Four rounds later Winslow was stumped. He said that if Lena could recite two verses, he would match her. She agreed. He was defeated.

Mr. Kelsey congratulated Lena. He seemed embarrassed as he abruptly handed her the prize. "I wish it could have been just what you wanted, because you deserve. . . . " It was a tie, a boy's blue tie, a tie for Winslow. "I don't want it," Lena said. She dropped it on the floor. Was it wrong to want to win? Was it wrong for a black girl to beat a white boy?

Words by Heart, by Ouida Sebestyen.

—*Barbara Hawkins*

WORKING ON IT   YA
By JOAN OPPENHEIMER

Tracy lived in a family of successful people—where she felt she was the *only* unsuccessful member.

Her father was a salesman and gone a lot. Her mother, in Tracy's eyes, was an attractive Superwoman. Her favorite words for Tracy were, "You're just a late bloomer." That made Tracy boil! That and the fact her mother didn't like Tracy's only friend, Carla.

But the real star of the family was her older brother Scott. He was all the things Tracy wished she could be—good-looking, poised, fun to be with. He never had trouble finding a date. He was a super-jock with a klutzy kid sister! Tracy had heard him make a crack about her to his friends once: "Tracy? She is waiting in the wings till Phyllis Diller retires. Good old Trace. If anything goes wrong with my wheels, she gives me a lift on her broom!" With a brother like that, how could Tracy help having a rotten image!

Tracy dreaded school starting. She especially wished she hadn't agreed to take a drama class. But she did promise Carla she would! Tracy got sick to her stomach every time she thought about getting up before a class to perform, and even the thought of having a partner in the class didn't help much.

Her partner for the first six-week period was Wylie Babcock. As she left class the first day he asked her about their assignment. (They were supposed to write in a journal about an emotion they felt often.) Tracy blurted out the first thing that popped into her head. "Terror! I could sure do a number on that. Do I know terror!"

Wylie cocked his head to study her, "Yeah, that's pretty obvious." Then added, "But do you plan to make it your life work?" Tracy walked out blindly. How dare he! What gave him the right to cut her like that? Didn't he think she had feelings? She vowed, "I'll show you, Wylie Babcock! You can't make me quit this class! I'll show you if it takes all semester to do it!"

Is Wylie trying to get Tracy to drop drama class? If so, will he succeed?

Read *Working on It*, by Joan Oppenheimer!

—Shirley Alley

THE WORLD IS MY EGGSHELL   YA
By PHILIPPA GREENE MULFORD

Abbey's biggest rival in life is her twin brother Sheldon. Shel is the popular, outgoing type; Abbey, the shy, noncompetitive type. It's easy for Shel to put down Abbey. For example, he calls her a hermit, and in front of the whole world he asks her when she is going to stop wearing pajamas with feet in them. Abbey never protests against outbursts like these or has any comebacks for Shel's nasty cracks.

Life begins to change, though, when Shel begins to date Crystal, a stuck-up girl Abbey doesn't like. Shy Abbey ends up competing, racing against Crystal at a track meet and trying to beat her out for an editorial position on their school newspaper.

So Abbey is becoming more like Shel. Abbey feels pretty good about this until one day Shel tells her that *he* wants to be more like *her*.

To find out what each twin is like by the end of the book, read *The World Is My Eggshell*, by Philippa Greene Mulford.

—Mary Hedge

THE WORLD'S GREATEST EXPERT   YA
ON ABSOLUTELY EVERYTHING . . . IS CRYING
By BARBARA BOTTNER

Tucker T. Cobbwebber marched up to Jessie's front door holding a giant tiger lily.

"Here," he said as he shoved it in her face.

"Thanks! Where did you get it? Did you pick it? Where?"

"You ask too many questions, Jessie Langston." Then Tucker grinned and tore off down the front lawn.

That had happened yesterday, and Jessie was elated . . . until she met Katherine Ann Millicent Franklin and her two different-colored eyes. When you looked at them, you couldn't make up your mind which was more gorgeous: her gorgeous blue eye, or her gorgeous brown one. But there was more to Katherine Ann than her gorgeous eyes—she was an impressive person who had done so much, making pottery the way they did in Africa and cooking breads from around the world, for a start. When Jessie's best friend, Rosey Roth, said, "Maybe we're too uninteresting. Too dull to be friends with Katherine Ann. What do you think, Jess?", Jessie didn't answer. She was wondering something else. Something she couldn't wonder out loud. Something that made her feel like there was a big hole inside her, and it was ready to get bigger. Jessie was wondering what Tucker would think of this beautiful creature.

To find out what Tucker *does* think and how Jessie learns to cope with Katherine Ann Millicent Franklin, read *The World's Greatest Expert on Absolutely Everything . . . Is Crying*, by Barbara Bottner.

—Verla M. Herschell

A WRINKLE IN TIME   Grades 6–8/YA
A WIND IN THE DOOR
A SWIFTLY TILTING PLANET
By MADELEINE L'ENGLE

It was a dark and windy night; Meg Murray was in her attic bedroom being miserable about the fact that she always seemed to be an oddball and never fit in anywhere. Her little brother Charles Wallace was the only person who really understood her. Sometimes he even seemed to know what she was thinking—and on this particular night, when she went downstairs to get some cocoa, he was already in the kitchen with the milk on, enough for both Meg and her mother, who appeared shortly. A noise in the basement a few minutes later announced Mrs. Whatsit, a very strange old lady who looked rather like a tramp in an assortment of rags, and who ate a liverwurst sandwich and left. But just as she walked out, she turned around and said to Mrs. Murray, "By the way, there *is* such a thing as a tesseract." Mrs. Murray nearly fainted, because the tesseract—the wrinkle in time—was the secret project she and her husband had been working on when he suddenly disappeared.

The next day, Meg and Charles Wallace went to the old house where Mrs. Whatsit and her friends were staying and met Calvin O'Keefe as well. He was to be the third human member of the rescue party. That's why Mrs. Whatsit, Mrs. Who, and Mrs. Which had come to earth—to take these three kids to the planet where the black thing and a force called "It" were holding Mr. Murray prisoner.

A Wind in the Door continues Meg and Charles Wallace's story— and describes their adventures with a cherub who looks more like a drove of dragons than an angel, a dark personage called a Teacher, and an old enemy of Meg's—Mr. Jenkins, the elementary school principal.

Once again, Meg, Calvin, and Charles Wallace are all called to battle the dark shadow that surrounds the earth.

A Swiftly Tilting Planet is the last book of the trilogy. It takes place years after the first two. Charles Wallace is now a teenager, and this is his adventure. Meg helps, but she's pregnant with her and Calvin's first child and so can't do too much. This time, Charles Wallace is pretty much on his own.

Madeleine L'Engle's books are like the Narnia Chronicles. There's more to them than just surface action. Every time I read them, I find something new.

—*Joni Bodart-Talbot*

YEAGER   YA/Adult
By CHUCK YEAGER and LEO JANOS

How many of you have watched World War II movies? How many of you have watched aerial dogfights? How many of you have wondered what it would be like to be shot down over enemy territory?

Chuck Yeager, the hero of this autobiography, was one of the fighter pilots who was shot down. On Sunday, March 5, 1944, while fighting German Messerschmitts over southern France, twenty-one-year-old Chuck Yeager parachuted from his burning plane. He landed in a forest infested with German patrols. The Germans had seen this American flyer parachute, but hadn't seen where he landed.

Everything had happened so fast. Yeager barely had time to release his seatbelt and jump from his burning plane when suddenly he was on the ground with shrapnel punctures in feet and hands from the shells that hit around his cockpit. He also had a deep hole in his right ankle. He sprinkled sulfur powder from his survival kit on his wounds and wrapped a bandage around his injured foot, then studied a silk map of the area that was sewn into his flight suit. He knew where he was, fifty miles east of Bordeaux, but could he reach safety?

Most downed flyers were caught and interrogated by the Gestapo, the Nazi secret police. Somehow, he had to contact the French underground, the native resistance group that could help him escape from France.

[A short booktalk could stop here.]

Alone and cold, he used his parachute for cover during a heavy rain. Then, hearing noises, he drew his revolver and stopped a French woodcutter who, as luck would have it, was a member of the resistance. He helped Yeager limp to a farmhouse and hid the American flyer in a secret barn room. Yeager was sheltered in two farmhouses before he finally reached a resistance group that lived in secret woodland camps. This group helped Yeager make it to the base of the Pyrenees mountains where he and some other escapees were left to cross into Spain on foot.

None were mountain climbers, and the mountains were steep and patrolled by German soldiers. The escapees had to be careful. Yeager and another American named Pat climbed together and hid out one night in an abandoned shed. But Pat made a terrible mistake. He hung his wet socks to dry outside the hut on an old tree limb. When a German patrol discovered the socks in the morning, they fired on the hut. Yeager and Pat fled out a back window. Pat was injured badly, and Yeager had to carry him to safety.

When Pat fainted in their hide-out, Yeager soon learned why. Pat's right leg was almost blown away at the knee. Yeager had to amputate the leg with a penknife, then bind the wounds and carry his unconscious companion the rest of the way to Spain. To this day, he doesn't know where he got the strength to do so.

In Spain Chuck Yeager was given a vacation at government expense and told that he would soon be sent home. But he didn't want to go. He wasn't through fighting and wanted his command back. This was an unprecedented request. To discover if it was granted, read *Yeager*.

—*Anne Raymer*

THE YEAR IT RAINED YA
By CRESCENT DRAGONWAGON

Elizabeth has it all. She even has the mother everyone wants. So, then, why has Elizabeth tried to commit suicide, over and over again?

—*Nancy Guffey*

THE YEAR OF SWEET SENIOR INSANITY YA
By SONIA LEVITIN

Senior insanity is a strange disease. Its symptoms appear gradually, growing in intensity until you are totally in its grip. Senior insanity is being smug in your new status, no longer having to impress anyone with fashion-magazine coordinates; it's learning to stand back and watch, criticizing and joking. It's sitting in class and not hearing a word. It's going to Senior Council meetings and having nothing to say. It's watching the clock, counting the days, multiplying by 24 and then again by 60 to figure out how many minutes remain until the Christmas formal.

This is exactly what happens to Leni during her senior year. What had seemed such a wonderful year suddenly becomes chaotic as she tries to juggle a new boyfriend, classwork, a job, being a cheerleader and, of course, her family life. Sound familiar?

The Year of Sweet Senior Insanity, by Sonia Levitin.

—Pam Spencer

THE YEAR OF THE GOPHER   YA
By PHYLLIS REYNOLDS NAYLOR

George's parents are convinced he belongs in college, and not just *any* college—in an Ivy League college, getting ready for law school! But George knows one thing for sure: while he may not know what he does want to be, he is *certain* he doesn't want to be a lawyer. So the day after graduation, he starts work at the Green Thumb Garden Center as a gopher. You know—go for this, go for that. His father won't speak to him, but George is determined to do things *his* way.

That spring, after he'd fixed it so he'd never be accepted at any of the Ivy League schools he applied for, he had spent a lot of time watching his friends and his family—and discovering they weren't always who they seemed to be. His little brother Ollie was slow—he just couldn't think as fast or make as good grades as his sisters and brother. He already knew what he wanted to do, though—he wanted to be a forest ranger, and that meant he didn't want to go to college either. Jeri, George's little sister, suddenly wasn't so little any more. She always made good grades, but she spent a lot of time sneaking out late at night, and George knew the guys she was with were older than she was—or he was! Trish, the oldest, had won a scholarship to an Ivy League college and then gotten married to a guy with Roman numerals after his name, a guy who had graduated from Cornell summa cum laude. She had it all, right? Well, maybe—but she also drank Maalox by the quart and had to watch what she ate. So maybe she wasn't happy either.

George decides he wants to do what will make him happy—and along the way see if he can't help Ollie and Jeri figure that out too, in spite of what their parents have already decided is best for them. Do they join Trish and the Maalox Brigade or do they learn to break their own paths? Find out in *The Year of the Gopher.*

—Joni Bodart-Talbot

THE YEAR WITHOUT MICHAEL   YA
By SUSAN BETH PFEFFER

Michael left to play baseball. "I won't be late for supper." But he was. He was late for supper—for bed—for his life. He was gone. Vanished, without a trace. And no one could have ever predicted the effects on his family.

Jody, his older sister, blamed herself and tried to hold the family together while they waited. Kay, his younger sister, prayed for his death, just so the waiting would be over. His mother went crazy, his father caved in and did nothing.

What happens to a family when a child vanishes? What's the story behind the headlines, the face on the street poster or the milk carton?

Have you ever wished your sister or brother would just go away and never come back? Be careful what you wish—you may read this and decide to wish something different.

—Joni Bodart-Talbot

YOU'LL MISS ME WHEN I'M GONE   YA
By STEPHEN ROOS

Sixteen-year-old Marcus has it all: popularity, a new car, a place on the Dean's List at school, and a gorgeous girl who's in love with him. He also has a bottle of vodka in his bedroom, hidden underneath his sweaters. Another day, another drink. First he just wants to get a buzz on; then he wants to block out the pain; finally he realizes he doesn't just have a drink any more—now the drink has him! He has to consume more and more alcohol just to get through the day—just to survive, to stop shaking, to act cool, to cope with his problems at school, his parents' divorce, and the loss of everything and everyone that was important to him. He's on a merry-go-round he can't get off—all he can do is hang on tight and hope for the best.

Does he survive, or will they all really miss him when he's gone?

—Joni Bodart-Talbot

YOUNG WITCHES AND WARLOCKS   YA/Adult
Compiled by ISAAC ASIMOV

These stories have one thing in common—magic. Magic used in different ways, sometimes for good, sometimes for evil. Have you ever done something and then wondered why? That's what happened to Cecy in Ray Bradbury's story, "April Witch."

Into the air, over the valleys, under the stars, above a river, flew Cecy. Invisible as new spring winds, fresh as the breath of clover rising over twilight fields, she flew. She soared in doves, stopped in trees, and lived in blossoms, showering away in petals when the breeze blew. She perched in a tiny green frog by a shining pool. She lived in new April grasses.

It's spring, thought Cecy. I'll be in every living thing in the world to-night—on this one evening of her life when she was just seventeen. "Oh, how I want to be in love," she had said to her parents. They had reminded her that she and her whole family were odd and remarkable. We can't mix or marry with ordinary folks—we would lose our ability to travel by magic!

Yes, she sighed. We sleep days and fly nights like black kites on the wind. I can leave my plain body behind and send my mind far out for adventure.

The wind whipped her away over fields and meadows.

If I can't be in love myself, because I'm plain and odd, then I'll be in love through someone else, she thought.

Outside a farmhouse in the spring night, a beautiful young girl named Ann was drawing up water from a deep stone well. Cecy fell as a water droplet into the girl's cup as she drank. Cecy looked out from Ann's eyes.

"Do you know I'm here?"

Ann shook her head. "I've rented my body to an April witch, for sure."

Just then Tom, Ann's rejected lover, rode by. "Did you change your mind, Ann? Would you like to go to the dance with me tonight?"

"No, um, I mean *yes!*" said Ann and then Cecy, through Ann's lips.

That night, for the first time in her life, Cecy knew what it was like to dance. Her mind made Ann say nice words to Tom (whom Ann didn't like). Before Tom took Ann home, Cecy knew what it was like to be kissed, too. She would trade all her magic to be Tom's own love. If only he knew that it was she, Cecy, who loved him!

Cecy's power was strong for only a few hours and now she was weakening. She knew she must go. But she made Ann do one last thing—give

Tom her name and address on a small slip of paper "Promise me you'll visit my friend," Ann heard herself saying to Tom. Tom promised.

Then Cecy let go.

Ann fled to her home and slammed the door, glad to be rid of Cecy and Tom.

Once more Cecy soared, this time as a nightbird. Deep in the night, she found herself just outside Tom's window. "Will you come someday and see me? Will you look into my face and remember that it is I who love you?"

He did not stir in his bed when the blackbird beat softly against the moonstruck window panes; she saw his hand gently close around a small scrap of paper; then, fluttering quietly, she flew away over the sleeping earth.

—Linda Lee

YOU'RE ALLEGRO DEAD Grades 4-6
By BARBARA CORCORAN

Stella had heard about Camp Allegro from her mother all her life. She could even sing the camp song in her sleep:

> We're Allegro born, we're Allegro bred,
> and when we die we're Allegro dead!
> So rah, rah for Camp Allegro,
> rah, rah, rah!

Yes, Stella's mother had fond memories about her summer camp, so fond that when one of her camp mates, Miss Davenport, bought the old place and reopened it, Stella and her friend Kim found themselves spending the summer at the new Camp Allegro.

Much to Stella's surprise, it wasn't half bad. There was tennis, horseback riding, basketball, and crafts. But there were also some unusual and mysterious things happening. And a frightened Stella begins to wonder if the camp song might not just come true: "Allegro born, Allegro bred, and when we die, we're Allegro dead. . . . "

—Vicki Rubottom

A ZOO IN MY LUGGAGE YA/Adult
By GERALD DURRELL

Gerald Durrell is an animal collector. He goes to strange places and captures exotic animals for various zoos. Then he writes hilarious books about his trips, which are guaranteed to have you rolling on the floor.

This book is about one of Durrell's expeditions to collect animals; he went to the island of Bafut off the coast of West Africa. However, he didn't do his collecting in a logical fashion—first he picked out the animals, then he proceeded to look for a zoo to put them in, resulting in the title of this book, *A Zoo in My Luggage*. There were marvelously funny consequences, and in the end Durrell kept some of the animals and opened his own zoo. Ralph Thompson illustrates most of Durrell's books, and if Durrell's descriptions don't make the animals come alive, these sketches surely do!

To give you an idea of what the animals were like—[read excerpts].

It takes someone with a particular sense of humor to appreciate these books—they aren't the run-of-the-mill animal stories. But if you get hooked, it may be a lifetime thing. I am, and one of my goals in life is to visit Durrell's zoo in Jersey, begun with the animals that are described in this book.

A Zoo in My Luggage, by Gerald Durrell.

—*Joni Bodart-Talbot*

BIBLIOGRAPHY BY AUTHOR

Aaron, Chester. *Lackawanna.* Harper 1986. (YA)

Abercrombie, Barbara. *Run for Your Life.* Fawcett 1986. (Adult)

Adler, Carole S. *Kiss the Clown.* Ticknor 1986. (YA)

————. *The Shell Lady's Daughter.* Putnam 1983, Fawcett 1984. (YA)

Ahlberg, Janet and Ahlberg, Allan. *Burglar Bill.* Greenwillow, Puffin 1979. (Grades 2-4)

Aiken, Joan. *The Kingdom and the Cave.* Abelard-Schuman 1960, Doubleday 1974. (Grades 3-6)

Alcock, Vivien. *The Cuckoo Sister.* Delacorte 1986. (YA)

Alexander, Lloyd. *The Book of Three.* Holt 1964, Dell 1980. (Grades 4-9)

Aliki. *Keep Your Mouth Closed, Dear.* Dial 1966, 1980. (Grades k-3)

Ambrus, Victor. *Grandma, Felix and Mustapha Biscuit.* Morrow 1982. (Grades k-1)

Anderson, Margaret J. *The Brain on Quartz Mountain.* Knopf 1982. (Grades 3-5)

Anderson, Mary. *Do You Call That a Dream Date?* Delacorte 1987. (YA)

Angell, Judie. *Secret Selves.* Ballantine 1986. (Grades 5-8)

Anthony, Piers. *Centaur Isle.* Ballantine 1982. (YA)

Asimov, Isaac. *I, Robot.* Fawcett 1978, Ballantine 1984 (YA/Adult)

————, comp. *Young Witches and Warlocks.* Harper 1987. (YA/Adult)

Averill, Esther. *The Fire Cat.* Harper 1960, 1983. (Grades k-3)

Avi. *Wolf Rider.* Bradbury 1986, Macmillan 1988. (Grades 6-9)

Babbitt, Natalie. *The Devil's Storybook.* Farrar 1984. (Grades 2-8)

Bach, Alice. *Waiting for Johnny Miracle.* Harper 1980. (YA)

"Bachman, Richard" (Stephen King). *Thinner.* NAL 1984, 1985, G. K. Hall 1986. (YA/Adult)

Baker, Russell. *Growing Up.* NAL 1983, 1984. (YA/Adult)

Banks, Lynne Reid. *The Indian in the Cupboard.* Doubleday 1981, Avon 1982. (Grades 3-6)

Barton, Del. *A Good Day to Die.* Doubleday 1980. (YA/Adult)

Battles, Edith. *The Witch in Room 6.* Harper 1987. (Grades 4-6)

Beattie, Ann. *Spectacles.* Workman 1985. (Grades 4-6)

Beatty, Patricia. *Wait for Me, Watch for Me, Eula Bee.* Morrow 1978. (Grades 5-9)

Begley, Kathleen A. *Deadline.* Dell 1979. (YA)

Bellairs, John. *The Treasure of Alpheus Winterborn*. Bantam 1985. (Grades 4–8)

Benjamin, Carol Lea. *Nobody's Baby Now*. Macmillan 1984. (YA)

Bennett, Jay. *The Death Ticket*. Avon 1985. (YA)

————. Jay. *The Executioner*. Avon 1982. (YA)

————. Jay. *Say Hello to the Hit Man*. Dell 1977. (YA)

Bethancourt, T. Ernesto. *The Dog Days of Arthur Cane*. Holiday 1976. (YA)

Blum, Robert S. *The Girl From the Emeraline Island*. Ballantine 1984. (YA)

Blume, Judy. *Forever*. Bradbury 1975. (YA)

————. *Freckle Juice*. Macmillan 1971, 1985; Dell 1986. (Grades 1–2)

————. *Just As Long As We're Together*. Watts 1987. (Grades 6–8)

Boatright, Lori. *Out of Bounds*. Fawcett 1982. (YA)

Bodecker, N. M. *Hurry, Hurry, Mary Dear! and Other Nonsense Poems*. Macmillan 1976, 1987. (Grades k–3)

Bonham, Frank. *Premonitions*. Holt 1984. (YA)

Bonsall, Crosby Newell. *Tell Me Some More*. Harper 1961. (Grades 1–4)

Borland, Hal. *When the Legends Die*. Lippincott 1963, Bantam 1972. (YA/Adult)

Bottner, Barbara. *The World's Greatest Expert on Absolutely Everything . . . Is Crying*. Harper 1984, Dell 1986. (YA)

Bowden, Nina. *Kept in the Dark*. Lothrop 1982, Scholastic 1984. (Grades 6–8)

Bowen, John. *Squeak*. Curley 1984, Viking 1984. (YA/Adult)

Bradbury, Peggy. *The Snake That Couldn't Slither*. Putnam 1976. (Grades 1–3)

Bradbury, Ray. *Fahrenheit 451*. S & S 1969, Ballantine 1979, 1981. (YA/Adult)

Bradford, Richard. *Red Sky at Morning*. PB 1983, Harper 1986. (YA)

Bradley, Marion Zimmer. *Hunters of the Red Moon*. DAW 1973. (YA)

Brancato, Robin. *Come Alive at 505*. Knopf 1980. (YA)

————. *Winning*. Bantam 1978. (YA)

Branscum, Robbie. *Johnny May*. Avon 1984. (Grades 3–6)

————. *To the Tune of a Hickory Stick*. Doubleday 1978. (Grades 6–8)

————. *Toby, Granny, and George*. Doubleday 1976. (YA)

Brittain, Bill. *Who Knew There'd Be Ghosts?* Harper 1985. (Grades 4–6)

————. *The Wish Giver: Three Tales of Coven Tree*. Harper 1983, 1986. (Grades 4–6)

Brontë, Charlotte. *Jane Eyre*. 1847; many editions. (YA)

Brookins, Dana. *Alone in Wolf Hollow.* Houghton 1978. (Grades 5–7)

Brooks, Bruce. *Midnight Hour Encores.* Harper 1987. (YA)

———. *The Moves Make the Man.* Harper 1984, 1987. (YA)

Brooks, Jerome. *The Big Dipper Marathon.* Dutton 1979. (YA)

Brooks, Terry. *The Sword of Shannara.* Random 1977, Ballantine 1983. (YA)

Brown, Claude. *The Children of Ham.* Stein & Day 1987. (YA)

Brown, Marc. *Arthur's Tooth.* Atlantic Monthly Press 1985. (Grades k–2)

———. *Arthur's Valentine.* Little 1980, 1988. (Grades k–3)

Bryan, C.D.B. *Friendly Fire.* Bantam 1977. (YA/Adult)

Bunting, Eve. *The Face at the Edge of the World.* Ticknor 1985. (YA)

———. *Ghost Behind Me.* PB 1984. (YA)

———. *Janet Hamm Needs a Date for the Dance.* Ticknor 1986, Bantam 1987. (Grades 6–8)

———. *Someone Is Hiding on Alcatraz Island.* Houghton 1984, Berkley 1986. (YA)

———. *Surrogate Sister.* Harper 1984. (YA)

Burns, Olive Ann. *Cold Sassy Tree.* Ticknor 1984, Dell 1986. (YA/Adult)

Byars, Betsy C. *Cracker Jackson.* Viking 1985, Penguin 1986. (Grades 6–8/YA)

———. *The Pinballs.* Harper 1977, Scholastic 1979, Harper 1987. (Grades 7–9)

Calhoun, Mary and Morrill, Leslie. *The Night the Monster Came.* Morrow 1982. (Grades 3–6)

Carleton, Barbee Oliver. *The Witches' Bridge.* Holt 1967. (Grades 3–5)

Carlson, Dale Bick. *Baby Needs Shoes.* Atheneum 1974. (Grades 3–5)

Carris, Joan. *When the Boys Ran the House.* Harper 1982, Dell 1983. (Grades 4–6)

Carter, Alden R. *Sheila's Dying.* Putnam 1987. (YA)

———. *Wart, Son of Toad.* Putnam 1985, Berkley 1987. (Grades 7–8/YA)

Catton, Bruce. *Glory Road.* Fairfax (dist. by Crown) 1984. (YA/Adult)

Chaback, Elaine and Fortunato, Mel. *The Official Kids' Survival Kit: How to Do Things on Your Own.* Little 1981. (Grades 4–6)

Chambers, Aidan. *Out of Time.* Harper 1985. (YA)

Chase, Mary. *Loretta Mason Potts.* Lippincott 1958. (Grades 3–6)

Clapp, Patricia. *Jane-Emily.* Dell 1973. (Grades 5–6)

Clark, Mary Higgins. *A Cry in the Night.* Dell 1983. (YA/Adult)

———. *Where Are the Children?* S & S 1975, Dell 1976. (YA/Adult)

Cleary, Beverly. *Beezus and Ramona.* Morrow 1955, Dell 1979. (Grades 3-6)

———. *Dear Mr. Henshaw.* Morrow 1983, Dell 1984, ABC-Clio 1987. (Grades 4-6)

———. *Ramona the Brave.* Morrow 1975, Dell 1984. (Grades 3-5)

———. *Ramona the Pest.* Morrow 1968, Dell 1982. (Grades 2-5)

Cleaver, Vera and Cleaver, Bill. *Ellen Grae.* NAL 1978. Also in *Ellen Grae and Lady Ellen Grae,* NAL 1987. (Grades 3-5)

Cobb, Vicki and Darling, Kathy. *Bet You Can't: Science Impossibilities to Fool You.* Lothrop 1980, Avon 1983. (Grades 4-6)

Cohen, Daniel. *Frauds, Hoaxes, and Swindles.* Watts 1979. Also published by Dell as *Frauds and Hoaxes and Swindles.* (Grades 3-6)

Cole, Joanne. *Bony-Legs.* Macmillan 1983, Scholastic 1986. (Grades k-3)

Collier, James Lincoln and Collier, Christopher. *My Brother Sam Is Dead.* Scholastic 1977, 1985. (Grades 6-8)

Colville, Bruce. *Spirits and Spells.* Dell 1983. (Grades 7-8/YA)

Conford, Ellen. *The Alfred G. Graebner Memorial High School Handbook of Rules and Regulations.* Little 1976, Archway 1977, PB 1983. (Grades 7-10)

———. *Lenny Kandell, Smart Aleck.* Little 1983, Archway 1987. (Grades 5-8)

———. *Strictly for Laughs.* Putnam 1985, Berkley 1987. (Grades 7-8/YA)

Conrad, Pam. *Prairie Songs.* Harper 1985, 1987. (Grades 7-9)

———. *What I Did for Roman.* Harper 1987. (YA)

Cooney, Caroline B. *Among Friends.* Bantam 1987. (YA)

Coontz, Otto. *Night Walkers.* Houghton 1982, Archway 1983. (Grades 7-8/YA)

Corcoran, Barbara. *You're Allegro Dead.* Atheneum 1981. (Grades 4-6)

Coren, Alan. *Arthur and the Great Detective.* Little 1979 (American edition). (Grades 1-2)

Cormier, Robert. *Beyond the Chocolate War.* Knopf 1984, Dell 1986. (YA)

Cosgrove, Stephen. *Cap'n Smudge.* French 1967, Price 1977. (Grades k-3)

Cross, Gillian. *Chartbreaker.* Holiday 1987. (YA)

Crutcher, Chris. *The Crazy Horse Electric Game.* Greenwillow 1987. (Ya/Adult)

———. *Running Loose.* Greenwillow 1983, Dell 1986. (YA)

———. *Stotan!* Greenwillow 1986. (Grades 6-8/YA)

Curry, Jane Louise. *Me, Myself and I.* Macmillan 1987. (Grades 7-8/YA)

Curtis, Philip. *Invasion of the Brain Sharpeners.* Knopf 1981. Originally published by Andersen Press in London as *Mr. Browser and the Brain Sharpeners.* (Grades 3-5)

Dahl, Roald. *The Magic Finger.* Harper 1966, 1983. (Grades 3-6)

D'Ambrosio, Richard. *No Language But a Cry.* Doubleday 1970, Dell 1987. (YA/Adult)

Dana, Barbara. *Necessary Parties.* Harper 1986, Bantam 1987. (Grades 6-8/YA)

Danziger, Paula. *The Cat Ate My Gymsuit.* Delacorte 1974, Dell 1986. (Grades 7-8/YA)

———. *There's a Bat in Bunk Five.* Delacorte 1980, Dell 1986. (Grades 7-8/YA)

———. *This Place Has No Atmosphere.* Delacorte 1986, Dell 1987. (Grades 7-8/YA)

Davis, Richard, comp. *Space 3: A Collection of Science Fiction Stories.* Abelard 1976. (YA/Adult)

DeClements, Barthe. *How Do You Lose Those Ninth Grade Blues?* Viking 1983, Scholastic 1984. (Grades 6-8/YA)

———. *Seventeen and In-Between.* Viking 1984, Scholastic 1985. (YA)

——— and Greimes, Christopher. *Double Trouble.* Viking 1987. (Grades 6-8)

Desbarats, Peter. *Gabrielle and Selena.* Harcourt 1974. (Grades 1-2)

Dickinson, Peter. *Healer.* Delacorte 1985, Dell 1987. (YA)

Dickson, Gordon. *The Dragon and the George.* Ballantine 1978. (YA/Adult)

D'Ignazio, Fred. *Chip Mitchell: The Case of the Stolen Computer Brains.* Lodestar 1982. (Grades 4-6)

Dixon, Jeanne. *The Tempered Wind.* Macmillan 1987. (YA)

Dragonwagon, Crescent. *Dear Miss Moshki.* Macmillan 1986. (Grades 4-6)

———. *The Year It Rained.* Macmillan 1985, PB. (YA)

Duncan, Lois. *A Gift of Magic.* Little 1971, Archway 1981. (Grades 6-8)

———. *I Know What You Did Last Summer.* Little 1973, Archway 1985. (YA)

———. *Killing Mr. Griffin.* Little 1978, Dell 1986. (YA)

———. *Locked in Time.* Little 1985, Dell 1986. (YA)

———. *Summer of Fear.* Little 1976, Dell 1986. (YA)

———. *The Twisted Window.* Delacorte 1987. (Grades 7-8/YA)

Durrell, Gerald. *A Zoo in My Luggage.* Penguin 1976, Peter Smith 1983. (YA/Adult)

Eckert, Allan W. *The Incident at Hawk's Hill.* Little 1971, Dell 1972, Bantam 1987. (Grades 6-8)

Elder, Lauren with Shirley Streshinsky. *And I Alone Survived.* Dutton 1978, Fawcett 1979. (YA/Adult)

Elfman, Blossom. *The Girls of Huntington House.* Houghton 1972, Bantam 1973. (YA)

Ellis, Mel. *No Man for Murder.* Holt 1973. (YA)

Essex, Rosamund Sibyl. *Into the Forest.* c1963. American edition Coward 1965. (Grades 3-6)

Eyerly, Jeannette. *See Dave Run.* Harper 1978, Archway 1986. (YA)

Farmer, Penelope. *Charlotte Sometimes.* Dell 1987. (Grades 3-5)

Ferris, Jean. *Invincible Summer.* Farrar 1987. (YA)

Fitzhugh, Louise. *Harriet the Spy.* Harper 1964, Dell 1986, ABC-Clio 1987. (Grades 5-7)

Fleischman, Paul. *Path of the Pale Horse.* Harper 1983. (Grades 7-8/YA)

Fleischman, Sid. *The Ghost on Saturday Night.* Little 1974. (Grades 4-6)

Fox, Paula. *The One-Eyed Cat.* Bradbury 1984, Dell 1986. (Grades 5-9)

———. *Slave Dancer.* Bradbury 1973, Dell 1975. (Grades 6-10)

French, Michael. *Pursuit.* Delacorte 1982, Dell 1986. (YA)

———. *Us Against Them.* Bantam 1987. (YA)

Gaeddert, Louann. *The Kid With the Red Suspenders.* Dutton 1983. (Grades 2-5)

Gaffin, Jane. *The Adventures of Chuchi.* Friesen 1985. (Grades 3-5)

Gallo, Donald R., comp. *Sixteen: Short Stories by Outstanding Writers for Young Adults.* Delacorte 1984, Dell 1986. (YA)

———, comp. *Visions: 19 Short Stories by Outstanding Writers for Young Adults.* Delacorte 1984, Dell 1984. (YA)

Gannett, Ruth Stiles. *My Father's Dragon.* Random 1986, Knopf 1987. (Grades 2-4)

Garden, Nancy. *Prisoner of Vampires.* Farrar 1985, Dell 1986. (Grades 4-8)

Garfield, Brian. *The Paladin.* Bantam 1986. (YA/Adult)

Garrigue, Sheila. *All the Children Were Sent Away.* Bradbury 1976. (Grades 7-8)

Gauch, Patricia. *This Time, Tempe Wick?* Putnam 1974, Shoe Tree 1986. (Grades 1-4)

George, Jean Craighead. *My Side of the Mountain.* Dutton 1967, 1975. (Grades 4–8)

———. *The Talking Earth.* Harper 1983, 1987. (Grades 6–9)

Giblin, James C. *Chimney Sweeps: Yesterday and Today.* Harper 1982, 1987. (Grades 4–6)

Giovanni, Nikki. *Gemini.* Bobbs-Merrill 1971. (YA/Adult)

Girion, Barbara. *A Handful of Stars.* Macmillan 1981, Dell 1986. (YA)

———. *In the Middle of a Rainbow.* Macmillan 1983, Putnam 1984, Berkley. (Grades 7–8/YA)

———. *Joshua, the Czar, and the Chicken-Bone Wish.* Scribner 1978; distributed by Macmillan. (Grades 3–5)

Green, Bette. *The Summer of My German Soldier.* Dial 1973, Bantam 1981. (Grades 7–8/YA)

Green, Gerald. *Girl.* Doubleday 1977. (Grades 3–5)

"Green, Hannah" (Joanne Greenberg). *I Never Promised You a Rose Garden.* Holt 1964, NAL 1977. (YA/Adult)

Greenberg, Jan. *No Dragons to Slay.* Farrar 1984. (YA)

———. *The Pig-Out Blues.* Farrar 1982, Dell 1986. (YA)

Greenberg, Joanne. *Simple Gifts.* Holt 1986, 1987. (YA/Adult)

Greene, Constance C. *Love Letters of J. Timothy Owen.* Harper 1986. (Grades 7–8/YA)

Greenwald, Sheila. *All the Way to Wit's End.* Little 1979, Dell. (Grades 4–8)

———. *Give Us a Great Big Smile, Rosy Cole.* Little 1981, Dell 1982. (Grades 4–6)

———. *It All Began With Jane Eyre, or The Secret Life of Franny Dillman.* Little 1980, Dell 1986. (YA)

———. *Will the Real Gertrude Hollings Please Stand Up?* Atlantic 1983 (dist. by Little); Dell 1985. (Grades 4–6)

Grillone, Lisa and Gennaro, Joseph. *Small Worlds Close Up.* Crown 1987. (Grades 4–6)

Guest, Judith. *Ordinary People.* Penguin 1982, Ballantine 1982, 1987. (YA/Adult)

Guy, Rosa. *The Friends.* Holt 1973, Bantam 1973. (Grades 7–9)

Haddad, Carolyn. *The Last Ride.* Dodd 1984. (YA)

Hahn, Mary D. *Daphne's Book.* Houghton 1983, Bantam 1985. (Grades 6–8)

Hallstead, William F. *The Launching of Linda Bell.* Fawcett 1983. (YA)

Halvorsen, Marilyn. *Cowboys Don't Cry.* Delacorte 1985, Dell 1986. (YA)

Hamilton, Virginia. *A Little Love.* Putnam 1984, Berkley 1985. (YA)

—————, coll. *The People Could Fly: American Black Folktales.* Knopf 1985. (Grades 4–8/YA)

—————. *Sweet Whispers, Brother Rush.* Putnam 1982, Avon 1983. (Grades 7–8/YA)

Hammer, Charles. *Me, the Beef, and the Bum.* Farrar 1984. (Grades 5–8)

Hanes, Mari. *Wild Child.* Tyndale 1982. (YA/Adult)

Harlan, Elizabeth. *Footfalls.* Fawcett 1984. (Grades 6–8)

Haseley, Dennis. *The Counterfeiter.* Macmillan 1987. (YA)

Hastings, Beverly. *Watcher in the Dark.* Putnam 1986, Berkley 1986. (YA)

Haugaard, Erik Christian. *Chase Me, Catch Nobody!* Houghton 1980. (Grades 6–8)

Hautzig, Deborah. *Second Star to the Right.* Greenwillow 1981, Avon 1982. (YA)

Hautzig, Esther. *A Gift for Mama.* Viking 1981, Penguin 1987. (Grades 2–4)

Hayden, Torey L. *Murphy's Boy.* Putnam 1983, Avon 1983. (Adult)

Hazen, Barbara Shook. *Last, First, Middle and Nick: All About Names.* Prentice-Hall 1979. (Grades 3–6)

Head, Ann. *Mr. and Mrs. BoJo Jones.* Putnam 1967, NAL 1973. (YA)

Heinlein, Robert. *The Past Through Tomorrow.* Putnam 1967, Berkley 1975. (YA/Adult)

Heller, Joseph. *Catch-22.* S & S 1961, Dell 1985. (YA/Adult)

"Henry, O." (William Sidney Porter). *Gift of the Magi and Other Stories.* RD Assn. 1987. Many other collections contain the story. (YA/Adult)

Hentoff, Nat. *American Heroes: In and Out of School.* Delacorte 1987. (YA)

Herbert, Frank. *Dune.* Chilton 1965, Putnam 1984, Ace 1987. (YA/Adult)

Hersey, John. *Hiroshima.* Knopf 1946, 1985; Bantam 1986. (YA/Adult)

Hewett, Joan. *When You Fight the Tiger.* Little 1984. (Grades 5–9)

Heyerdahl, Thor. *Aku-Aku.* Rand 1958, Ballantine 1974. (YA/Adult)

Higdon, Hal. *The Crime of the Century.* Putnam 1975. (YA/Adult)

Higgins, Colin. *Harold and Maude.* Avon 1975. (YA)

Hindle, Lee J. *Dragon Fall.* Avon 1984. (YA)

Hinton, S. E. *The Outsiders.* Viking 1967, Dell 1986. (YA)

Holman, Felice. *The Wild Children.* Scribner 1983 (dist. by Macmillan), Penguin 1985. (Grades 5–9)

Horowitz, Anthony. *The Devil's Door-bell.* Holt 1983, Putnam 1983, Berkley 1986. (Grades 7-8/YA)

Houston, James. *Frozen Fire.* Macmillan 1981. (YA/Adult)

Howe, James. *The Celery Stalks at Midnight.* Atheneum 1983 (dist. by Macmillan), Avon 1984. (Grades 3-7)

Hunter, Evan. *Me and Mr. Stenner.* Harper 1976, Dell 1986. (Grades 5-6)

Hunter, Mollie. *The Thirteenth Member.* Hamilton 1971, Canongate 1986. (Grades 3-5)

Hurmence, Belinda. *Tancy.* Houghton 1984. (Grades 6-8/YA)

Hurwitz, Johanna. *The Adventures of Ali Baba Bernstein.* Morrow 1985, Scholastic 1987. (Grades 3-4)

———. *Aldo Applesauce.* Morrow 1979, Scholastic 1983. (Grades 3-4)

———. *Tough-Luck Karen.* Morrow 1982, Scholastic 1984. (Grades 4-6)

Huynh Quang Nhuong. *The Land I Lost: Adventures of a Boy in Vietnam.* Harper 1982, 1986. (Grades 5-8)

Jewell, Geri with Stewart Weiner. *Geri.* Morrow 1984, Ballantine. (YA)

Johnson, Annabel and Johnson, Edgar. *The Danger Quotient.* Harper 1984, 1987. (YA)

Jones, Diana Wynne. *Howl's Moving Castle.* Greenwillow 1986. (YA)

———. *Witch Week.* Greenwillow 1982. (Grades 5-7)

Jukes, Mavis. *Blackberries in the Dark.* Knopf 1985, Dell 1987. (Grades 4-6)

Kerr, M. E. *Fell.* Harper 1987. (YA)

———. *I Stay Near You.* Harper 1985, Berkley 1986. (YA)

———. *Little Little.* Harper 1981, Bantam 1986. (YA)

———. *Night Kites.* Harper 1986, 1987. (YA)

Kidd, Ronald. *Dunker.* Lodestar 1982, Bantam. (Grades 7-8/YA)

King, Stephen. *Carrie.* Doubleday 1974, NAL 1976. (YA/Adult)

———. *Christine.* Viking 1983, NAL 1983. (YA/Adult)

———. *Misery.* Viking 1987. (YA/Adult)

———. *Night Shift.* NAL 1979. (YA/Adult)

———. *The Shining.* Doubleday 1976, NAL 1983. (YA/Adult)

———. *Salem's Lot.* Doubleday 1975, NAL 1983. (YA/Adult)

King-Smith, Dick. *Babe the Gallant Pig.* Crown 1985, Dell 1987. (Grades 3-4)

Klein, Norma. *My Life as a Body.* Knopf 1987. (YA)

———. *Older Men.* Dial 1987. (YA)

Koertge, Ron. *Where the Kissing Never Stops.* Little 1987. (YA)

Korman, Gordon. *A Semester in the Life of a Garbage Bag.* Scholastic 1987. (YA)

Krents, Hal. *To Race the Wind.* Putnam 1972. (YA/Adult)

L'Amour, Louis. *Ride the River.* Bantam, G. K. Hall 1984, Century 1986. (YA/Adult)

Lasky, Kathryn. *Beyond the Divide.* Macmillan 1983, Dell 1986. (YA)

LaVert, John. *The Flight of the Cassowary.* Atlantic 1986. (YA)

Lawrence, Louise. *Children of the Dust.* Harper 1985. (YA)

Leach, Maria. *The Thing at the Foot of the Bed.* World 1959, Dell 1977, Putnam 1987. (Grades 4-6)

Lee, Robert C. *It's a Mile From Here to Glory.* Little 1972. (YA)

Le Guin, Ursula K. *The Left Hand of Darkness.* c1969. Harper 1980, Ace 1983. (YA/Adult)

L'Engle, Madeleine. *Time Trilogy: A Wrinkle in Time; A Wind in the Door; A Swiftly Tilting Planet.* Farrar 1979. Individual volumes also published by Dell. (Grades 6-8/YA)

Lenski, Lois. *Strawberry Girl.* Harper 1945, Dell 1987. (Grades 4-8)

Levin, Ira. *The Boys From Brazil.* Random 1976, Dell 1978. (YA/Adult)

Levitin, Sonia. *The Year of Sweet Senior Insanity.* Macmillan 1982, Fawcett 1983. (YA)

Lionni, Leo. *Alexander and the Wind-Up Mouse.* Pantheon 1969, Knopf 1987. (Grades k-3)

Lipsyte, Robert. *The Contender.* Harper 1967, 1987. (Grades 6-9)

———. *Summer Rules.* Harper 1981. (Grades 7-8/YA)

———. *The Summerboy.* Harper 1982, Bantam 1984. (YA)

London, Jack. *The Sea Wolf.* 1904; many editions. (YA/Adult)

Lord, Beman. *The Trouble With Francis.* Walck 1958, Hale 1958. (Grades 3-6)

Lord, Betty Bao. *In the Year of the Boar and Jackie Robinson.* Harper 1984, 1986. (Grades 4-6)

Lord, Gabrielle. *Fortress.* Ballantine 1982. (YA)

Lorimer, Janet. *The Biggest Bubble in the World.* Watts 1982. (Grades k-3)

Lowry, Lois. *Anastasia, Ask Your Analyst.* Houghton 1984, Dell. (Grades 4-6)

———. *Anastasia At Your Service.* Houghton 1982, Dell. (Grades 4-6)

———. *Taking Care of Terrific.* Houghton 1983, Dell 1984. (YA)

Luenn, Nancy. *The Dragon Kite.* Harcourt 1982. (Grades k-3)

Lukeman, Tim. *Witchwood.* Timescape 1983, dist. by S & S. (YA)

McCaffrey, Anne. *Dragonsinger.* Atheneum 1977, Bantam. (YA/Adult)

———. *Dragonsong.* Macmillan 1976; Bantam 1986. (YA)

McCauley, Kirby, comp. *Dark Forces.* Viking 1980. (YA/Adult)

MacDonald, Betty. *Mrs. Piggle Wiggle.* Harper 1957. (Grades k–3)

McGuire, Paula. *Putting It Together: Teenagers Talk About Family Breakup.* Delacorte 1987. (YA/Adult)

McIntyre, Vonda N. *Dreamsnake.* Houghton 1978, Dell 1986. (YA)

McKinley, Robin. *The Hero and the Crown.* Greenwillow 1984, Ace. (YA/Adult)

MacLachlan, Patricia. *Sarah, Plain and Tall.* Harper 1985, 1987. (Grades 3–6)

MacLean, Alistair. *Ice Station Zebra.* Fawcett 1978, 1984. (YA/Adult)

Magorian, Michelle. *Back Home.* Harper 1984. (YA)

Mahy, Margaret. *Changeover: A Supernatural Romance.* Macmillan 1984, Scholastic 1985. (YA)

———. *The Haunting.* Macmillan 1982, Scholastic 1984. (Grades 6–8)

Marshall, James. *Summer in the South.* Houghton 1977. (Grades 3–5)

Martin, Ann M. *Slam Book.* Holiday 1987. (Grades 6–8/YA)

Mason, Anne. *The Stolen Law.* Harper 1986. (YA)

Mason, Robert. *Chickenhawk.* Viking 1983, Penguin 1984. (YA/Adult)

Matheson, Richard. *Bid Time Return.* Ballantine 1976, Buccaneer 1986. (YA)

Mathis, Sharon Bell. *A Teacup Full of Roses.* Viking 1972, Avon 1981, Penguin 1987. (YA)

Maupassant, Guy de. *Guy de Maupassant's Short Stories* (translated by Marjorie Laurie). Dutton 1934. (YA/Adult)

Maxwell, Edith. *Just Dial a Number.* Archway 1972, Pendulum 1978. (YA)

Mayer, Mercer. *There's an Alligator Under My Bed.* Dial 1987. (Grades 1–4)

Mayhar, Ardath. *Makra Choria.* Macmillan 1987. (Grades 7–8/YA)

———. *Medicine Walk.* Macmillan 1985. (Grades 7–8/YA)

Mazer, Harry. *I Love You, Stupid!* Avon 1983. (YA)

———. *The Island Keeper: A Tale of Courage and Survival.* Delacorte 1981, Dell 1986. (Grades 6–8/YA)

———. *The War on Villa Street.* Delacorte 1978. (YA)

———. *When the Phone Rang.* Scholastic 1985, 1986. (Grades 6–8/YA)

Mazer, Norma Fox. *After the Rain.* Morrow 1987, Avon 1987. (Grades 6–8/YA)

———. *Dear Bill, Remember Me? And Other Stories.* Delacorte 1976, Dell 1978. (Grades 6–8/YA)

———. *Downtown*. Avon 1984, Morrow 1984. (YA)

———. *When We First Met*. Macmillan 1982, Scholastic 1984. (YA)

Meyer, Carolyn. *Denny's Tapes*. Macmillan 1987. (YA)

Miklowitz, Gloria D. *Goodbye Tomorrow*. Delacorte 1987. (YA)

———. *The War Between the Classes*. Delacorte 1985, Dell 1986. (YA)

Mills, Claudia. *The One and Only Cynthia Jane Thornton*. Macmillan 1986, Bantam 1988. (Grades 4–6)

Morrison, Dorothy. *Whisper Goodbye*. Macmillan 1985. (Grades 4–8)

Mulford, Philippa Greene. *The World Is My Eggshell*. Delacorte 1986. (YA)

Myers, Walter Dean. *Crystal*. Viking 1987. (YA)

———. *Fast Sam, Cool Clyde and Stuff*. Viking 1975, Avon 1979. (YA)

———. *The Legend of Tarik*. Viking 1981, Scholastic 1982. (YA)

Nathanson, Laura. *The Trouble with Wednesdays*. Putnam 1986, Bantam 1987. (Grades 6–9)

Naylor, Phyllis Reynolds. *The Year of the Gopher*. Macmillan 1987, Bantam 1988. (YA)

Nelson, O. T. *The Girl Who Owned a City*. Lerner 1975, Dell 1977. (Grades 6–8)

Neufeld, John. *Lisa, Bright and Dark*. Phillips 1969, NAL 1970. (YA)

Niven, Larry and Pournelle, Jerry. *Lucifer's Hammer*. Playboy 1977, Fawcett 1985. (YA)

Nixon, Joan Lowery. *The Kidnapping of Christina Lattimore*. Harcourt 1979, Dell 1980. (Grades 7–8/YA)

———. *The Other Side of Dark*. Delacorte 1986, Dell 1987. (YA)

———. *The Stalker*. Delacorte 1985, Dell 1987. (YA/Adult)

Nostlinger, Christine. *Konrad* (trans. by Anthea Bell). Avon 1983. (Grades 3–6)

Oakley, Graham. *The Church Mice in Action*. Macmillan 1985. (Grades 2–5)

O'Dell, Scott. *Child of Fire*. Houghton 1974. (Grades 6–9)

Oppenheimer, Joan. *Working On It*. Harcourt 1980, Dell 1986. (YA)

Orgel, Doris. *A Certain Magic*. Viking 1976. (Grades 3–5)

Osborne, Mary Pope. *Love Always, Blue*. Dial 1983, Scholastic 1984. (YA)

Palin, Michael. *Mirrorstone*. Knopf 1986. (Grades 7–8/YA)

Palmer, David R. *Emergence*. Bantam 1984. (YA)

Panshin, Alexei. *Rite of Passage*. PB 1982. (YA)

Park, Barbara. *Skinnybones*. Knopf 1982, Avon 1983. (Grades 3–6)

Pascal, Francine. *The Hand-Me-Down Kid*. Viking 1980, Dell. (Grades 3–6)

————. *Hangin' Out With Cici.* Viking 1977, Dell 1986. (Grades 6–8)

————. *Love and Betrayal and Hold the Mayo!* Viking 1985, Dell 1986. (Grades 7–8)

————. *My First Love and Other Disasters.* Viking 1979, Dell 1986. (YA)

Paterson, Katherine. *Come Sing, Jimmy Jo.* Lodestar 1985, Avon 1986. (YA)

————. *Jacob Have I Loved.* Harper 1980, Avon 1981. (YA)

————. *Rebels of the Heavenly Kingdom.* Lodestar 1983, Avon 1984. (YA)

Paulsen, Gary. *The Crossing.* Watts 1987. (YA/Adult)

————. *Dancing Carl.* Bradbury 1983, Penguin 1987. (YA/Adult)

————. *Hatchet.* Bradbury 1987. (YA)

————. *Popcorn Days and Buttermilk Nights.* Lodestar 1983. (Grades 7–8/YA)

————. *Sentries.* Bradbury 1986, Penguin 1987. (YA)

Peck, Richard. *Are You in the House Alone?* Viking 1976, Dell 1986. (YA/Adult)

————. *Ghosts I Have Been.* Viking 1977, Dell 1986, 1987. (YA)

————. *Princess Ashley.* Delacorte 1987. (YA)

————. *Remembering the Good Times.* Delacorte 1985, Dell 1986. (YA)

————. *Representing Superdoll.* Viking 1974, Avon 1980, Dell 1986. (Grades 7–8/YA)

————. *Secrets of the Shopping Mall.* Delacorte 1979, Dell 1986. (Grades 7–8/YA)

————. *Through a Brief Darkness.* Viking 1973, Avon 1981, Dell 1986. (YA)

Peck, Robert Newton. *Millie's Boy.* Knopf 1973. (Grades 6–8/YA)

Peet, Bill. *Kermit the Hermit.* Houghton 1965. (Grades 1–4)

Peterson, P. J. *Going for the Big One.* Delacorte 1986, Dell 1987. (YA)

————. *Nobody Else Can Walk It for You.* Delacorte 1982, Dell 1986. (YA)

Pfeffer, Susan Beth. *A Matter of Principle.* Delacorte 1982. (YA)

————. *What Do You Do When Your Mouth Won't Open?* Delacorte 1981, Dell 1982. (Grades 4–8)

————. *The Year Without Michael.* Bantam 1987. (YA)

Pierce, Meredith Ann. *The Woman Who Loved Reindeer.* Atlantic 1985. (YA)

Pinkwater, Daniel. *The Snarkout Boys and the Baconburg Horror.* Lothrop 1984, NAL 1985. (Grades 7–8/YA)

Plath, Sylvia. *The Bell Jar.* Harper 1971, Bantam 1975. (YA/Adult)

Poitier, Sidney. *This Life.* Knopf 1980, Ballantine 1981. (YA/Adult)

Pope, Elizabeth. *The Sherwood Ring.* Houghton 1958, Ace 1985. (Grades 6-10)

Prelutsky, Jack. *The New Kid on the Block.* Greenwillow 1984. (Grades 2-6)

Randall, Florence Engel. *The Almost Year.* Atheneum 1971. (Grades 6-8)

Rather, Dan with Mickey Herskowitz. *The Camera Never Blinks: Adventures of a TV Journalist.* Ballantine 1984. (YA/Adult)

Rawls, Wilson. *Summer of the Monkeys.* Dell 1987. (Grades 4-8)

Reader, Dennis J. *Coming Back Alive.* Avon 1983. (YA)

Rice, Anne. *Interview With the Vampire.* 1976, Ballantine 1986. (YA/Adult)

Rinaldi, Ann. *The Good Side of My Heart.* Holiday 1987. (YA)

Roberts, Willo Davis. *Baby-Sitting Is a Dangerous Job.* Macmillan 1985, Fawcett 1987. (Grades 5-8)

――. *The Girl With the Silver Eyes.* Macmillan 1980, Scholastic 1982. (Grades 6-8/YA)

――. *The Pet-Sitting Peril.* Macmillan 1983, 1985. (Grades 5-7)

――. *View From the Cherry Tree.* Macmillan 1979, 1987. (Grades 7-8)

Robinson, Barbara. *The Best Christmas Pageant Ever.* Harper 1972; Avon 1973, 1979; Tyndale 1982. (Grades 4-7)

Robinson, Spider. *Callahan's Crosstime Saloon.* c1977. Enslow 1978, Berkley 1987. (YA)

Roos, Stephen. *You'll Miss Me When I'm Gone.* Delacorte 1988. (YA)

Roueche, Berton. *Feral.* Avon 1983. (YA/Adult)

Rounds, Glen. *Blind Outlaw.* Holiday 1980, Scholastic. (Grades 5-6)

Ruckman, Ivy. *Night of the Twisters.* Harper 1984, 1986. (Grades 4-6)

Rylant, Cynthia. *A Blue-Eyed Daisy.* Bradbury 1985, Dell 1987. (Grades 4-8)

Salassi, Otto R. *Jimmy D. Sidewinder and Me.* Greenwillow, 1987. (Grades 6-8/YA)

Sargent, Pamela. *Earthseed.* Harper 1983. (YA)

Saul, John. *Comes the Blind Fury.* Dell 1986. (YA/Adult)

Schwartz, Alvin. *Scary Stories to Tell in the Dark.* Harper 1981. (Grades 4-6)

Scoppettone, Sandra. *Playing Murder.* Harper 1985, 1987. (YA)

Sebestyen, Ouida. *Words by Heart.* Little 1979, Bantam 1987. (Grades 7-9)

Selsam, Millicent E. *Is This a Baby Dinosaur? and Other Science Picture Puzzles.* Harper 1972, 1984. (Grades k–2)

Senn, Steve A. *Circle in the Sea.* Atheneum 1981. (YA)

Shaara, Michael. *The Herald.* McGraw 1981, Avon 1984. (YA/Adult)

Shange, Ntozake. *Betsey Brown.* St. Martin 1985. (YA/Adult)

Shannon, Jacqueline. *Too Much TJ.* Delacorte 1986. (YA)

Sharmat, Marjorie. *He Noticed I'm Alive . . . and Other Hopeful Signs.* Delacorte 1984, Dell 1985. (Grades 6–8/YA)

———. *Scarlet Monster Lives Here.* Harper 1979. (Grades k–3)

Sherman, Eileen Bluestone. *Monday in Odessa.* JPS Phila. 1986. (YA)

Shyer, Marlene Fanta. *Adorable Sunday.* Scribner 1983. (Grades 6–8/YA)

Silverstein, Shel. *A Light in the Attic.* Harper 1981. (Grades 4–8)

Skorpen, Liesel Moak. *That Mean Man.* Harper 1968. (Grades k–3)

Sleator, William. *Fingers.* Macmillan 1983, Bantam 1988. (Grades 7–8/YA)

———. *House of Stairs.* Dutton 1974, Scholastic 1981. (YA)

———. *Interstellar Pig.* Dutton 1984, Bantam 1986. (YA)

Slote, Alfred. *Clone Catcher.* Harper 1982, 1986. (Grades 4–6)

Smith, Robert Kimmel. *Jelly Belly.* Delacorte 1981, Dell 1982. (Grades 4–6)

Snyder, Zilpha Keatley. *Eyes in the Fishbowl.* Macmillan 1974. (Grades 3–5)

Speare, Elizabeth. *Sign of the Beaver.* Houghton 1983, Dell 1984. (Grades 4–7)

Spiegelman, Art. *Maus: A Survivor's Tale.* Pantheon 1986. (YA/Adult)

Spinelli, Jerry. *Space Station Seventh Grade.* Little 1982, Dell 1984. (Grades 5–9)

———. *Who Put That Hair in My Toothbrush?* Little 1984, Dell 1986. (Grades 6–9)

Stearns, Pamela. *Into the Painted Bear Lair.* Houghton 1976. (Grades 2–5)

Steig, William. *The Amazing Bone.* Penguin 1977. (Grades k–2)

———. *The Real Thief.* Farrar 1973. (Grades 1–2)

Sterman, Betsy and Sterman, Samuel. *Too Much Magic.* Lippincott 1987, Harper 1987. (Grades 3–6)

Stevens, Kathleen. *The Beast in the Bathtub.* Gareth Stevens 1985, Harper 1987. (Grades 2–3)

Stewart, Mary. *The Crystal Cave.* c1970. Fawcett 1984. (YA)

———. *The Hollow Hills.* Morrow 1973, Fawcett 1984. (YA)

Stingley, Darryl with Mark Mulvey. *Darryl Stingley: Happy to Be Alive.* Beaufort 1983. (YA/Adult)

Stolz, Mary. *The Cat in the Mirror.* Dell 1978. (Grades 5-9)

———. *Cat Walk.* Harper 1983, 1985. (Grades 4-6)

Strang, Celia. *This Child Is Mine.* Beaufort 1981. (YA)

Strasser, Tod. *Friends Till the End.* Dell 1982. (YA)

Streiber, Whitley and Kunetka, Janos. *Nature's End.* Warner 1986, 1987. (YA/Adult)

Stren, Patti. *I Was a Fifteen-Year-Old Blimp.* Harper 1985, NAL 1986. (YA)

Swarthout, Glendon. *The Shootist.* Doubleday 1975. (YA/Adult)

Sweeney, Joyce. *Center Line.* Delacorte 1984, Dell 1985. (YA)

Swindells, Robert. *Brother in the Land.* Holiday 1985. (YA)

Switzer, Ellen Eichenwald. *How Democracy Failed.* Atheneum 1975. (Grades 7-8/YA)

Talbert, Marc. *Dead Birds Singing.* Little 1985, Dell 1988. (YA)

Taylor, Theodore. *The Trouble With Tuck.* Avon 1983. (Grades 5-8)

———. *Walking Up a Rainbow.* Dell 1988. (YA)

Terris, Susan. *The Pencil Families.* Greenwillow 1975. (Grades 3-5)

"Tey, Josephine" (Elizabeth Mackintosh). *The Daughter of Time.* Macmillan 1952, Washington Square 1982, PB 1987. (YA/Adult)

Thompson, Julian. *Simon Pure.* Scholastic 1987. (YA)

Thompson, Julian F. *A Band of Angels.* Scholastic 1986, 1987. (YA)

Tobias, Tobi. *Chasing the Goblins Away.* Warne 1977. (Grades 1-3)

Tolkien, J.R.R. *The Hobbit.* Houghton 1937, 1987. (Grades 4-8)

Trainor, Joseph. *Family Crypt.* Dell 1984. (YA)

Turkle, Brinton. *Do Not Open.* Dutton 1981, 1985. (Grades k-3)

Turner, Ann. *Dakota Dugout.* Macmillan 1985. (Grades 4-8)

———. *Nettie's Trip South.* Macmillan 1987. (Grades 4-8)

———. *Third Girl From the Left.* Macmillan 1986. (YA)

"Twain, Mark" (Samuel Clemens). *The Adventures of Tom Sawyer.* Many editions. (Grades 4-6/Adult)

Ure, Jean. *See You Thursday.* Delacorte 1983, Dell 1985. (YA)

Van Allsburg, Chris. *Jumanji.* Houghton 1981. (Grades 2-6)

Van Leeuwen, Jean. *The Great Cheese Conspiracy.* Random House 1969. (Grades 4-6)

———. *The Great Christmas Kidnapping Caper.* Dial 1975, Dell 1977. (Grades 2-7)

Vinke, Hermann. *The Short Life of Sophie Scholl* (trans. by Hedwig Pachter). Harper 1984. (YA)

Viorst, Judith. *Alexander and the Terrible, Horrible, No Good, Very Bad Day.* Atheneum 1983. (Grades k-3)

————. *My Mama Says There Aren't Any Zombies. . . .* Atheneum 1973, Macmillan 1977. (Grades 2-5)

Voigt, Cynthia. *Dicey's Song.* Macmillan 1982, Fawcett 1984. (YA)

Waber, Bernard. *Ira Sleeps Over.* Houghton 1972, 1975. (Grades k-3)

Walker, Sloan and Vesey, Andrew. *The Only Other Crazy Car Book.* Walker 1984. (Grades 4-6)

Walton, Todd. *Inside Moves.* Doubleday 1978. (YA)

Wartski, Maureen Crane. *A Long Way From Home.* Westminster 1980, NAL 1982. (Grades 7-8/YA)

Webb, Sharon. *Earth Child.* Atheneum 1982. (YA)

Wells, Rosemary. *None of the Above.* Dial 1974, Avon 1984. (YA)

————. *When No One Was Looking.* Dial 1980, Fawcett 1981, 1987. (Grades 7-8/YA)

Wersba, Barbara. *Love Is the Crooked Thing.* Harper 1987. (YA)

Wharton, William. *Birdy.* Knopf 1978, Avon 1979. (YA/Adult)

White, Ellen Emerson. *Friends for Life.* Avon 1983. (YA)

————. *Life Without Friends.* Scholastic 1987. (YA)

————. *President's Daughter.* Avon 1984. (YA)

White, Robb. *Deathwatch.* Doubleday 1972, Dell 1973. (YA)

————. *Fire Storm.* Doubleday 1979. (Grades 6-8/YA)

Wilcox, Fred A. *Waiting for an Army to Die.* Random 1983. (Adult)

Wilkinson, Brenda. *Not Separate, Not Equal.* Harper 1987. (Grades 6-8/YA)

Willey, Margaret. *The Bigger Book of Lydia.* Harper 1983. (Grades 6-8/YA)

————. *Finding David Dolores.* Harper 1986. (YA)

Windsor, Patricia. *Killing Time.* Dell 1983. (YA/Adult)

Wood, Phyllis Anderson. *A Five-Color Buick and a Blue-Eyed Cat.* Westminster 1975, NAL 1977. (YA)

Wouk, Herman. *The Caine Mutiny.* c1951. Doubleday 1954, PB 1983. (YA/Adult)

Wright, Betty Ren. *The Dollhouse Murders.* Holiday 1983, Scholastic 1985. (Grades 4-7)

Yeager, Chuck with Leo Janos. *Yeager: An Autobiography.* Bantam 1985, 1986. (YA/Adult)

Yep, Laurence. *Dragon of the Lost Sea.* Harper 1982. (Grades 5-9)

————. *Liar, Liar.* Morrow 1983, Avon 1985. (Grades 7-8/YA)

Yolen, Jane. *Heart's Blood.* Delacorte 1984, Dell 1986. (YA)

————. *Uncle Lemon's Spring.* Dutton 1981. (Grades 3-6)

York, Carol Beach. *Takers and Returners: A Novel of Suspense.* Nelson 1973. (Grades 6–8)

Zelazny, Roger. *Nine Princes in Amber.* Avon 1977. (YA)

Zindel, Paul. *The Amazing and Death-Defying Diary of Eugene Dingman.* Harper 1987. (YA)

———. *My Darling, My Hamburger.* Harper 1969, Bantam 1971. (YA)

BIBLIOGRAPHY BY AGE LEVEL

Young Children

Alexander and the Terrible, Horrible, No Good, Very Bad Day (Viorst)
Alexander and the Wind-Up Mouse (Lionni)
The Amazing Bone (Steig)
Arthur and the Great Detective (Coren)
Arthur's Tooth (Brown)
Arthur's Valentine (Brown)
The Beast in the Bathtub (Stevens)
The Biggest Bubble in the World (Lorimer)
Bony-Legs (Cole)
Burglar Bill (Ahlberg and Ahlberg)
Cap'n Smudge (Cosgrove)
The Celery Stalks at Midnight (Howe)
Chasing the Goblins Away (Tobias)
The Church Mice in Action (Oakley)
The Devil's Storybook (Babbitt)
Do Not Open (Turkle)
The Dragon Kite (Luenn)
The Fire Cat (Averill)
Freckle Juice (Blume)
Gabrielle and Selena (Desbarats)
A Gift for Mama (Hautzig)
Grandma, Felix and Mustapha Biscuit (Ambrus)
The Great Christmas Kidnapping Caper (Van Leeuwen)
Hurry, Hurry, Mary Dear! (Bodecker)
Into the Painted Bear Lair (Stearns)
Ira Sleeps Over (Waber)
Is This a Baby Dinosaur? (Selsam)
Jumanji (Van Allsburg)
Keep Your Mouth Closed, Dear (Aliki)
Kermit the Hermit (Peet)
The Kid With the Red Suspenders (Gaeddert)
Konrad (Nostlinger)
Mrs. Piggle Wiggle (MacDonald)
My Father's Dragon (Gannett)
My Mama Says There Aren't Any Zombies . . . (Viorst)
The New Kid on the Block (Prelutsky)
Ramona the Brave (Cleary)
Ramona the Pest (Cleary)
The Real Thief (Steig)
Scarlet Monster Lives Here (Sharmat)
The Snake That Couldn't Slither (Bradbury)
Summer in the South (Marshall)
Tell Me Some More (Bonsall)
That Mean Man (Skorpen)
There's an Alligator Under My Bed (Mayer)
This Time, Tempe Wick? (Gauch)

Middle Grades

The Adventures of Ali Baba Bernstein (Hurwitz)
The Adventures of Tom Sawyer (Twain)
All the Way to Wit's End (Greenwald)
Alone in Wolf Hollow (Brookins)
Anastasia, Ask Your Analyst (Lowry)
Anastasia At Your Service (Lowry)
Babe the Gallant Pig (King-Smith)
Baby Needs Shoes (Carlson)
Baby-Sitting Is a Dangerous Job (Roberts)
Beezus and Ramona (Cleary)
The Best Christmas Pageant Ever (Robinson)
Bet You Can't (Cobb and Darling)
Blackberries in the Dark (Jukes)
Blind Outlaw (Rounds)
A Blue-Eyed Daisy (Rylant)
The Book of Three (Alexander)
The Brain on Quartz Mountain (Anderson)
The Cat in the Mirror (Stolz)
Cat Walk (Stolz)
The Celery Stalks at Midnight (Howe)
A Certain Magic (Orgel)
Charlotte Sometimes (Farmer)
Chimney Sweeps (Giblin)
Chip Mitchell: The Case of the Stolen Computer Brains (D'Ignazio)
Clone Catcher (Slote)
Dakota Dugout (Turner)
Dear Miss Moshki (Dragonwagon)
Dear Mr. Henshaw (Cleary)
The Devil's Storybook (Babbitt)
The Dollhouse Murders (Wright)
Dragon of the Lost Sea (Yep)
Ellen Grae (Cleaver and Cleaver)
Eyes in the Fishbowl (Snyder)
Frauds, Hoaxes, and Swindles (Cohen)
The Ghost on Saturday Night (Fleischman)
Girl (Green)

Give Us a Great Big Smile, Rosy Cole (Greenwald)
The Great Cheese Conspiracy (Van Leeuwen)
The Great Christmas Kidnapping Caper (Van Leeuwen)
The Hand-Me-Down Kid (Pascal)
Hangin' Out With Cici (Pascal)
Harriet the Spy (Fitzhugh)
The Hobbit (Tolkien)
In the Year of the Boar and Jackie Robinson (Lord)
The Indian in the Cupboard (Banks)
Into the Forest (Essex)
Invasion of the Brain Sharpeners (Curtis)
Jane-Emily (Clapp)
Jelly Belly (Smith)
Johnny May (Branscum)
Joshua, the Czar, and the Chicken-Bone Wish (Girion)
Jumanji (Van Allsburg)
The Kid With the Red Suspenders (Gaeddert)
The Kingdom and the Cave (Aiken)
Konrad (Nostlinger)
The Land I Lost (Huynh)
Last, First, Middle and Nick (Hazen)
Lenny Kandell, Smart Aleck (Conford)
A Light in the Attic (Silverstein)
Loretta Mason Potts (Chase)
The Magic Finger (Dahl)
Me and Mr. Stenner (Hunter)
My Father's Dragon (Gannett)
My Mama Says There Aren't Any Zombies . . . (Viorst)
My Side of the Mountain (George)
Nettie's Trip South (Turner)
The New Kid on the Block (Prelutsky)
Night of the Twisters (Ruckman)
The Night the Monster Came (Calhoun and Morrill)
The Official Kids' Survival Kit (Chaback and Fortunato)
The One and Only Cynthia Jane Thornton (Mills)
The One-Eyed Cat (Fox)
The Only Other Crazy Car Book (Walker and Vesey)
The Pencil Families (Terris)
The People Could Fly (Hamilton)
The Pet-Sitting Peril (Roberts)
Prisoner of Vampires (Garden)
Ramona the Brave (Cleary)
Ramona the Pest (Cleary)
Sarah, Plain and Tall (MacLachlan)
Scary Stories to Tell in the Dark (Schwartz)
Secret Selves (Angell)
Sign of the Beaver (Speare)
Skinnybones (Park)
Small Worlds Close Up (Grillone and Gennaro)
Space Station Seventh Grade (Spinelli)
Spectacles (Beattie)
Strawberry Girl (Lenski)
Summer in the South (Marshall)
Summer of the Monkeys (Rawls)
The Talking Earth (George)
The Thing at the Foot of the Bed (Leach)
The Thirteenth Member (Hunter)
Too Much Magic (Sterman and Sterman)
Tough-Luck Karen (Hurwitz)
The Treasure of Alpheus Winterborn (Bellairs)*The Trouble With Francis* (Lord)
The Trouble With Tuck (Taylor)
Uncle Lemon's Spring (Yolen)
Wait for Me, Watch for Me, Eula Bee (Beatty)
What Do You Do When Your Mouth Won't Open? (Pfeffer)
When the Boys Ran the House (Carris)
When You Fight the Tiger (Hewett)
Whisper Goodbye (Morrison)
Who Knew There'd Be Ghosts? (Brittain)
The Wild Children (Holman)
Will the Real Gertrude Hollings Please Stand Up? (Greenwald)
The Wish Giver (Brittain)
The Witch in Room 6 (Battles)
Witch Week (Jones)
The Witches' Bridge (Carleton)
You're Allegro Dead (Corcoran)

Older Children

Adorable Sunday (Shyer)
After the Rain (Mazer)
The Alfred G. Graebner Memorial High School Handbook of Rules and Regulations (Conford)
All the Children Were Sent Away (Garrigue)
All the Way to Wit's End (Greenwald)
The Almost Year (Randall)
Alone in Wolf Hollow (Brookins)
Baby-Sitting Is a Dangerous Job (Roberts)
The Best Christmas Pageant Ever (Robinson)
The Bigger Book of Lydia (Willey)
A Blue-Eyed Daisy (Rylant)

The Book of Three (Alexander)
The Cat Ate My Gymsuit (Danziger)
The Cat in the Mirror (Stolz)
Chase Me, Catch Nobody! (Haugaard)
Child of Fire (O'Dell)
The Contender (Lipsyte)
Cracker Jackson (Byars)
Dakota Dugout (Turner)
Daphne's Book (Hahn)
Dear Bill, Remember Me? (Mazer)
The Devil's Door-bell (Horowitz)
Double Trouble (DeClements)
Dragon of the Lost Sea (Yep)
Dunker (Kidd)
Fingers (Sleator)
Fire Storm (White)
Footfalls (Harlan)
The Friends (Guy)
A Gift of Magic (Duncan)
The Girl Who Owned a City (Nelson)
The Girl With the Silver Eyes (Roberts)
Hangin' Out With Cici (Pascal)
The Haunting (Mahy)
He Noticed I'm Alive . . . and Other
    Hopeful Signs (Sharmat)
The Hobbit (Tolkien)
How Democracy Failed (Switzer)
How Do You Lose Those Ninth Grade
    Blues? (DeClements)
In the Middle of a Rainbow (Girion)
The Incident at Hawk's Hill (Eckert)
The Island Keeper (Mazer)
Janet Hamm Needs a Date for the Dance
    (Bunting)
Jimmy D. Sidewinder and Me (Salassi)
Just As Long As We're Together (Blume)
Kept in the Dark (Bowden)
The Kidnapping of Christina Lattimore
    (Nixon)The Land I Lost (Huynh)
Lenny Kandell, Smart Aleck (Conford)
Liar, Liar (Yep)
A Light in the Attic (Silverstein)
A Long Way From Home (Wartski)
Love and Betrayal and Hold the Mayo!
    (Pascal)
Love Letters of J. Timothy Owen
    (Greene)
Makra Choria (Mayhar)
Me, Myself and I (Curry)
Me, the Beef and the Bum (Hammer)
Medicine Walk (Mayhar)
Millie's Boy (Peck)
Mirrorstone (Palin)
My Brother Sam Is Dead (Collier and
    Collier)
My Side of the Mountain (George)

Necessary Parties (Dana)
Nettie's Trip South (Turner)
Night Walkers (Coontz)
Not Separate, Not Equal (Wilkinson)
The One-Eyed Cat (Fox)
Path of the Pale Horse (Fleischman)
The People Could Fly (Hamilton)
The Pinballs (Byars)
Popcorn Days and Buttermilk Nights
    (Paulsen)
Prairie Songs (Conrad)
Prisoner of Vampires (Garden)
Representing Superdoll (Peck)
Secret Selves (Angell)
Secrets of the Shopping Mall (Peck)
The Sherwood Ring (Pope)
Slam Book (Martin)
Slave Dancer (Fox)
The Snarkout Boys and the Baconburg
    Horror (Pinkwater)
Space Station Seventh Grade (Spinelli)
Spirits and Spells (Colville)
Stotan! (Crutcher)
Strawberry Girl (Lenski)
Strictly for Laughs (Conford)
The Summer of My German Soldier
    (Green)
Summer of the Monkeys (Rawls)
Summer Rules (Lipsyte)
Sweet Whispers, Brother Rush (Hamil-
    ton)
Takers and Returners (York)
The Talking Earth (George)
Tancy (Hurmence)
There's a Bat in Bunk Five (Danziger)
This Place Has No Atmosphere (Dan-
    ziger)
Time Trilogy (L'Engle)
To the Tune of a Hickory Stick (Bran-
    scum)
The Treasure of Alpheus Winterborn
    (Bellairs)
The Trouble With Tuck (Taylor)
The Trouble With Wednesdays (Nathan-
    son)
The Twisted Window (Duncan)
View From the Cherry Tree (Roberts)
Wait for Me, Watch for Me, Eula Bee
    (Beatty)
Wart, Son of Toad (Carter)
What Do You Do When Your Mouth
    Won't Open? (Pfeffer)
When No One Was Looking (Wells)
When the Phone Rang (Mazer)
When You Fight the Tiger (Hewett)
Whisper Goodbye (Morrison)

Older Children (cont.)
Who Put That Hair in My Toothbrush? (Spinelli)
The Wild Children (Holman)
Wolf Rider (Avi)
Words by Heart (Sebestyen)

Young Adults

Adorable Sunday (Shyer)
After the Rain (Mazer)
Aku-Aku (Heyerdahl)
The Alfred G. Graebner Memorial High School Handbook of Rules and Regulations (Conford)
The Amazing and Death-Defying Diary of Eugene Dingman (Zindel)
American Heroes (Hentoff)
Among Friends (Cooney)
And I Alone Survived (Elder)
Are You in the House Alone? (Peck)
Back Home (Magorian)
A Band of Angels (Thompson)
The Bell Jar (Plath)
Betsey Brown (Shange)
Beyond the Chocolate War (Cormier)
Beyond the Divide (Lasky)
Bid Time Return (Matheson)
The Big Dipper Marathon (Brooks)
The Bigger Book of Lydia (Willey)
Birdy (Wharton)
The Boys From Brazil (Levin)
Brother in the Land (Swindells)
The Caine Mutiny (Wouk)
Callahan's Crosstime Saloon (Robinson)
The Camera Never Blinks (Rather)
Carrie (King)
The Cat Ate My Gymsuit (Danziger)
Catch-22 (Heller)
Centaur Isle (Anthony)
Center Line (Sweeney)
Changeover (Mahy)
Chartbreaker (Cross)
Chickenhawk (Mason)
The Children of Ham (Brown)
Children of the Dust (Lawrence)
Christine (King)
Circle in the Sea (Senn)
Cold Sassy Tree (Burns)
Come Alive at 505 (Brancato)
Come Sing, Jimmy Jo (Paterson)
Comes the Blind Fury (Saul)
Coming Back Alive (Reader)
The Counterfeiter (Haseley)
Cowboys Don't Cry (Halvorsen)
Cracker Jackson (Byars)

The Crazy Horse Electric Game (Crutcher)
The Crime of the Century (Higdon)
The Crossing (Paulsen)
A Cry in the Night (Clark)
Crystal (Myers)
The Crystal Cave (Stewart)
The Cuckoo Sister (Alcock)
Dancing Carl (Paulsen)
The Danger Quotient (Johnson and Johnson)
Dark Forces (McCauley)
Darryl Stingley: Happy To Be Alive (Stingley)
The Daughter of Time (Tey)
Dead Birds Singing (Talbert)
Deadline (Begley)
Dear Bill, Remember Me? (Mazer)
The Death Ticket (Bennett)
Deathwatch (White)
Denny's Tapes (Meyer)
The Devil's Door-bell (Horowitz)
Dicey's Song (Voigt)
Do You Call That a Dream Date? (Anderson)
The Dog Days of Arthur Cane (Bethancourt)
Downtown (Mazer)
The Dragon and the George (Dickson)
Dragon Fall (Hindle)
Dragonsinger (McCaffrey)
Dragonsong (McCaffrey)
Dreamsnake (McIntyre)
Dune (Herbert)
Dunker (Kidd)
Earth Child (Webb)
Earthseed (Sargent)
Emergence (Palmer)
The Executioner (Bennett)
The Face at the Edge of the World (Bunting)
Fahrenheit 451 (Bradbury)
Family Crypt (Trainor)
Fast Sam, Cool Clyde and Stuff (Myers)
Fell (Kerr)
Feral (Roueche)
Finding David Delores (Willey)
Fingers (Sleator)
Fire Storm (White)
A Five-Color Buick and a Blue-Eyed Cat (Wood)
The Flight of the Cassowary (LaVert)
Forever (Blume)
Fortress (Lord)
Friendly Fire (Bryan)
Friends for Life (White)

ly Everything . . . Is Crying (Bottner)
Yeager (Yeager)
The Year It Rained (Dragonwagon)
The Year of Sweet Senior Insanity (Levitin)
The Year of the Gopher (Naylor)
The Year Without Michael (Pfeffer)
You'll Miss Me When I'm Gone (Roos)
Young Witches and Warlocks (Asimov)
A Zoo in My Luggage (Durrell)

Adults

The Adventures of Tom Sawyer (Twain)
Aku-Aku (Heyerdahl)
And I Alone Survived (Elder)
Are You in the House Alone? (Peck)
The Bell Jar (Plath)
Betsey Brown (Shange)
Birdy (Wharton)
The Boys From Brazil (Levin)
The Caine Mutiny (Wouk)
The Camera Never Blinks (Rather)
Carrie (King)
Catch-22 (Heller)
Chickenhawk (Mason)
Christine (King)
Cold Sassy Tree (Burns)
Comes the Blind Fury (Saul)
The Crazy Horse Electric Game (Crutcher)
The Crime of the Century (Higdon)
The Crossing (Paulsen)
A Cry in the Night (Clark)
Dancing Carl (Paulsen)
Dark Forces (McCauley)
Darryl Stingley (Stingley)
The Daughter of Time (Tey)
The Dragon and the George (Dickson)
Dragonsinger (McCaffrey)
Dune (Herbert)
Fahrenheit 451 (Bradbury)
Feral (Roueche)
Friendly Fire (Bryan)
Frozen Fire (Houston)
Gemini (Giovanni)

The Gift of the Magi (Henry)
Glory Road (Catton)
A Good Day to Die (Barton)
Growing Up (Baker)
Guy de Maupassant's Short Stories (Maupassant)
The Herald (Shaara)
The Hero and the Crown (McKinley)
Hiroshima (Hersey)
I Never Promised You a Rose Garden (Green)
I, Robot (Asimov)
Ice Station Zebra (MacLean)
Interview With the Vampire (Rice)
Killing Time (Windsor)
The Left Hand of Darkness (Le Guin)
Maus (Spiegelman)
Misery (King)
Murphy's Boy (Hayden)
Nature's End (Streiber and Kunetka)
Night Shift (King)
No Language But a Cry (D'Ambrosio)
Ordinary People (Guest)
The Paladin (Garfield)
The Past Through Tomorrow (Heinlein)
Putting It Together (McGuire)
Ride the River (L'Amour)
Run for Your Life (Abercrombie)
'Salem's Lot (King)
The Sea Wolf (London)
The Shining (King)
The Shootist (Swarthout)
Simple Gifts (Greenberg)
Space 3: A Collection of Science Fiction Stories (Davis)
Squeak (Bowen)
The Stalker (Nixon)
Thinner (Bachman)
This Life (Poitier)
To Race the Wind (Krents)
Waiting for an Army to Die (Wilcox)
When the Legends Die (Borland)
Where Are the Children? (Clark)
Wild Child (Hanes)
Yeager (Yeager)
Young Witches and Warlocks (Asimov)
A Zoo in My Luggage (Durrell)

SELECTIVE BIBLIOGRAPHY
BY THEME AND GENRE

Adventure/Survival

Aku-Aku (Heyerdahl) YA/A
All the Children Were Sent Away (Garrigue) 7-8
Alone in Wolf Hollow (Brookins) 5-7
And I Alone Survived (Elder) YA/A
Beyond the Divide (Lasky) YA
Brother in the Land (Swindells) YA
Center Line (Sweeney) YA
Chase Me, Catch Nobody (Haugaard) 6-8
Child of Fire (O'Dell) 6-9
Coming Back Alive (Reader) YA
The Crossing (Paulsen) YA/A
Deathwatch (White) YA
Dreamsnake (McIntyre) YA
Dune (Herbert) YA/A
Earthseed (Sargent) YA
Emergence (Palmer) YA
Fire Storm (White) 6-8/YA
Frozen Fire (Houston) YA/A
The Girl From the Emeraline Island (Blum) YA
The Girl Who Owned a City (Nelson) 6-8
Going for the Big One (Peterson) YA
Hatchet (Paulsen) YA
Heart's Blood (Yolen) YA
Herald (Shaara) YA/A
The Hero and the Crown (McKinley) YA/A
House of Stairs (Sleator) YA
Hunters of the Red Moon (Bradley) YA
Incident at Hawk's Hill (Eckert) 6-8
Into the Forest (Essex) 3-6
Into the Painted Bear Lair (Stearns) 2-5
Island Keeper (Mazer) 6-8/YA
The Kid With the Red Suspenders (Gaeddert) 2-5
Lackawanna (Aaron) YA
The Land I Lost (Hunyh) 5-8
Legend of Tarik (Myers) YA
A Long Way From Home (Wartski) 7-8/YA
Medicine Walk (Mayhar) 7-8/YA
Millie's Boy (Peck) 6-8/YA
My Side of the Mountain (George) 4-8
Nature's End (Streiber and Kunetka) YA/A
Night of the Twisters (Ruckman) 4-6
Nobody Else Can Walk It for You (Peterson) YA

The Official Kids' Survival Kit (Chaback) 4-6
Paladin (Garfield) YA/A
Path of the Pale Horse (Fleischman) 7-8/YA
Pursuit (French) YA
Rebels of the Heavenly Kingdom (Paterson) YA
Ride the River (L'Amour) YA/A
The Sea Wolf (London) YA/A
The Shootist (Swarthout) YA/A
Sign of the Beaver (Speare) 4-7
Someone Is Hiding on Alcatraz Island (Bunting) YA
The Stolen Law (Mason) YA
The Talking Earth (George) 6-9
To the Tune of a Hickory Stick (Branscum) 6-8
Us Against Them (French) YA
Wait for Me, Watch for Me, Eula Bee (Beatty) 5-9
Walking Up a Rainbow (Taylor) YA
The War on Villa Street (Mazer) YA
Who Knew There'd Be Ghosts? (Brittain) 4-6
The Wild Children (Holman) 5-9
Yeager (Yeager) YA/A

Aging

After the Rain (Mazer) 6-8/YA
Blackberries in the Dark (Jukes) 4-6
Earth Child (Webb) YA
Harold and Maude (Higgins) YA
Nobody's Baby Now (Benjamin) YA
Spectacles (Beattie) 4-6

Animals

The Adventures of Chuchi (Gaffin) 4-6
Babe, the Gallant Pig (King-Smith) 3-4
Blind Outlaw (Rounds) 5-6
Cat Walk (Stolz) 4-6
Circle in the Sea (Senn) YA
The Dog Days of Arthur Cane (Bethancourt) YA
A Five-Color Buick and a Blue-Eyed Cat (Wood) YA
The Flight of the Cassowary (LaVert) YA

Girl (Green) 3-5
Incident at Hawk's Hill (Eckert) 6-8
One-Eyed Cat (Fox) 5-9
The Pet-Sitting Peril (Roberts) 5-7
Squeak (Bowen) YA/A
Summer of the Monkeys (Rawls) 4-8
This Time, Tempe Wick? (Gauch) 1-4
The Trouble With Tuck (Taylor) 5-8
When You Fight the Tiger (Hewett) 5-9
A Zoo in My Luggage (Durrell) YA/A

Biography

And I Alone Survived (Elder) YA/A
The Camera Never Blinks (Rather) YA/A
Chickenhawk (Mason) YA/A
Darryl Stingley (Stingley) YA/A
Daughter of Time (Tey) YA/A
Deadline (Begley) YA
Gemini (Giovanni) YA/A
Geri (Jewell) YA
Growing Up (Baker) YA/A
No Language But a Cry (D'Ambrosio) YA/A
The Short Life of Sophie Scholl (Vinke) YA
This Life (Poitier) YA/A
To Race the Wind (Krents) YA/A
Yeager (Yeager) YA/A
A Zoo in My Luggage (Durrell) YA/A

Child Abuse

Center Line (Sweeney) YA
Cracker Jackson (Byars) 6-8/YA
Daphne's Book (Hahn) 6-8
Murphy's Boy (Hayden) A
No Language But a Cry (D'Ambrosio) YA/A
The Pinballs (Byars) 7-9
See Dave Run (Eyerly) YA
Seventeen and In-Between (DeClements) YA
To the Tune of a Hickory Stick (Branscum) 6-8
The Trouble With Wednesdays (Nathanson) 6-9
Wild Child (Hanes) YA/A

Death/Mourning

Blackberries in the Dark (Jukes) 4-6
Dead Birds Singing (Talbert) YA
Footfalls (Harlan) 6-8
Friendly Fire (Bryant) YA/A

Friends Till the End (Strasser) YA
Goodbye Tomorrow (Miklowitz) YA
Invincible Summer (Ferris) YA
Maus (Spiegelman) YA/A
No Dragons to Slay (Greenberg) YA
Remembering the Good Times (Peck) YA
Running Loose (Crutcher) YA
Sheila's Dying (Carter) YA
Waiting for Johnny Miracle (Bach) YA
When the Phone Rang (Mazer) 6-8/YA
The Year It Rained (Dragonwagon) YA
The Year Without Michael (Pfeffer) YA

Delinquency/Crime

Are You in the House Alone? (Peck) YA
Baby Needs Shoes (Carlson) 3-5
The Best Christmas Pageant Ever (Robinson) 4-7
Beyond the Chocolate War (Cormier) YA
Burglar Bill (Ahlberg) 2-4
Center Line (Sweeney) YA
Children of Ham (Brown) YA
The Counterfeiter (Haseley) YA
The Crime of the Century (Higdon) YA/A
Ellen Grae (Cleaver) 3-5
Fire Storm (White) 6-8/YA
Frauds, Hoaxes and Swindles (Cohen) 3-6
The Girls of Huntingdon House (Elfman) YA/A
I Know What You Did Last Summer (Duncan) YA
Jimmy D. Sidewinder and Me (Salassi) 6-8/YA
Killing Mr. Griffin (Duncan) YA
Liar, Liar (Yep) 7-8/YA
Life Without Friends (White) YA
One-Eyed Cat (Fox) 5-9
The Outsiders (Hinton) YA
Popcorn Days and Buttermilk Nights (Paulsen) YA
Say Hello to the Hit Man (Bennett) YA
A Semester in the Life of a Garbage Bag (Korman) YA
Through a Brief Darkness (Peck) YA

Eating Disorders

The Bigger Book of Lydia (Willey) 6-8/YA
I Was a 15-Year-Old Blimp (Stren) YA
Jelly Belly (Smith) 4-6
The Pig-Out Blues (Greenberg) YA
Second Star to the Right (Hautzig) YA

Stand Up? (Greenwald) 4-6
Winning (Brancato) YA

History

All the Children Were Sent Away (Garrigue) 7-8
Back Home (Magorian) YA
Betsey Brown (Shange) YA/A
Beyond the Divide (Lasky) YA
The Cat in the Mirror (Stolz) 5-9
Charlotte Sometimes (Farmer) 3-5
Chase Me, Catch Nobody (Haugaard) 6-8
Chickenhawk (Mason) YA/A
Chimney Sweeps (Giblin) 4-6
Dakota Dugout (Turner) 4-8
Glory Road (Catton) YA/A
A Good Day to Die (Barton) YA/A
Hiroshima (Hersey) YA/A
How Democracy Failed (Switzer) 7-8/YA
The Indian in the Cupboard (Banks) 3-6
In the Year of the Boar . . . (Lord) 4-6
Lackawanna (Aaron) YA
Me, Myself and I (Curry) 7-8/YA
Midnight Hour Encores (Brooks) YA
My Brother Sam Is Dead (Collier and Collier) 6-8
Nettie's Trip South (Turner) 4-8
Not Separate, Not Equal (Wilkinson) 6-8/YA
Paladin (Garfield) YA/A
Path of the Pale Horse (Fleischman) 7-8/YA
The People Could Fly (Hamilton) 4-8/YA
Prairie Songs (Conford) 7-9
Rebels of the Heavenly Kingdom (Paterson) YA
Sarah, Plain and Tall (MacLachlan) 3-6
The Shootist (Swarthout) YA/A
The Short Life of Sophie Scholl (Vinke) YA
The Sign of the Beaver (Speare) 4-7
Simple Gifts (Greenberg) YA/A
Slave Dancer (Fox) 6-10
The Summer of My German Soldier (Green) 7-8/YA
Tancy (Hurmence) 6-8/YA
Tempered Wind (Dixon) YA
Third Girl From the Left (Turner) YA
The Thirteenth Member (Hunter) 3-5
This Time, Tempe Wick? (Gauch) 1-4
Wait for Me, Watch for Me, Eula Bee (Beatty) 5-9
Walking Up a Rainbow (Taylor) YA
The Wild Children (Holman) 5-9
Words by Heart (Sebestyen) 7-9

Horror/Occult

The Almost Year (Randall) 6-8
Bid Time Return (Matheson) YA
Carrie (King) YA/A
The Celery Stalks at Midnight (Howe) 3-7
A Certain Magic (Orgel) 3-5
Changeover (Mahy) YA
Charlotte Sometimes (Farmer) 3-5
Chasing the Goblins Away (Tobias) 1-3
Christine (King) YA/A
Circle in the Sea (Senn) YA
Comes the Blind Fury (Saul) YA/A
The Crystal Cave (Stewart) YA
Dark Forces (McCauley) YA/A
The Devil's Door-bell (Horowitz) 7-8/YA
Double Trouble (DeClements and Greimes) 6-8
Dragon Fall (Hindle) YA
Family Crypt (Trainor) YA
Feral (Roueche) YA/A
Fingers (Sleator) 7-8/YA
Ghost Behind Me (Bunting) YA
Ghosts I Have Been (Peck) YA
A Gift of Magic (Duncan) 6-8
The Girl With the Silver Eyes (Roberts) 6-8/YA
The Haunting (Mahy) 6-8
Healer (Dickinson) YA
Interview With the Vampire (Rice) YA/A
Jane-Emily (Clapp) 5-6
Killing Time (Windsor) YA/A
Locked in Time (Duncan) YA
Loretta Mason Potts (Chase) 3-6
The Magic Finger (Dahl) 3-6
My Mama Says . . . (Viorst) 2-5
The Night the Monster Came (Calhoun) 3-6
Night Shift (King) YA/A
Night Walkers (Coontz) 7-8/YA
Out of Time (Chambers) YA
Portrait of Jennie (Nathan) YA
Premonitions (Bonham) YA
Prisoner of Vampires (Garden) 4-8
'Salem's Lot (King) YA/A
Scary Stories to Tell in the Dark (Schwartz) 4-6
Secrets of the Shopping Mall (Peck) 7-8/YA
The Sherwood Ring (Pope) 6-10
The Shining (King) YA/A
Spirits and Spells (Colville) 7-8
Summer of Fear (Duncan) YA
The Thing at the Foot of the Bed (Leach) 4-6

Thinner (Bachman) YA/A
The Thirteenth Member (Hunter) 3–5
Too Much Magic (Sterman) 3–6
Uncle Lemon's Spring (Yolen) 4–6
The Wish Giver (Brittain) 4–6
The Witch in Room 6 (Battle) 4–6
Witch Week (Jones) 5–7
The Witches' Bridge (Carleton) 3–5
Young Witches and Warlocks (Asimov)
   YA/A

Humor

The Adventures of Tom Sawyer (Twain)
   4–6/A
Alexander and the Terrible . . . Day
   (Viorst) k–3
The Alfred G. Graebner Memorial High
   School Handbook (Conford) 7–10
All the Way to Wit's End (Greenwald)
   4–8
The Amazing and Death-Defying Diary
   of Eugene Dingman (Zindel) YA
Anastasia series (Lowry) 4–6
The Beast in the Bathtub (Stevens) 2–3
The Best Christmas Pageant Ever (Rob-
   inson) 4–7
Catch-22 (Heller) YA/A
The Celery Stalks at Midnight (Howe)
   3–7
Centaur Isle (Anthony) YA
Cold Sassy Tree (Burns) YA/A
The Dragon and the George (Dickson)
   YA/A
A Five-Color Buick and a Blue-Eyed Cat
   (Wood) YA
Ghosts I Have Been (Peck) YA
The Hand-Me-Down Kid (Pascal) 3–6
Harriet the Spy (Fitzhugh) 5–7
How Do You Lose Those Ninth Grade
   Blues? (DeClements) 6–8/YA
Hurry, Hurry, Mary Dear (Bodecker) k–3
The Invasion of the Brain Sharpeners
   (Curtis) 3–5
It All Began With Jane Eyre (Greenwald)
   YA
Keep Your Mouth Closed, Dear (Aliki)
   k–3
Lenny Kandell, Smart Aleck (Conford)
   5–8
A Light in the Attic (Silverstein) 4–8
Little Little (Kerr) YA
Loretta Mason Potts (Chase) 3–6
Love and Betrayal and Hold the Mayo!
   (Pascal) 7–8
The Magic Finger (Dahl) 3–6

Mrs. Piggle Wiggle (MacDonald) k–3
My Darling, My Hamburger (Zindel) YA
My First Love and Other Disasters (Pas-
   cal) YA
The New Kid on the Block (Prelutsky)
   2–6
Ramona series (Cleary) 3–6
Simple Gifts (Greenberg) YA/A
Skinnybones (Park) 3–6
The Snarkout Boys and the Baconburg
   Horror (Pinkwater) 7–8/YA
Space Station Seventh Grade (Spinelli)
   5–9
This Place Has No Atmosphere (Dan-
   ziger) 7–8/YA
Tough-Luck Karen (Hurwitz) 4–6
The Trouble With Francis (Lord) 3–6
When the Boys Ran the House (Carris)
   4–6
Who Put That Hair in My Toothbrush?
   (Spinelli) 6–9
Witch Week (Jones) 5–7
The World's Greatest Expert . . . Is
   Crying (Bottner) YA
A Zoo in My Luggage (Durrell) YA/A

Identity

Adventures of Ali Baba Bernstein (Hur-
   witz) 3–4
Alexander and the Wind-Up Mouse
   (Lionni) k–3
The Amazing, Death-Defying Diary of
   Eugene Dingman (Zindel) YA
Chartbreaker (Cross) YA
Flight of the Cassowary (LaVert) YA
Give Us A Great Big Smile, Rosy Cole
   (Greenwald) 4–6
The Launching of Linda Bell (Hallstead)
   YA
Me, Myself and I (Curry) 7–8/YA
None of the Above (Wells) YA
The One and Only Cynthia Jane
   Thornton (Mills) 4–6
The President's Daughter (White) YA
Representing Superdoll (Peck) YA
Sentries (Paulsen) YA
The Trouble With Francis (Lord) 3–6
Wart, Son of Toad (Carter) 7–8/YA
When the Legends Die (Borland) YA/A
The World Is My Eggshell (Mulford) YA
The Year of the Gopher (Naylor) YA

Men/Boys

The Adventures of Tom Sawyer (Twain)
   4–6/A
The Amazing, Death-Defying Diary of

Eugene Dingman (Zindel) YA
Birdy (Wharton) YA/A
Blind Outlaw (Rounds) 5-6
The Caine Mutiny (Wouk) YA/A
Catch-22 (Heller) YA/A
Center Line (Sweeney) YA
Chickenhawk (Mason) YA/A
Christine (King) YA/A
Cracker Jackson (Byars) 6-8/YA
The Crossing (Paulsen) YA/A
A Good Day to Die (Barton) YA/A
I Love You, Stupid (Mazer) YA
Inside Moves (Walton) YA
It's a Mile From Here to Glory (Lee) YA
The Moves Make the Man (Bruce) YA
Night Kites (Kerr) YA
The Outsiders (Hinton) YA
Popcorn Days and Buttermilk Nights
  (Paulsen) YA
Running Loose (Crutcher) YA
Space Station Seventh Grade (Spinelli)
  5-9
Wart, Son of Toad (Carter) 7-8/YA
When the Boys Ran the House (Carris)
  4-6

Minorities:
Black
Betsey Brown (Shange) YA/A
Children of Ham (Brown) YA/A
The Contender (Lipsyte) 6-9
Crystal (Myers) YA
Denny's Tapes (Meyer) YA
Dicey's Song (Voigt) YA
Fast Sam, Cool Clyde, and Stuff (Myers)
  YA
The Friends (Guy) 7-9
Gemini (Giovanni) YA/A
A Little Love (Hamilton) YA
The Moves Make the Man (Bruce) YA
Nettie's Trip South (Turner) 4-8
Not Separate, Not Equal (Wilkinson)
  6-8/YA
The People Could Fly (Hamilton)
  4-8/YA
Slave Dancer (Fox) 6-10
Sweet Whispers, Brother Rush (Hamil-
  ton) 7-8/YA
Tancy (Hurmence) 6-8/YA
A Teacup Full of Roses (Mathis) YA
This Child Is Mine (Strang) YA
This Life (Poitier) YA/A
Words by Heart (Sebestyen) 7-9

Hispanic
Child of Fire (O'Dell) 6-9
The Crossing (Paulsen) YA/A
Red Sky at Morning (Bradford) YA
Sentries (Paulsen) YA

Jewish
The Boys From Brazil (Levin) YA/A
A Certain Magic (Orgel) 3-5
A Gift for Mama (Hautzig) 2-4
How Democracy Failed (Switzer) 7-8/YA
I Never Promised You a Rose Garden
  (Green) YA/A
Maus (Spiegelman) YA/A
Monday in Odessa (Sherman) YA
Summer of My German Soldier (Green)
  7-8/YA

Native American
A Good Day to Die (Barton) YA/A
Sentries (Paulsen) YA
The Sign of the Beaver (Speare) 4-7
The Talking Earth (George) 6-9
Wait for Me, Watch for Me, Eula Bee
  (Beatty) 5-9
When the Legends Die (Borland) YA/A

Oriental
The Dragon Kite (Luenn) k-3
Hiroshima (Hersey) YA/A
In the Year of the Boar . . . (Lord) 4-6
Land I Lost (Huynh) 5-8
A Long Way From Home (Wartski)
  7-8/YA
Rebels of the Heavenly Kingdom (Pater-
  son) YA
The War Between the Classes (Mi-
  klowitz) YA

Mystery and Suspense
Arthur and the Great Detective (Coren)
  1-2
Baby Sitting Is a Dangerous Job (Rob-
  erts) 5-8
Band of Angels (Thompson) YA
The Boys From Brazil (Levin) YA/A
Chip Mitchell: The Case of the Stolen
  Computer Brains (D'Ignazio) 4-6
Clone Catcher (Slote) 4-6
A Cry in the Night (Clark) YA/A
Daughter of Time (Tey) YA/A
Death Ticket (Bennett) YA
Do Not Open (Turkle) k-3

The Pinballs (Byars) 7-9
Second Star to the Right (Hautzig) YA
Secret Selves (Angell) 5-8
The Shell Lady's Daughter (Adler) 5-8
The War Between the Classes (Miklowitz) YA
Wild Child (Hanes) YA/A
Working On It (Oppenheimer) YA

Religion/Philosophy
American Heroes (Hentoff) YA
The Best Christmas Pageant Ever (Robinson) 4-7
Healer (Dickinson) YA
Monday in Odessa (Sherman) YA
The Sea Wolf (London) YA/A
The Talking Earth (George) 6-9

Romance
The Amazing, Death-Defying Diary of Eugene Dingman (Zindel) YA
Arthur's Valentine (Brown) k-3
Bid Time Return (Matheson) YA
The Counterfeiter (Hazeley) YA
Dear Bill, Remember Me? (Mazer) 6-8/YA
Do You Call That a Dream Date? (Anderson) YA
Finding David Delores (Willey) YA
Forever (Blume) YA
He Noticed I'm Alive . . . (Sharmat) 6-8/YA
I Love You, Stupid (Mazer) YA
I Stay Near You (Kerr) YA
In the Middle of a Rainbow (Girion) 7-8/YA
Jane Eyre (Brontë) YA
Janet Hamm Needs a Date for the Dance (Bunting) 6-8
Love Is the Crooked Thing (Wersba) YA
The Love Letters of J. Timothy Owen (Greene) 7-8/YA
Mr. and Mrs. BoJo Jones (Head) YA
My First Love and Other Disasters (Pascal) YA
Night Kites (Kerr) YA
None of the Above (Wells) YA
Portrait of Jennie (Nathan) YA
Premonitions (Bonham) YA
Running Loose (Crutcher) YA
Secret Selves (Angell) 5-8
See You Thursday (Ure) YA
Strictly for Laughs (Conford) 7-8/YA
The Summer of My German Soldier (Green) 7-8/YA

Where the Kissing Never Stops (Koertge) YA

Runaways
Back Home (Magorian) YA
Center Line (Sweeney) YA
The Crazy Horse Electric Game (Crutcher) YA/A
Denny's Tapes (Meyer) YA
Going for the Big One (Peterson) YA
Island Keeper (Mazer) 6-8/YA
Me, the Beef and the Bum (Hammer) 5-8
Secrets of the Shopping Mall (Peck) 7-8/YA
See Dave Run (Eyerly) YA
This Child Is Mine (Strang) YA
The Trouble With Tuck (Taylor) 5-8
Us Against Them (French) YA
The War on Villa Street (Mazer) YA

Science
Aku-Aku (Heyerdahl) YA/A
Bet You Can't (Cobb and Darling) 4-6
Chip Mitchell: The Case of the Stolen Computer Brains (D'Ignazio) 4-6
Circle in the Sea (Senn) YA
Nature's End (Streiber and Kunetka) YA/A
No Dragons to Slay (Greenberg) YA
Small Worlds Close Up (Grillone and Gennaro) 4-6
Waiting for an Army to Die (Wilcox) A
A Zoo in My Luggage (Durrell) YA/A

Science Fiction/Fantasy
Bid Time Return (Matheson) YA
The Book of Three (Alexander) 4-9
Brother in the Land (Swindells) YA
Callahan's Crosstime Saloon (Robinson) YA
The Cat in the Mirror (Stolz) 5-9
Centaur Isle (Anthony) YA
Charlotte Sometimes (Farmer) 3-5
Children of the Dust (Lawrence) YA
Circle in the Sea (Senn) YA
Clone Catcher (Slote) 4-6
The Crystal Cave/The Hollow Hills (Stewart) YA
Danger Quotient (Johnson) YA
The Dog Days of Arthur Cane (Bethancourt) YA
The Dragon and the George (Dickson) YA/A
Dragon of the Lost Sea (Yep) 5-9

Sex and Sexuality—Gay

Sex and Sexuality—Straight

Short Stories

Sports/Games

Substance Abuse

Friends for Life (White) YA
The Good Side of My Heart (Rinaldi) YA
The Last Ride (Haddad) YA
A Teacup Full of Roses (Mathis) YA
The War on Villa Street (Mazer) YA
You'll Miss Me When I'm Gone (Roos)
   YA

Women/Girls

Are You In the House Alone? (Peck)
   YA/A
Betsey Brown (Shange) YA/A
Dear Bill, Remember Me? (Mazer)
   6-8/YA
Dragonsinger/Dragonsong (McCaffrey)
   YA/A
Dreamsnake (McIntyre) YA
The Girl From the Emeraline Island
   (Blum) YA
The Girls of Huntingdon House (Elfman)
   YA
Hangin' Out With Cici (Pascal) 6-8
Howl's Moving Castle (Jones) YA
In the Middle of a Rainbow (Girion)
   7-8/YA
Just As Long As We're Together (Blume)
   6-8
Midnight Hour Encores (Brooks) YA
None of the Above (Wells) YA
Out of Bounds (Boatright) YA
Princess Ashley (Peck) YA
Second Star to the Right (Hautzig) YA

The Trouble With Wednesdays (Nathanson) 6-9
The War Between the Classes (Miklowitz) YA
Words By Heart (Sebestyen) 7-9

Working

Adorable Sunday (Shyer) 6-8/YA
The Camera Never Blinks (Rather) YA/A
Chartbreaker (Cross) YA
Chimney Sweeps (Giblin) 4-6
Come Sing, Jimmy Jo (Paterson) YA
Crystal (Myers) YA
Deadline (Begley) YA
Dunker (Kidd) 7-8/YA
A Five-Color Buick and a Blue-Eyed Cat
   (Wood) YA
Growing Up (Baker) YA/A
Love and Betrayal and Hold the Mayo!
   (Pascal) 7-8
Love Is the Crooked Thing (Wersba) YA
Me, the Beef and the Bum (Hammer) 5-8
My First Love and Other Disasters (Pas-
   cal) YA
The Pet Sitting Peril (Roberts) 5-7
Summer of the Monkeys (Rawls) 4-8
Summer Rules (Lypsyte) 7-8/YA
The Summerboy (Lipsyte) YA
Taking Care of Terrific (Lowry) YA
The Tempered Wind (Dixon) YA
There's a Bat in Bunk Five (Danziger)
   7-8/YA
When You Fight the Tiger (Hewett) 5-9
The Year of the Gopher (Naylor) YA

LIST OF PUBLISHERS

ABC-Clio. ABC-Clio, Inc., 2040 Alameda Padre Serra, Santa Barbara, CA 93140-4397

Abelard. Abelard-Schuman, Ltd. Harper & Row Publishers, Inc., 10 East 53rd St., New York, NY 10022.

Ace. Ace Books, 200 Madison Ave., New York, NY 10016

ALA. American Library Association, 50 E. Huron St., Chicago, IL 60611

Archway (PB). Archway Paperbacks, c/o Pocket Books, 1230 Avenue of the Americas, New York, NY 10020

Atheneum. Atheneum Publishers, 597 Fifth Ave., New York, NY 10017

Atlantic. Atlantic Monthly Press, 19 Union Sq. W., New York, NY 10003

Avon. Avon Books, 1790 Broadway, New York, NY 10019

Ballantine. Ballantine/Del Rey/Fawcett, 201 East 50th St., New York, NY 10022

Bantam. Bantam Books, Inc., 666 Fifth Ave., New York, NY 10103

Beaufort. Beaufort Books, Inc., 9 E. 40th St., St., New York, NY 10016

Berkley. Berkley Publishing Group, 200 Madison Ave., New York, NY 10016

Bradbury. Bradbury Press, 2 Overhill Rd., Scarsdale, NY 10583

Buccaneer. Buccaneer Books, P.O. Box 168, Cutchogue, NY 11935; P.O. Box 518, Laguna Beach, CA 92652

Canongate. Canongate Pub. Ltd., 17 Jeffrey St., Edinburgh EH1 1DR, Scotland

Coward. Coward, McCann & Geoghegan, Inc., 200 Madison Ave., New York, NY 10016

Crowell. Thomas Y. Crowell Co., c/o Harper & Row, 10 East 53rd St., New York, NY 10022

Crown. Crown Publishers, Inc., One Park Ave., New York, NY 10016

DAW. DAW Books, New American Library, 1633 Broadway, New York, NY 10019

Delacorte. Delacorte Press, c/o Dell Publishing Co., One Dag Hammarskjold Plaza, 245 East 47th St., New York, NY 10017

Dell. Dell Publishing Co., Inc., One Dag Hammarskjold Plaza, 245 East 47th St., New York, NY 10017

Dial. Dial Press, c/o Doubleday & Co., Inc., 245 Park Ave., New York, NY 10167

Doubleday. Doubleday & Co., Inc., 245 Park Ave., New York, NY 10167

Dutton. E. P. Dutton, 2 Park Ave., New York, NY 10016

Enslow. Enslow Publishers Inc., Box 777, Bloy St. & Ramsey Ave., Hillside, NJ 07205

Evans. M. Evans & Co., Inc., 216 East 49th St., New York, NY 10017

Fairfax. Fairfax Press, 1 Park Ave., New York, NY 10016

Farrar. Farrar, Straus, & Giroux, Inc., 19 Union Square West, New York, NY 10003

Fawcett. Ballantine/Del Rey/Fawcett, 201 East 50th St., New York, NY 10017

French. French & European Publications, Inc., 115 Fifth Ave., New York, NY 10003

Friesen. D. W. Friesen & Sons, Altona, Manitoba, Canada

Greenwillow. Greenwillow Books, 105 Madison Ave., New York, N Y 10016

Hall. G. K. Hall, Inc., 70 Lincoln St., Boston, MA 02111

Hamilton. Hamish Hamilton Children's Books, 27 Wrights Lane, London W8 5TZ, England

Harcourt. Harcourt Brace Jovanovich, Inc., 1250 Sixth Ave., San Diego, CA 92101

Harper. Harper & Row Publishers, Inc., 10 East 53rd St., New York, NY 10022

Holiday. Holiday House, Inc., 18 East 53rd St., New York, NY 10022

Holt. Holt, Rinehart, and Winston General Books, 521 Fifth Ave., New York, NY 10175

Houghton. Houghton Mifflin Co., One Beacon St., Boston, MA 02108

Knopf. Alfred A. Knopf, Inc., 201 East 50th St., New York, NY 10022

Lerner. Lerner Publications Co., 241 1st Ave. N., Minneapolis, MN 55401

Lippincott. J. B. Lippincott, East Washington Sq., Philadelphia, PA 19105

Little. Little, Brown & Co., 34 Beacon St., Boston, MA 02106

Lodestar. Lodestar Books, 2 Park Ave., New York, NY 10016

Lothrop. Lothrop, Lee & Shepard Books, 105 Madison Ave., New York, NY 10016; orders to William Morrow & Co., Inc., Wilmor Warehouse, 6 Henderson Dr., West Caldwell, NJ 07006

McGraw. McGraw-Hill, Inc., 1221 Avenue of the Americas, New York, NY 10020

Macmillan. Macmillan Publishing Co., Inc., 866 Third Ave., New York, NY 10022

Morrow. William Morrow & Co., Inc., 105 Madison Ave., New York, NY 10016

NAL. New American Library, Inc., 1633 Broadway, New York, NY 10019

Pantheon. Pantheon Books, 201 East 50th St., New York, NY 10022

PB. Pocket Books, Inc., 1230 Avenue of the Americas, New York, NY 10020

Pendulum. Pendulum Press Inc., P.O. Box 509, West Haven, CT 16516

Penguin. Penguin Books, Inc., 40 West 23rd St., New York, NY 10010

Peter Smith. Peter Smith Pub., Inc., 6 Lexington Ave., Magnolia, MA 01930

Playboy. Playboy Press, 747 Third Ave., New York, NY 10017; distributed by Harper & Row Pubs., Inc., Keystone Industrial Park, Scranton, PA 18512

Prentice. Prentice-Hall, Inc., Englewood Cliffs, NJ 07632

Price. Price/Stern/Sloan Pubs. Inc., 360 N. La Cienega Blvd., Los Angeles, CA 90048

Puffin. Puffin Books, 40 W. 23rd St., New York, NY 10010

Putnam. The Putnam Publishing Group, Inc., 200 Madison Ave., New York, NY 10016; orders to 390 Murray Hill Pkwy., East Rutherford, NJ 07073

Rand. Rand McNally & Co., P.O. Box 7600, Chicago, IL 60680

Random. Random House, Inc., 201 East 50th St., New York, NY 10022

RD Assn. The Reader's Digest Assn. Inc., Reader's Digest Rd., Pleasantville, NY 10570

S & S. Simon & Schuster, Inc., 1230 Avenue of the Americas, New York, NY 10020

St. Martin. St. Martin's Press, Inc., 175 5th Ave., New York, NY 10010

Scholastic. Scholastic, Inc., 730 Broadway, New York, NY 10003

Scribner. Charles Scribner's Sons, 115 Fifth Ave., New York, NY 10003

Shoe Tree. Shoe Tree Press, P.O. Box 356, Belvidere, NJ 07823 (now McDonald Pub. Co.)

Ticknor. Ticknor & Fields, 52 Vanderbilt Ave., New York, NY 10017

Timescape. Timescape Books, 1230 Avenue of the Americas, New York, NY 10020

Tyndale. Tyndale House Pubs. Inc., 336 Gundersen Dr., Wheaton, IL 60189-0089

Viking. Viking, Penguin, Inc., 40 West 23rd St., New York, NY 10010

Walker. Walker & Co., div. of Walker Pub. Co., 720 5th Ave., New York, NY 10019

Warne. Frederick Warne & Co., Inc., 40 West 23rd St., New York, NY 10010

Warner. Warner Books, Inc., 666 Fifth Ave., New York, NY 10103

Washington Square. Washington Square Press, Simon & Schuster Bldg., 1230 Avenue of the Americas, New York, NY 10020

Watts. Franklin Watts, Inc., 387 Park Ave. S., New York, NY 10016

Westminster. The Westminster Press, 925 Chestnut St., Philadelphia, PA 19107

Workman. Workman Co., Inc., One W. 39th St., New York, NY 10018

INDEX

Numbers in **boldface** type refer to pages in this volume; numbers in roman type refer to pages in Booktalk! 2 (1985) If a name or title appears in both volumes, two entries will appear in this index